KEYGUIDE TO INFORMATION SOURCES IN

Online and CD-ROM Database Searching

KEYGUIDE TO INFORMATION SOURCES IN

Online and CD-ROM Database Searching

Second Edition

C. J. Armstrong and R. J. Hartley

MANSELL
London and Washington

Mansell Publishing Limited, *A Cassell imprint*
Wellington House
125 Strand
London WC2R 0BB
PO Box 605, Herndon, VA 20172

First published 1991
Reprinted 1992
Second edition 1997

British Library Cataloguing in Publication Data
A catalogue record for this book is available from the British Library.

Library of Congress Cataloging-in-Publication Data
Armstrong, C. J.
Keyguide to information sources in online and CD-ROM database searching / C.J. Armstrong and R.J. Hartley.—2nd ed.
p. cm.
Rev. ed. of: Keyguide to information sources in online and CD-ROM database searching / John Cox. 1991
Includes bibliographical references and index.
ISBN 0-7201-2207-4
1. Online bibliographic searching—Bibliography. 2. Database searching—Bibliography.
3. Information retrieval—Bibliography.
I. Hartley, Richard J. II. Cox, John (John Joseph). Keyguide to information sources in online and CD-ROM database searching.
III. Title.
Z699.2.A76 1997
025.3'16—dc20 96-30568
CIP

ISBN 0 7201 2207 4

Typeset from disks supplied by the authors
Printed and bound in Great Britain by Biddles Ltd, Guildford and King's Lynn

Contents

Part II Bibliography

Part III Directory of Organizations

Introduction

Databases – by which this volume means databases produced by a third party and sold or licensed for use elsewhere – have become a fact of life. Not only, as John Cox wrote here in the first edition, are they a logical and essential application of computer and optical disc technology but their numbers are – in that most misused of phrases – growing exponentially. There are many more information providers and more online vendors or CD-ROM publishers today than there were when the last edition was printed; on top of that there have been some rapid growths in the associated networking technologies which have meant that databases are available from a number of non-traditional, alternative sources. No longer is the choice made simply from CD-ROM and online; now it is also possible to search via the Internet, via Campus-Wide Information Services and via academic or private hosts.

Clearly, databases represent an unrivalled resource for those who seek information electronically. Since the Internet has become almost universally available many reference librarians use it as an informal (and free) means of obtaining answers and many are the messages beginning 'REFQ' in the leading library-oriented lists such as LIS-IIS or BUSLIB-L. But this is, at best, a hit-and-miss approach to information retrieval and answers cannot be guaranteed by return. A more structured approach which – with the wealth of databases available – can offer a more certain response to all but the most specialist of queries is that of the formal database or databank. Queries dropped randomly into the electronic alphabet soup which is the Internet are a poor substitute for the presearch preparation of a strategy – which database, what search terms, what synonyms, what search structure – and the controlled search which is the more traditional tool of the reference librarian. No one would argue that the Internet is not a good alternative or top-up strategy and the literature is beginning to show evidence of such library use. Indeed, discussion on lists often demonstrate the desire to use such informal sources formally!

The Historical View

In the late 1960s and early 1970s the word 'online' meant either DIALOG or SDC and the few databases available were bibliographic and of a very similar structure and format. Now both those names have vanished (DIALOG has become Knight-Ridder Information although the product name of KR DIALOG remains) and the variety of database forms, formats and delivery mechanisms is, if not legion, then certainly more diverse than could have been imagined only twenty years ago.

In the early 1960s, printed indexes and abstracts began to be generated by means of computers; it quickly became apparent that the data stored could be used in other ways and tailored, on-demand search services began to appear. Among the first was the National Library of Medicine Medical Literature Analysis and Retrieval System or MEDLARS.

With the growth and advancement of telecommunications networks, dial-up access became possible and online searching had arrived. Undertaken initially on cumbersome teletype, paper-based terminals, online access has progressed through dumb terminals with screens and quasi- intelligent screen terminals to microcomputers – all, until recently, linked to telephone lines and international packet switching services and networks by a modem or an acoustic coupler. With the advent of wide and local area networks, access has, to some extent, moved beyond the modem and telephone-line link.

In the last decade, the emphasis of electronic information has changed: its scope now encompasses information from stock exchanges and wire feeds, credit and marketing information, transactional and home shopping databases and even interactive television. Technology has moved forward enough to permit images (for example chemical or patent) to be transmitted as a part of a record and it is quite common to find databases updated in near realtime or daily. There are even CD-ROM databases with updates delivered weekly.

At the beginning of 1995, the former Cuadra, now Gale, *Directory of Databases* covered more than 9,800 databases and database products accessible through an online vendor or available for direct lease, license or purchase on CD-ROM, diskette or magnetic tape from more than 3,400 database producers and offered by some 1,800 online services and database vendors. At the same time, the Bowker-Saur *Database of Databases* project with its wider remit contained over 12,000 records for discrete databases available in any electronic medium. While the number of sources has been growing, the traditional online vendors have been metamorphosing. Gone are the Maxwell companies of Pergamon Financial Data Services, Orbit and BRS; gone too is the independence of the Swiss-owned Data-Star; swallowed by DIALOG. At the time of writing in late1995, Data-Star continues to maintain a separate service and identity but, in its turn, gone too – subsumed by its parent's identity – is DIALOG. More recently BRS has been acquired by CD Plus (now known as Ovid Technologies) and ORBIT by Questel, while Knight-Ridder companies DIALOG and Data-Star have both become Knight-Ridder Information and their services have adopted the name of their parent and are thus known as KR DIALOG and KR Data-Star. Mead Data Central has become LEXIS/NEXIS and is now owned by the Reed-Elsevier Group; Disclosure has been sold by VNU to the Primark Corporation, the owners of Datastream; and during this time too, Derwent, Information Access Company (IAC), the Institute for Scientific Information (ISI) and Sandpoint have all become part of the Thomson Corporation group of companies. During the summer of 1995 the Lotus Development Corporation, and thus Lotus Notes, has been purchased by the computer giant, IBM and the US company Equifax Inc has, through Equifax Europe, acquired the UK-based Infocheck Group although in both these cases, company and product names (such as Global Scan) are currently being retained.

With this growth have come changes in the patterns of database use. A student leaving a School of Library and Information Studies in the late 1970s would have found the grounding received in online searching – probably via the DIALOG OnTap files – served them very adequately as they began work. By the late eighties, the same student's introduction to online would have done little more than demonstrate the principles – dipping into a few of the possible search services and database types and leaving the more specialized, database-specific or system-specific training to be accomplished in the workplace. As CD-ROM products grew in popularity and acceptance, it was evident that they provided a cheap means of training on a greater variety of databases as well as an information source to be introduced in their own right.

The proliferation of databases and the need for an appropriate telecommunications link kept access to databases in the library for some time. With the advance of the microcomputer into the workplace, the real users of the information began to demand personal use of databases: the end user was born. With CD-ROMs came the possibility of unlimited personal access to databases and the end user's position in the scheme of things was assured.

With new and changing systems come new softwares and even the professional searcher has pause for thought before logging on. For the end user searching less-frequently the variety is even more problematic and help is needed if the right command is to be used on the right system at the right time. CD-ROMs are less problematic as their near-intuitive, sometimes menu-driven search interfaces are easier to navigate but anywhere that a variety of online databases is being used, help will be required. The UK Online User Group (UKOLUG) produced their first *Quick Guide to Online Commands* in 1987 and the fourth edition is still proving popular (UKOLUG, 1994). In the early nineties, a software package called A-COM was developed to translate from one command language to another but despite its undoubted aptitude, did not seem popular with users. Perversely, a review of the *UKOLUG Guide* called for just such a package in 1995! (Owen, 1995).

Throughout the short history of online database, and perhaps increasingly since the advent of CD-ROMs and end users, a considerable amount of work has gone into front-end software and interfaces which sit above the host retrieval engine in order to smooth the way of the less-skilled user. Some emphasis has gone into alternatives to Boolean retrieval but much more labour has gone into disguising the existing Boolean logic. One attempt towards simplifying the search process has been the implementation of a retrieval mechanism in which the user inputs a series of search terms with no attempt at linking them logically with Boolean or proximity operators and the output of the system is a set of references ranked in decreasing order of similarity to the query. The way was led, as long ago as 1985, by ESA-IRS which developed its simple ranking system, QUESTQUORUM (Mulauser, 1985). This remains available today but is scarcely ever mentioned in the literature. In 1993, DIALOG offered the more sophisticated ranking system (DIALOG, 1993), TARGET and the legal system Westlaw introduced its own ranked retrieval system (Pritchard-Schoch, 1993).

The gradual increase in artificial intelligence and expert systems has also produced a series of search aids and expert interfaces; perhaps the earliest was the ill-fated TOME-Searcher (Robertson, 1990) while the latest, the subject of papers at the Online and CD-ROM '94 Meeting in London, are MenUSE (Menu-based User Search Engine) (Pollit, 1994) and CIDA (Company Information Database Adviser) (Tseng, 1994).

Following many years of third-party attempts to provide such front-ends, considerable effort has been made by the database providers and online vendors in the years following 1993. Both the European Space Agency (ESA-IRS) and Knight-Ridder have entered the arena; the former with BRAQUE (BRowse And QUEry) advertised as 'an intelligent navigation tool for the information space' and the latter with KR ProBase, a front-end which, running under Windows, will integrate access to both KR DIALOG and KR Data-Star by 1996. Particular market sectors are catered for by KR ScienceBase and KR BusinessBase. Other systems on the market are the FT Profile *freeway* and FT Discovery systems which provides a Windows, form-fill access to their products (Bjorner, 1994); Chemical Abstract's SciFinder; the TRW Smart Search and Smart Charts (for the Pharmaprojects database), Questel-Orbit's Windows-based Imagination and LEXIS/NEXIS' AnswerPaks which provide tailored interfaces for particular types of client or data, with offline search strategy preparation and invisible connecting to the online system (Quigley, 1994).

Taking things a stage further and linking the old concept of Selective Dissemination of Information (SDI) with the idea of information delivered in real-time are the filtered information services with data delivered via electronic mail to a local product such as Lotus Notes. Examples available in 1995 are the SandPoint Hoover system, MAID for Notes and Individual UK's First! and HeadsUp.

Anyone visiting one of the major trade shows for the database industry in the last two years cannot have failed to be impressed with these miriad front-ends. But all is not well at the PC. Just as years ago, users complained of the variety of command languages they were called on to learn, now they may well moan about the many software packages that have to be loaded. Nancy Garman has pointed out that we have traded one set of complexities for another (1995). Moving the interface to the desktop and 'putting the power of the search software on the client computer has created a greater burden for the searcher ... empowering [the user] means that the end-user and the software on his computer do the work that was once done remotely by the search service.' Clearly it is the direction in which things are moving and, more work or more lost disk space notwithstanding, these front ends *do* empower the user in a way which could not have been envisioned even a few years ago. As I recall it, the first stage in coping with disparate CD-ROMs used to be to create an operating system-level menu which autoloaded the relevant package; only when you are satisfied with this does the common search interface front end arrive.

A final trend to emerge in today's online marketplace, and one which to some extent answers Nancy Garman's point, is an extension of the gateways which have nearly-always existed between major online vendors. Cooperative agreements, initially between ESA-IRS, DIMDI and Questel, are intended to allow the customers of any service to access the databases of the others with a single command language and single billing. From the user's point of view, it should appear as a single mega-host.

The Alternatives to Online

As computer databases became available to remote users, they were with some justification viewed as doubtful alternatives to traditional print sources: those abstracting and indexing journals which were and are the basis of so much information unit and library research work. In due course as technology advanced, CD-ROMs and optical publishing underwent a similar reception before being welcomed. In 1994 and 1995 – although in terms of a medium, it is not really an alternative to, but an extension of, online – the Internet is the subject of much similar discussion.

The computer industry governs so many of the advances made in the world today that it seems unnecessarily carping to complain that advances in the information industry are technology- rather than application-led. A favourite quotation from Douglas Adams noted that 'Multimedia is an invention looking for a necessity to mother it' and although this is largely no longer true, it does encapsulate the idea that the information industry simply takes advantage of technologies presented to it. Without suggesting that such chances should be ignored, it must be recognized that such chance, unplanned utilisation brings with it the possibility of diminished quality control. Where a new technology is developed specifically to criteria set by an industry, quality control is indemic and the product will have to meet preset standards; where a general-purpose technology is utilized, parameters are discovered and accepted as use advances; users and providers may well be working to differing expectations.

There is no doubt, given the technological and marketing forces that lie behind them, that CD-ROMs would have been successful at any level; marketed as end-user tools, they became a force that was unstoppable. Today they are used as delivery mechanisms for everything from public-domain software to typefaces and from electronic books to clip art, as well as for conventional databases of every shape and size. With multimedia driving the computer and the computer games industries, CD-ROM has gained an added life force.

Although applications rather than technologies, services such as Campus Wide Information Services, JANET and SuperJANET, closed/private services such as the Bath Information and Data Services (BIDS), and electronic document ordering and delivery, for example, the UnCover service from Blackwells (also with a front end – the imaginatively named, Personal UnCover Navigator) are also extensions of the traditional online service.

All such advances are to be welcomed if they improve the services provided to library and information service users or if they extend such services to end users outside of the conventional library's control. And if they provide a service which is accurate, reliable and dependable. A virtual library is acceptable if the virtual users can be virtually certain of their results! Trouble looms when end users, unused to evaluating information and possibly seduced by the technology of the information superhighway, make use of materials which an information professional might have rejected as incomplete, invalid or unsafe. If information sources are placed on the desks of the real users of the information, they must be secure (Armstrong, 1991).

Current Issues

New technologies and applications in the areas of information retrieval and database use give rise to a range of management and industry issues. Management issues include all aspects of use and control of the new technologies: how to integrate them into library services, problems of public access, decisions relating to existing print-based services which could be dropped in favour of electronic forms and so on.

An issue which is more wide ranging in its ramifications is that of quality. As has already been noted, many of today's users of electronic information sources come to them from industries which traditionally have located information by way of a company library or information specialist. Their education and experience is not likely to encompass the evaluation or selection of information sources. With the ever-increasing pressures within both industry and academia, even the professional information worker may be hard pressed to review all information critically and while many of the larger, more responsible information providers, publishers and venders have quality management routines in place, there are also many which do not.

With the vast amounts of information involved, even the most rigourous routines have to be rationalized against information currency and costs. As David Minkoff of Datastream International noted, 'We don't set ourselves targets other than zero. Why do we do this? If we set ourselves a target, say, we are allowed 1 per cent errors per month and we met that target no doubt we would be patting ourselves on the back for a job well done, but 1 per cent of 720 million data items works out to be 7 million complaints in a month, which is obviously stupid' (1992). Quality – the ability to guarantee performance against user requirements – is clearly something which has to be addressed in the ever-expanding information industry and this is one of the reasons behind the setting up of The Centre for Information Quality Management (CIQM) by The Library Association and UKOLUG. It is the Centre's role to monitor and report on database quality issues and their long-term aim to develop a methodology for guaranteeing quality. To this end they have developed a methodology first suggested by Jacsó (1993) which will provide users with a visible determinant of the quantitative and qualitative capabilities of a given database. Database Labelling – intended to remove the gap between user expectations and the on-screen reality of a database – also provides both self-regulating guarantees of quality and a means for third-party venders to check the viability of updates and reloads. It is described briefly in a paper by Armstrong (1994, 1996).

Information Sources

The activity of database searching has generated a substantial body of literature and is a significant subject in its own right. The literature, although largely rooted in the disciplines of librarianship and information science, also extends to virtually every subject area in which such databases are used. Many are the articles and papers which describe databases relevant to a particular subject area, which alert searchers to new databases, which offer advice on search equipment and software, which document the experience of more expert searchers, which advise on end-user training, and which demonstrate appropriate search techniques.

Journals, newsletters, directories, conference proceedings, books, reports and databases themselves are the most significant media for publication of this information. It is the purpose of this *Keyguide,* to describe and evaluate such material as well as the bibliographies or abstracting and indexing services in printed or database format which provide the key to finding specific information. The newsletters and other documentation published by commercial organizations such as online hosts, CD-ROM publishers and database producers are largely excluded from consideration as not only will readers need no particular help in locating them but they represent a single point of view and are aimed at users of the publishing company's services rather than the database user community as a whole. Publications of this type are, of course, important for searchers who use particular services and addresses for online hosts and CD-ROM publishers can be found in Part III of this guide.

The *Keyguide* is a summary of the most influential, important and useful information sources at the time of writing and as such should prove helpful to anyone wanting to find out more about online or CD-ROM database searching or to contribute to the literature, particularly librarians and information professionals responsible for delivering and administering database search services, teachers and students of library and information science, employees of companies active in the database industry and the growing number of end user searchers. The guide is organized in three parts.

The short Part I is introductory in nature and identifies the characteristics of the literature and describes the major sources of information available. These sources are evaluated and compared, their strengths and weaknesses being noted according to criteria such as the level of detail they contain, their subject and geographical scope and the currency of their information. Secondary sources which point the way to further published information are examined in some detail and a separate chapter discusses ways of keeping up to date with new developments.

The body of the guide, Part II, is the annotated bibliography. It begins with a general section, primarily for sources on database searching but also including many items whose wider coverage removes them from consideration in more targetted sections. This is followed by separate sections for publications on specific concerns such as CD-ROM, the database industry, microcomputer hardware and software and search techniques. The emphasis throughout is on more recent publications or those which continue to be issued at regular intervals. Individual journal articles are included only selectively, usually when they provide overviews or leads to further information.

The evaluations or annotations are, in all cases, intended to give sufficient evaluative information for readers to assess relevance to their own circumstances. In several cases, third-party reviews are quoted to add to the picture being built up.

Part III contains addresses of organizations concerned with online and CD-ROM database searching worldwide as online hosts, CD-ROM publishers, advisory or membership bodies for searchers, industry associations, market research companies or publishers of major information sources. Such organizations will in many cases be able to supplement information contained in printed sources.

References

Armstrong, C.J. 'CD-ROM: An effective use of technology?' *Journal of Information Systems,* 1991, 1 (4).

Armstrong, C.J. 'Databases and Quality: Why not try 'What You See Is What You Get'?' *Managing Information,* 1994, 1 (11/12), pp. 28-30.

Armstrong, C.J. 'Databases: Fit for use or fit for us?' *Library Management,* 1996, 17 (2), pp. 40-42.

Bjorner, S. 'The .where and .why of freestyle'. *Online,* 1994, 18 (2), pp. 88-91.

DIALOG Target: A new way to search DIALOG. A 'How-to' Guide. Palo Alto: DIALOG, 1993.

Garman, N. 'The Inverted File: Whatever Happened to Common Command Language?' *Online,* 1995, 19 (6), pp. 7-8.

Jacsó, P. 'A Proposal for Database 'Nutrition and Ingredient' Labeling'. *Database,* 1993, 16 (1), pp. 7-9.

Minkoff, D. 'Quality: Participation plus Change'. *In Total Quality Management: Based on papers given at a one day conference on Total Quality Management in library and information services with additional material.* Hatfield: HERTIS Information and Research, 1992 pp. 70-81. (The Information Business: Key Issue 92).

Mulhauser, G. 'Dawn of Next Generation Information Retrieval'. *In* D.I. Raitt (ed) *9th International Online Information Meeting Proceedings London 3-5 December 1985.* Oxford: Learned Information, 1985 pp. 365-371.

Owen, T. [Review of UKOLUG Quick Guide to Online Commands (4th ed.)]. *UKOLUG Newsletter,* 1995, 6 (1), pp. 22-23.

Pollitt, A.S., Smith, M.P. and Ellis, P. 'Peek-a-Boo revived – end- user searching of bibliographic databases using filtering views'. *In* D.I. Raitt and Jeapes, B. (eds) *Online Information 94: 18th International Online Information Meeting Proceedings London 6-8 December 1994.* Oxford: Learned Information, 1994 pp. 63-74.

Pritchard-Schoch, T. 'Natural Language Comes of Age'. *Online,* 1993, 17 (3), pp. 33-43.

Quigley, M. 'New Features on Lexis and Nexis: Frequency Searching, Capitalization and Pluralization'. *Online,* 1994, 18 (1), pp. 56-61.

Robertson, A.M. et al. *Effectiveness of retrieval in statistically-based and knowledge-based retrieval systems.* Sheffield: Sheffield University, Department of Information Studies. Report for the period October 1989 to September 1990 to the British Library Research and Development Department on Project SI/G/871. 1990.

Tseng, G., Morris, A. and Drenth, H. 'Expert selection of databases for UK company news'. *In* D.I. Raitt and Jeapes, B. (eds) *Online Information 94: 18th International Online Information Meeting Proceedings London 6-8 December 1994.* Oxford: Learned Information, 1994 pp. 75-86.

UKOLUG Quick Guide to Online Commands (4th ed.) Compiled by S. Webber, C. Baile, A. Cameron and J. Eaton. London: UK Online User Group, 1994.

Acknowledgements

Guides such as this are not the product of the authors only; *they* tend to be only the agents through which countless other opinions come to light. So, the first acknowledgement to be made is to all those individuals who suggested all the titles and pointed to all the useful articles and volumes over which we poured in creating the main part of the *Keyguide.* Thanks are also certainly due to John Cox, the author of the last edition, who provided us with his text as a starting point; I am sure he will recognize several of his original titles! Thanks are also due to the libraries of the University of Wales Aberystwyth, Department of Information and Library Studies – the Thomas Parry Library – and the University of Northumbria at Newcastle. We must also thank the staff at Mansell Publishing, particularly Veronica Higgs, for their patience and help.

Glossary

This glossary does not aim to serve as a comprehensive guide to the terminology of online and CD-ROM information retrieval. Its objective is rather to define the acronyms and other jargon commonly used throughout the book.

Access time – The length of time taken for data to be read from a database or CD-ROM drive and displayed on a computer screen following a search request.

Artificial intelligence – The programming of computers to perform quasi-intelligent tasks by 'learning' and 'reasoning'. (*See also* Expert system)

ASCII – American Standard Code for Information Interchange. Uniform code used to represent alphabetic, numeric or other characters in computer files, allowing exchange of data between different computers and software. Extended ASCII refers to characters not immediately accessible from, or visible on, the keyboard: those with accents, for example. The ability of computers to display different character sets or fonts is achieved at a level which is above ASCII.

Baud rate – A measure of the speed of data transmission (as for example, in online information retrieval) over telecommunications networks. Speeds – which depend on both network capabilities and modems – are increasing rapidly and the 2,400 baud (a speed of 240 characters per second) which was typical when this volume was last published is slow compared with the current 14,400 and 28,800 baud which greater quantities of data demand.

Bibliographic database – Database which contains bibliographic data for primary documents rather than their full text. Abstracts are frequently included.

BLAISE-LINE – An online host

BLDSC – British Library Document Supply Centre.

BRS *see* CDP Online

BUBL – Bulletin Board for Libraries. A JANET facility offering a major resources and links to documents and institutions relevant to information workers, libraries and librarians. Also accessible via TELENET and WWW.

Bulletin Board System (BBS) – the electronic equivalent of a pin board where subscribers (not necessarily paying subscribers) can leave messages to be read by fellow users. In essence, a bulletin board is a topical focal point where users with similar interests can communicate usefully.

Campus-Wide Information System/Service (CWIS) – A communications tool existing to link all members of a community. Most CWIS provide access to reference tools – usually via the library or the library catalogue – as well as to other users and external resources such as the Internet.

CCL – Common Command Language.

CDP Online – An online host, formerly BRS and now owned by CD Plus, a CD-ROM publishing company.

CD-ROM – Compact Disc-Read Only Memory. A data storage medium which allows databases of information (text, images, fonts, video clips, etc) to be stored on compact discs and read by means of laser technology. CD-ROM can be accessed by searchers using retrieval software in much the same way as online databases. The discs are 'read only' in the sense that data can only be read from, and never written to, them by users. Discs are normally twelve centimetres in diameter and can store over 600 megabytes of data although smaller discs are used with portable devices such as the Sony Data Discman.

CD-ROM drive – Device which reads data from CD-ROM discs for display on computer screens. Drives can be external or built into a microcomputer. More modern drives may have dual-speed capability. Drives can also be stacked and accessed logically in 'juke-boxes'.

CD-ROM publisher – Organization which is responsible for the production and distribution of CD-ROM discs containing data supplied by an information provider. Examples are CD Plus, Information Access Company (IAC) and SilverPlatter Information. The publisher may employ the services of a systems integrator to perform some or all of the processes involved in producing a CD-ROM database.

CD-ROM SPAG – CD-ROM Standards and Practice Action Group.

Centre for Information Quality Management (CIQM) – a clearing house set up under the aegis of The Library Association and the UK Online User Group to monitor database quality issues and develop a means of guaranteeing databases to their users.

Command language – The set of instructions which is available to searchers for retrieval of information from a database and which varies according to the software used by the host or CD-ROM publisher through which the database is accessed. Command language searching demands that the user knows the vocabulary and syntax and it is thus, especially on CD-ROMs, frequently disguised by a menu-driven interface. (See also Front-end software and Filtered information service)

Communications software – Software which manages the processes of connection to host computer and the interchange of data between it and the searcher's workstation or microcomputer.

Compatibility – The ability of a particular microcomputer or operating system to run a specific software program or to operate with certain peripheral equipment.

Connect time – The length of time for which the searcher's equipment is connected to the host computer in online information retrieval. Historically, this has been a major element of the charges for online searching but more recently, led by an ESA-IRS initiative, pricing for the information retrieved is being viewed as a fairer mechanism.

Controlled vocabulary – A uniform set of terms or phrases used to index the subject matter of documents in a database. Such terms are sometimes referred to as descriptors and may be listed in a published thesaurus to aid searchers.

Data preparation – Part of the CD-ROM disc production process in which data are prepared for conversion to CD-ROM format by the conversion of digital code and the addition of error correction codes. Also known as pre-mastering.

Data-Star – Formerly an online host in its own right, Data-Star is now owned by Knight-Ridder Information and has become a service name: KR Data-Star.

Databank – Term sometimes used to describe a numeric database but also used as a synonym for database.

Database – Traditionally, a collection of information in machine- readable format which is usually structured into fields and records for searching on a computer. Such databases may be bibliographic, full-text or numeric. With the advent of multimedia, databases can contain a combination of images, sounds, video clips, animation as well as textual data. Databases can be accessed online (conventional online information retrieval or on the Internet), on CD-ROM or on local microcomputers (personal databases).

Database labelling – Proposed methodology for database quality assurance where information providers and vendors jointly produce a mini-specification containing both quantitative and qualitative information on a database image. This would serve as a statement of a quality below which user may be certain the database will not slip, and will also ensure users know exactly what they can expect from a database. The methodology is being proposed by CIQM (see).

Database producer – Organization which owns and compiles the information contained in a database. It usually employs a host or CD- ROM publisher to make the database accessible to searchers, although both functions may be served by the same organization, especially for smaller databases.

Descriptor *see* Controlled vocabulary.

DG XIII – Directorate General for Telecommunications, Information Industries and Innovation.

DIALOG – Formerly an online Host and, as DIALOG OnDisc, a CD-ROM publisher in its own right but, like Data-Star, now owned by Knight- Ridder Information. KR DIALOG is the online service name and KR OnDisc the CD-ROM product range.

Document delivery – Provision of the original documents about which information has been retrieved in a database search can be by electronic mail, facsimile or conventional mail. Frequently undertaken on behalf of an online service by a third party organization.

Downloading – Transfer of search results from online or CD-ROM databases to the disk of the searcher's own computer.

EARN – European Academic Research Network.

EDI – Electronic Data Interchange.

E-mail – Electronic mail. Messages transferred to and from personal addresses on networks. With access to the Internet, computer users world-wide can communicate with each other and receive answers in a very short space of time.

End user – The actual user of data retrieved from an online or CD-ROM database search.

ESA-IRS – The European Space Agency Information Retrieval Service, an online Host based in Frascati, Italy and represented in the UK by IRS-DIALTECH at the British Library Science Reference information Service.

Expert system – Software system based on artificial intelligence logic which is able to infer and draw conclusions by using a knowledge base of rules and facts while operating interactively with the user.

E-Zines – term coined for an electronic magazine for which there is (usually) no paper equivalent. In some cases, the content as delivered may be governed by the subscriber's profile.

False drop – A Record which is retrieved by a search for a particular keyword or combination of keywords but whose subject matter is nevertheless irrelevant – perhaps because the keywords were mentioned in a different context in a text field such as the abstract.

Field – Data element within a database record, for instance title, author, descriptor or abstract. Sometimes known as 'Paragraphs'. Some databases are unstructured (with no fields in records), each record being simply a single text element.

Filtered information service – delivery of relevant information, usually according to a profile, from a remote service via electronic mail to local software product such as Lotus Notes. The local database created may be updated in real time or overnight invisibly to users.

Free-text searching – Retrieval of terms or phrases from any field in a database record as opposed to from a descriptor (controlled vocabulary) field only. Search terminology will not be standardized and the searcher needs to allow for numerous possibilities such as variant spellings and the use of singular or plural forms.

Front-end software – Software which mediates between searcher and system and provides an easier interface than that offered by a command language, guiding the searcher through the retrieval process by presenting choices to be selected from a screen menu or perhaps by interacting with the searcher in natural language. (See also Filtered information service)

FTP – File Transfer Protocol. A service which allows users to transfer large files or documents from a host computer to a user's local machine.

Full-text database – Database which contains the entire text of documents (for example, newspaper articles). Distinction should be made between full-text and full-content, only the latter implying everything to be found between the covers of the paper equivalent.

Gateway service – System which enables the searcher to link to a host computer other than the one initially connected to and for which a password is owned. ESA-IRS has long maintained a gateway to FT Profile, for example.

Gateway software *see* Front-end software

GIS – Geographical Information System.

GNS – Global Network Service.

Gopher – a menu-driven search tool used on the Internet to enable users to choose the service they wish to access. Once the user selects a service, the Gopher will process the request. Most Gopher servers are publicly available.

GUI – Graphical User Interface.

High Sierra standard – An internationally agreed standard format for placing files and directories on CD-ROM discs.

Host – An organization which is commonly also described as a vendor and which provides computer services, storage facilities and retrieval software through which online databases, usually produced by other organizations, can be accessed remotely by searchers. Examples are STN International, ESA-IRS and BLAISE-LINE.

Hypermedia – Associative information retrieval and management system in which interconnecting links are established between related items of information. Items may be in different media, for example, text, sound or graphics. A form of hypermedia is used in the World Wide Web system on the Internet; in this case links may be to data on a completely different computer site.

Hypertext – Associative information retrieval and management system in which interconnecting links are created between related concepts for easy identification by users who can diverge from the main sequence in which information is presented in order to access related data at any point.

In-house database – Locally stored database of information for use by any person in an organization. Within the confines of the copyright laws, these may be developed by adding data downloaded from commercial databases.

Information broker – Company or individual operating independently of any library or information centre to provide fee-based information services, including database searches, on behalf of clients.

Information provider – The owner of the data in databases.

Interface – Physical or electronic link between a microcomputer and a peripheral. (See User interface for the link between system and user.)

Intermediary – Person who conducts a search on behalf of the client who will be the end user of the data retrieved by the search.

Internet – Developed from the US Arpanet, the Internet is best defined as a worldwide, interconnected series of networks which allow users to communicate unilaterally. Capable of storing and transmitting all kinds of data – from electronic mail to moving images and sound – the Internet is a constantly evolving, anarchistic collection of computer sites. Users and information providers continue to 'join' in huge numbers and some calls are being made for control. This definition may no longer be accurate!

JANET (and SuperJANET) – Joint Academic NETwork. A major UK network linking higher education institutions, publicly-funded bodies and other non-commercial organizations. JANET links to the Internet.

Keyword – Term or phrase which represents a subject and can be used in a database search for information about that subject.

LAN – Local Area Network. A data communications system which links computers and computer equipment within a local area such as a building or campus in order to share computing resources.

Laserdisk *see* Optical disc

Mastering – Production of a master disc for replication in CD-ROM publishing.

Memory – The capacity, measured in bytes or megabytes, which a computer has for running programs or the temporary storage of data. Disk capacity or storage is the size of the non-volatile storage media on which software and data are stored.

Menu – A set of choices presented on a computer screen from which the user can select in order to direct the system to perform a particular function. Choice may be made by initial letter, number or, within a Windows environment, by pointing and clicking on the desired item.

Microsoft Extensions – Software devised by the Microsoft Corporation to enable MS-DOS to read CD-ROM discs by extending the capacity of this operating system to read files whose size exceeds 32 megabytes and whose labelling is more extensive than that found within MS-DOS, as is usually the case with CD-ROM databases.

Modem (MOdulator/DEModulator) – A device which is connected to the searcher's terminal, workstation or microcomputer to enable communication with a remote host computers via telecommunications networks. The modem converts digital signals to analog when sending data to the host computer and performs the reverse process (that is, analog to digital) when receiving data.

Monitor – Screen which displays information sent to and received from a computer.

Mouse – Hand-held peripheral device whose shape resembles a mouse and which is manoeuvred by the user in order to transmit instructions to a computer. (See also Trackball)

MS-DOS – Microsoft Disk Operating System. (See Operating System)

Multimedia – The combination in a single database of a variety of data formats, questionably 'media', such as text, sound, photographs, images, animations, maps, music and video clips together with software which integrates them to provide the user with a cohesive display of data in different forms. Seen to best advantage in products such as encyclopaedia and educational packages, multimedia is most often distributed on CD-ROM although World Wide Web Internet browsers allow for non-text clips within material.

Networked Information Retrieval (NIR) – A generic term applied to Internet search tools such as Gopher, WAIS and WWW.

Networking – The sharing of computing resources and services such as CD- ROM databases between separate locations, often by means of a local area network (LAN).

NISS – National Information on Software and Services. A focal point for a wide range of information on the Internet accessible by gopher and WWW.

NUA – Network User Address. A numeric address of a computer on an X.25 network.

NUI – Network User Identifier. A means of identifying a network user.

Numeric database – Database of statistical, numeric or factual data. Sometimes described as a factual database or a databank.

Ondisc – In CD-ROM format.

Online information retrieval – The process of interactively retrieving information from databases stored on remote computers in real time, that is while the searcher's own equipment is 'online' to the computer via a telecommunications network.

Operating system – Set of programs which manages the operations of a computer and its peripheral devices. The most common operating system currently in use is DOS (Disk Operating System) whose IBM and Microsoft versions are known as PC-DOS and MS-DOS respectively.

Optical disc – Disc containing data written or read by a laser. The 'disk' spelling is also used and is likely to indicate that data can be written as well as read by the user, an example being the WORM (Write Once Read Many) disk. The alternative spelling, disc, should denote an optical storage medium from which data can only be read, for instance Compact Disc-Read Only Memory (CD- ROM). In practice, however, the use of both spellings varies among individual authors!

ORBIT – Originally an online host in its own right but now owned and being integrated with its own system by Questel as Questel/ORBIT. Eventually, the two database families should all run under a single software.

Peripheral – Device attached to a computer which enables it to perform extra operations. Examples are a Modem or CD-ROM drive.

Personal database – Database of information, often composed of data captured by downloading search results from online or CD-ROM databases, for use by an individual who usually stores it on a local microcomputer.

Pre-mastering *see* Data preparation.

Post-processing – The manipulation of data obtained from an online or CD-ROM search by downloading. Post-processing may involve reformatting of data or their importation into word processing, spreadsheet or personal database software.

Questel/ORBIT – Both Questel and ORBIT were online hosts but they are now being integrated as Questel/ORBIT. Eventually, the two database families should all run under a single software.

Record – Discrete block of information about a particular item in a database. This information is usually separated into a number of fields which represent different data elements. One record may represent a bibliographic citation or the full text of an article.

Replication – Production of copies of CD-ROM discs from the original master disc.

SDI – Selective Dissemination of Information. Current awareness facility whereby a search strategy is established for a particular subject and run against each update of a database in order to deliver the most recent information on that subject. This may be done in-house or remotely by the host with results shipped to users by mail or e-mail. (*See also* Filtered information services)

Search results – The information retrieved by a database search.

Search strategy – Set of database search instructions, composed of database selections and controlled vocabulary and/or free-text terms in appropriate combinations, devised in order to retrieve information relevant to a specific enquiry.

Searching – The process of retrieving information from a database.

SilverPlatter Information – A CD-ROM publisher.

Systems integrator – Organization which provides support services necessary for the production of CD-ROM databases, namely data preparation, mastering and replication.

Telecommunications network – Long distance data communications service which allows searchers to transmit data to and from host computers in online information retrieval. Examples are TYMNET in the United States and the Global Network Service (GNS) Dialplus in UK.

Telnet – An Internet service which acts as an intermediary and allows users to connect to a remote computer and use its facilities.

Thesaurus – A structured controlled vocabulary with hierarchical use of terms. Thus some terms may denote broader concepts than others and related concepts will be highlighted. For example, arm is a narrower term than limb, while a related term may be leg. This structure may be used by searchers to control the breadth of their search. (See also controlled vocabulary)

Trackball – Peripheral device resembling an inverted computer mouse and which is rotated by the user in order to move a screen pointer and transmit instructions to a computer. (See also Mouse)

UKOLN – UK Office for Library Networking. Established by the British Library Research and Development Department with the primary goal to develop a coherent strategy for the effective use by the UK library and information community of the national and international computer and telecommunications network infrastructure for the provision of services.

UKOLUG – UK Online User Group. A group formed by the Institute of Information Scientists to enable database searchers – whether online, CD-ROM or Internet – to communicate. Organizes regular meetings and a biannual conference and produces the *UKOLUG Newsletter* and other occasional publications.

User aid – Documentation which assists searchers, for instance a thesaurus, host manual or database guide.

User group – Group of users of a particular technology, product, host or database. Such groups organize meetings, produce publications and represent members' interests to companies in the database industry. Many countries or areas have Online User Groups, for example the UK Online User Group (UKOLUG).

User interface – The way in which a retrieval system is presented to the searcher and through which the searcher may interact with that system. The user may need a detailed knowledge of the system command language or may be guided through the retrieval process by menues or front-end software.

Utility software – Software which enables users to perform common computer operations such as file management in a more efficient and straightforward manner than by directly using the operating system.

Vendor *see* Host

WAIS – Wide Area Information Server. A distributed information retrieval system which helps users search databases over networks by providing an easy-to-use interface.

Workstation – Collection of equipment necessary to use computer systems at a single physical location. A CD-ROM workstation typically consists of a microcomputer, CD-ROM drive and printer.

World Wide Web (WWW or W3) – A hypertext search system for the Internet which means that documents prepared using the HyperText Markup Language (HTML) can be accessed using special software such as Mosaic. Users can move from document to document (and thus site to site) by pointing and clicking.

X.500 – An integrated standard designed to provide a distributed global directory service.

Z39.50 – A standard protocol for accessing and searching remote information sources.

Zero hits – Phrase used to describe the result of a database search which retrieves no records.

PART I

Survey of Information Sources in Online and CD-ROM Database Searching

1 The Nature of the Literature

This opening chapter of the guide introduces the literature by considering the reasons that people write about online and CD-ROM database searching; that is to say, that it examines the types of issues about which people write. As will become apparent in the succeeding pages, an interesting feature of the literature is that it ranges from the newsy through the practical to what might be termed the academic or research paper. The news items will appear in sources such as the indispensable monthly *Information World Review* [102] or the American equivalent *Information Today* [100], the practical in journals such as *Online* [83] or *Database* [71] and the research-based in journals such as *Journal of the American Society for Information Science* [424] or the British equivalent *Journal of Information Science* [423].

1.1 Changes in the Literature over Time

The whole industry of electronic information exists because of the databases and so it should be obvious that one of the major topics in the literature is the databases themselves. Information about databases varies from the extensive evaluative reviews to brief news items. The extensive reviews are best exemplified by the series *CD-ROM Information Products* [196] in which an attempt was made to evaluate the entire product: data, software and documentation and to make subjective statements about the data, the ease of use of the software and general value for money of the product. Much more typical is the short review which does not go into so much detail of the component parts of the package but simply introduces readers to the product's aims and good or bad points; examples appear in *Information World Review* as well as in the more general, *CD-ROM Magazine.* At the other extreme, brief news items might cover matters such as the appearance of a new CD-ROM product, the change of ownership of a database producer or a new product linking the existing information products to the Internet. In between these two extremes are various general articles: for example the December 1995 issue of *Database* contained a comparison of four multimedia encyclopaedias which are priced for the smaller library or the domestic market. Earlier in the same year the same journal carried an article about image databases. These articles give an indication of the considerable changes which have taken place in the electronic information industry since the early days when the databases were exclusively text-based and aimed solely at information professionals.

1.2 Retrieval and Performance

Another obvious topic for coverage in the literature is the retrieval facilities available to searchers. In the early days of the online industry this was a question of the facilities available in a particular command language, perhaps a comparison of the retrieval facilities available in two different command languages or even, as with Krichmar (1981), an investigation of the apparent ease of use of different command languages. Another early paper, by Rouse and Lannom (1977), compared the retrieval differences of the same search undertaken on ostensibly the same databases mounted on different search services, examining and explaining the differences in retrieval performance. As CD-ROMs became widely available this process was repeated with discussions of the retrieval facilities available and speed of operation of a particular CD-ROM product. In addition there was the occasional investigation of the retrieval performance of the same search undertaken on CD-ROM and on the apparently equivalent online product. At the time of writing this approach has been adopted for a third time with regard to information access over the Internet. As both the traditional online market and the CD-ROM market have matured so have the access mechanisms and, thus, so has the consideration given to their search facilities; so that consideration of retrieval facilities has given way to discussions of such matters as the utility of the help messages and in the case of CD-ROM the acceptability or otherwise of the search interface. Thus there might be considerations of matters such as onscreen and context-sensitive help, screen design, output facilities, etc. Large's paper is a good example of this approach [171]. The fullest framework for evaluating CD-ROM products is that given by Jacsó [151]. To date similar frameworks have yet to be published for the evaluation of information available via the Internet although at least one has been established. The extensive and thorough guidelines given to reviewers of resources to be added to the Organising Medical Networked Information (OMNI) site cover all aspects of evaluating in some depth.

In various incarnations searcher software has existed since the early 1980s. Initial products were aimed firmly at the professional searcher and offered facilities to speed up the log-on process and enable offline search strategy preparation. Such software has now been developed so that at least some of it is aimed squarely at the end user. In recent years there has been a surge of Windows-based products such as FT Profile's Freeway or ESA-IRS's BRAQUE and ProBASE from KR Data-Star. Such products are again reported both in a brief in the industry's news media such as Stoker's review of FT Freeway in *Information World Review* (Stoker 1995) and in a more detailed and academic manner as in the discussion of the same product in *Program* by Davies and Hepworth (1993).

The technology has always been a topic of the practical if not the research literature of online and CD-ROM searching. The changes have been dramatic: from the use of teletypewriters to sophisticated laptops; modems now function at nearly 100 times the speed of the original; and telecommunications networks have increased bandwidth enabling much faster communication and substantially more data – images, for example – to be passed. A recent paper in *Online* discussed the use of mobile phones in online searching. Indeed, an interesting phenomenon has been the broadening of the range of material covered within the online literature. Again taking *Online* as an example, another recent article offered tips on the creation of electronic presentations using software such as Powerpoint. In some senses not only do some of the search service seek to offer one-stop shopping for electronic information but some of the associated journals seem to seek to offer one-stop shopping for information about information technology for the information professional, whether or not the topic falls strictly within the traditional area of electronic database searching.

Search techniques and search styles were much discussed in the literature most especially in the early days of the online industry. The general periodicals such as *Database* and *Online* included database search guides (for example Yarborough, 1977 or Savage and Pemberton, 1978), while *On-Line Review* offered search tips and sample searches. In addition there was considerable interest in academic studies of the search styles and techniques used by experienced searchers. The most impressive and valuable of these studies have been those by Marcia Bates and more recently by Raya Fidel. The former's discussions of search tactics (Bates 1979b) and search ideas (Bates 1979a) are presented in a highly academic style but she also writes in a more practical style (Bates, 1987). Fidel's extensive research into how searchers take decisions and choose search terms should be read by all serious online searchers (Fidel 1985, 1991a, 1991b, 1991c). The relative paucity of recent literature on the topic might lead one to suppose that the search process is well understood. Nothing could be further from the truth. Given the plethora of search tools available with all the variants on, for example, truncation and word proximity, the searcher is faced with difficult decisions on how best to achieve the desired search outcome. It remains the case that there is little understanding of how to search successfully. This fact should not be lost among all the enthusiasm for 'glitzy' search interfaces.

1.3 The Searcher

At its inception, online searching was viewed as the sole province of the information professional who acted as a search intermediary for the end user. The rationale was that a detailed knowledge of command languages, database structures, indexing practices and, of course, the mechanics of logging on to the remote systems constituted a body of knowledge with which the practising professional, whether geologist, physicist or market researcher, had little experience or interest. Over time this situation has changed. Logging on has become much more reliable and the speed of interaction has increased. Interest in searching by end users really started with the emergence of CD-ROMs. Even the most dyed-in-the-wool intermediary who was convinced that end users did not have the skills for searching and who was not prepared to recognise that they could acquire them fairly easily had to admit that it was no longer possible for an intermediary to undertake all the searches. Proponents of end-user searching might prefer to say that end users have been liberated from the interference of the intermediary in their information hunting. Accordingly the literature changed from discussions about whether end users should or could search to discussions of training programmes to ensure that they had at least a basic understanding of the search process together with discussions of how to offer them support in their searching. Enthused by the searching of CD-ROMs and aided by the emergence of Windows-based search interfaces such as FT Freeway, end users are now searching remote systems in increasing numbers. Obviously this is a cause for some pleasure to the online hosts who have long needed to widen the market beyond the confines of a select group of information professionals and reach out to end users. Whilst no-one disputes that end-user searching is here to stay, there remains concern about the quality of the searches which are being undertaken. A concern which has been cogently expressed by Hepworth (1992). This should be no surprise. Whilst the interfaces might make the search process appear simpler most of the complex issues still remain. No interface which we have yet seen is capable of taking decisions about how to use word proximity facilities appropriately in a given search, how to truncate each search term, which synonyms to choose or whether or not to take advantage of the descriptors in the controlled vocabulary for a particular search. Obviously the late TOME-Searcher achieved some but not all of these functions. Searching remains a tricky business. Hiding it behind the shiny facade of a Windows interface does little to remove the complexity of searching.

1.4 Quality

It is a curious phenomenon of the electronic information literature that whilst there have been attempts to evaluate command languages, help facilities, CD-ROM interfaces and so on, there have been far fewer attempts to evaluate the quality of the information in the databases themselves. A few early articles were written, for example, Bourne's examination of the impact of spelling errors in databases (1977) but, then as now, this is not a frequent topic. In the United States, the Southern California Online Users' Group (SCOUG) [519] has undertaken pioneering work in this direction. In the United Kingdom considerable work is being undertaken by the Centre for Information Quality Management (CIQM) [204]. Yet relatively little has been written on the subject and relatively little overt interest has been displayed in quality by the host of other players in the electronic information industry; though happily there are encouraging signs that this might be about to change (Armstrong, 1996).

Management issues have moved on from the initial concerns about matters such as the choice and location of equipment, ensuring access to direct telephone lines and which information professionals should undertake the searches to discussions about the choices between access mechanisms: CD-ROM versus online host versus closed services such as BIDS and to concerns about methods of offering training and support to end users in their searching. More recently there has been considerable interest in the impact of electronic information services both on the services offered by a library or information centre and on organisational structures and job descriptions.

The development of reference management software or bibliographic software such as EndNote, Pro-Cite and Reference Manager has become another area of concern to those interested in online and CD-ROM database searching [499]. The literature includes descriptions of particular products and comparison of different products. Reviews have appeared in many journals intended for audiences far wider than the traditional community of information professionals with descriptions of various products aimed at different professional communities such as biologists or geologists. Each of the major products has spawned its own well used discussion list on the Internet as well as contributing to a general discussion list on the use of bibliographic software.

1.4.1 Legal Issues

On the surface it might be surprising that the literature of such a practical topic as the searching of commercial databases might include publications on legal matters. However there are numerous areas where there are serious legal concerns. The first relates to the uses to which the data may be put. Database producers became particularly concerned about this as software developed to facilitate the easy downloading of search output and subsequently the easy storage and retrieval of that data. Quite rightly database producers do not wish to see others making profits from their effort in record creation and validation. As CD-ROM products have been networked, the issue of license agreements for networked access has emerged. A good summary of the complexity and some sound advice on licence negotiation is offered by Lewis (1994). At the time of writing different CD-ROM companies have different licensing agreements based on matters such as the number of potential PCs which may access the data or the number of simultaneous searchers which the system can support. Attempts have been made to produce a standard model for such licensing agreements and these are outlined in an appendix to a British Library Research and Development Department report (Smith, 1994). This would certainly be welcomed in the library community. The publishers also commissioned a report through their standards and practices action group (CD-ROM SPAG, 1995).

1.5 Theory and Practice

From the foregoing pages it is apparent that there are many concerns for those in the electronic information industry and it is no surprise that there is a healthy literature. If there is a concern, it is that there appears to be an increasing gap between researchers and practitioners. How many practitioners read papers in *Journal of Information Science* or *Journal of the American Society for Information Science.* Conversely how many researchers regularly read *Information World Review* or *Database?* This lack of interaction between researchers and practitioners is neither a healthy nor a desirable state of affairs. If this *Keyguide* helps in some small way to promote interaction between the different communities with their different perspectives on the electronic information world then it will have achieved something positive.

Chapter 2 provides a discussion of the primary literature of online and CD-ROM database searching. In Chapter 3, the secondary literature or navigational aids are outlined. In writing Chapters 2 and 3, we have made one major change from the approach adopted in the first edition and that is that we have sought to discuss print and electronic sources side by side rather than separately. This would seem to reflect the increasing importance of electronic information as opposed to print information. The main body of the work, the bibliography, follows Chapter 3. This has been substantially revised and reorganised since the first edition to reflect both the changing nature of the literature and our differing perception of the most useful way in which to present the references. Finally the glossary and references have been updated since the previous edition of the work.

References

Armstrong, C. J. 'Database Labels in use: a trial'. *Information Technology Solutions,* 1996 (in press).

Bates, M. J. 'Ideas tactics'. *Journal of the American Society for Information Science,* 1979a 30 (5) pp. 280-289.

Bates, M. J. 'Information search tactics'. *Journal of the American Society for Information Science,* 1979b 30 (4) pp. 205-214.

Bates, M. J. 'How to use information search tactics online'. *Online,* 1987 11 (3) pp. 47-54.

Bourne, C. P. 'Frequency and impact of spelling errors in bibliographic data bases'. *Information Processing & Management,* 1977 13 (1), pp. 1-12.

CD-ROM SPAG. *CD-ROM Licensing Issues for Publishers. A report prepared for the CD-ROM Standards and Practices Action Group by Electronic Publishing Services and Bird & Bird.* London: EPS, 1995.

Davies, A. D. and Hepworth M. 'PC based interfaces to online information services and the development of FT Profile's Freeway'. *Program,* 1993 27 (2) pp. 149-163.

Fidel, R. 'Moves in online searching'. *Online Review,* 1985, 9 (1), pp. 61-74.

Fidel, R. 'Searchers' selection of search keys: 1. The selection routine'. *Journal of the American Society for Information Science,* 1991a, 42 (7), pp. 490-500.

Fidel, R. 'Searchers' selection of search keys:2. controlled vocabulary or free text searching'. *Journal of the American Society for Information Science,* 1991b, 42 (7), pp. 501-514.

Fidel, R. 'Searchers' selection of search keys: 3. Searching styles'. *Journal of the American Society for Information Science,* 1991c, 42 (7), pp. 515-527.

Hepworth, J. B. 'Developing information handling courses for end users'. *In* C. J. Armstrong and R. J. Hartley (eds). *Database 2000 UKOLUG State-of-the-Art Conference 1992, University of Surrey 1992.* Oxford: Learned Information. 1992 pp. 67-75.

Krichmar, A. 'Command language ease of use: a comparison of DIALOG and ORBIT'. *Online Review,* 1981, 5 (3), pp. 227-240.

Lewis, M. 'CD-ROM networking: licensing issues'. *In* C. J. Armstrong and R. J. Hartley (eds). *Changing patterns of online information UKOLUG State-of-the-Art Conference, University of Edinburgh 1994.* Oxford: Learned Information. 1994 pp. 131-139.

Rouse S. H. and Lannom L. W. 'Some differences between three online systems: impact on results'. *Online Review,* 1977, 1 (2), pp. 117-132.

Savage, G. S. and Pemberton, J. 'SciSearch on DIALOG'. *Database,* 1978, 1 (1), pp. 50-67.

Smith, N. R. 'Guidelines for suppliers for licence agreements for Electronic Publishers' (Appendix 5). *In* P. Vickers and J. Martyn (eds). *The Impact of Electronic Publishing on Library Services and Resources in the UK. Report of the British Library Working Party on Electronic Publishing.* (Library and Information Research Report 102). London: British Library, 1994 pp. 60-67.

Stoker, D. A. 'FT Profile and Chadwyck Healey offer an information freeway'. *Information World Review,* September 1995, No. 106, pp. 21-22.

Yarborough, J. 'The Novice's Guide to ERIC'. *Online,* 1977, 1 (3), pp. 24-29.

2 The Literature of Online and CD-ROM Database Searching

In this chapter, the major primary sources of information about online and CD-ROM database searching are discussed.

2.1 Journals

Journals are the dominant medium of publication. Their frequent publication enables rapid communication of practical information about online and CD-ROM database searching. The value of journals specifically for hardware and software product information is discussed later in this chapter in section 2.4.4, their role as current awareness tools is examined in Chapter 3 (section 3.5) and their contribution to the location of new publications is described later in this chapter in section 2.3.1. The current section looks at the main features of the journal literature, with particular emphasis on the specialist titles for online and CD-ROM and a more general discussion of the different types of journal outside this core in which relevant literature may be published.

2.1.1 Specialist Journals for Online Database Searching

Four specialist journals can be identified, three of them established in the late 1970s. *Online: the Magazine of Online Information Systems* [83] was first published by Online Inc. in January 1977, appearing on a quarterly basis until 1982 when a bimonthly publication schedule was assumed. As its subtitle suggests, online information is treated in the broadest sense with feature articles on topics such as hypermedia and local area networks colour printers, colour LCD panels supplementing those more directly concerned with online searching. Articles are frequently published on subjects of general concern, examples being pricing of online information in the January 1990 issue, common command languages in July 1989 and the use of cellular telephones in online searching in September/October 1995. Most of the feature articles, which number between four and eight per issue, are written by contributors from the United States whose backgrounds are a mixture of libraries, schools of librarianship and information science, information consultancy firms and telecommunications or computing companies.

Online's president and publisher Jeff Pemberton, interviewed by the journal's editor at the time of the journal's tenth anniversary, Gordon (1987), sees its biggest contribution as providing a forum where people in the online industry can help each other to solve mutual problems, acting in effect as 'an information clearinghouse'. The practical nature of the journal is especially evident in its regular columns and sections. The 1995 volume contained sections on the Internet (Inside the Internet), Industry Trends and Technology, practical computing and the online searcher. This range of topics indicates both the broad definition of online which is used by the publisher and the scale of development of 'online' from those early days when it referred only to the use of DIALOG, ORBIT and a few other systems. Current awareness is provided in an extensive news column (Online News), a column titled 'Journal Watch' in which recent literature is selectively abstracted and an 'International Notes' feature which reports on developments outside the United States. Reviews of new publications and software are also included. In general, the practising online searcher will find something of interest in just about any issue of Online.

The same is true of its sister publication, *Database: the Magazine of Database Reference and Review* [71]. *Database* began publication more than a year later than *Online,* in September 1978, and changed from a quarterly to a bimonthly schedule in 1986. The two journals are in many ways similar but *Database's* subtitle gives an indication of its greater concern with individual databases, the broader issues of searching being more the province of *Online.* Articles may focus on particular databases, for instance Washington Post Online in the August 1989 issue. An examination of recent issues indicates how technological development has caused the re-definition of database as is illustrated by an article on the evaluation of multimedia encyclopaedias in the December 1995 issue. *Database* comparisons are another regular feature and once again a recent issue indicates the changing nature of electronic information with an article which compares LEXIS, WESTLAW and the Internet as sources of information for lawyers. Creation and management of in-house and personal databases are other regular topics and software for these purposes is frequently reviewed or compared. Authors are usually based in the United States and sometimes include software experts as well as librarians, information consultants and educators.

Some of the columns in *Database* are the same as those in *Online,* at present these include the 'Dollar Sign' and 'Consumer Online'. It must be noted that these columns change to reflect the changing developments in the ever expanding world of electronic information: a section labelled 'On the Net' would have been fairly Spartan at the time of the previous edition of this book! These are supplemented by 'Chemcorner' for chemical information and in some issues by 'Database Design' in which advice is offered about local databases. Some coverage of CD-ROM databases is to be found in the 'CD-ROM Report' feature. As in *Online* there is a strong news section, while columns containing reviews of recent journal articles and of new book publications are common to both journals. The text of the two journals was added to the full-text database Trade and Industry ASAP [63] in 1988.

Online and CD-ROM Review, which began life as *Online Review: the International Journal of Online Information Systems* [81], was first published by Learned Information in March 1977, shortly after the first issue of *Online.* Like *Online* and *Database* it began as a quarterly journal but became bimonthly in 1981. Its original subtitle is almost identical to that of *Online* but the word 'international' reflects one of the differences between the two. Although many of its articles are written by American authors, there are many contributors from other parts of the world notably Europe. The journal has joint editors and separate news editors for the United States and Europe to ensure a balanced coverage geographically. The title was changed to reflect the growing importance of CD-ROM publishing in 1993.

The type of article published in *Online and CD-ROM Review* is often markedly different from that to be found in *Online.* The comments of Tenopir (1989) remain applicable despite the change in journal name:

> the focus of *Online Review* is often on research results rather than how-to-do-it searching. This means the articles are more scholarly (and sometimes less readable) than most of the articles in *Online,* but perhaps of more lasting value.

It is true to say that its articles tend to be fewer in number, lengthier and more detailed, frequently examining areas of general concern in online information retrieval. For example, the first issue of 1996 contains one paper discussing browsing in hypertext systems and another considering information storage and retrieval on the World Wide Web whilst there was a CD-ROM user interface evaluation in October 1995. Nevertheless, articles of a practical nature are published on topics which have included documentation for end-user searchers in February 1989 and on techniques for corporate family searching in December 1989. Therefore it would be inaccurate to label *Online and CD-ROM Review* as a scholarly journal with a concentration on the theoretical rather than the practical. This point is further borne out by the balance of librarians, researchers in library and information science and representatives of the information industry among its contributors. Current awareness is supplied through an extensive news section which follows the main articles in each issue and is supplemented by a calendar of forthcoming events. Book reviews and reports of relevant conferences are a feature of some issues. The journal is shorter than *Online* or *Database* and this results in an absence of specialist columns of the type found in those journals.

Database Searcher: the Magazine for Online Database Users [70] is the newest of the specialist journals for online searching. It began life in 1985 as *Database End-User,* changing to its present title in 1987, and is published monthly with combined issues for February/March (July/August prior to 1990) and November/December. In addition to informing its readers it aims to represent their interests to database producers and host services. It has been described by Jack (1987) as a journal which 'holds no punches in taking a consumerist approach to databases and online services' and this is evident from a reading of the editorial and readers' letters in any issue. Its 'Caveat Searcher' column also monitors the value for money and quality offered by producers and hosts - a topic which is not covered in many other places - *Searcher: The Magazine for Database Professionals* [276] edited by Barbara Quint, a long-time campaigner for quality, and the new *db-Qual* available from CIQM and on the Internet where the URL is http://www.fdgroup.co.uk/ciqm.htm are the only two of note. Most issues only contain one or two articles and these are usually about matters of very topical concern to searchers. They may focus on a particular area of searching, as in the case of full-text retrieval in September 1989, or on a more general issue such as pricing of online information in January 1989. Nevertheless the greater part of the journal consists of news columns which serve to keep readers up to date with online host and database developments and with new hardware and software products. The emphasis throughout is on developments and services in the United States. *Database Searcher* can be accessed in full-text format online in the Trade and Industry ASAP [63] database.

2.1.2 Specialist Journals for CD-ROM Database Searching

Although CD-ROM technology features prominently in industry journals like *Inform: the Magazine of Information and Image Management* [181], two titles have emerged specifically for users of CD-ROM systems who are more interested in the data than the technology. *CD-ROM Professional: the Magazine for CD-ROM Publishers and Users* [178] was established in May 1988 and is published bimonthly. It changed its title from *Laserdisk Professional* in the May 1990 and more recently has changed its subtitle to reflect changing developments in the industry. Its publisher is Pemberton Press, an affiliate of Online Inc, publishers of *Online* and *Database* whose format it resembles in many respects. The publisher's promotional material emphasizes that this is a journal for information professionals rather than end users. Its articles focus on practical concerns such as CD-ROM security in the July 1989 issue and drive selection in January 1989. More general issues are also covered, with user instruction and networking being featured in March 1990. Coverage has been extended in 1990 to include articles on CD-ROM publication processes and trends. This trend seems to have become more marked in recent years so that for example the

February 1996 issue contains a review of new CD-ROM drives and also a detailed examination of the design and evolution of a new CD-ROM product and the hurdles which had to be overcome so that it could see the light of day.

Reviews of CD-ROM databases have been a regular feature in each issue until recently. The more detailed reviews usually contained screen illustrations and may compared related databases or versions of databases, for instance MEDLINE in March 1990. Shorter reviews are featured in a separate column, 'CD-ROM in Brief'. Like *Online* and *Database,* this publication contains a number of shorter columns which examine new hardware and software associated with CD-ROM, answer user problems, report on recent conferences and review new books and recent journal articles. A separate news section keeps track of database and other announcements. Full-text searching of the whole journal is possible online in the Trade and Industry ASAP [63] database.

CD-ROM Librarian originated in 1986 as *Optical Information Systems/Library and Information Center Applications,* a title which never exactly tripped off the tongue! The title, *CD-ROM Librarian,* was adopted in mid-1987, with publication frequency moving from bimonthly to monthly from 1988 onwards, although the July/August issue is combined. More recently it changed its title to *CD-ROM World* and in 1995 it became *Multimedia World* [184, 476]. The number of articles rarely exceeds three per issue, generally of less than five pages. Their themes are a mixture of specific concerns like setting up a CD-ROM workstation in the February 1988 issue and general trends, as exemplified by an article on the adoption of CD-ROM by European libraries in January 1990. Applications other than information retrieval are featured and the January 1990 issue contains a number of contributions on retrospective catalogue conversion although since its last change of title the emphasis has tended towards the games end of multimedia. Background on other optical media may be provided.

Database reviews are the strongest feature of the journal and are usually illustrated with sample screen displays. Some reviews are detailed and, in addition to showing a typical search, will discuss installation, hardware considerations, searching capacities and documentation. One or two products per issue receive this treatment. The other main section of the journal is the 'Optical News' column which informs readers of developments in CD-ROM database and associated products. Like some other journals major online and CD-ROM journals it is available in full-text format in the Trade and Industry ASAP [63] database.

There are many other CD-ROM journals, as a glance at the magazines in any railway station will testify. The longevity of such journals is not yet proven and so such titles are not discussed. The demise of the journal *CD-ROM EndUser* which featured prominently in the first edition of this book is but one example of a journal in this field which proved to have a brief life. For the same reason, it seems premature to discuss any of the burgeoning number of Internet magazines which are appearing in newsagents. At the time of compilation, those listed in the bibliography [404-407] appear to be reasonably stable publications.

2.1.3 Other Journals

Literature about online and CD-ROM topics can be found in many journals outside the core titles already identified. General and specialist journals in librarianship are obvious sources. In addition to publishing occasional articles on online and CD-ROM retrieval, some of the more traditional librarianship titles contain regular columns. Examples are *Library Journal* [79] and *RQ* [84]. Columns are written by leading authors in the online field and keep readers informed of news and trends, while *RQ* has a separate section for reviews of online and CD-ROM databases. Those library and information studies journals which focus on computer applications are often useful sources of information. Useful examples are *Computers in Libraries* [448], *The Electronic Library* [454] and *Program* [453]. Journals for subject specialisms within librarianship may feature online and CD-ROM searching in their articles, news sections or book reviews. *Bulletin of the Medical Library Association* [607] carries relevant articles in many issues, while *Science and Technology Libraries* [627] has a special news section titled 'Sci-Tech Online'.

The major information science journals namely *Information Processing and Management* [421], *Journal of Documentation* [422], *Journal of Information Science* [423] and *Journal of the American Society for Information Science* [424] publish papers of relevance to searchers. Whilst these are usually about information retrieval and in particular novel retrieval systems, there are significant reports of research into the thorny problem of how people search electronic information sources. Whilst these papers are usually reports of research rather than practical articles they ought to be of considerable interest to practitioners. Online and CD-ROM retrieval may feature in review articles or may be the subject of special issues in which a group of articles examines developments. For example the January 1988 issue of *Journal of the American Society for Information Science* contained a series of articles on CD-ROM whilst more recently the January 1996 issue is devoted to the thorny problem or the evaluation of information retrieval systems. It is interesting to note that whilst there is considerable change in the content of the more newsy journals, the topics covered in the more academic journals changes more slowly. This could scarcely be viewed as a new subject having been the subject of much debate since the first Cranfield tests in the late 1950s. Whilst the subject of this debate remains, there are now far wider approaches to evaluation.

Many countries publish information science journals and these are often an important source for articles and perhaps news or book reviews relevant to online and CD-ROM searching in these countries. Examples are *Nachrichten für Dokumentation* [80] for Germany, *Documentaliste* [72] for France, and *Joho Kanri* [76] for Japan. Such titles are significant in the absence of specialist journals about online and CD-ROM information in many countries. In other cases they supplement the coverage provided by specialist news services which are the more common medium for regular communication of information about database searching at a national level.

Outside librarianship and information science, the importance of computing journals and magazines is recognized in the list of journals indexed for the 'Journal Watch' column in *Online* and *Database* where they account for about a third of the titles listed. Those included are titles such as *Byte, Datamation, PC Magazine, PC Week* and *PC World.* In addition to coverage of developments in microcomputer technology, such titles may include overviews of online database sources and descriptions of new CD-ROM databases. For the rest, a perusal of the annual *Online Information Retrieval Bibliography* [31] before it ceased in 1990 would show that relevant articles can occasionally appear in the journals of most disciplines. Examples have included *Fortune, Bankers Monthly, Archives of Ophthalmology* and *Investigative Radiology.* Such articles most often discuss individual databases or groups of databases in a particular field, an example being 'Advances in Computerized Information Retrieval in Remote Sensing', published in *International Journal of Remote Sensing* in 1988. This bears out the point made by Hawkins (1978) that there will always be papers 'advertising' online searching to different subject areas as databases become available for searching in these areas. Electronic information, whether from CD-ROM or online search services, is now an accepted part of the working environment of many professional groups such as lawyers, geologists and doctors. Whilst the first edition noted examples of papers in journals outside the library and information press which prompted the use of electronic information, it is noticeable that the approach to electronic information in the literature of other professions has advanced considerably since 1990. Thus, for example, the American *International Law Journal* for the 2nd October 1995 has a paper about the place of CD-ROM jukeboxes in legal research whilst two or three years earlier journals such as *Law Practice Management* contained several papers about the place of CD-ROM in the legal environment. Conferences such as the Annual Symposium on Computer Applications in Medical Care also include such papers; for example, on electronic information delivery over institutional networks in 1993.

2.2 Conference Literature

Conference papers are of value in providing reviews of trends and in describing particular databases and services offered by companies in the information industry. The proceedings of a particular conference can provide a 'state-of-the-art' summary in the field at a given time. Writing about the *International Online Information Meeting* [45] series, Raitt (1989) makes the point that such meetings can 'serve as barometers or gauges to measure the online information industry's progress, development, growth and maturity'.

The conference literature of online and CD-ROM searching is dominated by three long-established publications each of which emerged in the early days of online searching. These are supplemented by smaller publications and the presence of a considerable body of relevant information in the mainstream library and information science literature although like any other subject it should not be forgotten that many conference papers are never published formally whilst a selection of others will appear in journals such as *Information Services and Use.* Sometimes preprints may be issued to delegates but not made available elsewhere. Reports of some events will be written up in a number of relevant journals or newsletters though this is rarely a substitute for the full text of the paper. As the World Wide Web becomes more pervasive, the possibility exists that authors can make electronic versions of papers available whether or not the conference proceedings are published in more conventional ways.

The patchy nature of publication of conference literature is not exclusive to the online and CD-ROM fields. Oseman (1989) has studied the problems which this form of literature poses in any discipline. The best source for finding conference proceedings, whether issued in full, as preprinted abstracts or in special issues of journals, is the *Index of Conference Proceedings Received* [9] compiled by the British Library Document Supply Centre. Individual papers are indexed by many of the abstracting and indexing services discussed in Chapter 3.

The International Online Information Meeting [45], referred to as IOLIM by many who have been regular attendees over the years, is the longest established of the three major online conferences. It has been held in London each December since 1977. Its proceedings are published by the organizers, Learned Information. The first proceedings volume contained twenty-seven papers but the number has risen steadily since and peaked in 1988 when more than 90 papers were published in two volumes. In 1994 the figure had declined to 63 and the 1995 figure was 62. The international nature of the conference is evident from the list of authors in any volume. The European countries are especially well represented. Most of the papers are contributed by members of companies in the information industry, librarians and staff of the LIS departments. In addition to these groups papers may be accepted from people outside the information industry whose applications of online or optical systems are of particular interest. Raitt (1989) cites doctors, lawyers and astronomers as examples.

The range of topics covered in the proceedings is diverse and Raitt (1989) has fully documented its evolution over the years to take account of new developments. Certain subjects have been featured throughout, notably search techniques, education and training, chemical and substructure searching, database descriptions and in the last decade CD-ROM products and their utilisation. Topics which have emerged strongly in recent times are microcomputer applications, end-user searching and the Internet. It is also possible for subjects to achieve prominence quite suddenly, a clear example being hypertext which did not feature in the subject index in 1987 but had twelve entries in 1988. Inevitably the recent rise in interest in the Internet is mirrored both in the papers in the conference and its presence at the attendant exhibition. The level of the papers included shows a balance between presentations of research, descriptions of products and accounts of experience or practice.

The proceedings of the National Online Meeting [46] in the United States are also published by Learned Information. The conference is normally held in early May, although some of the earlier meetings took place in late April. A collection of abstracts was published for the first meeting in 1980 but since then the full text of most of the papers presented has been published in the proceedings. In a few cases abstracts only are supplied, while there is no text at all for about ten to fifteen of the papers presented. The 1989 proceedings volume, for instance, contains text for only sixty eight of the original seventy eight papers, although the titles of the missing papers are included, along with the names and affiliations of their authors. The opening paper in each proceedings volume, titled 'Highlights of the Online Database Industry' in recent years, reviews the technological and market trends in the industry in the previous year. Remaining papers follow in alphabetical order of first-named author. Occasionally some papers may be clustered around a particular theme such as end user searching in 1985 or online sources of business information in 1987. More usually, however, they cover a similarly wide range of topics to that found in the International Online Information Meeting with a corresponding evolution towards newer concerns such as gateways, CD-ROM, personal databases and hypertext. Database presentations, searcher training and management of online services in libraries have been recurrent themes. Like its European counterpart recent conferences have seen a sudden increase in the number of papers about the information superhighway. Most of the speakers are based in the United States so a less world-wide perspective is offered compared to the International Online Information Meeting.

The Online [47] conference has been held in October or November each year since 1981 and is organized by Online Inc, publishers of the proceedings. The title of the conference was changed to Online/CD-ROM in 1990. The proceedings consist mostly of preprinted summaries rather than the content of the full paper as presented by the author at the conference, although this can be purchased on audiotape from the publisher. The reason given for publishing summaries only is that Online/CD-ROM is an invited paper conference whose authors are less likely to put their whole presentation on paper than is the case for submitted paper conferences like the two already discussed. Attempts in the first two years of the conference, 1981 and 1982, to publish full presentations were abandoned when forty per cent of the authors failed to meet the deadline for publication. The result nowadays is that papers vary greatly in length and quality of presentation in the proceedings. Some appear to contain most if not all of the original paper and can be seven or eight pages long. Others are only one page in length and occasionally have no title! The proceedings usually contain about forty papers which are arranged in alphabetical order of first-named author. Almost all of the speakers are from the United States. They are mostly either information professionals or representatives of companies in the database industry. There are markedly fewer presentations by LIS department faculty than in the other two online conferences. The emphasis is on product presentations and reports of technological developments. As in the publisher's journals *Online* and *Database,* software products and applications are featured prominently. Other topics are search techniques, end user searching and, increasingly, CD-ROM databases and technology. Host and database updates are always strongly represented.

Apart from these three major online conferences, there are occasional regional conferences. In Australia, the Australasian Information Online and OnDisc conference and exhibition is held in January in alternate years. The 1997 conference is the eighth in the series. In addition Learned Information have organised the East-West Online Information Meeting and an Asian Information Meeting, the second of which is scheduled for September 1996. On a smaller scale, UKOLUG organises a biennial State-of-the-Art conference in the UK [204, 205]. The 1996 conference is the 7th and as with its three immediate predecessors, the proceedings will be edited by the authors of this book.

Inevitably other conferences contain material which is relevant to online and CD-ROM searchers. Two regularly published events which usually contain relevant papers are the ASIS Annual Meeting and Computers in Libraries. The ASIS Annual Meeting [43], organized by the American Society for Information Science since 1964 and published in recent times by Learned Information, normally contains about fifty papers in its proceedings. Of these it is typical to find about ten of direct relevance to online and CD-ROM searching. The emphasis is less on individual databases than on more general issues such as searcher performance, relevance of search results, end user searching and system-user interface. Computers in Libraries [442] and Computers in Libraries International [441] are similar events held annually in the United States and England in March and February respectively. The US event began in 1986 and the international conference has been held since 1987. They changed from SCIL (Small Computers in Libraries) and SCIL International to their present titles in 1989 and 1990 respectively. Proceedings in both cases consist of extended abstracts rather than full papers but contact information is provided for authors. Microcomputer applications in libraries are the common theme throughout and topics include CD-ROM, expert systems for information retrieval, communications software and microcomputer selection and management.

2.3 Books

Books can offer a convenient introduction to, or overview of, online or CD-ROM searching or some aspect of it and have been included in many sections of Part II of this guide with this purpose in mind. Single-author works may also be able to give a more coherent and consistent picture than a series of journal articles or conference papers by different authors. Unfortunately, this medium does not lend itself to currency. The information contained in books tends to date very quickly and, as Jack (1987) observes, 'their reference value is questionable because of the volatility of the industry'. Whilst this may be true of books which concentrate on the details of a particular command language or the databases offered on a particular search service, it is less so of books which concentrate on the principles of searching rather than the details of practice. Two books which have considerable relevance today are those by

Harter [542] and by Hartley et. al. [37]. Information retrieval textbooks such as Lancaster and Warner [416] are less susceptible to rapid dating and so may provide useful background information of lasting value.

In addition to general overviews of online searching and CD-ROM technology, book publication has tended to concentrate on search techniques and management of search services in libraries. As far as management issues are concerned, the collection of papers edited by Hanson and Day [149], of which the second edition is in preparation at the time of writing this book, offers a good example. Although many books are still aimed at students of librarianship and information science and at information professionals, there has been an upsurge in the publication of introductions to online retrieval methods and resources for end users, usually in a particular subject field. Examples are *The Electronic Business Information Sourcebook* [350] and *A Basic Guide to Online Information Systems for Health Care Professionals* [345], both of which are written by and for end users. In practice works of this nature contain much which is of value to the information professional also. *How to Look it up Online: Get the Information Edge with Your Personal Computer* [556], for instance, offers lots of helpful advice on how to find factual data online.

Advice on online searching in many subject areas is contained in *Manual of Online Search Strategies* [546], first published in 1988 with a second edition in 1992. Its chapters are written by experienced searchers and cover databases in over fifteen specialities. Chapters are assigned to types of information such as patents and citation data or, more commonly, to subject disciplines which include chemistry, health sciences, engineering, law and humanities. In the second edition, both law and business have separate chapters for the UK and the USA. The narrative in each chapter is liberally interspersed with sample records and searches from relevant databases, while tables are frequently used to identify and compare databases. Less commonly used features such as full-text searching, statistical analysis, chemical structure searching and retrieval from databanks of numeric or factual data are well covered. The wide scope of this publication gives it a definite reference value for searchers needing from time to time to use databases other than those with which they are most familiar. Commentary on individual databases or hosts can be located by using a separate index for this purpose whose 500 entries illustrate the extensive coverage provided.

Guides to search strategy in particular subject areas have also been published. Examples are *Fast Facts Online: Search Strategies for Finding Business Information* [579] and *Online Searching in Science and Technology an Introductory Guide to Equipment and Search Services* [625]. Retrieval strategy in online databases is sometimes governed by search costs. It is important to be able to compare the cost of searching different databases or of accessing the same database on different hosts. Ideally price data for the various hosts and database will be coordinated in some way. Assistance can be obtained from some of the database directories which are examined later in this chapter in section 2.4.

The recent upsurge of interest in the Internet and the services which are offered has resulted in a rash of books. Some are brief introductory texts such as Bradley's *UKOLUG Quick Guide to the Internet* published by the UK Online User Group [391] whilst others are much more substantial. Of the many detailed books about the Internet, Krol [397] is particularly recommended. As the World Wide Web has become widespread, books about Web browsing software such as Netscape and about the tagging language used to create WWW pages are becoming more widespread. At the time of writing two books which are commended are *The Complete Idiot's Guide to Netscape* (Dupoy 1995) and *HTML for Dummies* (Tittel and James 1995), though the situation changes all the time and at any time the best source of recent books in these areas is the computing section of a large bookshop.

2.3.1 Finding Out about Books

Arguably the material covered in this section ought to be in chapter three. However since it relates specifically to books and did not fit readily into the structure of chapter three it has been included here. It should be noted that in addition to the sources mentioned here, many of the navigational aids which are discussed in chapter three will also provide guidance about books within the field.

Cumulative Book Index [117] is a monthly listing, with quarterly and annual cumulations, of books published in the English language world-wide. Its scope extends to directories and conference proceedings. These publications are listed, with bibliographic and price details, in a single alphabetical sequence by author, title and subject keyword or phrase. Among the terms offering subject access are 'On-Line Bibliographic Searching' and 'CD-ROM', while related material may be found under 'Information Retrieval', 'Information Services' or 'Optical Disks'.

National bibliographies will often identify extra material published in a particular country and some are likely to be more current. An example is the *British National Bibliography* [1] which is published weekly, with monthly, four-monthly and annual cumulations. Currency is further enhanced by the inclusion of Cataloguing in Publication (CIP) entries which contain basic bibliographic data for works whose publication is imminent. Entries are arranged according to the Dewey Decimal Classification (20th edition), to which a subject index is provided. The main number for automated information storage and retrieval is 025.04, while 025.06 is the root number for automated information storage and retrieval in specific subjects. The other section to bear in mind is 025.524 which is information search and retrieval as a subdivision of services to library users.

New books may be announced or reviewed in journals and news publications. *Information Today* [100] includes a 'Bookshelf' section in which publications from Learned Information and other publishers are announced and briefly described. Book review sections, in which new publications are evaluated as well as described, are a feature of *Database* [71], *Online* [83], and *CD-ROM Professional* [178] among other journals. Reviews published in a wide range of journals can be identified through a feature in *Journal of Academic Librarianship* called 'The JAL Guide to the Professional Literature' [21]. This feature summarizes book reviews and includes the reviewer's recommendation in each case. Thirty subject groupings are used, among which 'Online Information Systems' is clearly relevant. CD-ROM can be found under general headings such as 'Nonprint Media', 'Information Storage and Retrieval' and 'Information Technology'. *Library and Information Science Annual* [16] is a significant source for keeping track of book literature in a given year. One of its objectives is to review all English-language monographs and reference books in library science published in the previous year. Coverage has been increasing in each year since publication began in 1985 and now includes material published in Canada, Britain and Australia as well as in the United States. The main subject section of interest carries the general heading 'Computers' but includes subdivisions for databases, microcomputers and online searching. Reviews of CD-ROM publications are included as a subsection within the main category titled 'New Technologies'.

2.4 Reference Material

The types of reference material examined in this section serve as aids to support searchers in their activities. Their purpose is highly practical in that they act as a point of reference in problem solving with regard to command languages, search strategies and costs, and definitions of terminology. Reference material frequently brings together in a compact and consistent format information which would otherwise have to be culled from many separate sources. Directories constitute an important form of reference material and not surprisingly constitute the major part of this section of the chapter. The reference materials have been arranged under six headings to reflect the needs of electronic database searchers.

2.4.1 Finding Out about Databases

Database directories are important to searchers for a number of reasons. They allow identification of databases available in a particular subject area or from a specific producer. Where the name of a database is known they can be used to find out more about it. Standard data provided by directories are database name, hosts through which access can be obtained, producer, timespan covered, updating frequency and a summary of subject content. Additional data may include price information, special access conditions, published user guides or other documentation and equivalent printed sources. Often directories provide the only description of a database available to a searcher. Alternatively, they can bring together in a more convenient and objective format basic essential data which may be scattered among a series of host and producer newsletters, leaflets and other documentation. Database information is, however, subject to frequent change and many directories advise the searcher to contact the host or producer for more current and detailed information before undertaking a search. The journals and news services outlined in section 2.4.3 are also of value in keeping abreast of the latest database information.

The need for database directories has grown with the rapid and continuing increase in the number of databases themselves. The 1979/80 issue of the predecessor of the *Directory of Databases* [226] listed 400 databases from fifty-nine hosts; the figures for its January 1990 issue were 4,465 databases and 645 hosts. Online files have been joined by CD-ROM databases of which more than 800 were listed in the 1990 edition and more than 8,000 in the 1995 edition of *The CD-ROM Directory* [248]. Identification and selection of databases have become more complex and have called for a wider range of general and specialist directories. This call has been met. Ingebretsen, Borgman and Case (1985) found that the number of directories had increased from one in 1976 to almost forty in 1985. New online database directories have continued to be published, while the emergence of CD-ROM has spawned a new set of directories for that medium, a selection of which can be found in Part II of this guide under the heading Database Directories [208-250].

The remainder of this lengthy section examines the different categories of database directory now available. It begins with the major general directories for online and CD-ROM databases, proceeds to examine directories for specific countries, subjects and types of information and ends with a look at methods of identifying databases by searching online, on CD-ROM or on diskette. At the outset it may be wise to bear in mind a note of caution from Glossbrenner (1987):

> Directories vary widely in quality and depth of coverage none of them is 100% comprehensive. Directory A may include databases that Directory B leaves out, and vice versa. Directory C's coverage of a given database may include important details not found in the write-ups of the identical database offered by A and B.

Several directories of databases are described in the following pages. Initially two general directories of databases are discussed, these is followed by a brief description of a new directory of databases on the Internet. Directories of CD-ROM databases are then outlined and finally there is a discussion of directories which provide details of databases on a national or regional basis or by subject.

The Directory of Databases [226] is a merger of a number of former directories namely the *Directory of Online Databases* which was initially published by Cuadra/Elsevier and was often simply referred to as 'Cuadra', the *Directory of Portable Databases* from the same publisher and Gale Research's *Computer Readable Databases.* It is published in full twice yearly with a quarterly supplement between editions. This updating schedule aims to ensure currency. More recently it has been taken over by Gale Research Inc. An indication of the growth of the electronic information industry is given by the fact that whilst there were more than 4,400 databases described in the January 1990 issue, which was published as a single volume of manageable size the January 1996 edition is published in 2 volumes each of which are in 2 parts and together list more than 8,500 databases. Entries are listed in alphabetical order of database name, each having a clear and uncluttered layout. This is largely effected by the presentation of only the most vital data to describe each database. Thus extra details such as user aids and search costs are not included.

Indexes offer access by a number of routes. There is an index of database producers which gives contact addresses, telephone and fax numbers and a list of the databases for which each producer is responsible. Similarly, the index of online services provides an alphabetical listing of providers with contact information and lists of available databases. The geographic index is organised by country and indicates the databases which originate from each country. The main subject index is organised by subject heading and for each heading lists the databases which fall into that category and indicates the type of each database (for example, full text, numeric or bibliographic). Finally there is a master index which includes names, keywords in database names, acronyms, former names and search services. A helpful feature in each index is the highlighting of new or changed databases by the use of special symbols. International coverage is a definite strength of this directory and is an area in which it has traditionally outperformed its competitors. Around forty countries are represented in its vendor geographic index.

DataBase Directory [235] from Knowledge Industry Publications is newer than either of the directories already discussed. It was first published in 1984 and is issued as part of an annual subscription service operated by the publisher which provides an inter-edition supplement and a monthly newsletter called *DataBase Alert.* Every effort is therefore made to keep up to date with new database developments. The use of a small typeface gives entries a somewhat crammed appearance, however, making it difficult sometimes to pick out a particular element of data. One helpful feature in terms of presentation is the use of a symbol to identify new databases in the alphabetical listing and in the indexes. The amount of information provided in each entry is comparable with that in *Directory of Databases,* an extra data element being the names of telecommunications networks through which a database can be accessed. CD-ROM versions are mentioned, with brief details, in the 'Producer/Producer Services' section of entries as appropriate. Subject, host, producer and alternate name indexes are provided. Contact information is included in the host and producer indexes. The subject index contains over 500 terms and is of variable quality. On the credit side, some specific headings are included, for example, 'AIDS'. Country names are also used as subject headings. The introductory notes to this directory state that more than a third of its entries are for databases produced outside the United States. Nevertheless, the international coverage which it offers is compromised by its main criterion for inclusion of databases which requires that they should be accessible from the United States.

Whilst not a directory, it is useful to note at this juncture *Online Files: Comparative Cost Analysis* [328] and its electronic equivalent OFCCA (diskette version) [329]. These products are useful for searchers in Britain since they offer comparative cost data on a large number of databases available from major British and American search services. They can be obtained from Effective Technology Marketing in Grimsby. All prices are given in pounds sterling. Separate columns for each database cover connect time, online and offline printing of references and estimates for 'browsing'. Some of the prices in the chart may not take account of discounted rates available for certain types of organization.

A new directory is the *Gale Guide to Internet Databases* [382]. In addition to information on more than 2,000 databases accessible over the Internet it includes a bibliography of the latest Internet books, a glossary of Internet terms and a Web Home pages section divided into 24 major categories. Given the rapidity of change of the Internet it is a moot point whether of not there is a long term future for a print based directory to it. It is perhaps not surprising that the appearance of this directory and the larger Gale's *Directory of Databases* on the Internet has been announced. (http://www.galenet.gale.com).

Directories of CD-ROM databases exhibit some different characteristics from those which describe online databases. Since CD-ROM databases are accessed on local equipment rather than from remote computers over telecommunications networks it is necessary to provide full information about types of microcomputer hardware and software needed to support them. In fact CD-ROM database directories are more likely to be used as an aid for database purchase rather than search decisions. As a result there is often a greater concentration on technical and price data rather than on subject coverage and database content. *The CD-ROM Directory* [248] typifies the tendencies just noted. Its 1990 edition lists 817 databases in a section titled 'CD-ROM Products'. This number had risen to approximately 6,000 in the 1993 edition and to more than 13,000 in the 1996 edition. The listing is international and includes test or demonstration databases and some products aimed at the entertainment market such as novels or music catalogues on disc. Another point to note is that not all products listed are commercially available. Entries are presented in alphabetical order of product name. It is noticeable that the narrative description of database content is sandwiched between details of organizations associated with the product and specifications of hardware necessary for using it. Information may be scanty for a small number of products. In such cases further information will be obtainable from any organization named in the entry. Full contact information is given for publishers, distributors and information providers in the separate Company Information section. There are indexes of multimedia CD-ROMs, retrieval software, Macintosh compatible titles, country, company activity and advertisers in the directory in addition to an extensive subject index.

CD-ROMs in Print: an International Guide [233] commenced publication in 1988, a year later than *The CD-ROM Directory,* and is also published annually. The 1990 cumulated edition of the directory doubled its number of CD-ROM products covered to 600 titles. By the 1995 edition it had grown to include more than 8,000 products. Its coverage is slightly less international but the strength of the directory lies in the amount of detail which it provides for each database listed. Up to twenty-five elements of data may be specified in an entry. These include foreign distributors, availability of demonstration products, site license conditions and networking facilities. Operating requirements are fully specified and recommended drives and peripheral equipment such as mouse or type of monitor are given. Readability is enhanced by the clear separation of data elements from each other in each entry. There is a separate section detailing CD-ROM companies. Indexes are provided by subject, audience level – a novel approach, by Macintosh compatibility and of multimedia CD-ROMs. Both are available on CD-ROM as well as in print.

A further directory of value and interest is the annual *CD-ROM Marketplace* [232]. This provides an alphabetical listing of those organisations involved in the CD-ROM industry whether as producers, distributors, publishers or consultants. More than 3,500 organisations are listed. Indexes are provided by subject,geographic location and activity. The names and numbers section claims to be a white pages of the CD-ROM industry. A claim which did not stand the test when the first name checked, Hatvany, was not present. One can only assume that he is sufficiently well known to have gone ex-directory! Nicholls (1990) describes others in an excellent article which also identifies journals and newsletters in which database listings and reviews regularly feature.

Some countries or more commonly groups of countries produce their own database directories. These publications supplement the coverage offered by the general directories discussed earlier. They provide convenient listings of databases from and perhaps about a country and often identify smaller databases, databanks or hosts which may not be described elsewhere. The United States is deliberately omitted here since its databases dominate the general directories examined earlier and are also well documented in the *Datapro Directory of On-Line Services* [57]. One regional example is the *Directory of Australian and New Zealand Databases* [236]. *The Directory of European Databases and Databanks* [237] lists nearly 1,000 files offered by hosts in the European countries, while *Nordguide: Nordic Databases* [246] provides information about databases from the Scandinavian countries Denmark, Finland, Iceland, Norway and Sweden. The number of databases emanating from Scandinavia has increased from some 207 in 1985 to 704 in 1995. It is perhaps surprising that the two major database producing countries in Scandinavia are Finland and Norway. A slight variation is provided by the Canadian directory *Espial Canadian Database Directory* [239] which lists more than 500 databases which contain Canadian material. A final point to note is that more current versions of most of these directories are available as online databases. Two databases, *Alphaline Database of Databases* [222] which offers information on more than 3,000 databases accessible from Germany and *Databas* [223] which gives information on databases accessible in Spain are only available in this format.

Database directories covering a particular discipline, as opposed to all subject areas, have become increasingly prominent, especially in the field of business information. Aslib, the Association for Information Management, has produced a series of directories of this type for databases in business and company information [567, 568], management and marketing [570], law [596], medicine [606], patents and trade marks [622], engineering [621], environment [592], building constructions and architecture [617]. However by far the most ambitious series is the *World Databases* series from Bowker-Saur. A total of 17 separate titles are planned of which 11 have been published to date. The include *World Databases in Medicine, World Databases in Physics and Mathematics* and *World Databases in Patents.* The level of detail provided for each databases far exceeds that offered in other directories and where possible includes either extracts from, or references to, third party evaluative reviews. There is a highly detailed description of each master database and this is linked to a less detailed description of each manifestation of the database whether on CD-ROM or a number of different search services. Where one database is a subset of another this is explicitly stated. In the medium term the publisher plans to make the entire series available online.

Business [406] and technology [428] databases are covered in two annual German-language directories from Hoppenstedt. Advantages are offered by such publications. Their narrower focus often allows them to give a more detailed treatment than can be provided in a more general source. Examples are *Online/CD-ROM Business Sourcebook* [573] and *European Business Information Sourcebook* [572]. The latter, for instance, often provides detailed narrative descriptions with helpful commentary on search features or peculiarities within a database. Comparison of databases may also be easier, as in the *Directory of Online Healthcare Databases* [605] which employs a tabular format across each page in which essential facts are provided for each database. Finally, there is always the chance of finding out about less obvious sources, often from outside the main discipline, which may not be noticed in larger directories. An example is *CD-ROM and Online Management and Marketing Databases 1993* [570] which includes some relevant databases from the engineering and health and safety fields.

Two other specialized types of database directory warrant mention. The first covers information from government sources which is made available in database form, sometimes via commercial hosts as in the case of the government report literature database NTIS [126]. In many other instances access from the searcher's own site is not possible but government organizations will run searches, sometimes free of charge, on request. The *Directory of United Nations Databases and Information Systems (DUNDIS)* [225] focuses on information services generated by United Nations organizations. These include more than 300 databases, notably of statistical information. The directory is available for online searching as the DUNDIS database on the ECHO host.

Another specialized form of directory puts the emphasis on source documents, more particularly periodicals, covered by databases rather than on the databases themselves. The aim of such directories is to indication databases in which a specific periodical is featured. The nature of the coverage afforded by the database, namely indexing, abstracting or presentation of the full text of the periodical, will also be shown. Directories of this kind are useful when a particular periodical or group of periodicals is considered likely to contain information relevant to a search topic. An excellent source of information about full-text coverage of periodicals is *Fulltext Sources Online* [240], updated twice yearly and indicating databases on fifteen hosts in which 2,000 publications, including newspapers, newsletters and newswires can be located. For other types of coverage there are separate volumes of the annual *Directory of Periodicals Online: Indexed, Abstracted and Full-Text,* one of which covers news, law and business [583] and the other science and technology [623]. A complementary source for business and legal databases is 'Books and Periodicals Online: a Guide to Publication Contents of Business and Legal Databases', which appears as one of four separate directories in *Books and Periodicals Online* [228], which is updated annually and is also available as a CD-ROM.

A significant number of database directories can be searched online. Those available on CD-ROM/diskette are included in the bibliography as entries [214-218] whilst those available online are included as entries [219-227]. Thus there are electronic versions of some of the major directories including CD-ROMs in Print [216], CD-ROM Directory [214], Gale Directory of Databases [226] databases and DIANEGUIDE [224] which is the electronic product from which the irregular print publication *Directory of European Databases and Databanks* [237] is generated.

Online access to database directories allows more specific searches to be conducted. Since most fields of data can usually be searched it is possible to specify search criteria such as timespan, language and geographical coverage which are not likely to be indexed in the printed version. Descriptive summaries of database content can also be searched in free text online, greatly expanding subject access. Another significant advantage of online directories is that they are usually more up to date than their print counterparts. However Houck (1987) has suggested some disadvantages of searching the electronic version of directories. One of these is search costs. Another factor is that databases are sometimes discovered by browsing through printed directories. Browsing is a somewhat less common activity online. Houck also cited subject access as a problem due to the lack of printed lists of subject descriptor terms for the major electronic directories.

2.4.2 Finding Out about Organizations

Many organizations are connected with the generation of online and CD-ROM information world-wide, the majority of them on a commercial basis. Numerous directories exist to identify commercial companies and their activities. Information on non-profit organizations is often harder to find. Part III of this guide includes the addresses of some of the major organizations in both categories.

Some of the more obvious commercial organizations are online search services, database producers and telecommunications network service suppliers. CD-ROM database production demands a chain of processes which involves publishers, information providers and service companies for data preparation, mastering and replication.

Regularly updated profiles of varying length for companies in the online industry can be found in the *Datapro Directory of On-Line Services* [57]. The approach taken is to provide detailed reports on online hosts and shorter profiles of database producers. The detailed reports may run to over ten pages in length and can be located in the first section of the directory service in a section titled 'Information Retrieval Services'. They number forty and focus almost entirely on US hosts. In each case there is a delineation of company background, competitive position, resources and facilities and a detailed description of services provided. Charts are sometimes used to show the range of databases offered and the cost of accessing them. Over 900 companies world-wide, mostly database producers or telecommunications network services, are profiled in a separate section, 'Company Profiles' in the second volume. A standard format is employed to summarize details of size, key personnel, subject emphasis, primary customers, products and sales concentration in geographic terms. The section is arranged alphabetically by company name, although a subject index to the whole directory offers alternative access.

A convenient international listing of CD-ROM organizations is to be found in the Company Information section of *The CD-ROM Directory* [248] which was described earlier in section 2.4.1 of this chapter. Another useful source of information about organizations is the annual *CD-ROM Marketplace* [232] which was also noted in section 2.4.1.

Non-commercial organizations exist to promote or advise on database searching or to represent providers and users of database services. For example, most European countries have a national online advisory centre, while online and, increasingly, CD-ROM user groups are commonplace at national and regional level. Professional bodies such as the American Society for Information Science and trade associations like the Australian Database Development Association are other significant categories of non-profit organization.

The North American Online Directory [60] includes some trade and professional organizations involved in providing courses on the creation and utilization of information products and services. Details given include services to members, publications and date of foundation. Unfortunately this directory has not been updated since 1987. It also contains a listing of some user groups in the United States.

Search services exist to meet the needs of people who require a database search but do not have the necessary equipment or staff to conduct it from within their own resources. They are also likely to be used even if an organization has its own search service but needs occasional access to a database on a host to which it does not subscribe. The search service is usually, although not necessarily, a library or information centre which has invested in search equipment and host and database subscriptions and employs trained staff to conduct searches on a commercial basis on behalf of clients. Increasingly this type of service is also being offered by companies or individuals commonly known as information brokers. Directories which aim to identify search services provided by organizations and individuals should provide indexes by geographic region, subject and names of hosts and, ideally, main databases searched. Their entries should indicate contact person, hosts accessed, subject specialisms, charging policy and conditions of service availability.

Impressive by these criteria is *UK Online Search Services* [61] providing essential contact and service data for organizations in the UK which offer fee-based online brokerage service. Entries are listed alphabetically by organization name and providing details of type of service available, client types served, charging policy and other information about the service. There are indexes organized by online services, CD-ROM, subject and region.

Europe is well served by the database, BROKERSGUIDE [55]. This is a database of individuals and organizations offering fee-based information services. It is compiled by the European Information Market Development Group and can be searched on the ECHO host. Thirteen of the seventeen data elements in each record can be searched, including country and town of broker, working language and subject specialism. Hosts and databases searched can also be named in each entry to a maximum of five and ten respectively and can be specified in searching. Cornelius (1989) describes the compilation and development of the database.

The Directory of Fee-Based Information Services is of more manageable size with 684 entries in its 1989 edition. The United States dominates but twenty-nine other countries are represented. Entries provide contact information, subject areas and a narrative description of the service. Indexes are by city, company name, contact person, subject and service category. Details of new services are included in the publisher's bimonthly newsletter *Information Broker* [96].

Individual information brokers or consultants in the United States are identified and described in the American Library Association's *Directory of Library and Information Professionals* [58] which contains a consultancy/freelance index. The *Directory of Library and Information Professionals* is also available on CD-ROM, as reviewed by Jacsó (1989) who notes some problems in record structure.

2.4.3 Finding Out about the Information Industry

Information about developments in the database industry is needed by companies already active in the industry or intending to enter it as online hosts, database producers or CD-ROM publishers. Sources of data for market intelligence and competitor analysis are important to such companies. They will help to establish the state of the market in particular subjects or geographic areas and to monitor the activities, policies and fortunes of other companies. Market studies and industry newsletters are the main categories of source for such information and are now discussed.

The complex task of delivering current and accurate statistical data on the online and CD-ROM database markets is undertaken in a growing number of market studies. Re'em (1988) points out the lack of data at their disposal: basic usage and revenue data are just not available .... the online industry is keen to provide information about almost everything – but not itself.The implication is that revenue figures provided in market studies will be based on estimates rather than on actual figures in the case of the online industry at least.

A selection of market studies for CD-ROM and online information can be found in Part II of this book [261-267, 292-304]. The database industry in Japan is discussed in [261] and in Europe in [265, 303] whilst the marketing strategies used by the online industry have been examined by Saunier [267]. Market indicators and studies of the information industry appear in other reports listed in the bibliography. The likely impact of the Internet on business information services is the subject of a recent study by Adamson and Pearce (1996). At approximately £300.00 sterling this study is conservatively priced when many market research reports are priced at more than $1,000. A pattern which will not change, however, is the high price of market studies which are expensive to compile and usually cost more than $1,000 to purchase.

What types of data are contained in these costly publications? Market share may be studied, as in *Online Database Markets: Expanding U.S. Market Opportunities for Online Database Vendors* [304] which includes current and projected estimates for the share of the online market by databases in different categories (bibliographic, full-text and numeric) and subject areas. A recent market research report seeks to relate online information to the emerging electronic library (*Online Information and the Electronic Library*, 1996). It examines potential use of the Internet, CD-ROM and online search services as information sources for incorporating into the electronic library. Business opportunities and internal organisational issues are addressed. However, at a price of nearly £700, this is targetted at the commercial rather than the academic or public library.

Data on specific companies can also be found in market studies. Over 250 CD-ROM companies, including large and small publishers, hardware providers and systems integrators, are examined in the annually updated research report, *State of the CD-ROM Industry: Applications, Players and Products* [301]. Profiles give information on company background, product development and CD-ROM uses. *Information Market Indicators* [296] is a quarterly service which monitors usage of online host and database services. Its estimates are based on statistical analysis of usage data supplied by a panel of 500 to 700 user organizations. A series of figures is delivered to service subscribers every quarter and includes rankings of hosts, producers and databases according to both revenue and amount of usage time. Reports tailored to individual needs can be prepared for subscribers for an additional fee on a one-time or regular basis. Revenue estimates for selected US companies in the database industry are a feature of the yearbook, *Information Industry Factbook: the Information Industry's Annual Report* [305]. Statistical data supplied by this publication can be obtained in machine-readable format on a separate Factbook Data Disk. Data are supplied in the Lotus 1-2-3 file format and can be imported into nearly all spreadsheet and database management packages which run on IBM and compatible microcomputers.

Directories of market research publications can be consulted to locate studies on the database industry. Two which cover online and CD-ROM industry reports regularly are *FINDex* [256] and *Marketsearch* [258]. FINDex provides descriptive abstracts for each publication listed. Abstracts in Marketsearch usually take the form of single-line lists of keywords but a better coverage of market studies from outside the United States is offered by this source. In addition to these directories, new studies are frequently announced and reviewed in the newsletters *Infotecture Europe* [103], *IDP Report* [227] and *CD-ROM Newsletter* [189] (it should be noted that the producers of *CD-ROM Newsletter* announced in April 1996 that this useful newsletter will only be available by e-mail once current subscriptions end – they are also increasing the price for this less convenient format). Addresses of leading market research companies for the database industry are provided in part III of this guide.

Company news is strongly featured in industry newsletters which provide brief reports of marketing activities, orders received, contracts negotiated, appointments of new staff and company reorganizations, mergers or takeovers. They may also feature product innovations and government policy and regulation in relation to the information industry. These sources are less expensive and more easily accessible than market studies. *Online Newsletter* [112] and *Infotecture Europe* [103] are two concise newsletters which offer specialist coverage of developments in the database industry. The scope of both is international but the former emphasizes events in the United States while the latter favours Europe. They were originally established to monitor the online industry but have integrated CD-ROM into their coverage in more recent times. The full text of *Online Newsletter* can be searched online by three different routes while *Infotecture Europe* is also published in French as *Infotecture: Lettre Bimensuelle d'Actualite des Banques de Données.*

Learned Information (now known in the States as Information Today, Inc) publishes two newspapers, *Information Today* [100] and *Information World Review* [102] which keep track of industry and company activity in the United States and Europe respectively. *Information World Review* includes a regular column on the online market and contains frequent interviews with leading figures in the industry. Many issues profile a particular company with discussion of its policies and products. Appointments of new staff by companies are also documented, although the headline 'Five Sign for Hampden' in the July 1989 issue could be mistaken for news of the Scottish football scene! Another Learned Information publication, *Monitor* [288], makes excellent reading with lively commentary on industry developments worldwide in each issue. It concentrates more on analysis of trends than on news reporting. *Optical Memory News* [291] provides an international perspective with emphasis on product development in the optical memory industry. It includes a column titled 'Industry Developments' whose range of topics is defined in the newsletter as 'shipments, prices, plans, profits, losses, standards, new alliances, new firms, new entrants, new plants'. Another column, 'New Products', announces new and forthcoming optical memory products and services. Despite its title, *CD-ROM International* [188] focuses mainly on Europe, for which it is the best source of information on company activities. News stories are sometimes grouped under country name. A French-language version is published as *CD-ROM: la Lettre Mensuelle du CD-ROM, CD-I, CD-V....*

Government policy in the United States and its effects on the information industry as a whole receive regular attention in *Information Times* [287], the newsletter of the Information Industry Association, which has a special column titled 'Washington Report', while *Information Today* [100] carries a feature called 'The Federal Scene'.

European Community initiatives are communicated through *I & T Magazine* [286] This 2-volume newsletter describes the activities and policies of the European Commission's Directorate General XIII: Telecommunications, Information Industries and Innovation. One of the volumes provides a glossy overview of developments whilst the other is a newsletter/directory of developments, opportunities, conferences, publications and other useful information.

Industry information in newsletters is coordinated in a number of abstracting and indexing services and online databases. More than thirty online database sources for information on the CD-ROM industry are comprehensively documented and evaluated in an excellent article by Ojala (1988). One valuable source omitted was *Electronic Publishing Abstracts* which has subsequently become *World Publishing Monitor* [260]. It is available online as a part of the PIRA Abstracts file on ORBIT and as a CD-ROM. The major point in favour of this service is that its source coverage includes a higher proportion of online and CD-ROM industry newsletters than any of its competitors. Their coverage is international and is supplemented occasionally by market research reports. Other relevant abstracting and indexing services, also searchable online, include the online and CD-ROM database industries within a general coverage of business sectors. The most extensive of these is the *F & S Index* series which is split into separate publications for the United States [255], Europe [253] and the rest of the world [254]. All three publications are arranged in the same way with subject grouping of entries based on a modified version of the US Standard Industrial Classification. The most specific code is 73750, 'Database Vendors', although 3679140, 'Optical Recording Media', should be considered for coverage of developments in CD-ROM technology. Entries are also listed in each publication under company name. Articles on a diversity of topics, including new product developments and company marketing strategies, can be located in these publications. Source coverage concentrates on journals and newsletters from a variety of business and industrial sectors. All three printed publications can be searched simultaneously in the online database IAC PROMT [279] whose records contain abstracts. Other factors in favour of the online version are daily updating and inclusion of news releases in its source coverage.

Two other general sources in which articles on the online and CD-ROM database industries can be located are ABI/INFORM [251] and Business Periodicals Index [252] which index 800 and 300 English-language journals or newsletters respectively. Both can be searched online and on CD-ROM. Indeed ABI/INFORM has no printed equivalent. Its main assets are that it provides detailed abstracts and maintains a short time lag from publication to abstracting. Business Periodicals Index has an easy to use printed version in which details of articles, without abstracts, can be found under a few specific headings, including 'CD-ROM', 'Database Publishers' and 'Database Vendors', or by company name.

2.4.4 Finding Out about Hardware and Software

Knowing about databases is a major part of the searcher's job; a knowledge of the hardware and software necessary to access them is also important. The arrival of CD-ROM databases on the scene heightened the importance of this knowledge. Database searchers will probably be involved in operating, and perhaps evaluating, purchasing and maintaining, microcomputers and peripheral equipment such as printers, modems and CD-ROM drives. They may also use and advise upon software for a variety of applications, including communication with online hosts, reformatting of downloaded data and creation of personal databases.

Ideally an all-purpose directory of online and CD-ROM hardware and software would exist for easy location of relevant information. This, unfortunately, is not the case. Information about microcomputer hardware and specific software packages is scattered among a number of directories and a wide range of journals which will now be described. It is also worth noting that the major online and CD-ROM conferences, the proceedings of which were discussed earlier in this chapter, have attendant exhibitions which offer a wealth of product information to attendees. Some of the major exhibitions within library and information science and microcomputing will provide useful information. Details of these events is readily available from calendars of meetings in the professional press or from advertisements in newsletters such as *Information World Review*.

Directories which aid in the selection and evaluation of hardware and/or software for library and information applications are not in plentiful supply. One of the few is the *European Directory of Software for Library and Information Services* [445], compiled at Loughborough University in England and published at irregular intervals. Over 500 software packages are described. Their applications include online communications, downloading and post-processing of data and database management. A narrative description is provided for each package to indicate the main features of the software. This information may be supplemented by bibliographic details of reviews published in mainstream library and information journals. Specifications such as hardware, memory and operating system requirements are also given.

Buyer's Guide to Micro Software (SOFT) [443] is another online directory of software with many access points. The database is produced by Online Inc, publishers of the major journals *Database* [71] and *Online* [83], and can be searched on KR DIALOG. Updating is monthly. The database contains over 6,000 records of software for business applications, but library and information science is one of the fields to which particular attention is paid. A criterion for inclusion is that packages should be rated at least 'good' by the technical press. Software must also be available in the United States. Each record offers a detailed description of the package concerned including a note of published reviews and brief abstracts of their evaluations. Sometimes reviews are selected to represent different points of view. It is also possible to limit retrieval to packages with published reviews and, within this, to those rated 'very good' or 'excellent'.

The annual Computers in Libraries Buyer's Guide and Consultant Directory [444] serves as a guide to suppliers of library hardware and software in the United States. (***is this still the case???***) This publication is published as the July/August issue of the journal *Computers in Libraries* [442]. Its first two parts list hardware by category and software by application. In each case only supplier names are provided without any product specifications. Full contact information for more than 200 suppliers is provided in a separate section. In terms of the requirements of database searchers this source is stronger on hardware than on software. Also relevant for information on hardware is the *Datapro Directory of On-Line Services* [57]. Its feature reports section includes regularly updated reports and comparison charts for microcomputers and modems which run to over seventy and fifty pages respectively.

For CD-ROM specifically, it was noted earlier in this chapter that entries in database directories usually include technical information regarding the hardware and software operating requirements of each database listed. Some sources supplement this information with separate listings of drives. The best example is *The CD-ROM Directory* [248]. It is safe to say that there has been considerable growth in the marketplace since the first edition of this keyguide when it was noted that the 1990 edition of *The CD-ROM Directory* listed more than fifty drives from twenty seven companies world-wide. The 1995 edition of the same directory contains a hardware section arranged by company but it is difficult to know which of the available products should be referred to as CD-ROM drive since many offered complex packages such as a complete multimedia workstation of which a CD-ROM drive was but one element. Many of the entries contain useful information on access times and compatibility of the products.

While directories concentrate on giving specifications and descriptions, journals can go further by providing evaluative reviews and advice on selection and, especially, use of microcomputer hardware and software. Leading the way are *Database* [71] and *Online* [83], published by Online Inc. in alternate months. Both journals have liberal interpretations of their subject matter and include regular reviews of technological developments including microcomputers in a number of longer articles and columns or sections which have changed over time. Examples of relevant topics include advice on microcomputer purchase, colour printers, colour LCD panels and even cellular telephones for online searching. *Database* also publishes articles on local database creation and maintenance and associated software. Advice on these topics is also offered in a 'Database Design' column in many issues. Information on hardware and software is prominently featured in another specialist journal, *Database Searcher* [70]. Its 'Connecting Gear' column frequently announces new products, notably modems, printers and communications software. In addition it offers advice on practical concerns such as data transfer, hard disk maintenance and file management. Contact data for all organizations cited can be found at the end of the journal. New microcomputers, modems and peripheral equipment for online searching are also regularly announced and reviewed in two newspapers from Learned Information, *Information Today* [100] and *Link-Up* [107].

Anyone concerned with CD-ROM databases will find find lots of valuable information in *CD-ROM Professional* [178]. There are announcements of new drives or product developments such as networking solutions in its news column. Its articles often advise on product use and selection.

On a more general level it is worth considering some of the library automation journals in particular *Computers in Libraries* [442] which has published relevant practical papers. Moore (1990) provides a convenient summary of topics covered by some of these articles. *The Electronic Library* [454] also contains useful information in its hardware corner and software review sections. In-depth reviews of individual software packages are the province of *Library Software Review* [450]. Finally, there is much to commend regular perusal of some of the more general microcomputing magazines. Two of the many such titles are *Personal Computer World* [452] and *Personal Computing,* published in England and the United States respectively. They contain news of the latest developments in microcomputer technology and include advertisements and reviews of hardware and software. Maintenance and upgrading of equipment are also common themes.

It is appropriate to indicate a few sources which help to bring together some of the product information which is dispersed among many journals. A bibliography on text information management software has been published in *The Electronic Library* [434]. Its scope embraces software for communications, post-processing of data and information storage and retrieval. References from a broad cross-section of computing and library literature sources are listed under software package name or application. Over 1,000 references have been identified in the first two issues of the bibliography. Software which intermediates between searchers and databases is the subject of a bibliography titled *Online Searching Aids* [344] which was compiled from four computer and library science databases in early 1989. Among the software applications for which references are identified are downloading, post-processing and menu-driven online searching. On a more general but ongoing level, the quarterly *Microcomputer Index* provides abstracts for articles, product announcements and hardware or software reviews from more than seventy magazines and journals. In addition to general computing titles these sources also include *Online, Online and CD-ROM Review, Database, Database Searcher, Link-Up* and *The Electronic Library.* This makes it possible to locate articles on a wide range of relevant hardware and software. Indexes cumulate annually to aid retrospective searching. An online database version [653], bearing the same title, is also available. Another online source, also searchable on CD-ROM, is Computer Database [457] which emphasizes product information from the more popular computing journals, some of which are included in full-text format online. An article type subfield in each record includes the categories 'Product Announcement' and 'Evaluation' to which search results can be limited if required.

Current awareness columns in journals are discussed in section 3.5 of Chapter 3, but two which are especially significant for information about recent literature on microcomputing are published in *The Electronic Library* [454] and *Library Hi Tech News* [105].

2.4.5 Finding Out about Command Languages

The importance of command languages in the retrieval process is clearly in decline. CD-ROM products have led to a revolution in the search interface from the era of command languages and idiosyncratic error messages: menus, forms and onscreen guidance make the search experience much simpler. Menu driven interfaces appeared on many search services many years ago and now Windows-based communication and retrieval packages such as KRProbase and BRAQUE are becoming widespread. At the time of writing of this book it appears that Web-based retrieval interfaces such as WebSPIRS will be of increasing importance. Nevertheless command languages still retain an important role and so assistance in identifying search commands for a number of different systems is important. Indeed it might be argued that as command languages become less common then there is an increasing need for reference tools which enable people to use several command languages any one of which they may not use frequently. The *UKOLUG Quick Guide to Online Commands* [552], which is updated at irregular intervals and is produced by the UK Online User Group, provides details of more than thirty system features on each of fifteen hosts in its 4th edition. Each host receives four pages within which a standard format is followed so that a particular command is located in the same place for each host. Additional information includes help desk telephone numbers, postal addresses, Network User Addresses and hours of availability for searching.

2.4.6 Finding Out about Acronyms

Acronyms, are an established part part of the jargon of most disciplines and so it is no surprise that the electronic information industry has spawned its own acronym vocabulary. The perplexed searcher may find that the sources listed in this section are of value.

Over 500 of those in common use in online searching, notably database names, are expanded to their full form in the *North American Online Directory* [60]. A more general but international source is the *New International Dictionary of Acronyms in Library and Information Science and Related Fields* [54]. Definitions of more than 1,200 terms are included in *Online Searching: a Dictionary and Bibliographic Guide* [24], published in 1983. Unfortunately this source, although including a number of standard database terms of enduring significance, fails to reflect current terminology, especially in the area of microcomputer applications. A new edition is due to be published and will include CD-ROM terminology. The *Datapro Directory of On-Line Services* [57] is of greater value at present since it includes an eighty-page glossary in which over 1,500 online, microcomputing and telecommunications terms are defined. The directory is described at greater length later in this section of chapter two. A similar range of topics is covered by a glossary of gateway and telecommunications software which is included in a study titled *Gateway Software and Natural Language Interfaces* [346]. The number of terms defined is only around seventy but explanations are detailed. Finally, it is hoped that the glossary in this volume will be of value to some searchers.

2.5 Grey Literature

This category of literature consists of a mixture of publication types which includes reports of research, seminars or study visits, policy guidelines and database guides and evaluations. Essentially this is literature whose origin lies outside the mainstream publication channels. Among the types of organization which publish it are national libraries, such as the British Library, and individual libraries conducting their own or sponsored research. Government organizations are another source. These may be at an international level as in the case of the United Nations Educational Scientific and Cultural Organization (UNESCO), or national bodies like the Educational Resources Information Center (ERIC) of the United States Department of Education. Other sources are schools of librarianship and information science, professional bodies such as the Medical Library Association, and industry associations, for instance the European Association for Information Services (EUSIDIC) which has been responsible for issuing guidelines on CD-ROM supply conditions and pricing. The diffuse nature of this literature can make it difficult to locate but a number of finding tools are available and are now described.

2.5.1 Finding Out about Grey Literature

The bibliographical control of grey literature is notoriously difficult and complex. Whilst some of the major abstracting and indexing services include some grey literature most make no attempt to be comprehensive. Accordingly a separate bibliographic apparatus has grown up to document this form of literature. Therefore it seems more appropriate to discuss bibliographical control of this literature here rather than in the next chapter. *Resources in Education* [19] is an abstracting and indexing service which is coordinated by the Educational Resources Information Center (ERIC) in the United States and is published monthly with twice-yearly cumulations. It consists of sixteen broad subject groupings, each representing one of the clearinghouses which submit information to ERIC. One of these clearinghouses covers information resources and its section represents a full range of grey literature, including investigations of individual online or CD-ROM databases, seminar papers and instructional materials, mostly produced in the United States. Virtually all of the material listed can be acquired through the ERIC Document Reproduction Service (EDRS) or borrowed from a large number of national and other libraries, usually on microfiche. Entries contain abstracts, document type designations and the names of the organizations conducting and sponsoring research. Indexes allow entries to be located by subject, author, institution and publication type. Relevant terms in the subject index are 'Databases', 'Information Retrieval', 'Online Searching' and 'Optical Data Disks'. Resources in Education is a subfile of the ERIC [119] database which can be searched online and on CD-ROM.

Government Reports, Announcements and Index [8] can be used to locate reports from organizations outside the educational sector. It is published fortnightly by the National Technical Information Service (NTIS) in the United States and cumulates annually. The emphasis is on detailed reports produced by government departments and research organizations or by non-government bodies such as universities carrying out contracted research on behalf of the government. Coverage is international but is strongest for the United States. Entries include abstracts and contract or grant numbers. They represent less in the way of ephemeral material than *Resources in Education* but concentrate on detailed research reports on topics which have included gateway software, CD-ROM applications, optical disc production processes and the establishment of research databases. Reports can be acquired from NTIS and are also collected by many major libraries. A separate 'Library and Information Sciences' section exists, but a fuller range of entries can be found through the subject index which uses the same headings as those in Resources in Education. The NTIS [126] database offers online or CD-ROM access and includes some material from ERIC.

A special database for European grey literature, SIGLE [128], is compiled by the European Association for Grey Literature Exploitation from information submitted by national documentation centres in European Community countries. Chillag (1985) provides an insight into the establishment of the database and the way in which it is compiled. The database name is an acronym for System for Information on Grey Literature in Europe. It is strongest on material published in Britain and Germany but France and Italy are also represented in its coverage of publications about online and CD-ROM searching. Research reports, database directories, meeting reports and user aids for individual databases are among the types of document included in the database. Copies can usually be borrowed through national documentation centres. Hard copy abstracting and indexing services are produced by countries which contribute to the database. An example is *British Reports, Translations and Theses* [2].

Current Research in Library and Information Science [52] can sometimes identify relevant publications which are not documented elsewhere. This is not an abstracting or indexing service for published literature as such but serves as a register of current research projects in more than fifty countries. Its entries can include a section in which any publications emanating from the research are listed. The final issue of each year is cumulative and updates existing projects with details of the final report produced where appropriate. Until recently it was arranged by a faceted classification scheme which has now been replaced by a simpler system of subject headings. Separate indexes allow searching by subject headings or by researcher and organization name. Full postal addresses are supplied for research organizations, a helpful feature if publications cannot be obtained through other sources.

2.6 Theses

Doctoral theses account for a small proportion of the literature of online and CD-ROM searching. Indeed the number listed in the main abstracting and indexing service for theses, *Dissertation Abstracts International* [6] and its electronic equivalent [118], is never much in excess of 100 annually for library and information science as a whole. Those which are relevant have included evaluations of specific databases or of the effectiveness of online information retrieval systems in general, analyses of searcher behaviour and retrieval strategies, investigations into the success or otherwise of end-user searching and studies of the use of gateway software and expert systems in online information retrieval. CD-ROM and the Internet have not, as yet, received much attention (about 30 titles each) but this situation can be expected to change.

2.6.1 Finding Out about Theses

Schlachter (1988) observes that 'doctoral dissertations are cloaked by fragmented and sluggish bibliographic announcements and distribution channels'. As a consequence it may take a year from acceptance of a thesis to its recording in *Dissertation Abstracts International* [6, 118], already mentioned as the major abstracting and indexing service. This service is divided into three parts of which Section A, covering the humanities and social sciences, is the most relevant. It includes separate subject groupings for 'Library Science' and 'Information Science' in which theses are listed with lengthy abstracts in many cases. The majority of theses are from the United States or Canada, but doctoral theses from British universities have been included since 1988. Limited coverage of other countries is contained in section C of the service whose subtitle changed from European Abstracts to Worldwide in 1989. Author and subject indexes are included. Unfortunately the subject index is not cumulated each year, a situation which slows down retrospective searching appreciably and makes either the online or CD-ROM version [118] more attractive. More specific listings are compiled from Dissertation Abstracts International in two other sources. The journal *Library and Information Science Research* occasionally publishes lists compiled from the database version. For example its July-September 1989 issue contains a list of 211 doctoral dissertations on library and information science accepted in 1986 and 1987. Arrangement is by author name and abstracts are not included. This journal also has a section in which detailed reviews of a small number of theses are published in each issue. *Library and Information Science Annual* [16] contains a section titled 'Abstracts of Library Science Dissertations'. This section provides abstracts for a selection of theses accepted two years previously. The abstracts are different from those in *Dissertation Abstracts International* and are divided into four sections which outline purpose, procedure, findings and conclusions. National listings can be used for fuller coverage of individual countries. For example *Index to Theses* [11] provides abstracts for theses from universities in the United Kingdom and Ireland, including some at masters as well as at doctoral level. Another source for Britain is *British*

Reports, Translations and Theses [2] which records theses submitted by more than forty UK universities to the British Library Document Supply Centre for microfilming. This source does not contain abstracts.

References

Adamson, M. and Pearce, F. *Online Services in Europe: The impact of the Internet on business information services.* London: Financial Times Telecoms and Media Publishing. 1996.

Chillag, J. P. 'Grey literature: its supply and bibliographic access at the BLLD'. *Catalogue and Index,* no. 78-79, Autumn/Winter 1985, pp. 6-8.

Cornelius, P. 'BROKERSGUIDE: experiences in developing a database to improve the European information market, part 1'. *Infomediary,* 3 (1), September 1989, pp. 21-28.

Dupoy, J. *The complete idiot's guide to Netscape.* Indianapolis, Indiana: Que Corporaton, 1995.

Glossbrenner, A. *How to Look it up Online: Get the Information Edge with Your Personal Computer.* New York: St. Martin's Press, 1987. 486pp.

Gordon, H. A. 'Online magazine 1977-1987. An interview with Online's creators, Jeff and Jenny Pemberton'. *Online,* 11 (1), January 1987, pp. 8-16.

Hawkins, D. T. 'Bibliometrics of the online information retrieval literature'. *Online Review,* 2 (4), December 1978, pp. 345-352.

Houck, M. 'A look at the database directories online'. *Database,* 10(3), June 1987, pp. 67-75.

Ingebretsen, D. L., Borgman, C. L. and Case, D. 'Database guides: an annotated bibliography'. *Database,* 8(3), June 1985, pp. 89-100.

Jack, R. F. *Essential Guide to the Library IBM PC. Volume 4. Data Communications: Going Online.* Westport, Connecticut: Meckler, 1987. 245pp.

Jacsó, P. 'Directory of Library and Information Professionals on CD-ROM'. *Laserdisk Professional,* 2 (4), July 1989, pp. 63-73.

Moore, C. 'Bibliographic update'. *UK Online User Group Newsletter,* 1(1), January 1990, pp. 12-13.

Nicholls, P. T. 'A buyer's guide to CD-ROM selection: CD-ROM product directories and review tools'. *CD-ROM Professional,* 3 (3), May 1990, pp. 13-21.

Ojala, M. 'Laserdisks online: searching for the information not handed to you on a silver platter'. *Laserdisk Professional,* 1 (2), July 1988, pp. 48-58.

Online Information and the Electronic Library. Cambridge: Cambridge Market Intelligence, 1996.

Oseman, R. *Conferences and Their Literature: a Question of Value.* London: Library Association, 1989. 146pp.

Raitt, D. 'The evolution and development of the International Online Information Meetings'. *Online Review,* 13 (3), June 1989, pp. 235-245.

Re'em, D. 'The online market column'. *Information World Review,* no. 31, November 1988, p.9.
Schlachter, G. A. 'Abstracts of library science dissertations'. *Library and Information Science Annual,* 4, 1988, pp. 289-301.
Tenopir, C. 'The database press'. *Library Journal,* 114 (4), 1 March 1989, pp. 56-57.
Tittel, E. and James, S. *HTML for Dummies.* Foster City, California: IDG Books. 1995.

3 Access to the Primary Literature

3.1 Introduction

In this chapter the tools which give access to the primary literature of online and CD-ROM database searching are outlined. Since the first edition of this book, electronic information resources have increased in importance; this is particularly the case with bibliographic information sources. Accordingly this chapter does not treat electronic sources separately but seeks to integrate them into the text and refers to them alongside print products.

It is widely recognised that the bibliographic tools which provide a means of navigating around the primary literature have been created principally for one or other of two purposes. Firstly there are those such as bibliographies, abstracts and indexes which have been created to provide retrospective access to material that has been published over time. Secondly there are the current awareness tools which have been created to enable researchers to keep abreast of recent developments within their field.

3.2 Abstracting and Indexing Services

The major sources for retrospective searching are the abstracting and indexing services which are available in various combinations of print product, CD-ROM database and online access via the commerical search services. These databases can be viewed as belonging to one or other of three major groups and this section of the chapter is organised into three parts matching those three groups which are:

1. Library and Information Sciences
2. Other Disciplines
3. National Services.

It should not be forgotten that no single service will be comprehensive in its coverage: not only is each service selective in the journals which it indexes but many may also be selective in how they cover a journal. Finally many of these services do concentrate heavily on journals to the exclusion of other types of material: reports, theses, books and so on. Thus there might be many occasions when it may be necessary to search in several databases in order to complete a comprehensive search.

In deciding whether to search an electronic or a print product, the advantages of each approach should be borne in mind. Obviously searching an electronic product is faster than searching its print equivalent. Another point to bear in mind is that apparently identical products are in fact different. For example the electronic version of LISA [125] includes not just the material in *Library and Information Science Abstracts* but also the material in *Current Research in Library and Information Science.* Electronic products have the possibility of being more up-to-date than their print equivalents though it should not be automatically assumed that the possibility has become reality for each and every information product. Electronic products have far more search possibilities than do their printed equivalents. For example it is possible to search many databases using criteria such as document type, intellectual approach (for example, review, practical, theoretical, etc) or language of retrieved item. Searchers of electronic products can undertake searches with far more complex retrieval criteria than is practical with the print equivalents. In addition online search services offer the possibility of searching not just many years of the same database simultaneously but of searching several databases together. However this approach has obvious pitfalls. A simultaneous search across multiple databases usually demands that the searcher uses only natural language search criteria and that search statements must be developed without recourse to any of the database specific features which enhance the value of many databases. For example, someone who chose to search ERIC, LISA and INSPEC as a single search would not be able to use the controlled terms in the ERIC or INSPEC thesauri or take advantage of any database features such as INSPEC's Treatment Codes.

The major advantage of the print product is that it is far simpler to browse through a printed indexing or abstracting publication. In most cases this is facilitated through the classified arrangement of the items. This should help in those situations where the searcher knows what is sought and would recognise relevant material but is unable to articulate the information need in a manner which can be translated into a search statement. The classified arrangement also facilitates keeping up-to-date in a field or sub-field rather than on a very specific topic.

On those very rare occasions when a comprehensive search is necessary, it should not be forgotten that in terms of retrieval performance as measured through recall and precision, print and electronic products perform at about the same level as each other. Worse, there is considerable evidence that there is remarkably little overlap in items retrieved from the print and electronic versions of the same product. This leads to the unpleasant conclusion that to be completely thorough a searcher needs to search in both the print and electronic versions of the same product (Hartley 1983).

3.2.1 Library and Information Sciences

Library and Information Science Abstracts (LISA) [15] is one of three established services which specialize in monitoring the literature of librarianship and information science. Originally compiled by The Library Association it is published now by Bowker-Saur and began publication in 1950. It has been issued on a monthly basis with annual cumulations since 1982. Online and CD-ROM versions, are available [125]. Its entries contain essential bibliographic details with informative abstracts. One useful data element which is lacking is author affiliation. In the printed version entries until the end of 1992 are arranged according to a faceted classification which uses alphanumeric notation. Separate sections group most literature on online and CD-ROM searching at Zm, 'On-Line Information Retrieval' and Zjjc, 'CD-ROMs'. This classification scheme can be broken down to more specific levels so that entries can be found within the Zm, online searching, section for ZmHz&, 'End Users', and ZmOtn, 'Expert Systems and Front End Systems'. These designations should not, however, be considered to contain everything on the topics which they represent. The dominant facet in a document dictates its position in the classification so that an article on the user-system interface in end user searching would be found at ZmVr& rather than ZMHz&. The message which this example conveys is that, instead of relying solely on the most obvious section of the classification scheme, the searcher should use the subject index to group related items which are scattered by the classification. This scatter is an inevitable consequence of any classification scheme. The subject index contains a mixture of general and specific terms, among them 'Data Bases', 'Command Languages' and 'Strategies', although the system of chain indexing which is employed means that such terms may be embedded in other headings, for example 'Patents: Information Services: Data Bases: On-Line Information Retrieval'. Clearly it is possible to find very specific concepts represented in the subject index but the searcher must be prepared to exercise plenty of imagination to allow for the possibility of relevant references being indexed within less obvious headings. Since January 1993 the faceted classification system has been replaced by a simpler system of broad subject categories, most of which are divided to a further level of subheadings. The important section is 13.0 – Computerized Information Storage and Retrieval with subsections 13.14 Searching; 13.15 Downloading; 13.17 Non-Bibliographic Databases, Databanks; 13.21 Multimedia; and 13.26 CD-ROM Databases of note. Subsection14.16 Online Systems is also worth checking. Subject searching can therefore become very hard work and it is difficult to dissent from Prytherch's (1987) observation that 'to use the service online or on CD-ROM will save an enormous amount of time in a large-scale search'. Though the searcher would be well advised to remember that faster searching does not necessarily mean more effective searching.

The other search route which is available in *LISA* up to the December 1992 issues is the the name index. Apart from author names this index very helpfully contains database and host names and makes it easy to locate references about a particular file or the host. However in the simplification of the print product in 1993 the name index was replaced by the more conventional author index and names of information products and services should be checked in the subject index from that date. Both indexes cumulate annually. In the 1995 issues *LISA* indicates that 550 journals are indexed though it should be noted that this figure has varied somewhat over recent years. The major specialist online and CD-ROM titles are included in *LISA's* coverage. Although many journals are indexed selectively, this does not appear to be true of the main online and CD-ROM titles whose articles are virtually all included. A selection of newsletters is also covered, including *Library Hi Tech News, Information Today* and *Information World Review.* The established online conferences are also covered, with abstracts for individual papers as well as for the proceedings volumes as a whole. The international nature of source coverage is a recognized strength of *Library and Information Science Abstracts* which has been further improved by the recent extension of coverage. Until recently it was known that *LISA* often suffered from serious time lags. It is pleasing to note that there has been considerable improvement in this respect and as an example there are many items in the September 1995 issue which record items published in the June or July 1995 issues of journals.

Library Literature: an Index to Library and Information Science [17] is published every two months by the H.W. Wilson Company in New York. Its first issue was in 1934 and bimonthly publication has been established since 1969. The publisher also produces it online and on CD-ROM [124], although retrospective coverage only extends to 1984. The printed version is arranged in a single alphabetical listing in which entries are grouped under headings for subjects, authors or proper names such as databases. This saves the searcher's time by removing the need to switch back and forth between separate indexes and relevant entries. The whole publication, as opposed to only the indexes in the case of *Library and Information Science Abstracts,* is issued in cumulated form annually. This, in combination with the single author and subject sequence of entries, eases retrospective searching. In the absence of any abstracts uninformative titles are expanded to clarify their subject matter. Subject access is served by headings of varying specificity. Some of those with many entries are subdivided by subheadings though some of these are curious choices and of limited value. Why, for example, is country or state used as a subdivision of the section on OPACs? Two of the more important headings were changed in 1988. 'Online Searching' was introduced to replace two less obvious headings, 'Searching, Computer' and 'Searching, Microcomputer'. The term 'Information Storage and Retrieval Systems' was superseded by 'Information Systems' in the same year. These changes need to be borne in mind in retrospective searching. 'Online Searching' is a general heading underneath which cross-references are provided to guide the searcher to related, often more specific, terms such as 'End-User Searching', 'Information

Systems' and 'Online User Groups'. Surprisingly, there are no cross-references to the headings 'CD-ROM' or 'Reference Services' in the 1993 cumulation although a substantial number of relevant items are listed under each heading. They list some relevant references which are not to be found under the heading 'Online Searching'. It is evident that entries in *Library Literature* can appear under subject headings which are none too obvious so that the searcher needs to take full note of 'See' and 'See also' references from other headings and to think carefully about other possibly relevant headings for any given search. *Library Literature* covers less sources than *Library and Information Science Abstracts,* but its relevance for topics concerned with the online and CD-ROM fields has been increased by the addition of *Database Searcher, CD-ROM World* (now *Multimedia World*) and *CD-ROM Professional* to the list of journals indexed. This expansion took effect in 1989, bringing the number of journals covered to more than 200 and ensuring that there is now a good coverage of core journals about online and CD-ROM searching. The remaining source journals are largely traditional librarianship titles, about thirty of which are in languages other than English. Newsletters are excluded but some books, conferences and directories from leading US publishers are listed. *Library Literature* performs well on two counts. Firstly, it aims to index its journals fully. This means that it provides access to items, notably reports of conferences or trade exhibitions which are not indexed elsewhere. Secondly, the time lag between publication and indexing of entries appears to be kept within acceptable bounds. A figure of 4.3 months was cited by Ernest, Lange and Herring (1988). Certainly the journals *Online* and *Database* are often indexed within four months of publication.

Information Science Abstracts (ISA) [13], which first appeared as *Documentation Abstracts* in 1966 and changed to its present title in 1969, is the final abstracting and indexing service in this section. Its coverage is less rooted in librarianship than the services already discussed and includes computer science literature probably to a greater extent than does *LISA* even after its recent expansion. *ISA* is sponsored by a number of professional organizations, including the American Society for Information Science and the American Library Association. The whole timespan from 1966 is accessible online [121] via KR DIALOG. Thomas and Rosenberg (1988) provide some general background information about the printed service. Entries are clearly presented with full bibliographic details, which sometimes includes author affiliations, and informative abstracts which vary in length but are typically in the range of 100 to 150 words. Arrangement is by a classified system based upon eight main sections seven covering information science and the eighth related subjects such as mathematics and psychology. The most obviously relevant subsections are 3.2, 'Bibliographic Search Services, Databases', within the main section titled 'Information Systems and Applications', and 6.10, 'Searching, Search Strategy, Retrieval', in the 'Information Storage and Retrieval' section, within which another division, 6.6, 'Storage', contains some coverage of CD-ROM specifically. Cross-references are provided at the end of sections to guide the searcher to relevant entries in other sections and these should be heeded since they may help to pick out useful abstracts for specific topics like searcher education and training and for more general aspects which find their way into sections like 1.1, 'Conferences, Documentation, Bibliographies'. The subject index is arranged by broad subject heading amongst which 'CD-ROM', 'Online retrieval' and 'Searching' are obviously relevant whilst 'Online Systems' is more computer science than information science. Headings such as 'Legal Information' and 'Medical Information' may be useful for some searchers. Reference title is supplied in addition to the accession number in the monthly subject listing, a feature which can save search time significantly. More than 400 journals are now indexed as a result of a doubling of coverage in the 1980s. This expansion has ensured better international coverage, with a good representation of literature in European languages. The journals indexed are a cross-section of librarianship, information science and computer science titles. Coverage of the major online journals is good and the coverage of the CD-ROM journals has improved in recent years. Some general librarianship and library automation titles are included, as are a selection of personal computing magazines. Papers from the major online conferences are also indexed. Unlike most other abstracting and indexing services, *ISA* contains a high proportion of abstracts for report literature, most of it emanating from the ERIC and NTIS clearinghouses, and for theses recorded in *Dissertation Abstracts International* [6, 118]. Books are sometimes listed, with abstracts for individual chapters if appropriate. The introductory notes for the service state explicitly that the intention is to index source publications selectively rather than comprehensively, the criterion for inclusion of individual items being their subject relevance. The time lag between publication of a journal and the recording of its contents in *ISA* appears to be a problem. Delays of six months and over are common for the specialist journals in online and CD-ROM. Whilst this is quite typical of abstracting and indexing publications in many fields it does seem that *ISA* does not perform as well as *LISA* or *Library Literature* in this respect.

3.2.2 Other Disciplines

Online and CD-ROM database searching have applications in virtually any subject area. This is reflected in the publication of articles about them in journals from many different fields outside library and information science. Consequently, abstracting and indexing services from many disciplines are potentially useful as sources of information. Substantial coverage of online and CD-ROM searching occurs in three abstracting and indexing services from the computing, social science and education fields as outlined below.

Computer and Control Abstracts [3], published each month by the Institution of Electrical Engineers, is the leading source for computer science literature containing approximately 70,000 abstracts annually. Publication began in 1969 and searching is possible as far back as that date in the online database INSPEC [122] which includes *Computer and Control Abstracts* as a subfile. A classified subject arrangement is used for grouping entries and the major section for 'Information Science and Documentation' is 72.00. Most of the coverage of literature on online and CD-ROM searching is concentrated within this section although some abstracts on CD-ROM technology are included in 53.20K, 'Optical Storage'. Cross-references to related entries in other sections are also provided at the end of each section. Section 72.00 is divided into a number of more specific sections of which the most relevant are 72.10. 'Information Services and Centres' and 72.50 'Information Storage and Retrieval'. The former contains abstracts of literature on individual databases and on database coverage of subject areas while the latter also covers individual databases but emphasizes retrieval techniques and search strategies in different subjects. In addition it is a good place to look for reviews of reference management software. Its scope is wider than the others in section 72.00 as reflected by its further subdivision into the sections 72.50C 'Bibliographic Systems', 72.50L 'Non-Bibliographic Systems' and 72.50N 'Front End Systems for Online Searching'.

Users of *Computer and Control Abstracts* are likely to become familiar with its classified sequence, since there is no subject index to the monthly issues. Instead a cumulated subject index is issued twice yearly for the January to June and July to December periods.Terms in this index are of variable specificity as far as aspects of online and CD-ROM searching is concerned. CD-ROM is straightforward with the heading 'CD-ROMs' added in 1986. Unfortunately, there is no specific heading for online. A cross-reference is supplied from 'Online Literature Searching' to 'Information Retrieval'; a general heading within which references on online searching must be located in a lengthy list in which theoretical and experimental information retrieval features prominently. Some assistance is provided by the permutation of database names and terms or phrases such as 'end users' to the beginning of references listed under this and other headings. Other relevant subject headings are 'Bibliographic Systems', 'Information Services' and 'Information Retrieval System Evaluation'. The author index is provided on a monthly as well as a cumulated basis. There are also lists of books and conference proceedings indexed in each issue. These too cumulate twice yearly. *Computer and Control Abstracts* excels in its coverage of journal literature relevant to online and CD-ROM searching, not so much for core publications, although many are included in the coverage, as for other publications within and outside library and information science. Library automation titles like *Computers in Libraries* and *Library Software Review* are strongly represented as are general computing titles such as *Byte* and *PC User* which may contain relevant items from time to time. These are supplemented by a selection of trade and company periodicals from corporations like Hitachi, NEC and IBM which are active in CD-ROM or general microcomputer product development. Foreign-language material is well covered throughout *Computer and Control Abstracts.* Papers from the established online conference proceedings are indexed. Relevant papers are included from conferences which are unlikely to be indexed by *Library and Information Science Abstracts* such as the IEEE Information Visualisation conference held in Atlanta, Georgia in October 1995 and indexed in the January 1996 issue.

Social Sciences Citation Index [20] provides considerable coverage of the literature of online and CD-ROM database searching. The extensive coverage of LIS sources includes the main journals on online information retrieval. It has been published since 1966 by the Institute for Scientific Information. Its online and CD-ROM versions [129] extend back to 1972 and 1986 respectively. Academics in the United Kingdom have easy access to this database via the Bath Information and Data Services (BIDS) system which has had a major impact on information access in the United Kingdom academic community (Morrow 1995). The printed version consists of four separate parts: the Source Index which contains the bibliographic data and 3 indexes which provide access to that data by subject, corporate source and citations. The Source Index contains bibliographic data organised by first author of each item. Basic bibliographic data is provided together with the corporate address of the first author. There were no abstracts until 1991. Two data elements are of interest. One is a document type designation which indicates the approach taken in the document, for example, 'book review', 'hardware review', 'software review' or 'meeting abstract'. The second feature is far more unusual and valuable. It is the presence of a list of all the citations from the end of a paper.These can form a valuable indicator of the relationship of the document to other documents and by implication the subject content of the document.

Subject access to items in the Source Index is given by the Permuterm Subject Index which appears as a separate volume for each issue. This is an easy to use but limited index. All possible pairs of keywords in the titles of items in the Source Index are permuted and listed with a note of the name of the first author.This facilitates simple subject searching. For example the location of items about a particular database or software package should not be a problem provided that the name appears in the paper title. However for most searches, it does place considerable onus on the searcher to check all possible synonyms and spelling variants for a sought concept.For example it is worth looking under CDROM, CDROMS and CD-ROMS as well as CD-ROM and it may be worth searching for 'optical' too.

Another separate index which identifies literature in a unique way is the Citation Index. This enables the searcher to start with a known relevant paper and to retrieve those items which have cited it. The paper needs to be searched according to its first-named author where multiple authorship is involved. The papers which have cited it in the period covered by that issue or volume of *Social Sciences Citation Index* will be listed in a brief format enabling the full bibliographic citation to be retrieved from the Source Index. The Citation Index allows searches to be conducted forward in time from a particular reference and can be valuable if the citing authors are writing about and expanding upon the topic of the original paper. This will not necessarily be the case and Small (1982) identifies numerous other reasons for citation.

The final index in *Social Sciences Citation Index* is an index of corporate source of authors in the Source Index. The whole service cumulates annually to make retrospective searching easier. Searching of cumulated volumes or single issues can be a time-consuming process since it involves a lot of switching between indexes which are published in separate volumes.

Source coverage consists mainly of 1,400 journals in the social sciences although relevant articles from any of the 3,300 titles indexed by its sister publication *Science Citation Index* will be included. This makes *Social Sciences Citation Index* a good source for articles about applications of online and CD-ROM searching in any of the social sciences. Over fifty library and information science titles are also indexed, among them *Online, Database, Online and CD-ROM Review* and *The Electronic Library*. The value of this service is enhanced by its policy of total indexing of all its journals. This allows retrieval of shorter items like editorials, software, hardware, database and book reviews and meeting reports. Only *Library Literature* of the other services can approach this level of comprehensiveness.

Current Index to Journals in Education [5] is a more orthodox abstracting service whose strength in terms of information about online and CD-ROM searching lies in the areas of searcher education and training and end-user searching activities. It began publication in 1969, is issued monthly and forms part of the ERIC [119] database which can be accessed online and on CD-ROM. The whole service cumulates twice yearly. Data are coordinated by the Educational Resources Information Center (ERIC) in the United States from sixteen ERIC Clearinghouses each of which is allocated a particular educational speciality. One of these is information resources. Entries include brief abstracts. Standard bibliographic details are provided but entries do not indicate any corporate source. An additional feature is the inclusion of all identifiers and descriptor terms assigned to the entry. Terms preceded by an asterisk are included in the subject index. Arrangement of entries is by Clearinghouse name, 'Information Resources' being the section of most interest. Within this section entries are simply listed by accession number with no subject divisions. A separate subject index is provided. Its main term for CD-ROM is 'Optical Data Disks'. Online retrieval has two obvious terms, 'Online Searching' and 'Online Systems'. The former emphasizes the practice of searching by intermediaries and end users, while the latter concentrates on individual databases and groups of databases for particular subject areas. Relevant items can be found at other headings such as 'Databases', 'Search Strategies', 'Information Science Education' and 'Library Schools'. Other indexes are by author and journal source. A total of 740 journals in all fields of education is indexed. Coverage of other types of document is the province of its companion publication *Resources in Education* [19]. Articles on the use of online and CD-ROM databases in organizations at all educational levels from schools to universities are indexed from these journals and particularly from the eighty titles covered by the Information Resources Clearinghouse. All of these are in English and include the main online titles apart from *Database Searcher,* while *CD-ROM Professional* and *Optical Information Systems* represent CD-ROM. The remainder is a mixture of established librarianship journals, especially those associated with education and a selection of library automation titles. Indexing of most journals, including all of those for which the Information Resources Clearinghouse is responsible, is selective with only those items relevant to educational contexts included. A look at the journal contents index makes this clear with, for instance, only two articles listed from the May 1989 issue of *Laserdisk Professional* (now titled *CD-ROM Professional*). Currency is not a strength of *Current Index to Journals in Education* as can be seen by the absence of any articles published in 1989 under the headings 'Online Systems' and 'Optical Data Disks' in the subject index to the January to June 1989 cumulation.

3.2.3 National Services

The services discussed so far, although international in their source coverage, give more attention to the literature of the countries in which they are compiled, namely the United States and Britain. Consequently a literature search on online and CD-ROM developments in another country is more likely to yield comprehensive results if conducted in an abstracting or indexing service compiled in that country. This is true even when the service extends its source coverage to publications from many other countries. Examples from France, Germany and Russia are examined now.

PASCAL THEMA T205: Sciences de l'Information Documentation [18] is part of the multidisciplinary *PASCAL* abstracting and indexing service compiled in France by the Centre National de la Recherche Scientifique. The source coverage of the whole service is international and extends to a total of 4,500 journals. French-language material in fact only accounts for 12 % of the eight million references indexed by the whole service. *PASCAL THEMA T205* replaced *Bulletin Signaletique Section 101: Sciences de l'Information. Documentation* in 1985. It is published ten times a year and each issue contains about 350 entries. In addition to the major English-language journals, these entries represent French journal and conference literature and a selection of French government reports. Theses are also included. Entries are arranged by a subject classification whose headings are listed in both French and English. There are eight subject sections of which section 07, 'Recherche de l'Information', deals with general aspects of information retrieval such as search strategy and evaluation. Section 03, 'Sources Documentaires', is divided into subsections, including one titled 'Bases et Banques de Donnees' which covers references about individual databases or groups of databases. Short abstracts in French are provided for most references, along with translated English titles for documents whose original language is not English. The subject index is in both French and English and is supplemented by both name and author indexes. All indexes cumulate annually. The whole *PASCAL* service can be searched online [127], with descriptor terms in English, French and more recently Spanish.

Dokumentationsdienst Bibliothekswesen (DOBI) [7] is the best source for coverage of German literature on librarianship and information science. It took over in 1982 from *Fachbibliographischer Dienst Bibliothekswesen.* Originally publication was only annual but two issues per year are now produced. This change occurred in 1987. The whole publication is in German. Source publications are all published in the former German Federal Republic and, in addition to eighty journals and newsletters, include books, reports, yearbooks, conference proceedings and press releases. Entries, which totalled over 2,000 in 1987, contain full bibliographic details, subject headings and, usually, an abstract of between 100 and 200 words. They are arranged in fifteen subject sections. Section 6, 'Uberortliche Informations-und Literaturversorgung Informationssysteme', concentrates on online and other information systems. Online and CD-ROM databases are featured in the subsections 'Informationssysteme (einzelne), Dialogretrievalsdienste' and 'Elektronisches Publizieren' respectively. Cross-references to relevant entries in other sections are provided. The subject index can be used for more specific subject access and includes the terms 'CD-ROM', 'Datenbanken' 'Online-Literaturrecherchen' and 'Online-Informationssysteme'. Host, database and software package names can be searched in the subject index, as can geographic location. The other index is by author. Both indexes cumulate annually.

Informatics Abstracts [4] is a cover-to-cover translation of the Russian abstracting publication *Referativnyi Zhurnal: Informatika.* The translation has been published since 1967. It is issued monthly, usually about three or four months after the Russian edition. Like the French *PASCAL* service, the full *Referativnyi Zhurnal* series of abstracting and indexing publications is multidisciplinary and international in its coverage. *Informatics Abstracts* reflects this with a strong coverage of major English-language journals in information science, including the specialist journals in online information retrieval. Journal and report literature from the Soviet Union and from other countries in Eastern Europe is, however, more strongly featured than in other abstracting and indexing services.

Entries contain abstracts which vary greatly in length, sometimes extending to 300 words. Broad subject groupings are used and references on online and CD-ROM searching are scattered. Search techniques are emphasized in the section titled 'Information Retrieval', while databases figure strongly in the section for 'Information Service'. CD-ROM databases and technology are covered in a subsection titled 'Information Storage' within the 'Information Technology' grouping. The subject index can be used to overcome this scatter and contains several relevant terms, among them 'CD-ROM', 'Databases' and 'Online Search'. This index is cumulated annually, as are the other indexes by author and source publication.

3.2.4 Choosing an Abstracting or Indexing Service

The preceding pages have given some indication of the merits and defects of the major abstracting and indexing services. It is precisely because each has at least one area of weakness that previous studies have concluded that more than one of them needs to be used in order to get a full perspective on the literature. Not everybody has the time, inclination or need to find out absolutely everything written about the sought aspect of online or CD-ROM searching and accordingly may only search one service. Sometimes the choice is dictated by the range (or lack of range) of abstracting and indexing services available. Where a choice is offered the situation is one of 'horses for courses', the nature of the search being the deciding factor. For example, literature about individual databases or hosts is most easily found in either *Library and Information Science Abstracts* [15] or *Social Sciences Citation Index* [20] whose indexes are well suited for this type of search. Topics which are likely to be covered in the computing literature are well served by *Computer and Control Abstracts* [3]. End user searching is strongly featured in *Current Index to Journals in Education* [5].

If a single service had to be recommended above the others for general use then *Library and Information Science Abstracts* [15] seems to be the best option. The recent expansion in coverage by *LISA* means that it is now the source of choice at least for recent material. For pre-1990 material and particularly for computer science oriented literature then *Computer and Control Abstracts* [3] would be a good choice. Despite the absence of one or two specialist journals from its source list and its scattered indexing of online searching. The sources which it covers are international and highly relevant. In addition to most of the specialist journals and conferences its source coverage represents the more computer-oriented librarianship and information science titles and supplements them with computer science journals which may contain features on searching or, more likely, its associated technology. Current information on microcomputer hardware and software is essential for anyone involved with online and CD-ROM databases. The relatively rapid inclusion of recent literature in *Computer and Control Abstracts* is another significant point in its favour. Although not perfect, it can be used to find a lot of relevant journal and conference literature on various aspects of online and CD-ROM searching.

3.3 Bibliographies

Bibliographies can bring together literature from a wide range of sources in a convenient format. In particular they can be helpful to anyone seeking a perspective of online and CD-ROM developments over a period of time. They appear in a variety of formats: some being issued as publications in their own right, perhaps as part of a series, and others appearing incidentally as sections of books or reports. An invaluable source for literature on online searching from its earliest days has been the Online Information Retrieval Bibliography compiled by D. T. Hawkins each year as a supplement to the journal *Online Review*. It began in March 1977 with a supplement to the very first issue of *Online Review,* covering literature in the period from 1965 through 1976. Annual updates were published until 1990. They appeared in the journal itself until 1985 when the size of the bibliography warranted publication as a supplement to each August issue of *Online Review.* To aid retrospective searching a number of cumulations have been published. Those for 1983-1986 [26] and 1987-89 [27] have been listed in the bibliography. Earlier ones covered the periods 1964-1979 and 1964-1982. References were listed in seven subject sections originally but this number was increased in 1983 to eleven, reflecting the expansion of coverage into newer areas, notably microcomputer applications. The first section was a general one which was used to record new books, reviews, conference proceedings and directories, although these types of publication also featured in the more specific subject sections if appropriate. Of the remaining sections the largestwas always the second one, 'Descriptions of Online Systems, Databases and Services'. This section dealt with databases in all disciplines and best shows the wide source coverage of the bibliography. In addition to the major online and CD-ROM titles there is a good representation of articles in titles from other disciplines such as business, medicine, law and chemistry. A notable feature was the listing of relevant articles from some of the popular computing magazines. Conference literature was also strongly featured and included papers from the major proceedings. The remainder of the bibliography comprised a selection of books, reports and a few theses. English-language literature dominated throughout, although items in European languages and in Japanese were included. The bibliography normally contained about 900 references each year. There were no abstracts. The author and permuted (enriched) title indexes make it easy to identify papers by individuals or on specific databases but are of more limited value for finding literature on a particular topic since it depended to some extent on the occurrence of appropriate keywords in the title. Some literature from the year in which the bibliography was published was included and its proportion increased in the later years. In the main, however, the emphasis was on literature from the previous year. Overall, this is a valuable record of publishing activity in the online searching and CD-ROM fields up until August 1990.

Retrospective coverage is also provided by a series of bibliographies compiled by J. L. Hall between 1976 and 1986. The first two covered 1965-1976 and, with A. Dewe, 1976-1979. Together they document almost 2,000 earlier references on online searching taken from journals, conference proceedings and reports, predominantly in the English language, although representing many countries in Europe and internationally. Two differences to note are that report literature is significantly more prominent in the first publication than in the second, while brief abstracts are an additional feature of the 1976-1979 volume. In each case entries are arranged alphabetically by author name. There are author, report number and general indexes, the last-named allowing retrieval by database or host name or by subject. Two further bibliographies were compiled by Hall as part of the third and fourth editions of *Online Bibliographic Databases: a Directory and Sourcebook,* published in 1983 and 1986 [22] respectively. The 1983 edition included references to articles on individual databases within the entries for those databases in the directory section of that publication together with a separate bibliography of 215 references to more general material. Most were published between 1979 and 1982. However the 1986 [22] edition was arranged as a single listing of references with cross references in the database directory section. This bibliography extends to over 1,000 references published in the whole period from the early 1960s through to 1985. It is thus a selection of literature from the previous bibliographies as well as an update. Entries are arranged alphabetically according to first-named author with indexes by subject and co-author. There are no abstracts.

The other major bibliography on the early development of online information retrieval is *Online Searching: a Dictionary and Bibliographic Guide* [24] published in 1983. It restricts its coverage to English language journals only. Significantly, for articles to mid-1982 from the major journals author, subject and source journal indexes are provided. The subject index contains names of databases and hosts and illustrates a definite bias towards information about US systems. For instance, seventy-nine entries are listed under the heading 'DIALOG INFORMATION RETRIEVAL SERVICE' but only two under that for 'ESA-IRS', the similarly long-established European host.

A further very useful bibliography is the *Online Searching for End Users: an Information Sourcebook* [23] which covers a selection of the literature from 1983 to 1987. Its scope is more general than the title might suggest to an information professional since it is a book for end-users rather than about end-users and so emphasis is placed on listing references of practical value to searchers. Over 500 references, mostly in English, are included from a diversity of types of publication, notably a selection of books, reports, theses, search kits and directories in addition to journal articles and conference papers. Most entries are annotated with informative abstracts. Indexes are by author, title and subject. An extra feature is the provision of a suggested core collection of literature for online searchers.

Not surprisingly, there are fewer major retrospective bibliographies for CD-ROM since little was published in this area until the mid-1980s. One bibliography which covers all aspects of CD-ROM up to the end of 1987 is *CD-ROM: an Annotated Bibliography* [139] This is a substantial bibliography containing 725 annotated references from a mixture of librarianship and computing sources. Its strength is its coverage of CD-ROM applications in particular subject areas, of which forty are identified by separate sections. Access to specific items can be obtained through author, title and subject indexes. Literature from the period 1985 to 1988 is covered in *A Guide to the Literature of Electronic Publishing: CD-ROM, Desktop Publishing, and Electronic Mail, Books and Journals* [140]. Ostensibly *CD-ROM 1992: an Annotated Bibliography of Resources* [141] is more up-to-date. In fact, very little of the material listed is post-1990.

Other useful retrospective coverage of CD-ROM literature can be found in *Optical Storage Technology: a State of the Art Review* [143]. Though it should be noted that this publication concentrates on the technology. CD-ROM is a topic which has featured in two ongoing series of bibliographies, *Library Hi Tech Bibliography* [28] and NTIS Published Searches [30]. Volumes in the *Library Hi Tech* series are published annually and contain about fifteen bibliographies on library automation topics. Its bibliographies are selective but usually contain detailed abstracts. Subjects have included CD-ROM and end-user searching. NTIS Published Searches are the result of retrieval by staff at the US National Technical Information Service (NTIS) from any of a range of the major international science and technology databases. The series may be of interest as a means of identifying literature from outside the mainstream library and information science sources. Published Searches are included in the abstracting and indexing service *Government Reports, Announcements and Index* [8], although a more convenient listing is to be found in the *Published Search Master Catalog* which can be obtained free of charge from NTIS. It is published annually, with a semiannual update, and contains subject headings for 'Compact Disks', 'Optical Storage', 'Information Retrieval' and 'On-Line Systems'. Updates of the bibliographies themselves are issued regularly for fast-developing fields like CD-ROM and purchasers of a search are automatically informed of any new editions.

The final category of bibliography is that which is included in books or reports about online or CD-ROM searching. Substantial bibliographies may be identified in this way. The approach may be to provide a general bibliography on a subject as in the case of *End-User Searching: Services and Providers* [347] and in *The Librarian's CD-ROM Handbook* [146]. Alternatively, it may be that the whole work contains extensive bibliographies for all or most of its chapters. Examples are *Online Information Retrieval: an Introductory Manual to Principles and Practice* [34] and *Guidelines for Teachers of Online Information Retrieval* [360].

3.4 Review Literature

Review literature performs the valuable function of documenting developments in a subject area, describing the current state of the art and indicating the main organizations and individuals responsible for major advances. A review paper usually end with a sizeable bibliography of published work on its subject. Special publications exist to act as vehicles for the publication of reviews only and in addition many journals publish review papers which contain many references. There are three annual reviews which are relevant to online and CD-ROM databases searching. Firstly the *Annual Review of Information Science and Technology (ARIST)* [133] contains detailed reviews of developments in library and information science. As Bellardo (1988) notes, it

> 'has chronicled not only most of the theories and empirical investigations of the past twenty years, but also the technological advances and innovations, the important social and economic issues, information policies, applications and services in the field.'

Thus it is not surprising that it has included topics pertinent to this book. The 1988 volume contained a thorough review of developments in CD-ROM technology [197] with 180 references and an article titled 'Quality Control in Online Databases' which analyzed errors in data included in online files and their implications for search quality and searcher liability, appending 150 citations. More recent examples include a review of expert systems as search tools [361] and a review of the human computer interface for information retrieval [362]. These examples illustrate the detailed treatment accorded to issues in online and CD-ROM technology and services.

It might be thought that the review journal *Advances in Librarianship* would be a likely source of review papers for online and CD-ROM database searching. Unfortunately to date only volume 17 in 1993 has contained anything of obvious relevance (Potter, 1993). However given that the publication seems to have resumed regular publication again after a hiatus in the mid-1980s and is giving increased emphasis to electronic communication, it would seem appropriate to spend a few minutes checking through recent volumes for potentially relevant reviews.

Perspectives in Information Management promised to be a useful annual review since it complemented *ARIST* both by being produced and largely written in Europe and in a style more useful to students and practitioners than researchers. Alas this does not seem to have progressed beyond the inaugural volume published in 1989. Its thirteen reviews covered a number of themes of practical concern to searchers, including retrieval of standards and patent information, developments in chemical structure searching and online sources of business information.of articles in the first volume contained substantial bibliographies.

A major review source for CD-ROM developments is *Optical Storage Technology: a State of the Art Review* [198], published annually since 1985. This publication examines developments in optical disc technology as a whole but CD-ROM features prominently in one of its main categories: read-only discs. Developments in CD-ROM technology, products and markets are fully reviewed. This publication serves as a review of the technology and its associated literature. New literature is included in a general bibliography of more than 1,000 recent and older references which is updated each year.

In addition to the specialist review journals, many review papers appear in general journals. Of the mainstream online and CD-ROM journals, *Online and CD-ROM Review* [81] is probably most likely to contain review papers whilst other such papers may also appear in the major information science journals: *Information Processing and Management* [420], *Journal of Documentation* [422] and *Journal of the American Society for Information Science* [423]. For example, *Journal of Documentation* regularly features review papers under the general heading of Progress in Documentation; valuable relevant examples are the paper by Efthimiadis [355] on online search aids and Enser's review of pictorial information retrieval [472].

It can be argued that the practical nature of online and CD-ROM searching generates two types of literature. There is the scholarly research for example on the process of searching as typified by the work of Fidel (1985, 1991). This literature will generate scholarly reviews with many references. However there is a substantial literature which is practitioner-orientated which tends not to contain large numbers of references to other publications. This might even extend to papers which can be termed review papers in the sense that they review a topic and summarize the key developments but without the panoply of references to original literature.

Some of the major abstracting and indexing services aid the location of review papers. Thus *Computer and Control Abstracts* [3] contains a bibliography index in each issue which gives a separate list of articles with substantial bibliographies.*Social Sciences Citation Index* [20] applies the document type designation 'Review' to all articles in its Source Index which have been published in review serials or which contain bibliographies of over 100 references.

3.5 Current Awareness Services

Whilst the products discussed so far in this chapter enable the searcher to undertake retrospective searches, they are not always appropriate for keeping track of current developments within a field. The lack of currency which has been noted precludes this despite the fact that many electronic products offer retrieval facilities for searching only the newly added material. The person seeking to keep up-to-date with recent developments in online and CD-ROM database searching has a variety of options. There are several print and electronic products have merged to enable people to track current developments in addition some information is recorded in the primary journals and newsletters. More recently services have emerged on the Internet which make it possible to track recent publications. Finally many people find it useful to visit conferences and exhibitions as sources of current information.

The latest literature and research are monitored by a small number of current awareness publications which are examined in this section. Current awareness publications perform a valuable role since they bridge the gap between the publication of literature and its appearance in print or electronic versions of abstracting and indexing services. Two current awareness services are available for literature in library and information science. Aslib's *Current Awareness Abstracts of Library and of Information Management Literature* [53] provides a good coverage of the literature germane to readers of this book featuring items from some 300 core journals. Its groups articles in subject sections covering 'CD-ROM', 'Online Equipment', 'Online Hosts and Databases' and 'Online Searching Techniques'. Bibliographic details and abstracts are provided. Source coverage centres on the main online and CD-ROM titles but supplements them with library automation journals and some newsletters. Most of the articles listed will have been published within the last three months.

Recent library and information science literature is also monitored by *CABLIS: Current Awareness Bulletin for Library and Information Staff* [49], compiled by the British Library Information Sciences Service which is based at The Library Association. It includes a section in which the main contents of recent issues of about fifty journals are listed by journal title. Regular columns and news sections are not included in the contents listings. The subject range of the journals covered extends across the full spectrum of library and information science and includes most of the specialist titles for online and CD-ROM purposes. In addition it contains a list of recent additions to the stock of the British Library Information Sciences Service. This section is arranged by subject groupings, the most significant being 'Automation in Libraries' and 'Information Searching and Retrieval'.

The other major collection of Librarianship and Information Science literature in the United Kingdom and probably Europe is that of the Thomas Parry Library of the University of Wales Aberystwyth. That library's regular listing, *Periodical Alert: Contents Pages of Serials Received at the Thomas Parry Library,* provides notification of the contents of a large number of journals relevant to online and CD-ROM and of course has the benefit of also including many titles which upon occasion contain material within the sphere of searching electronic information sources.

Current Contents: Social and Behavioural Sciences [51] also employs the contents page approach to current awareness. As indicated by its subtitle, coverage extends well beyond library and information science but this is included as one of the categories in which journal contents are listed. Within this category contents pages from the latest issues of any of thirty journals can be scanned, among them *Online, Database* and *Online and CD-ROM Review*. The contents listing for each journal is fuller than in *CABLIS* and includes the subjects of all columns and the titles of any publications reviewed. The weekly publication schedule enables *Current Contents* to display journal contents for new issues very quickly. In the United Kingdom it is not uncommon to see the contents page of an American journal in *Current Contents* before the original journal arrives in the library. Article title word and author indexes are also provided. The service can be searched online [50] using KR Data-Star or KR Dialog.

Current Research in Library and Information Science [52] complements these current awareness services by providing details of ongoing research whose results may not have been published. Entries describe the nature of the research and include a contact person for further information. A telephone number may be included. Otherwise the address of the organization at which the research is being conducted can be obtained in the name index.

Recognizing a gap in the marketplace, a number of organisation have developed new current awareness products in recent years. These new products are often linked to other services making attractive packages for information managers. One example is the British Library's Inside Information service which offers access to approximately 1 million items each year from approximately 10,000 journals at the British Library Document Supply Centre. Obviously notification of the existence of articles is supported by a document delivery service. Another example is Swetscan from the large subscription agency Swets. This product offers access to the contents of some 7000 journals and adds about 110,000 items to its database each month. There are other services and further information can be gleaned from the paper by Rowley (1994).

A recent development is the use of the Internet to provide a current awareness service. The well known Bulletin Board for Libraries (BUBL) includes two sections of current awareness information. The first provides data about forthcoming books. The data includes bibliographic details and an abstract of the content. The service provided from BookData information is so current that in November 1995 it is possible to read about books which will not be published until early 1996! Secondly there is a journals contents page service which offers access to the contents pages of several hundred library and information science oriented journals. Again this is very up-to-date so that in November 1995 it was possible to view the contents of the October 1995 issue of journals such as *Library Manager*. Most of the major online and CD-ROM journals are covered by this service. This service can also be obtained as e-mail by subscribing to LIS-BUBL-E2; in which case the mostly abstracted tables of contents simply arrive in the user's mail box.

Some journals and newsletters include sections which are designed to alert readers to recent literature of relevance to online and CD-ROM searching. They usually list articles from related journals and, like the current awareness services described in the last section, do so more rapidly than abstracting and indexing services. The widest coverage until a few years ago was once offered by *Library Hi Tech News* [105] whose 'Information and Instruction Technologies' column included articles from any of eighty journals and magazines in library and information science, supplementing its coverage of some of the main online and CD-ROM journals with library automation titles and industry newsletters like *CD Data Report* and *Optical Memory News*. Each issue contained about seventy entries, mostly with descriptive abstracts. Coverage of online and CD-ROM literature could be found throughout, the emphasis being on microcomputing aspects. *Online* [83] and *Database* [71] share a column called 'Journal Watch' which summarizes articles mostly selected from a core list of thirty highly relevant journals. These journals are a mixture of core online and CD-ROM titles, librarianship journals which emphasize computer applications and microcomputing magazines such as *Byte, PC Week* and *Personal Computing*. There is a definite bias towards literature published in the United States. Relevant European titles like *Online and CD-ROM Review, The Electronic Library* and *Information World Review* are excluded. Between ten and fifteen recent articles are featured in each issue and are arranged according to subject headings such as 'Microcomputers', 'Modems', 'Printers and Printing' and 'Workstations' which illustrate the emphasis of this column on product information. Full descriptions are provided for each article featured. These descriptions are evaluative and often include quotations from the article. *CD-ROM Professional* [178] also has a 'Resources in Brief' section which highlights useful or valuable journals, books, Web sites and services. This is usually a side-bar to a main article – 'The Resource Directory' – which deals with a different topic in each issue. After the introduction this and then the side-bar have much the same format with each entry followed by a description.

Recent literature on developments in Britain and Europe is reported in the UKOLUG Newsletter [114] whose current awareness column has been expanding and may contain 30-35 abstracts of journal articles or conference papers. The column caters for a full range of interests with entries organized under headings such as 'CD-ROM', 'Database Creation', 'Downloading and Post-Processing' and 'Online: Subject: Business' although there is current discussion on the value of such headings and the column may become a single sequence. As well as the specialist titles for online and CD-ROM searching, sources include European news publications like *Information World Review* and a number of popular computing magazines.

For current literature published in other countries it is best to consult journals from these countries, some of which have current awareness features of the type described in this section. The German title *Nachrichten für Dokumentation* [80] displays the contents pages of a number of journals in a section titled 'Media-Info', while a separate column, 'Literaturauslese zur Informationswissenschaft und -praxis', contains over 100 references per issue from the INFODATA [120] database. Online and

CD-ROM searching and associated hardware and software are fully featured in this column. For France, *Documentaliste* [72] has a separate section in which abstracts of recent articles from journals such as *Infotecture* and *Memoires Optiques et Systemes* are presented under the journal title. Literature in Japanese and other languages is listed in an ongoing bibliography of references on online and CD-ROM information retrieval in *Online Kensaku* [82]. Finally, recent articles relevant to particular subject areas may be monitored in specialist journals such as *Bulletin of the Medical Library Association* [607] and *World Patent Information* [628].

3.6 Newsletters

The *UKOLUG Newsletter* was mentioned earlier because of its utility in keeping up-to-date with the literature. The other use of this newsletter is keeping the UKOLUG membership abreast of recent developments within the world of electronic information. Much useful information in this field is short term ephemeral information which is best gleaned from such sources. Another vital source of information for European searchers in Learned Information's monthly newspaper *Information World Review* which keeps a close watch on industry developments. American searchers will wish to keep a close eye on its American equivalent *Information Today*. These are not sources for those who wish a detailed exposition on search techniques but they offer unrivalled coverage of news about the financial status of major players in the electronic information business, news of new products and forthcoming exhibitions and conferences.

Many searchers will find it important to keep abreast of the various newsletters produced by the major online suppliers such as Knight-Ridder and FT Profile, database producers such as INSPEC and some of the larger suppliers of CD-ROM products such as SilverPlatter and Ovid.

Finally there are a small number of expensive newsletters such as *Monitor* [288] which provide detailed analysis and commentary on the electronic information industry by acknowledged experts. These are not essential reading for the users of electronic products but for anyone tracking the developments and trends in the industry they are indispensable reading.

3.7 The Internet

In recent years the importance of the Internet as a means of communication has become increasingly obvious. The use of services such as BUBL for current awareness have already been noted. 1995 has been the year in which the World Wide Web has threatened to ensnare all in its threads and thus it should be no surprise that many players in the electronic information business have a presence on the Web. Major players such as Disclosure, Dun & Bradstreet, SilverPlatter and Knight-Ridder and consumer organisations such as UKOLUG have a presence on the Web where people can locate information about those organisations. The URL for UKOLUG is http://www.bubl.bath.ac.uk/BUBL/UKOLUG.html. Currently the use of the Web is largely as a means of awareness, almost the marketing, of organisations although it is being extended beyond that to include information in electronic form.

Finally the various discussion lists which are on the Internet offer a means whereby people with a shared interest can swap information or indeed seek help in the solution of a problem. Of interest to online searchers will be UKOLUG's discussion list: LIS-UKOLUG and for the many in the British higher education community who take advantage of the BIDS services then the list LIS-BIDS-USERS may be of interest. Valuable information and guidance is available to users of reference management software from the various lists associated with packages such as Endnote (endnote-interest@niles.com) and ProCite (Pro-Cite@ubvm.indiana.com) and the general discussion list about bibliographic software (BIBSOFT@indycms.iupui.edu).

It is reasonable to suppose that the Internet will increase in importance as a means of communication. As a part of that increase it will become more important as a source of information about electronic information sources; inevitably so since users of electronic information sources are likely to feel comfortable using their workstation as their source of information. Whilst this prediction can be made with some confidence, it is much less clear how the prediction will be met. No one at the turn of the decade could have predicted the phenomenal growth of the World Wide Web, who would be so bold as to predict what might occur by the turn of the century? Perhaps the only thing which can be said with any confidence is that the Internet will become increasingly important as a source of informal and ephemeral information. Its role in the transfer of more formal information is likely to be slower because of the additional problems relating to economics and ownership which surround this type of information.

References

Bellardo, T. 'Keeping up in information science'. *Library and Information Science Annual*, 1988, 4, pp. 3-8.

Ernest, D. J., Lange, H. R. and Herring, D. 'An online comparison of three library science databases'. *RQ*, 1988 28 (4), pp. 185-194.

Fidel, R. 'Moves in online searching'. *Online Review*, 1985, 9 (1), pp. 61-74.

Fidel, R. 'Searchers selection of search keys: 3 Searching styles'. *Journal of the American Society for Information Science*, 1991, 42 (7), pp. 515-527.

Hartley, R. J. 'A laboratory method for the comparison of retrieval effectiveness in manual and online searching'. *In Proceedings of the 7th International Online Information Meeting London 6-8 December 1983*. Oxford: Learned Information, 1983, pp. 157-166.

Morrow, T. 'BIDS: the growth of a networked end-user bibliographic database service'. *Program*, 1995, 29 (1), pp. 31-41.

Potter, W.G. 'Access to electronic information:exploring the options'. *Advances in Librarianship,* 1993, 17, pp. 61-77.

Prytherch, R. *Sources of Information in Librarianship and Information Science* (2nd edn). Aldershot: Gower, 1987. 153 pp.

Rowley, J. E. 'Revolution in current awareness'. *Journal of Librarianship and Information Science,* 1994, 26 (1), pp. 7-14.

Small, H. 'Citation context analysis'. *Progress in Communication Sciences,* 1982, 3, pp. 287-310.

Thomas, D. and Rosenberg, M.D. 'Information science abstracts: an overview of history purpose and goals Part 1'. *Information Service and Use,* 1988, 8 (5/6), pp. 249-255.

PART II

Bibliography

Bibliography

The second and major part of this Keyguide is an annotated bibliography of information sources on online and CD-ROM searching and topics related to them such as the Internet, Downloading and Personal Bibliographic Software. Many of these topics have been discussed in Part I. Entries in the bibliography are grouped and numbered as follows:

The divisions have increased since the first edition, principally to include newer topics of interest to database searchers such as the Internet, alternative hosts and quality. As might be expected the older, traditional areas dominate with larger numbers of entries as the literature in newer areas – although growing fast – is not as established. The General section with which the bibliography begins is the longest as many sources are equally relevant to online, CD-ROM, the Internet and other later divisions. After the two General sections, the remaining division headings are treated in alphabetical order as indicated above.

The listing in each section is, of course, selective; this means that entries are either for the main sources (as in the case of abstracting and indexing services where those identified are the most likely to provide further information) or are deemed to be the most useful to readers. While the emphasis is on conventional sources, some electronic versions have been included; this is, to some extent, an indication of the way things are moving – much of the better information *about* the Internet is *on* the Internet and not available elsewhere. The database industry has changed and is changing extremely fast – while this bibliography has been in preparation three major names have changed ownership (one of them twice!) so that Data-Star was purchased by DIALOG before both parties became identifiably Knight-Ridder subsidiaries known as KR Data-Star and KR DIALOG, while Mead Data Central was purchased by Reed-Elsevier and became LEXIS/NEXIS. To some extent, these and other, technological changes are responsible for the enormous amount of writing, the mere tip of which is reflected in this bibliography. Some older works which were in the first edition have been kept if they are deemed relevant and important and are still in print. If nothing else, they will provide a historical perspective to the more recent items.

GENERAL

Abstracting and Indexing Services

1. *British National Bibliography.* London: British Library National Bibliographic Service, 1950-. Weekly, with monthly, four-monthly and annual cumulations.

Titles are arranged by subject according to the Dewey Decimal Classification as new books and conference proceedings published in Britain and received by the British Library each receive a Dewey 20 classification number. They are catalogued according to the Anglo-American Cataloguing Rules. Among the classification numbers used for works on online and CD-ROM information retrieval the most relevant are 025.524 and 025.00285456 respectively. An alphabetical joint author/title index is provided, along with a subject index – The Compass Index – to the month's titles in the Monthly Index. Available online and on CD-ROM.

2. *British Reports, Translations and Theses.* Wetherby, West Yorkshire: British Library Document Supply Centre, 1969-. Monthly, with quarterly and annually cumulated indexes.

According to the Introduction, this indexes, without abstracts, 'British report literature and translations produced by British government organizations, local government, universities, and learned institutions and most doctoral theses accepted at British universities and polytechnics during and after 1970'. Almost 1,500 items are listed each month under broad subject categories. The relevant section is 05B, 'Documentation, Information Science and Librarianship'. A keyterm index is issued monthly at the end of each issue with separate author, report number and keyterm indexes on microfiche in March, June, September and December, the last issue being an annual cumulation.

3. *Computer and Control Abstracts.* Stevenage, Hertfordshire: Institution of Electrical Engineers, 1969-. Monthly, with twice yearly cumulated indexes.

One of the INSPEC Abstracts Journals, this is a valuable source for international coverage of articles and papers on online and CD-ROM information retrieval, with a particular emphasis on technological developments such as enhancements in host services, search software and equipment. Many journal and conference publications in the field, representing a wide range of countries, are included in its source coverage, along with a small selection of report and book literature. Informative abstracts are supplied and entries are arranged according to a subject classifications scheme whose most relevant headings are 72.10, 'Information Services and Centres' and 72.50, 'Information Storage and Retrieval'. Latest issues need to be searched according to the classification since subject and author indexes are not provided monthly, but appear in cumulated form twice a year. The subject index allows retrieval via headings such as 'Information Retrieval', 'Information Services' and, since 1986, 'CD-ROMs'. About 72,000 references are added each year. Also available on microfiche, and as a part of INSPEC, online and on tape and CD-ROM. *Current Papers on Computing and Control* gives full bibliographic references only, arranged by subject and available monthly.

4. *Cumulative Book Index: a World List of Books in the English Language.* New York: H. W. Wilson, 1898-. Monthly, with quarterly and annual cumulations.
A listing of English-language books published worldwide, including reference works and conference proceedings with over 50,000 books are added annually. Entries are listed in a single alphabetical sequence arranged by Library of Congress Filing Rules by author and title under Library of Congress subject headings, the fullest bibliographic details being provided under author name. A generous range of subject headings is available and these are further subdivided by document type. The most appropriate headings begin 'Online', 'Optical disk' and 'CD-ROM'. Available online and on CD-ROM.

5. *Current Index to Journals in Education.* Phoenix: Oryx Press, 1969-. Monthly, with twice yearly cumulations.
CIJE indexes and abstracts journals in education and related fields while a companion title, *Resources in Education,* covers other types of document. Information is supplied by the sixteen clearinghouses of the Educational Resources Information Center (ERIC) in the United States. Many of the major journals in the field of information retrieval are indexed, selectively in most cases and with an emphasis on practical rather than theoretical aspects. Entries are grouped by Clearinghouse Subject Area and indexed by subject, author and source journal. A wide range of terms pertinent to database searching is included in the subject index. These consist of the major descriptors and identifiers assigned to each reference and displayed with an asterisk in each entry and include 'Online Searching' and 'Optical Data Disks'. Available online and on CD-ROM as part of the ERIC database.

6. *Dissertation Abstracts International Section A: The Humanities and Social Sciences.* Ann Arbor, Michigan: University Microfilms International, 1938-. Monthly.
Until 1988 this service concentrated on listing doctoral dissertations from nearly 500 primarily US and Canadian institutions. Since then doctoral dissertations from UK universities have been included. Abstracts are lengthy and descriptive and are compiled by authors. Entries are arranged under broad subject headings, of which 'Information Science' and 'Library Science' are the most relevant. A subject index, compiled from title keywords, key phrases and acronyms, is included in each monthly issue but is not cumulated annually. A monthly and annually cumulated author index is, however, provided. Further coverage may be provided in the other two sections of Dissertation Abstracts International, Section B: The Sciences and Engineering and

Section C: Worldwide (known as European Abstracts until 1989). The whole service can be searched online and on CD-ROM.

7. *Dokumentationsdienst Bibliothekswesen (DOBI): Informationsdienst zum Bibliothekswesen der Bundesrepublik Deutschland und des Auslands.* Berlin: Deutsches Bibliothekinstitut, 1982-. Quarterly.

Succeeds *Fachbibliographischer Dienst Bibliothekswesen (FD)* which was published annually between 1966 and 1983 to provide coverage of literature published in the period between 1965 and 1981. *DOBI* appeared annually until 1987 when twice yearly publication began; quarterly publication began in 1992. It documents general German librarianship literature. Source coverage features over eighty German-language journals and newsletters, conference proceedings, books and reports. Entries are grouped under broad subject headings, the most relevant group being that '06.03. 0n Informationssysteme, which are sub-sections within the heading 'Uberortliche Informations- und Literaturversorgung, Informationssysteme'. Most entries include abstracts, while subject keywords are always listed as, for books, are bibliographic details of published reviews. Indexes are by subject and by author.

8. *Government Reports, Announcements and Index.* Springfield, Virginia: U.S. Department of Commerce. National Technical Information Service, 1946-. Twice monthly, with annually cumulated indexes.

This is the major, general index to published US and other government- sponsored research reports with about 2,500 entries added each issue. All technological disciplines are included and, although US research is emphasized, reports from the major industrial countries figure prominently. NTIS Published Searches are also listed. Entries contain full bibliographic details, abstracts and contract or grant numbers. Prior to 1987 entries were arranged under COSATI categories and subcategories, the likeliest section being subcategory 5B, 'Documentation and Information Technology'. Since the beginning of 1987 NTIS has employed its own subject categories, and the appropriate heading is now 'Library and Information Sciences'. Because of the scatter of some reports on online services for individual disciplines, however, the thorough indexing of Government Reports, Announcements and Index is welcome. Monthly and annually cumulated indexes are provided, including keyword, personal author, corporate author and contract/grant number. Available online and on CD-ROM.

9. *Index of Conference Proceedings Received.* Wetherby, West Yorkshire: British Library. Document Supply Centre, 1964-. Monthly with annual cumulation.

Indexes proceedings (as opposed to individual papers) published in various forms and received by the British Library Document Supply Centre (BLDSC) in all subject areas. Entries are listed under keywords or key phrases taken from the conference titles, and a useful feature is the inclusion of proceedings under the acronyms of prominent institutions or societies, for example ASIS (American Society for Information Science). Conferences are posted under as many key phrases as is deemed useful. As keywords are drawn from conference titles it is difficult to list specific places to look, but clearly phrases beginning 'Information', 'Online', 'Internet' and 'CD-ROM' would be useful starting points. Details given are the title, date, location and sponsor of the conference; ISBN are included where available. Available online and on CD-ROM with 25-year cumulations on microfiche.

10. *Index to Social Sciences and Humanities Proceedings.* Philadelphia: Institute for Scientific Information, 1979-. Quarterly, with annual cumulation.
This service indexes both individual conference papers and published proceedings, including those appearing in journals, reports and books: some 3,000 conferences or 23,000 papers per year. Papers are listed in contents page format under the title of the conference whose full publication details are provided. Proceedings with papers on online information retrieval are included in most issues and can be located in the category index. The best way to retrieve individual papers is via the Permuterm Subject Index, which operates on the basis of matching title words. Other indexes allow access by author/editor, sponsor, location and corporate body. A CD-ROM version is now available which indexes some 115,000 papers published since 1990. The CD-ROM is also updated quarterly adding some 6,000 papers at each update.

11. *Index to Theses.* London: Aslib, 1950-. Quarterly.
Indexes doctoral and masters theses from British and Irish universities and polytechnics. Arrangement of entries is by broad subject classifications with author and subject keyword indexes in each issue. Abstracts for most theses have been available on a separate microfiche publication, *Abstracts of Theses,* from 1977 to 1986 after which significant improvements were introduced, including the publication of abstracts in hard copy with each entry, more detailed subject indexing, and quarterly instead of twice yearly frequency. The subject index is of variable quality and it is probably best to combine use with the most relevant subject section in the classified sequence, 'A1: Library and Information Science. Bibliography'. Available as online and CD-ROM databases.

12. *Informatics Abstracts.* Moscow: All-Union Institute of Scientific and Technical Information, 1967-. Monthly, with annually cumulated indexes.
The English version of the Russian abstracting service for information science, Referativnyi Zhurnal: Informatika, which has been published since 1963. A separate section covers information retrieval, typically containing about seventy references per issue. This section is further subdivided into headings such as 'IR Processes' and 'IR Systems. Databanks' which include references on online and CD-ROM information retrieval. The subject index offers access under specific headings such as 'CD-ROM', 'Online Information Retrieval Systems' and 'Online Search'. Author and source publication indexes are also available. As well as indexing and abstracting Russian literature, this service covers articles in a range of journals from other

countries, notably the United States, Britain, France, the Federal Republic of Germany, Poland, Australia and Japan. In total, over 500 journals are indexed, along with a selection of conference proceedings, reports and books.

13. *Information Science Abstracts.* New York: Plenum, 1966-. Monthly, with annually cumulated indexes.

On average, between 800 and 1,000 references are listed, with detailed abstracts, in each issue. Apart from 450 journals, coverage of US reports and dissertations is strong. Information science is broadly treated and many computer science and engineering references are included. A new subject classification scheme was introduced in January 1993 and relevant material can now be found in '3.10 Optical and Laser Techniques'; and in most areas of 'Section 6 Information Systems and Applications'. Retrieval is enhanced by a system of cross-referencing at the end of each section and by subject and author indexes. *Information Science Abstracts* is also available online.

14. *Informationsdienst Bibliothekswesen.* Leipzig: Deutsche Bucherei, 1971-. Bimonthly, with annually cumulated indexes.

Originating in the German Democratic Republic, *Informationsdienst Bibliothekswesen* complements the German-language coverage of *Dokumentationsdienst Bibliothekswesen (DOBI)* by virtue of its more frequent publication and by more extensive source journal coverage. In fact many of the journals abstracted are in English or in European languages other than German. All entries contain abstracts and, where necessary, translated German titles, the aim being to provide German speakers with access to foreign-language literature. Entries are arranged according to the Universal Decimal Classification, the relevant section being 025.4.036, 'Maschinelle Recherchierverfahren'. Annually cumulating author and subject indexes provide access, while bimonthly issues also contain an index by journal source.

15. *Library and Information Science Abstracts (LISA).* East Grinstead, Bowker-Saur, 1950-. Monthly, with annually cumulated indexes.

Taken over from The Library Association but remaining under the same editor, *LISA* has completely revised its layout and structure from January 1993. It continues to offer thorough source coverage worldwide, with over 350 journals and conference literature in librarianship and information science indexed and abstracted from thirty-four languages and sixty countries. The new layout, subject arrangement and terminology have been introduced partly in response to demand from users and invloves the dropping of the Classification Research Group's unpublished draft version of *A Classification of Library and Information Science* (1971) in favour of a scheme involving broad subject headings. At the same time terminology has been updated (for example on-line and data bases have changed to online and databases). Finally it was decided to revert to the pre-1979 practice of having an Author index instead of a Name Index. While most sections are relevant, particular subject headings are those from

13.15 Searching to 13.29 Other Storage Systems which span specific areas for both online and CD-ROM databases. All indexes cumulate annually. *LISA* is available online and on CD-ROM.

16. *Library and Information Science Annual.* Englewood, Colorado: Libraries Unlimited. Annual.

Prefixed by a series of contributed essays, the bulk of this publication is devoted to descriptive book reviews which have been divided into subject sections for all aspects of library and information science, including online searching, CD-ROM, database applications and reference services. Reviews describe each work in detail, evaluating it and comparing it with similar publications and listing reviews where appropriate. Separate sections provide reviews of between twenty and forty journals in each volume and abstracts of over fifty significant doctoral dissertations. Consolidated author/title and subject indexes allow access to all reviews. Publication of this annual commenced in 1985 as *Library Science Annual,* changing to its present title in 1987.

17. *Library Literature: an Index to Library and Information Science.* New York: H. W. Wilson, 1934-. Bimonthly, with annual cumulation.

An index in which entries are listed in a single alphabetical sequence by subject, author, organization, host and database name. No abstracts are provided. Among the headings used are 'Online Searching', 'End-User Searching', 'Front-end Systems', 'Information Systems' and 'CD-ROM'. All sections are subdivided for more specific access by geographic area and publication types such as 'Aims and objectives', 'Case studies', 'Evaluation' and 'Reviews'. Extensive cross references are provided between the headings. Journals indexed are listed and coverage centres on about 240 journals, including most of the major titles on online and CD- ROM information retrieval. Conference proceedings are indexed only sporadically but numerous monograph and reference publications are listed. A separate index of book reviews is included at the end. Online and CD-ROM versions are offered by the publisher.

18. *PASCAL THEMA 205: Sciences de l'Information Documentation.* Vandoeuvre-les-Nancy: Centre National de la Recherche Scientifique. Institut de l'Information Scientifique et Technique, 1985-. Ten issues per year, with annually cumulated indexes.

Supersedes *Bulletin Signaletique Section 101: Sciences de l'Information Documentation* (1963-1984) and now forms part of the PASCAL THEMA series whose aim is to provide exhaustive coverage of its subject areas. Source coverage is extensive and includes journals from most countries. The emphasis is on English-language titles, although French, Russian and German sources are also said to be well represented. Conference, book, report and thesis literature receive selective treatment. About 350 items are added each issue, most of which contain French abstracts. Many items in French or other languages contain translated titles in English. A classified subject arrangement is used, with entries on database searching most likely to be grouped at 03.B.04, 'Bases et Banques de Donnees', and 07, 'Recherche de l'Information'. Indexes provide access by subject (in both French and English), author and name of host or database service. A separate subject index covers references by French or French-speaking authors. Available on CD-ROM and online.

19. *Resources in Education.* U.S. Department of Education. Office of Educational Research and Improvement. Educational Resources Information Center, 1966-. Monthly, with twice yearly cumulative indexes.

This service operates on the same basis as its sister publication *Current Index to Journals in Education* with information supplied by sixteen clearinghouses. Abstracts are listed according to clearinghouse and can be searched via subject, personal author, institution and publication type indexes. The focus is on report literature, most of which emanates from US organizations, including library schools and academic libraries. As well as state-of-the-art reviews, much of this literature takes the form of guides to searching particular online or CD-ROM databases. Some other document types also feature and include conference proceedings, theses, bibliographies and directories. Unless otherwise indicated all abstracted documents are obtainable from the ERIC Document Reproduction Service (EDRS). Can be searched online and on CD-ROM as a part of the ERIC database.

20. *Social Sciences Citation Index.* Philadelphia: Institute for Scientific Information, 1966-. Three times per year, with annual cumulation.

This service indexes some 1,500 journals in the social sciences, supplemented by relevant articles from 3,300 science titles. Relevant sources include *Database, Online* and *Online Review,* all among the longest-established titles in the online field, within a source list of over fifty information science periodicals. Like all citation indexes, it is unique in that it enables the user to search forward in time from a known article to find more recent references that cite the original. The usefulness of this feature is based on the premise that the citing author will be writing on a similar topic. Subject searches can be conducted via the Permuterm Subject Index in which title words of articles are matched against each other, an approach which is useful when a subject is identified by very specific keywords such as database names. Available online and on CD-ROM.

21. 'The JAL Guide to the Professional Literature.' Published in *Journal of Academic Librarianship: Articles, Features and Book Reviews for the Academic Library Professional.* Bimonthly.

This feature runs at about ten to fifteen pages in each issue of *Journal of Academic Librarianship* and serves as a reviewer of new or recent publications. Most of its coverage takes the form of summaries of book reviews, with the reviewer's recommendation in each case, already published in other journals of librarianship and higher education. These reviews are grouped under thirty-six broad subjects, including 'CD-

ROM Product and Services', 'Internet', 'Electronic Texts', 'Information Technology', 'Networks and Bibliographic Utilities' and 'Reference Services' of interest for online and CD-ROM purposes. A name index to items reviewed is provided at the end.

Bibliographies

22. Hall, J. L. *Online Bibliographic Databases: a Directory and Sourcebook.* (4th ed.). London: Aslib, 1986. 509pp.

This work provides a major ninety-page bibliography of published literature on online information retrieval as well as a database directory. This edition of the bibliography lists 1,011 references from the early 1960s through 1985. Most of these references appeared in refereed publications and represent a good proportion of the core journal and conference literature in the field. The emphasis is on publications about specific databases or database coverage in particular subject field, and references are made from database entries in the directory section to relevant papers listed in the bibliography. Retrieval is also assisted by a listing of comparative studies of individual databases in the early part of the work. This listing is in order of author name, as is the bibliography itself. A co-author index and general subject index are also supplied. The directory covers all subject fields and concentration on the most heavily used databases is deliberate in order to keep the work within manageable proportions. Useful features contained in each entry are sample record, file name or number on different hosts, indicative search costs, and references to published work relating to the database in the separate bibliography. Indexing is by database producer, title keyword and general subject. Other sections of note provide contact information for hosts, sample searches on nine major systems, and a statistical profile of available databases.

23. Batt, F. *Online Searching for End Users: an Information Sourcebook.* Phoenix: Oryx Press, 1988. 116pp. (Oryx Sourcebook Series in Computer and Information Science; 1).

Despite its title this work is of interest to intermediaries at least as much as to end users. 510 entries, the majority of them with annotations, are listed in ten sections within four chapters: 'Searching by Intermediaries' briefly indicates the major journal and reference sources for online searching; 'Online Searching by End Users' lists some 159 citations. Chapter three is the core of the work with seven sections on the major aspects of online searching which concern the practitioner, including equipment, databases and vendors, front-end and gateway systems, search strategies, an analysis by dsiciplines, a section on ergonomics and on one future prospects in which CD-ROM receives particular attention. The final chapter recommends a core library collection selected from the foregoing listings. Throughout the bibliography the emphasis is on literature from the mid-1980s onwards, primarily selected from US journals and conference proceedings. Author, title and subject indexes are provided.

24. Byerly, G. *Online Searching: a Dictionary and Bibliographic Guide.* Littleton, Colorado: Libraries Unlimited, 1983. 288pp.

Well organized early work whose contents are divided between a dictionary of terms used in online searching and an annotated bibliography. The dictionary contains over 1,200 terms, briefly defined and including some terminology from the computing field but would have to be seen as incomplete in 1995. The American bias of this work is reflected in the appearance in the dictionary section of descriptions for databases and commands for the then BRS, DIALOG and SDC hosts. Over 700 journal articles are descriptively annotated in the bibliography. These are grouped in two parts, the first of which contains thirty-two sections relevant to searching in all subjects, while the second consists of ten sections which include more than 250 articles on databases in specific subject disciplines. Articles cover the period from 1970 to mid-1982, including all of those published in *Database, Online* and *Online Review.* In addition to the bibliography proper, a selection of books, directories, bibliographies, conference proceedings and journal titles is identified. Indexing is by source journal, author and subject (including database name). An updated edition, to be titled *Online and Ondisc Searching: a Dictionary and Bibliographic Guide,* is in press from the same publisher.

25. Cruger, I. *Online für Neulinge: Literaturzusammenstellung aus der Datenbank INFODATA. 2. uberarbeitete Auflage.* Frankfurt: Gesellschaft für Information und Dokumentation, 1986. 55pp.

Introductory bibliography, with abstracts, of over 200 references on online searching. References are taken from the INFODATA database and consist mainly of German- and English-language documents with abstracts in the language of publication. Sources are a balance of books, conference papers and journal articles. The bibliography is arranged in seven subject sections which cover introductory texts, databases in individual subject areas, online terminology, microcomputers and communications software, telecommunications networks, command languages, and directories and reference works. There are no author or subject indexes.

26. Hawkins, D. T. *Online Information Retrieval Bibliography, 1983-1986.* Medford, New Jersey: Learned Information, 1987. 300pp.

Consolidates the three annual online information retrieval bibliographies in the series published in *Online Review* in the period from 1984 to 1986. 2,619 references are listed under eleven categories with access via permuted title and author indexes.

27. Hawkins, D. T. *Online Information Retrieval Bibliography, 1987-1989.* Medford, New Jersey: Learned Information, 1990. 355pp.

A merger of the three annual bibliographies in the series published in *Online Review* between 1987 and 1989. Bibliographic details are provided for 2,795 references on online searching in eleven broad subject headings: Books; Reviews; Conferences;

Directories; Descriptions of Online Systems; Databases and Services; Microcomputer Applications; CD-ROM Databases; Gateways; Front Ends; and User Education and Training. There is also an author and a permuted title indexes.

28. *Library Hi Tech Bibliography.* Ann Arbor, Michigan: Pierian Press, 1986-. Annual.

Library Hi Tech and *Library Hi Tech News* were founded with the intention of providing an awareness of books, articles and resources appearing elsewhere in the literature. This Bibliography includes the longer bibliographies submitted to the journals where space is not often available for them. Volumes in the series are published annually and consist typically of between twelve and fifteen separate bibliographies on various aspects of library automation with consolidated title and author indexes at the end. Topics covered have included CD-ROM and end user searching. The latest in the series (Volume 9, 1994) included chapters on Tape Loaded Databases and Numerical and Statistical Databases in Libraries.

29. McNab, A. (ed.) 'Current Awareness Column.' *UKOLUG Newsletter.* London: UK Online User Group, 1979-. Bimonthly.

The regular column, which includes relevant items drawn from Current Cites, contains abstracted citations to articles of interest to users of online and CD-ROM databases and the Internet. Typically running to thirty or forty references contributed by a team of reviewers, the column is divided by headings such as Campus Wide Information Services, CD-ROMs: General, Multimedia, Networked Information: Applications, and Online: Business. Many of the reviews run to over half a column and all are sufficient to indicate the likely relevance of articles.

30. *NTIS Published Searches.* Springfield, Virginia: U.S. Department of Commerce. National Technical Information Service.

This is a series of subject bibliographies compiled from searches of 23 databases in high technology areas, including NTIS, INSPEC and Computer Database, by NTIS information specialists. Subjects are chosen according to their timeliness and information retrieval, via online or CD-ROM access, is represented in the annual *Published Search Master Catalog* (available free of charge from NTIS with semi-annual supplements) through which these publications may be traced. The latest *Catalog* lists over 3,000 such bibliographies under appropriate subject headings. Published searches are typically on quite specific aspects of a subject over a period of about ten years or, if the subject is more generally treated, two or three years and are updated regularly. The bibliography is compiled from a single database and usually contains from 50 to 100 technical reports, conference proceedings and journal articles with full bibliographic details and abstracts as well as document delivery information. Subjects covered in the series include CD-ROM technology, database gateway systems, bibliographic software, full-text database searching and online search strategies.

31. *Online Information Retrieval Bibliography.* Compiled by D. T. Hawkins. Oxford: Learned Information, 1977-1990. Annual.
Published on an annual basis as a supplement to the August issue of *Online Review,* this bibliography offered an excellent way of keeping abreast of the literature published about online searching in any given year. The first bibliography appeared as a supplement to thc inaugural issue of the journal in 1977 and contained 615 items from the period 1965 to 1976. Updates typically listed around 900 references, without abstracts, arranged in author order within eleven subject sections whose coverage encompasses most topics of concern to the searcher. Source coverage represents major books, conferences and directories along with the core journals in the field, supplemented by articles from titles in other disciplines such as computer science as appropriate. Subject access is available via permuted title keyword. An author index is also included. Four cumulations have been produced of which the two latest for the periods 1983-1986 and 1987-1989 are included.

32. Prytherch, R. *Sources of Information in Librarianship and Information Science.* (3rd ed.). Aldershot: Ashgate, 1993. 300pp.
An introductory guide to the wide range of information sources available in librarianship generally whose the main strength is its thorough and detailed examination of the major abstracting and indexing services in the field. Since the second edition there has been a clear shift of emphasis towards technology-based services, information as a marketable commodity and closer links between the users and the providers of information. This means that the background literature has shifted to include material from communications, computing and marketing.

33. 'Reference Sources'. In *Going Online and CD-ROM.* London: Aslib. Irregular.
A listing of information sources which is updated in each edition of *Going Online and CD-ROM* and is of value to online searchers of all levels of experience. There are sections on database directories, introductory texts, subject guides, bibliographies and periodicals. Records contain abstracts and, for ordering purposes, prices and publisher addresses. These sections are normally supplemented by lists of references, mainly journal articles, on specific topics, notably charging and equipment.

Books

34. Convey, J. *Online Information Retrieval: an Introductory Manual to Principles and Practice.* (4th ed.) London: Library Association Publishing, 1992. 310 pp.
An introduction to online searching which is organized in two parts. The first part contains chapters on the development of online information retrieval; databases; the online information retrieval industry; CD-ROM; hardware and software; general principles of searching; the search; the costs; advantages and disadvantages of online; and the future of online. As Sheila Webber points out (Reviews. *Program* 27(4) (October 1993) 443-445), the first and third of these chapters, while providing a useful

overview of online history, overlap while all the chapters seem not to have been as thoroughly revised as they might have been. She also points out that a number of topics have not been covered: the Joint Academic Network (JANET); IXI; the Internet; the emergence of academic hosts (for example, BIDS); site-licensing; online public access catalogues; and the emergence of new types of host (for example, the Manchester Host). The second part of the book is designed to 'show practical applications of the principles outlined in Part 1, and to form part of the training programme of searchers new to information retrieval' and describes and illustrates search features on seven hosts: BLAISE-LINE, BLAISE-LINK, KR DIALOG, ESA-IRS, Questel-ORBIT, Pergamon Financial Data Services (since closed down) and KR Data-Star. While covering some advanced features (perhaps better left out for new searchers?) some details are glossed over or lost in the search annotations. As Webber says, 'the book has useful, accurate information in it' but also some shortcomings which detract from its intended uses.

35. Fecko, M. B. *Electronic Resources: Access and Issues.* East Grinstead: Bowker-Saur, 1992. 200pp.

An overall introduction to electronic resources, this book covers topics such as electronic mail, online databases, cataloguing utilities and networks. Each chapter looks at electronic resources in depth from a practical, 'hands-on' point of view.

36. Fenichel, C. H. *Online Searching: a Primer.* (3rd ed.). Medford, New Jersey: Learned Information. 1990.

Earlier editions of this work have provided a compact overview of online information retrieval for beginners by delineating the component links in the online industry and the major databases, explaining search strategy and discussing management issues.

37. Hartley, R. J., Keen, E. M., Large, J. A. and **Tedd, L. A.** *Online Searching: Principles and Practice.* East Grinstead: Bowker-Saur, 1990. 387pp.

Offers a general overview, from a UK perspective, of online searching with coverage also of CD-ROM and locally stored databases. The book is arranged in thirteen chapters dealing with the history and development, database structure, basic searching, retrieval facilities, search strategy, online sources, searching and the search process; management aspects of using external search services; online searching of locally stored databases; videotext and teletext systems; online public access catalogues; and systems which go beyond the Boolean approach to searching. Case studies are provided in an appendix. *C&L Applications* called the book, 'the work we have been waiting for' and recommended it to anyone beginning or needing guidance with any aspect of online searching. At the time of going to press, a new edition is under consideration.

38. Olle, J. G. and **Dixon, D.** A *Guide to Sources of Information in Libraries.* (2nd ed.). Aldershot: Ashgate, 1993. 180pp.
This book is intended to show the characteristics of each of the various types of information sources for every branch of knowledge. It shows how to recognise the most suitable type of information for a particular need, how best it may be used and how to locate it. Following an introduction on the pattern of sources of information, four main sections deal with Information and its packaging; Information sources; Bibliographic control; and Copyright. CD-ROM, online and viewdata all receive attention and Part 3 contains guides to online and CD-ROM databases.

39. *Online and CD-ROM Databases in School Libraries: Readings.* Compiled by A. Lathrop. Littleton, Colorado: Libraries Unlimited, 1989. 375pp. (Database Searching Series; 2).
A collection of over forty reprints which describe experiences with online and CD-ROM databases in school libraries. Contributions are grouped in nine sections in which issues such as instructional methods and management of search services are addressed. Other sections contain reports of individual projects and evaluations of particular databases or services. The final sections provides details of published literature, computer software and database hosts. Although dated, much of this material is still relevant – more especially so in the UK were uptake in schools has been slower due to funding difficulties.

40. Tedd, L. A. *An Introduction to Computer-Based Library Systems.* (3rd ed.) New York: Wiley, 1993. 316pp.
With each edition, Lucy Tedd's text book on the current state of computers in libraries is faced with the problem of reflecting the many changes taking place – as the author herself notes, such changes mean that a text such as this can only provide a snapshot of the topic. That the snapshot is in its third edition testifies to the success of the author's eye. The book concludes with a section on local information retrieval and online and CD-ROM databases which, like the other sections, provides the reader with an effective overview. As George Geddes says, this is a book that 'can be confidently recommended to anyone requiring a readable account' (*Library Association Record* 96 (4) April 1994. p. 219).

41. Tenopir, C. *Issues in Online Database Searching.* Englewood, Colorado: Libraries Unlimited, 1989. 188pp. (Database Searching Series; 1)
A collection of fifty short articles, the majority of which are reprinted from the author's 'Online Databases' column in *Library Journal.* Dates of publication range from 1980 through 1989 and the articles deal withsuch topics as search techniques, end-user searching, CD-ROM databases and microcomputer software for searching or personal database creation and management.

Conferences: Proceedings

42. Armstrong, C. J. and **Hartley, R. J.** (eds.). *Changing Patterns of Online Information: UKOLUG State-of-the-Art Conference 1994.* Oxford: Learned Information, 1994. 145pp.

The United Kingdom Online User Group (UKOLUG) holds a State-of-the-Art conference every other year with, since 1986, published proceedings. As in previous years, the proceedings contain not only the papers, but summaries of the discussions which took place after the formal presentations as well as a complete programme, delegate list and biographical details of the speakers. The theme in 1994 was reflected both in the title and in the choice of papers which coverd the Internet, Campus-Wide Information Services, SuperJANET, electronic document delivery and CD-ROM networking. A student paper – by the second winner of the UKOLUG Student Award – is also included in the proceedings.

43. ASIS Annual Meeting. Organized by the American Society for Information Science. Medford, New Jersey: Learned Information, 1964-. Annual.

A long-established information science conference whose proceedings began to be published in 1964 by Greenwood Press. Since then publication has been by the Society itself or, most recently, by Learned Information. The proceedings usually contain all contributed papers accepted by the panel of referees and may be supplemented by abstracts for presentations to the Society's various Special Interest Groups. All papers are audiotaped and can be ordered from the Society. Typically, there might be fifty full papers and twenty abstracts in a proceedings volume. The emphasis is on research findings rather than product presentations. Online information retrieval figures prominently within a general information science framework. Topics which feature on a regular basis are search strategy, evaluation of search results and of the performance of information retrieval systems, database indexing, expert systems, document delivery and international and national information policy. The most recent two conferences have been entitled *Networking, Telecommunications, and the Networked Information Resource Revolution;* and *People Understanding Information Systems and Information Systems Understanding People.* Location of papers is assisted by subject and author indexes.

44. *First East-West Online Information Meeting.* Oxford: Learned Information, 1989. 280pp.

The proceedings of a pioneer event organised jointly by Learned Information and the International Centre for Scientific and Technical Information (ICSTI) and held in Moscow in October 1989.

45. *International Online Information Meeting.* Organised by Learned Information (Europe). Oxford: Learned Information, 1977-. Annual.

The conference and exhibition, which are held in London in December each year, have both grown larger by the year, expanding to embrace optical publishing, information networking and the Internet. Each volume of proceedings offers a mix of papers covering a broad spectrum of topics of concern to the online industry at the time of presentation. Recurrent themes throughout the series have been database descriptions and evaluations, education and training, search techniques and chemical and substructure searching. More recently there has been a focus on databases from Eastern Europe and on the Internet, while in 1993 the opening session dealt with database quality. Each volume contains about fifty papers. Although presentations from the US and UK still dominate, this is far less true than it was in the earlier years of the conference and each volume contains contributions representing activities in a wide range of countries, notably those in Scandinavia and, now, Eastern Europe. An author index has been included since 1979 and a subject index since 1984. The title of the proceedings is now normally *Online Information '93, '94 ...: Proceedings of the First, Second ... International Online Information Meeting.*

46. *National Online Meeting.* Organized by Learned Information. Medford, New Jersey: Learned Information, 1980-. Annual.

This conference usually takes place in May each year and the proceedings volume typically consists of about seventy papers plus a listing of those not included in full. A single index offers access via author, author affiliation, title words and author-supplied keywords. The first paper reviews developments in the online information industry in the preceding year and includes usage and revenue figures. The rest of the papers are arranged alphabetically by author name and represent a range of subjects such as CD-ROM applications, individual database products, different categories of online information, management of online services in libraries, expert systems and gateway services. As indicated by the conference title, the majority of contributors are from the United States, representing libraries, library schools and companies in the online information industry.

47. *Online.* Organized by Online Inc. Weston, Connecticut: Online, 1981-. Annual.

Held in October or November each year since 1981, this conference contains many product presentations from database producers and online hosts. CD-ROM databases and technology have been featured with increasing prominence in recent years and is reflected in a change of title to Online/CD-ROM from 1990 onwards. The organisers say that the 'conference emphasises practical, how-to information and new trends and technologies.' In addition topics such as developments in microcomputer hardware and software, search techniques and new database information sources for specific subject areas receive an airing. The proceedings typically contain forty papers and in most cases take the form of preprinted summaries rather than entire presentations which are available on audiotape from the publisher from 1985 onwards. Papers appear in alphabetical order of author's surname. No subject index is provided.

48. *Pacific Conference on New Information Technology.* Newton, Massachusetts: MicroUse Information, 1987-. Biennial.

Many papers in this conference represent the experience of Asian and Pacific countries in the application of microcomputers to library and information operations, including information retrieval. The remainder summarize the state of the art in the United States and Europe.

Current Awareness

49. *CABLIS: Current Awareness Bulletin for Library and Information Staff.* London: British Library Information Sciences Service. Monthly.

A large part of this bulletin consists of contents listings from a selection of journals taken by the British Library Information Sciences Service (BLISS) library (until 1988 known as The Library Association library). Core online and CD-ROM titles are represented. Catalogue records are also supplied for new books, periodicals, theses and British Library research reports added to stock. These are listed under subject headings of which 'Automation in Libraries' and 'Information Searching and Retrieval' are relevant. An additional feature is a news section which includes digests of news from the online and CD-ROM information industries.

50. *Current Contents Search.* Philadelphia: Institute for Scientific Information. Weekly.

Contains the whole Current Contents service, including Social and Behavioral Sciences to whose subfile searches can be restricted if required. Individual articles or whole tables of a journal's contents can be retrieved. Abstracts are included where available. The database is offered for searching on CDP Online, KR Data-Star and KR DIALOG.

51. *Current Contents: Social and Behavioral Sciences.* Philadelphia: Institute for Scientific Information. Weekly.

Lists the tables of contents of the latest issues of over 1,400 journals, including *Database, Online* and *Online Review* among thirty information science titles featured. Journals covered are mainly in the English language and are selected on the basis of their international impact. Tables of contents are grouped under broad subject headings, including one entitled 'Library and Information Sciences', to facilitate scanning. An alphabetical title word index, based on single words or phrases occurring in article titles, is provided, as are an author index and address directory. The database is available online, on CD-ROM, diskette and tape. The electronic versions also contain abstracts.

52. *Current Research in Library and Information Science: Including Initiatives and Investigations.* East Grinstead: Bowker-Saur. Quarterly, with annual cumulation. (Formerly published by The Library Association.)

This publication serves as an index to research projects in progress internationally. Projects at various levels from funded academic work, mainly at doctoral level at least, to in-house or action research are listed. Automated information retrieval features in each issue and over 100 projects in this area are reported annually. Most entries can be located under online or CD-ROM headings in the classification. More specific access is available via a subject index. A name index enables searches to be conducted by name of researcher or country. Entries, which are updated annually, are submitted by researchers and include details of project personnel, duration, financial support, a summary of aims and any relevant publications emanating from the research. Available on the LISA Plus CD-ROM.

53. Hyams, M. (ed.) *Current Awareness Abstracts of Library and Information Management Literature.* London: Aslib. Monthly.
Bibliographic details with, from April 1990, lengthy abstracts of recent information science publications are provided in subject sections which include online and CD-ROM, with coverage of databases, hosts, search techniques, equipment and communications software. The majority of references are taken from a core of 300 online and CD-ROM journals, although articles from other sources are featured as appropriate. There are author and subject indexes.

Dictionaries

54. Sawoniak, H. and **Witt, M.** (eds.) *New International Dictionary of Acronyms in Library and Information Science and Related Fields* (2nd ed). East Grinstead: Bowker-Saur, 1991. 511pp.
The second edition of this work covers more than 30,000 acronyms in 34 languages with expansions listed in the appropriate language. The acronyms represent institutions, library and information systems, methods, programming languages and titles of publications and include hosts and other online organizations, along with database names and networks. Expansions are followed by the name of the country of usage if they are not international.

Directories: Online Format

55. *BROKERSGUIDE.* Luxembourg: European Information Market Development Group. Monthly.
Established in 1986, this databank can be freely searched online via the ECHO host. It consists of records for 1,136 information brokers active in the countries of the European Community, and who offer fee-based services, especially database searching, either as individuals or companies. Detailed descriptions are provided and records can be searched by name, country, hosts used, or areas of specialization. Some records also contain a narrative description of the service offered.

Directories: Print

56. *CICI Directory of Information Products and Services.* Harlow: Longman. Every two years.

Similar in many respects to Inside Information, this directory lists more than 1,800 UK bodies which provide various information services. Among these are database producers, online hosts, information consultancies, CD-ROM publishers, and organizations which conduct online searches. Corporate and individual contact data are provided, along with brief details of size, services, and print or non-print products. A single index allows retrieval by product or service, interest group served and general subject area.

57. *Datapro Directory of On-Line Services.* Delran, New Jersey: Datapro Research Corporation. Monthly updates to base volumes.

Two information-packed volumes constitute this directory service. Each volume is in looseleaf format to facilitate the insertion of monthly updates. The volumes are divided into a number of sections. One of these is 'Information Retrieval Services' and contains a series of reports of up to thirty pages in length on online services, either in information management or retrieval. These sevices are offered by forty companies, the majority of which are based in the United States. A separate section, 'Company Profiles' offers brief company data for a wider range of organizations worldwide, including hosts, telecommunications network services and database producers. This information includes key personnel, number of employees, primary customers and sales concentration geographically. The other major section gives standard descriptions of over 2,500 online databases. All of this information is accessible via a company and database name index and a general index which contains subject categories. The other features of the directory service comprise state-of-the-art thematic reports on technological trends, including one on microcomputers which runs to over seventy pages and compares over 120 different systems, an eighty-page glossary and a monthly newsletter which helps to keep the service up to date with interpretative commentary on company, market and product developments in the online field.

58. *Directory of Library and Information Professionals.* Woodbridge, Connecticut: Research Publications in collaboration with the American Library Association, 1988. 2 vols.

Over 23,000 biographical sketches of professional librarians or information specialists based in the United States and Canada, compiled from questionnaire responses, are contained in the first volume. These are supplemented by the names and addresses of 20,000 individuals from whom questionnaire responses were not received. The second volume contains four indexes, including one by keyword which offers access by professional or subject expertise and one by geographical area. A CD-ROM version is also available.

59. Stewart, J. and **Oxley, S.** *Electronic Sources of Information for Australian Business.* Melbourne: Royal Melbourne Institute of Technology, 1992.
Dealing with databases on CD-ROM, diskette or online from Australia and New Zealand as well as some international products, the guide is aimed mainly at users in the antipodes but will also prove valuable to users trying to research the Australian scene from abroad. Coverage includes management and industrial relations, finance and accounting, law and legislation, and statistical and numeric databases.

60. *The North American Online Directory: a Directory of Online Information Products and Services with Names and Numbers.* New York: Bowker, 1987. 379pp.
A general purpose directory which aims to describe the main products and services of the information industry in the United States and Canada. Its longest section is an alphabetical listing of over 2,000 databases which is followed by a general subject index. Other sections provide directory-type information for database producers, hosts, telecommunications networks, information brokers, consultants to the information industry and online user groups. Additional features are a calendar of courses and conferences for the coming year, a list of organizations offering courses on database creation and access, an annotated bibliography of reference works, periodicals and newsletters, and a glossary of acronyms. The work ends with a directory of addresses and telephone numbers for companies and individuals listed in the previous sections.

61. *UK Online Search Services.* (5th ed.). London: Aslib, 1991. 72pp.
A listing of organizations in the UK which offer a fee-based online brokerage service to people whose own institution cannot provide access to online databases. Entries comprise contact data, types of client to whom service is available, subject and host coverage, charging policy, speed of service, number of searches conducted annually, staff, and any back-up services provided by the organization. Indexes are by online services, CD-ROM, subject and region.

Handbooks

62. Bradley, P. and **Hanson, T. A.** (eds.) *Going Online and CD-ROM.* (9th ed.). London: Aslib, 1994. Irregular. 124pp.
A valuable handbook on online and CD-ROM searching for the UK user. The first half of the considerably updated work addresses such practicalities as 'What is online and CD-ROM?' 'Why choose online or CD-ROM?' 'What is a database?' and the different types of databases; explains costs; telecommunications; and the necessary equipment; as well as new topics such as networking CD-ROMs; downloading and post-processing; and copyright. Much of the remainder serves as a directory of contact organizations, including hosts, user groups, equipment suppliers and advisory cen-

tres. Other extensive sections are a glossary and an annotated listing of the major published sources of information on general and specific aspects on online information retrieval.

Journals: Online/CD-ROM Full-Text

63. *Trade and Industry ASAP.* Foster City, California: Information Access Company, 1983-. Monthly.

A major expansion of information science journal coverage in 1988 and 1989 saw the following titles added to this database:

CD-ROM Professional (January 1989-)
CD-ROM World (previously *CD-ROM Librarian*) (July 1988-)
Computers in Libraries (January 1988-)
Database (August 1988-)
Database Searcher (July 1988-)
Datamation
Information Technology
Libraries Information Today (July 1988-)
Library Software Review (July 1988-)
Link-Up (July 1988-)
Online (January 1988-)
RQ (January 1988-)
Searcher

CDP Online, CompuServe, KR Data-Star, KR DIALOG, Dow Jones News/Retrieval, LEXIS/NEXIS and Westlaw offer the file for searching either as a part of a larger file or in its own right. Most of the publications listed here can be searched for the time span shown in parentheses on KR DIALOG and LEXIS/NEXIS. January 1989 is the usual starting point on CDP Online and Dow Jones.

Journals

64. *Archimag: Les Technologies de l'Information.* Paris: Archmag, 1985-. Ten per year plus three special issues.

A journal for documentalists containing a series of articles covering archives, documentation, the Internet, CD-ROMs, multimedia and optical discs. Sections cover innovations and new techniques for information handling, the Internet, management of information and optical technology and applications. Book reviews are also included.

65. *Aslib Information.* London: Aslib, 1973-1993. Ten issues per year.

A source of current awareness on developments in online and CD-ROM information industry through a combination of news features and longer articles, those covering online and CD-ROM tending to be grouped to form a special issue on CD-ROM/ online developments in the final issue of each year. Areas of strength were professional development, with details of a range of courses run by Aslib, and news of database developments in individual subject disciplines. Most issues contained a number of evaluative reviews of new publications in the information field.This journal ceased publication at the end of 1993 in favour of a new title, *Managing Information.*

66. *Aslib Proceedings.* London: Aslib, 1949-. Monthly.
Consists mainly of papers presented at Aslib meetings or conferences on a variety of information management topics. Issues related to online information retrieval such as end-user searching and database pricing policies are sometimes addressed.

67. *Bibliotheksdienst.* Berlin: Deutsches Bibliotheksinstitut, 1966-. Monthly.
A general librarianship title whose main function in terms of online and CD-ROM information retrieval is to provide current awareness of developments and applications in Germany. This is achieved through reports of recent meetings and conferences, announcements and previews of forthcoming events, book reviews and copies of the contents pages of recent issues of journals from Germany and other countries.

68. *Bulletin of the American Society for Information Science.* New York: Wiley, 1974-. Bimonthly.
Most issues examine information science issues and policies and contain five or six short articles, a feature article and columns. Although articles dealing with online and CD-ROM are not a major feature, they are included and its current awareness sections provides news of new technological developments and policies, descriptions of recent publications and a listing of forthcoming events.

69. *cogito: Neue Wege zum Wissen der Welt. Informationen wirtschaftlich nutzen.* Darmstadt: Hoppenstedt. Bimonthly.
A mixture of news and informative articles, this German-language journal has regular news items under headings such as as 'CD-ROM', 'Online-Datenbanken', and 'Termine'. Articles take up the bulk of each issue – normally eight or nine – and are of a practical rather than a theoretical nature.

70. *Database Searcher: the Magazine for Online Database Users.* Westport, Connecticut: Mecklermedia, 1985-. Ten issues per year.
Until 1987 titled *Database End-User,* this journal advertises itself as a watchdog of the online industry. Its features represent the consumer viewpoint and are written by and for users of online databases. One of the features which reflects this is 'Reader Feedback' which contains letters from searchers whose points are often followed up

by the journal. Much of each issue consists of announcement and interpretation of new databases and host search features. Separate features entitled 'Connecting Gear' and 'Searcher Support' review telecommunications equipment and other hardware, software or service aids for online searching respectively. Contact information is provided at the end of the journal for all companies mentioned. Most issues also contain two or three articles analyzing trends or reviewing specific products or services. The full text of the journal can be searched online in the Trade and Industry ASAP 100 file and on LEXIS/NEXIS.

71. *Database: the Magazine of Electronic Database Reviews.* Weston, Connecticut: Online, 1978-. Bimonthly.
A key title in the field, *Database* covers a wide range of topics in the online area, complementing Online from the same publisher with treatment of CD-ROM, microcomputers and corporate or personal database design as well, increasingly, of the Internet. Although most of its contributors are based in the United States, its articles and regular columns are relevant internationally, keeping track of developments in database publishing both in general terms and also in individual subject disciplines. Many provide invaluable advice on database selection or on search techniques for specific files. Long-established and new databases are critically evaluated by experienced searchers in every issue. News stories typically account for ten pages per issue and announce new or enhanced databases, publications, and people or company moves in the information industry. The December 1994 issue contained annual reviews of database developments, bibliographic formatting software, CD-ROMs and PC and Macintosh developments. Regular columns, Caduceus (biomedical databases by Bonnie Snow) and The Dollar $ign (business databases by Marydee Ojala), also both reviewed the year. Its text can be searched online as part of The Online Chronicle and Trade and Industry ASAP databases.

72. *Digital Publisher.* Oxford: Learned Information, 1992-. Monthly.
For four years published as *Electronic Documents* and containing a standalone report on topics such as Image Filing; Text Indexing; Hypertext; ISDN; Online Books; SGML or Optical Character Recognition (OCR), in 1996 the journal was renamed and repositioned with a slightly changed emphasis. Learned Information say, 'We are all publishers now, and that is why Electronic Documents has become Digital Publisher in its fifth year.' The four fields of interest are assembling the raw material for publications (including OCR, etc.); indexing, markup languages and authoring systems; distribution options; and user access. Each issue has about four articles; additionally, there is news of latest products and technical developments.

73. *Documentaliste: Sciences de l'Information.* Paris: Association Francaise des Documentalistes et des Bibliothecaires Specialises, 1964-. Bimonthly.
Provides an overall view of information science, storage and retrieval. Short articles cover online information retrieval, the database industry and developments in CD-

ROM storage and retrieval capabilities. Regular features include reviews of new publications, abstracts of articles in other journals, reports of major conferences and tradeshows, and listings of forthcoming events.

74. *I'year.* Prague: Ministry of Economic Politics and Development of the Czech Republic and National Information Centre of the Czech Republic, 1990-. Monthly.
Formed in 1990 by the merger of *Ceskoslovenska Informatika: Teorie a Praxie* and *Technicka Knihovna.* Each issue contains three or four research articles on Librarianship and information science topics, including some on online information retrieval techniques and their application in Czech industrial settings. Individual databases are occasionally featured. The articles are in Czech or Slovak and article abstracts in Russian and English are included at the end of the journal. News is provided of new publications, products and databases. Complemented by the newsletter *Online Kontakt* from the same publisher.

75. *Information Services and Use.* Amsterdam: IOS Press, 1981-. Bimonthly.
Articles are detailed and academic in style and examine information systems, including databases, and their applications worldwide. Developments in the database industry are also examined. Reviews of new publications are included in most issues and special issues occasionally contain papers from conferences such as the the European Information Brokers Meeting and Information Online: the Australasian Online Information Conference.

76. *Joho Kanri (Journal of Information Processing and Management).* Tokyo: Japan Information Center of Science and Technology, 1958-. Monthly.
Issues contain a series of articles in Japanese on information science topics, at least one of which usually features online or CD-ROM information retrieval. Developments in Japan are reported and sometimes compared with those in other countries. English titles, keywords and abstracts are provided. The contents pages are also in both Japanese and English. Product information is a regular feature of each issue, with brief descriptions of hardware and software which are frequently accompanied by illustrations. Other columns contain book reviews, Japanese abstracts of recent journal articles from Europe and the United States, events listings and conference reports.

77. *LASIE: Library Automated Systems Information Exchange.* Haymarket, New South Wales: LASIE, 1970-. Bimonthly.
As its title indicates, this bulletin acts as a medium for the exchange of information on experience with automated systems in Australian libraries and includes articles on the use and management of online and CD-ROM services, the Internet and OPACs.

78. *Library Hi Tech.* Ann Arbor, Michigan: Pierian Press, 1983-. Quarterly.
This is primarily a general library automation journal which frequently includes articles on the application of CD-ROM for information storage and retrieval by

individual libraries in the United States. These articles offer background information on optical disc technology and on its range of applications. Generally, this journal offers a more detailed subject treatment than its sister title, *Library Hi Tech News.*

79. *Library Journal.* New York: Bowker, 1876-. Twice monthly.
US title with general coverage of librarianship which includes IT applications and CD-ROM and online databases. Occasional articles on the online scene and CD-ROM reviews complement a regular 'Online Databases' column dealing with practical issues associated with database searching. Brief announcements of new CD-ROM and online databases frequently appear.

80. *Nachrichten für Dokumentation: Zeitschrift für Information und Dokumentation mit Schriften zu den Informationswissenschaften.* Weinheim: Deutsche Gesellschaft für Dokumentation, 1950-. Bimonthly.
Detailed articles cover a wide spectrum of information science topics. Subjects include those relevant to databases. The language of publication is German, although English summaries are provided at the beginning of articles. Current awareness is a strong feature, especially in the case of published works. Contents pages of related journals from Japan, Germany, France, Britain and the United States are listed in each issue, and are supplemented by a listing of relevant references in numerous languages which have been recently added to the INFODATA database. Additional columns contain book reviews, news of new products and databases, reports of recent conferences and a listing of forthcoming events.

81. *Online & CD-ROM Review: the International Journal of Online and Optical Information Systems.* Oxford: Learned Information, 1977-. Bimonthly.
Formerly simply *Online Review,* this is one of the major titles in the field, offering a balance of refereed theoretical articles and practical contributions on information retrieval systems or techniques, end user searching, search strategies for specific subject areas or overviews of types of online information. The editors (Martha Williams and Forbes Gibb) and their editorial board bring together authors from many countries thus providing a global insight into the electronic publishing industry. Each issue contains a news section which highlights major database and service developments from online hosts or CD-ROM publishers and new hardware and software products with full contact information. Other sections critically review new publications and announce forthcoming conferences and exhibitions worldwide. A notable supplement to the August issue each year is the 'Online Information Retrieval Bibliography'.

82. *Online Kensaku.* Tokyo: Japan Online Terminal Research Association, 1980-. Quarterly.
Articles report on developments in online and CD-ROM information services worldwide, especially in the medical field, and on their application in Japan. Reviews of new databases and comparisons of established files are regular features, as are book

reviews, conference reports, events listings and an ongoing bibliography of references in Japanese and other languages on online information retrieval. The journal is published in Japanese with English-language abstracts at the end of each article.

83. *Online: the Magazine of Online Information Systems.* Weston, Connecticut: Online, 1977-. Bimonthly.

Along with its sister publication *Database,* this is the leading US journal in the online field. Although there is no duplication in coverage, the structure of both journals is very similar. Features include 'Hardcopy', reviewing recent writings, 'Journal Watch', providing summaries of recent articles in related journals – recommended readings, 'The Dollar $ign', in which online sources of business information are spotlighted, and 'CD-ROM and Multimedia' which offers commentary on CD-ROM developments. The Internet features prominently. News of market moves and new hardware, software, and online databases is also given extensive treatment, both in separate review sections and as part of the journal's news section. Each issue contains numerous practical articles on a broad range of themes, some of which 'test drive' new products or provide tips on search techniques, others deal specifically with related areas such as post-processing of search results or document delivery or in more general terms with themes like end-user training or information broking. Although the emphasis is on the United States, an 'International Notes' column is published in many issues and provides current awareness of developments worldwide. An annual subject index is published in each January issue, while the text of the journal is offered for online searching within The Online Chronicle and Trade and Industry ASAP files. *Online* shares a gopher address on the Internet with *DATABASE, MultiMedia Schools* and *CD-ROM Professional* (online.lib.uic.edu); this offers free browsing of selected articles and columns.

84. *RQ.* Chicago: American Library Association. Reference and Adult Services Division, 1960-. Quarterly.

Treatment of reference service provision in libraries includes ample coverage of online developments. Its primary value here is as a reviewer of new online and CD-ROM databases. This is achieved through a separate section in which typically three or four brief evaluative reviews are provided, with details of special search features, cost and system requirements. Reviews of new books on database searching are also published. Can be searched in full-text form online in the Trade and Industry ASAP database.

85. *Scientific and Technical Information Processing.* New York: Allerton Press, 1974-. Bimonthly.

Selectively translates articles from the journal *Nauchno-Tekhnicheskaya Informatsiya, Seriya 1: Organizatsiya i Metodika Informatsionnoi Roboty* which is published monthly in Moscow by VINITI, the All-Union Institute of Scientific and Technical Information. Each issue of *Scientific and Technical Information Processing* therefore usually contains articles selected from two earlier issues of the Russian title. Articles deal with a range of information science topics and are written typically at research level.

86. *Special Libraries.* Washington, DC: Special Libraries Association, 1910-. Quarterly.
The journal of the US Special Libraries Association covers general topics with an emphasis on broad management issues in US special libraries but there are still occasional reports of experience with online and CD-ROM management issues and searching.

87. *Tudomanyos es Muszaki Tajekoztatas (Scientific and Technical Information).* Budapest: Orszagos Muszaki Informacios Kozpont es Konyvtar, 1953-. Monthly.
Covers developments in the automation of library procedures, especially information retrieval via online or CD-ROM databases, in Hungary and worldwide. Each issue contains three or four detailed articles, including state-of-the-art reviews. Articles are in Hungarian, with abstracts in English, German and Russian. The contents page of the journal is also translated into these languages.

88. *Wilson Library Bulletin.* New York: H. W. Wilson, 1914-. Monthly.
General librarianship journal whose main significance lies in its 'Connect Time' column which reviews developments in the online industry and its services. General issues of concern to searchers are also addressed. The column is published regularly in the 'Technology' section of the journal. This section also includes coverage of the Internet, document delivery and microcomputing.

Newsletters: Online/CD-ROM Full-text

89. *Newsletter Database.* Foster City, CA: Information Access Company, 1988-. Daily.
Information Access (a Ziff company) took over all Predicasts' databases in 1993. The *Newsletter Database* contains the full text of over 530 specialized industry newsletters, including the following:

Advanced Information Report (April 1988-)
CD-ROM Databases (August 1988-)
Data Storage Report (January 1988-)
Electronic Services Update (May 1988-)
Online Libraries and Microcomputers (January 1989-) and
Online Newsletter (January 1989-)

The database can be searched on KR Data-Star and KR DIALOG as well as on CompuServe, ESA-IRS and I/PLUS Direct. In all cases from 1988 onwards except for

I/PLUS which offers 1987- and CompuServe which has coverage from 1993. It should be noted that coverage of individual journals within the database varies.

90. *NewsNet.* Bryn Mawr, Pennsylvania: NewsNet, 1982-. Daily
An online news service whose function is to offer access to the full text of more than 760 industry newsletters, in many cases prior to publication in printed form. Included in its coverage are:

CD Computing News (June 1987-)
CD-ROM Databases (September 1987-)
Friday Memo (January 1982-)
LAN Product News (January 1990-)
Online Libraries and Microcomputers (January 1989-)
Online Newsletter (January 1988-) and
Worldwide Videotex Update (December 1982-)

91. *Online Hotline News Service.* Phoenix: Information Intelligence, 1980-. Monthly.
Includes retrospectively the full text of the newsletters *Online Libraries and Microcomputers* and *Online Newsletter.* In the case of *Online Newsletter* coverage runs from 1980 through 1981 and from 1988 onwards, the intervening period being covered by the daily *Online Hotline.* An additional feature of the database is 'Joblines', a listing of employment opportunities in the online field in the United States and Canada. Access to the database can be arranged via the publisher for a fixed annual subscription with no further connect hour charges or via CARL Systems. An equivalent CD-ROM version, updated annually, is available from the publisher.

Newsletters

92. *Australian Database Development Association Newsletter.* Hawthorn, Victoria: Australian Database Development Association, 1983-. Bimonthly.
A regular source of news on new or changed databases on Australian and New Zealand hosts and of forthcoming training courses and conferences, this newsletter acts as a channel for communication of information among members of the Australian Database Development Association.

93. *Bases: Connaitre et Bien utiliser les Banques de Donnees.* Paris: Bases Publications, 1986-. Eleven per year.
A twelve-page, French-language newsletter containing a series of short articles for searchers on CD-ROMs, online searching, videotex and databases. The table of contents is divided into fives sections with a major article, a book review, news releases from online hosts and database producers, a section on Videotex and a diary of events.

94. *Database Canada: a Forum for Database Users and Creators.* Toronto: Database Canada, 1988-. Bimonthly.
As its subtitle indicates, this publication is of interest to database searchers and producers alike. A couple of articles of a practical nature are usually published but a large part of each issue is concerned with the communication of database developments in Canada and of news from host and gateway services. A list of forthcoming conferences, training courses and workshops is provided. The emphasis throughout is on online rather than CD-ROM databases.

95. *Inform.* London: Institute of Information Scientists, 1978-. Ten issues per year.
Not to be confused with *Inform: the Magazine of Information and Image Management,* this publication is mailed to members of the Institute of Information Scientists. It is essentially used to report on meetings and members but there is normally one brief article and the final page usually includes online and CD-ROM industry news. A diary of forthcoming meetings and conferences is also included. Coverage extends across a full range of information science topics. Book reviews are a regular feature. The November issue each year contains a supplement devoted to online information, coinciding with the annual International Online Information Meeting in London.

96. *Information Broker.* Houston: Burwell Enterprises, 1978-. Bimonthly.
Essentially a journal for, by and about companies that offer information for a fee and previously entitled *The Journal of Fee-Based Information Services,* this newsletter regularly identifies new information services and databases in the United States and, through a regular column, 'Window on the World', Europe. New entries for the publisher's annual 'Directory of Fee-Based Information Services' are included in each issue. Other features are advice for information brokers, book reviews and reports and listings of conferences.

97. *Information Hotline.* New York: Science Associates International, 1969-. Ten issues per year.
Includes news stories from the database industry about people, companies, market moves, forthcoming shows and conferences, new or enhanced online and CD-ROM databases, and host services. The first few pages of each issue contain brief announcements of latest developments, while the remainder offer more detailed descriptions of new information products or services with contact data at the end of each. Coverage is international with an emphasis on the United States. Other features are details of new research grants and contracts, mainly from the National Science Foundation or the British Library, and descriptive reviews of about ten new publications, most commonly reference works, per issue.

98. *Information Management Report.* Amsterdam: Elsevier, 1991-. Monthly.
Edited by Ray Prytherch and John Meyer, this newsletter provides comprehensive coverage of new developments in the information world with analysis of the

implications of new technology. The subject scope takes in areas such as artificial intelligence, multimedia systems and desktop publishing, as well as online and CD-ROM product and market developments internationally. Issues contain a balance of surveys of a particular area of technology or a general theme which is usually related to searching, reports of major trade shows, product and database news and reviews of new publications. This newsletter succeeds *Communication Technology Impact* and incorporates *Outlook on Research Libraries* and *Advanced Information Report,* and can be searched online in the PTS Newsletter Database.

99. *Information Retrieval and Library Automation.* Mount Airy, Maryland: Lomond, 1965-. Monthly.
Aims to provide current awareness on computer products and applications in libraries, with a US emphasis, through a series of brief news stories. New databases and host service enhancements are announced, while a special optical disc technology section updates CD-ROM developments. Other regular features list new books and forthcoming events.

100. *Information Today: The Newspaper for Users and Producers of Electronic Information Services.* Medford, New Jersey: Information Today, 1984-. Monthly.
Complements *Information World Review* from the same publisher with news of the US information industry. Apart from announcements and analysis of host and database developments, there are interviews with leading figures from the industry and reviews of individual databases and new hardware and software of interest to information professionals. Other special features are company profiles, 'Federal Scene' which reports on US and international government policy in relation to the information industry, 'PeopleLine', indicating changes of personnel within the industry, book reviews, and job advertisements. The publisher, Information Today Inc, was originally known as Learned Information Inc.

101. *Information World en Español.* Oxford: Learned Information, 1993-. Monthly (combined issue for July/August).
Edited in Spain by a team led by Francisca Garcia-Sicilia and Tomäs Baiget and published by Learned Information, this Spanish-language newsletter derives in part from *Information World Review* but over half of the material comprises original items covering Spanish news and news from other sources relating to the Spanish information industry. As the only Spanish-language publication in this area, *Information World en Español* covers such areas as libraries, online and CD-ROM databases, telecommunications, information systems and services and information policies. *Information World en Español* is the Spanish-language counterpart of *Information Today* and *Information World Review.*

102. *Information World Review: The Information Community Newspaper.* Oxford: Learned Information, 1986-. Monthly (combined issue for July/August).

A valuable source of current awareness on developments in the information industry with an emphasis on Europe, particularly Britain. Correspondents regularly supply reports on developments in France, West Germany and the Netherlands. The rest of the newspaper consists primarily of brief news stories covering new online and CD-ROM databases, search software, multimedia news, electronic document delivery, library automation (some), networking, publications and trade show previews and reviews. There are some regular and semi-regular columns, such as those by Tim Owen, Barry Mahon, Charles Ashley (The Internet) and Chris Armstrong (Database Quality). Each issue also has a main focus, extending over several pages and articles. Of particular interest is the regular coverage of developments in telecommunications networks and of company and market moves in the information industry. Information World Review is also available on CD-ROM with retrospective coverage to January 1990. See also *Information Today,* which is the US counterpart and *Information World en Español* which is a Spanish-language newsletter largely based on *Information World Review.*

103. *Infotecture Europe: Fortnightly European Newsletter on the Electronic Information Industry.* Paris: Transtex International, 1981-. Twice monthly.
Separate sections contain the latest news on European online and CD-ROM companies, markets, databases and services. Other features are summaries of new market research reports, reports on major EEC programmes, figures on the European information market and a diary of forthcoming conferences and exhibitions around Europe. Information on CD-ROM tends to replicate that provided in its sister publication CD-ROM International. News of developments in France features strongly and a longer-established French-language version of the newsletter is published as *Infotecture: Lettre Bimensuelle d'Actualite des Banques de Donnees* (Paris: A Jour, 1979-).

104. *Lesko's Info – Power Newsletter.* Kensington, Maryland: Information USA, 1984-. Monthly.
Formerly, *Data Informer and Data Base Informer,* this newsletter contains information on little-known databases in all subject areas, many of them available from US federal, state or local government and provides current awareness between editions of the publisher's directory, *The Federal Database Finder.* Markets, companies, demographics and technology are the main areas covered.

105. *Library Hi Tech News.* Ann Arbor, Michigan: Pierian Press, 1984-. Eleven issues per year.
This newsletter consists of a series of news briefs on library automation whose scope includes news from the online industry, developments in telecommunications services and announcement of new CD-ROM databases and equipment.

106. *Library Monitor: an Analytical Review of Current Interest in the Library World.* Calne, Wiltshire: Infonortics, 1988-. Monthly.

Similar in style and layout to *Monitor*, this publication reports on developments in online and CD-ROM technology and services and examines the implications for libraries of database industry policies in areas such as pricing and downloading. General issues such as liability in the provision of electronic information services and charging for library services are also addressed. New databases and publications are regularly reviewed. An author and subject index to the previous twelve issues is published.

107. *Link-Up: the Newsmagazine for Users of Online Services: Business, Educational, Personal.* Medford, New Jersey: Learned Information, 1983-. Bimonthly.

A newsletter with news and hints for the business, home and casual online searcher. Each issue includes a detailed software review, along with a series of briefer descriptions of new products, sometimes arranged in categories such as modems or communications software. As well as news of new or enhanced host and database services and updates on bulletin board systems with information on how to gain access to them. Databases for business, research and home use are featured, as indicated by the subtitle of the newsletter. Other regular features are profiles of individual host services, surveys of databases aimed at particular subject fields or types of information, and book reviews.

108. *Nordisk Online: Organ for Brukere av Elektronisk Informasjon i de Nordiske Land.* Oslo: AXESS Information Services, 1987-. Quarterly.

Offers updates on developments in online and CD-ROM information retrieval sources and services in Denmark, Finland, Norway and Sweden. Reports from conferences and trade shows in Scandinavian and other European countries are a regular feature. The newsletter runs to sixteen pages, with news stories and articles in the Scandinavian language of origin. A shorter international edition is also published in English at irregular intervals under the translated title *Nordisk Online: Periodical for Users of Online Information in the Nordic Countries.*

109. *Online and CD-ROM Notes.* London: Aslib, 1978-. Monthly.

Originally simply *Online Notes,* this time-saving publication consists mainly of a series of news digests of database and other product or service developments from the major online hosts used by UK searchers. A special column deals with new and planned databases, summarizing their subject coverage and hosts through which they are likely to become available. Meetings and training courses in the UK are listed. In addition, book reviews are a regular feature.

110. *Online Kontakt.* Prague: Ustredi Vedeckych Technickych a Ekonomickych Informaci, 1986-. Bimonthly.

Until 1989 *Online Informator,* this newsletter complements the coverage of online information retrieval afforded by its sister publication, *I'year.* Brief news and announcements of databases, search products and publications rather than detailed articles constitute this newsletter, with an emphasis throughout on the practical aspects of online searching.

111. *Online Libraries and Microcomputers.* Phoenix: Information Intelligence, 1983-. Ten issues per year.
Covers library automation in general but includes a section on databases which announces and concisely describes new online and CD-ROM files considered to be significant for US libraries. Its sister publication, *Online Newsletter,* offers fuller and more international coverage. Available online for varying time periods via the publisher's Online Hotline News Service, NewsNet and PTS Newsletter Database.

112. *Online Newsletter.* Phoenix: Information Intelligence, 1980-. Ten issues per year.
The major function of this newsletter is the provision of brief announcements of new, forthcoming and withdrawn online or CD-ROM databases, with details of subject content, availability, cost, and user aids. News of new equipment, developments in telecommunications, information industry trends, forthcoming events, and new publications makes up the rest of each issue. Like *Online and CD-ROM Notes* it brings together news digests from a variety of scattered sources but aims to be more international in its coverage. Its full text can be searched online via the Online Hotline News Service, NewsNet and PTS Newsletter Database. An annual index to the print version is published.

113. *SCANNET Today.* Espoo, Finland: SCANNET, 1979-. Irregular.
Although published typically only once or twice a year, this publication supplements the *Nordisk Databasguide* with announcements of new databases and databanks available in the Scandinavian countries, including details in each case of who to contact for further information. These announcements are grouped by subject area. Other sections of the newsletter report on conferences and exhibitions, new publications and projects supported by NORDINFO, the Nordic Council for Scientific Information and Research Libraries. The language of publication is English.

114. *UKOLUG Newsletter.* London: UK Online User Group, 1979-. Bimonthly.
An invaluable and information packed source of current awareness which runs the full gamut of online topics. Contributions frequently convey the consumer's view to providers of online information services. Regular columns are devoted to Internet, CD-ROM and telecommunications developments, detailed book and occassional product reviews, abstracts of recent journal articles, reports of meetings, and conference and course listings. Digests of news from the online industry are conveniently provided, encompassing details of new or enhanced databases, documentation and other services.

Online and CD-ROM Databases

115. *BNBMARC.* London: British Library Bibliographic Services, 1950-. Weekly.
Originally known as UKMARC, this is the online version of the *British National Bibliography* and can be accessed on BLAISE-LINE. The database is segmented into the following time periods: 1950-1970; 1971-1976; and 1977 onwards. A direct service known as Catalogue Bridge enables users to find full MARC records from a control number (ISBN, ISSN, BNB number or LC card number) and users of the Dynix Library System have access to the system from within the existing cataloguing and acquisitions software over the Internet. When a record is located, users are then given the option of purchase and automatic transfer to their database. A CD-ROM version launched by the British Library in 1989 and covering the whole period from 1950 and updated at quarterly intervals is available from Chadwyck-Healey.

116. *Conference Proceedings Index.* Wetherby, West Yorkshire: British Library Document Supply Centre, 1964-. Monthly.
Provides access to the *Index of Conference Proceedings Received* through the BLAISE-LINE host. Subject searching is best conducted via relevant free-text keywords since there is no subject indexing or classification scheme.

117. *Cumulative Book Index.* New York: H.W. Wilson, 1982-. Twice weekly.
Offers the same coverage from January 1982 onwards as the print version and can be searched on WILSONLINE. Greater currency is offered online through more frequent updating. CD-ROMs coresponding to the online file are issued by the publisher and SilverPlatter, covering the same time period but only updated quarterly.

118. *Dissertation Abstracts Online.* Ann Arbor: Michigan: University Microfilms International, 1861-. Monthly.
Online access to *Dissertation Abstracts International* – the definitive source to virtually every American dissertation accepted at an accredited institution since 1861, when academic doctoral degrees were first granted in the United States – is offered by CDP Online, KR Data-Star, KR DIALOG, OCLC and STN International, with abstracts from mid-1980. Citations for thousands of Canadian dissertations and an increasing number from the rest of the world are also included. The publisher produces a twice yearly updated CD-ROM version of the whole database on three discs as well as Humanities/Social Sciences and Sciences and Engineering subsets.

119. *ERIC.* Washington, DC: U.S. Department of Education. Office of Educational Research and Improvement. Educational Resources Information Center, 1966-. Monthly.
ERIC comprises the catalogue of the educational materials collected by the Educational Resources Information Center of the United States Department of Education and consists of the contents of *Resources in Education* and *Current Index to Journals*

in Education. As a result, a full range of document types is represented, including a significant amount of 'grey' literature. The database contains significant coverage of online and CD-ROM database searching although naturally, it is set in the educational context. The educational level discussed can be specified in searching as can target readership. A detailed thesaurus is published at irregular intervals to assist searching. It provides alphabetical, rotated keyword and hierarchical listings and shows the frequency with which a term has been assigned in the database. CDP Online and KR DIALOG make the file available online and CD-ROM versions are published by KR OnDisc (DIALOG) and SilverPlatter.

120. *INFODATA*. Frankfurt: Gesellschaft für Mathematik und Datenverarbeitung. Informationszentrum fur Informationswissenschaft und -praxis, 1976-. Monthly.
Contains over 55,000 records with abstracts on information science and related fields. Source documents include journal articles, monographs, reports and conference proceedings in German, English and other languages. Abstracts are supplied in German or English depending on the original language of the document. Topics covered include specialist databases, information systems, training, electronic publishing, communications and new media. Access is via FIZ Technik.

121. *Information Science Abstracts.* Alexandria, Virginia: IFI/Plenum, 1966-. Monthly.
Corresponding to the hard copy abstracting and indexing service of the same name, this source can be searched on KR DIALOG as File 202. A database user guide is available from the publisher.

122. *INSPEC.* Stevenage, Hertfordshire: Institution of Electrical Engineers, 1969-. Monthly.
INSPEC is an acronym for Information Services for the Physics and Engineering Communities and this is reflected in the fact that the full database (over 4.8 million records) contains extensive coverage of physics and electrical and electronic engineering as well as computer science and applications. Because of this it is a good idea to limit database searches to the appropriate subject classification codes indicated in the description of Computer and Control Abstracts, one of its printed equivalents or to Section D, Information Technology which office automation, computer terminals, electronic mail and teleconferencing among other topics. INSPEC can be searched on a variety of hosts and on CD-ROM with earliest availability is from 1969. Online hosts are CDP Online, CAN/OLE, CEDOCAR, KR Data-Star, KR DIALOG, ESA-IRS, Questel-ORBIT and STN. The CD-ROMs are provided by University Microfilms International (UMI) who offer various possibilities of subscribing to the complete INSPEC Ondisc, INSPEC – Electronics and Computing Ondisc, or IEEE/IEE Publications Ondisc; the latter providing the scanned images of the full text of some eighty journals and conference papers published by the US Institute of Electrical and Electronics Engineers and the UK-based Institution of Electrical Engineers. Approximately 25,000 records are added each year with monthly updates averaging 15,000

pages and coverage extending back to 1988. User aids include a user manual, a thesaurus of preferred indexing terms and a list of source journals. Standard Topics or profiles can be searched every two week by INSPEC staff and mailed to subscribers, alternatively for customers with very specific or narrower interests, A personalised SDI profile can be used. The set topics are Communications, Electronics, Imaging and display, Optics and lasers, Computers and Computing, Geophysics, Material science, and Power engineering.

123. *LCMARC.* Washington, DC: Library of Congress, 1968-. Weekly.
Consists of records catalogued by the Library of Congress from 1968 onwards on KR DIALOG and BLAISE-LINE and from 1977 on WILSONLINE. Access is offered to monographs, reference works and conference proceedings in a range of languages, primarily European, as well as in English. The file is segmented on BLAISE-LINE at 1977 and 1983, the latest section, from 1984 onwards, being updated monthly rather than weekly as on KR DIALOG.

124. *Library Literature.* New York: H. W. Wilson, 1984-. Twice weekly.
More frequently updated than its printed counterpart of the same title and searchable online through the publisher's WILSONLINE system from November 1984 onwards as well as via OCLC and, in the UK, BIDS. A CD-ROM version is also available from the SilverPlatter and from WilsonDisc. Although the latter is only updated quarterly, subscribers to it receive free access (apart from telecommunications charges) to the online database for more current information. Articles are indexed under specific library/information science subject headings with extensive cross-references. According to Reid, there is relatively little overlap between this database and ISA or LISA – certainly less than fifty per cent (Reid, B. J. 'Information and Library Literature on CD-ROM'. *Refer* 9 (3) 7-8, 10-13).

125. *LISA.* East Grinstead: Bowker-Saur, 1969-. Monthly.
Corresponds to the printed abstracting and indexing service *Library and Information Science Abstracts.* Abstracts are included from 1976 onwards. A point to note in searching is that the form 'On-Line' was preferred to 'Online' in the controlled vocabulary until this was updated in January 1993. From this date, 'Online' and 'Databases' (not Data Bases) have been used and the term 'Online databases' replaces the need to combine the two separate terms. LISA can be searched online via KR DIALOG, while a CD-ROM version, updated twice yearly, is available from the producers.

126. *NTIS.* Springfield, Virginia: U.S. Department of Commerce. National Technical Information Service, 1964-. Twice monthly.
The electronic version of *Government Reports, Announcements and Index* is offered by a range of hosts, some with the complete backfile to 1964. CD-ROM databases are provided with quarterly updating by KR DIALOG from 1980 and by SilverPlatter from 1983; the database is also available on tape.

127. *PASCAL.* Vandoeuvre-les-Nancy: Centre National de la Recherche Scientifique. Institut de l'Information Scientifique et Technique, 1973-. Monthly.
Offered for searching by KR DIALOG, ESA-IRS, Westlaw, CompuServe and Questel/ORBIT as well as via Minitel, this multidisciplinary file contains over ten million references from worldwide sources and includes *PASCAL THEMA T205: Sciences de l'Information Documentation.* Retrieval can be made more specific by searching the classification codes subfield of the database. Titles of all references are in their original language with French and/or English translations. French-language descriptors are employed throughout the database and are supplemented by English terms from 1982 and by Spanish from 1987, enabling effective searches to be conducted in languages other than French. Abstracts are always in French.

128. *SIGLE.* Seilles, Belgium: European Association for Grey Literature Exploitation, 1981-. Monthly.
SIGLE stands for System for Information on Grey Literature in Europe and the database is the result of the co-operative effort of national documentation centres in the European Community, chiefly those of the UK and Germany and, to a lesser extent, France. Types of document included are theses, internal reports, reports of meetings and some manuals and directories for online searching. The search language of the database is English, with original and translated titles for foreign-language items. From a UK perspective it is worth noting that the database includes most of the items in *British Reports, Translations and Theses.* The other major print version of SIGLE is the German publication *Forschungsberichte aus der Technik und Naturwissenschaften.* Over 3,000 records are added monthly and access is offered through BLAISE-LINE, SUNIST and STN International as well as on a SilverPlatter CD-ROM.

129. *Social Scisearch.* Philadelphia: Institute for Scientific Information, 1972-. Weekly.
Access to the online database version of Social Sciences Citation Index is offered by CDP Online, KR Data-Star, KR DIALOG and DIMDI, as well as by the UK BIDS service. A discounted rate for online searching can be requested by print subscribers who can also benefit from a reduced price for the CD-ROM version which covers the period from 1986 onwards and is updated quarterly. The CD-ROM version can also be obtained with abstracts added.

Reports

130. **Martyn, J.** (ed.) *Information UK Outlook.* London: Library Information Technology Centre, 1993-. Irregular.
The *Information UK Outlook* series, edited by John Martyn – one of the three editors of the British Library's *Information UK 2000 Report,* extends the original report with ten articles per year focussing on areas in which rapid change is taking place. Each

article is written by an acknowledged expert and, following some introductory statistics to establish context, covers the developments in the recent past and the trends which can be expected in the future. The consequences, the likely impact and the major issues involved for libraries and information services are discussed at length. Of particular interest in the first year are 'Online and CD-ROM Databases' by Harry East; 'Interlending and Document Delivery' by David Brown; and 'OPACs' by Micheline Hancock-Beaulieu.

131. Sigurdson, J. and **Greatrex, R.** *Electronic Databases in Japan: an Information Resource to be Reached On-Line.* Springfield, Virginia: NTIS, 1988. 143pp.
Also published as NTIS Report PB88-112065, this work describes an exploratory project, undertaken by the Research Policy Institute at the University of Lund in Sweden, to access Japanese-language databases online. It contains an overview of the Japanese database industry and its future prospects, sample searches in Japanese databases, including advice in search methods, and search evaluations. Appendices list the premier Japanese databases and give details of search costs and published search aids. This work, although some years old, complements the more recent *Databases in Japan* showing growth and progress.

Review Publications

132. *Advances in Librarianship.* San Diego: Academic Press, 1969-1984, 1991-. Annual.
Volumes of around seven or eight chapter-length reviews covering topics in librarianship and information science. Some articles are general in nature, covering the entirety of the discipline while others deal with anything from air quality in libraries to the information needs of children. All are lengthy and detailed and are usually divided into sections covering all aspects of the topic. Each article ends with a bibliography – typically anything from 25 to 150 references.

133. *Annual Review of Information Science and Technology.* Medford, New Jersey: Learned Information, 1966-. Annual.
This publication is coordinated by the American Society for Information Science, was originally published by Elsevier and has been edited for some years by Martha Williams. Its purpose is 'to describe and to appraise activities and trends in the field of information science and technology' (Preface, vol. 23, 1988, p. viii). Substantial reviews, typically of thirty pages, on topics related to information retrieval are usually included. Examples are 'CD-ROM' (1988) and 'End-user searching' (1987). Lengthy bibliographies accompany all contributions. The latest edition of *ARIST* (Volume 29, 1994) includes sections on 'Information Retrieval Techniques', 'Relevance and Information Behaviour', 'Database Access Systems', 'Health Informatics', and 'Managing information Systems'.

Yearbooks

134. Elias, A. W. (ed.) *The NFAIS Yearbook of the Information Industry 1993.* Medford, New Jersey: Learned Information, 1993. 130pp.

In this second *NFAIS Yearbook,* information professionals are provided with a global insight into significant events that have impacted the information community during the year, with some comments on how these may affect the future of the industry. Nine major chapters (Governmental Influence; New Technologies; The Marketplaces; Publishers, Producers and Distributors; Databases; Research; Communications; Legal Actions; and Worldview) draw information from an extensive collection of press releases, primary literature, newsletters, reports, online sources and other references. All material is reviewed and screened by an editorial board.

GENERAL – CONFERENCES
Guides to Forthcoming Events

Directories: Online Format

135. *EventLine. Amsterdam*: Elsevier Science. Monthly.
A multidisciplinary database of references to forthcoming conferences, exhibits, trade fairs, symposia and major sporting events worldwide, which from late 1994 has included cultural and artistic events. Sourced partly from other Elsevier journals, the database is available on OCLC, Questel/Orbit, KR DIALOG and KR Data-Star. Details in each record include the title, subject, type of event, date, venue, agenda or programme, past attendance figures and contact information.

136. *FAIRBASE.* Hannover: FAIRBASE Datenbank. Monthly.
Of particular interest to prospective attendees and exhibitors, FAIRBASE is an online directory of worldwide trade fairs, exhibitions and conferences from some 3,100 organisers in all subject areas which have taken place since 1986 or which will be held in the current year or the next twenty-five years. Details provided include event title, location, organizer, date and featured product category. The database can be searched using any of these elements of data and is available on CDP Online, KR Data-Star and FIZ-Technik. Searches for events in a particular product or subject area can be conducted by product codes based on those used in the US Standard Industrial Classification or by descriptors in English, French or German and in the case of FIZ-Technik and KR Data-Star search results are automatically placed in date order.

Directories: Print

137. **Webster, V. J.** (ed.) *Tradeshows Worldwide: an International Directory to Events, Facilities and Suppliers.* Detroit: Gale. Annual.
Much of the content of this directory is aimed at trade exhibition organizers rather than visitors, although it covers a wide range of events and is worth bearing in mind as a hard copy alternative to FAIRBASE and EventLine as it contains details of over 5,700 events from 4,600 organisers. Details provided in each entry include frequency, usual size of attendance, target audience, number of exhibitors, registration fees and dates and locations for current and, where known, future years. Date, location, subject and master name indexes are also provided. Prior to 1990 known as *Trade Shows and Professional Exhibits Directory.* The directory is also available on diskette or magnetic tape.

Journals

138. *Professional Calendar: Forthcoming Courses and Conferences for the Library and Information Professions.* Aberystwyth: Thomas Parry Library. Bimonthly.

An alerting service which provides details of forthcoming conferences, courses, meetings, exhibitions and study visits in all areas – and the coverage has been made as wide as possible – of interest to library and information professionals. The emphasis is on events in Britain, although major international and national meetings in other countries are included. Coverage of training courses in online searching from hosts and professional bodies is a strong feature. Events are listed in date order and provide details of event title, organizing body, contact information, location and cost. Indexes offer access by subject, organizer and location. The period of time covered normally exceeds one year from the date of each issue.

CD-ROM

Bibliographies

139. Elshami, A. M. *CD-ROM: an Annotated Bibliography.* Englewood, Colorado: Libraries Unlimited, 1988. 138pp.

Valuable and well arranged compilation of 725 references, representing literature on CD-ROM up to the end of 1987. Abstracts are provided in each case. Most of the references are articles from journals, newspapers or newsletters, the majority of which are published in the United States. Computing titles feature prominently alongside publications in information science. A selection of conference, dissertation and report literature is also included. All aspects of CD-ROM are covered and are assigned separate sections in the bibliography. Twelve parts, further subdivided into more specific sections, deal with CD-ROM technology, types of optical media, comparisons with other media, production, applications and markets. Applications receive most attention, with nearly 300 references listed in forty categories. Indexing is by author, title and subject. Alternatively, the bibliography can be purchased in diskette format for use on IBM and Macintosh computers.

140. Gabriel, M. R. *A Guide to the Literature of Electronic Publishing: CD-ROM, Desktop Publishing, and Electronic Mail, Books, and Journals.* Greenwich, Connecticut: JAI Press, 1990. 187pp. (Foundations in Library and Information Science; 24.)

Includes a bibliography of over 600 references, without abstracts, on optical media. All are in the English language and most date from the period 1985-1988. Sources are newsletters, magazines and journals in librarianship, optical publishing and computing. The bibliography is arranged by author.

141. Langlois, J. *CD-ROM 1992: An Annotated Bibliography of Resources.* Westport, Connecticut: Mecklermedia, 1992. 298pp.

An annotated bibliography of some 1,360 journal articles and 31 books and other materials dealing with CD-ROM use in libraries ostensively covering the period from 1983 to 1992. In fact, only four per cent of the content stems from 1991 while thirty percent comes from 1990 and no references are included from 1992; 56% date from 1987 to 1989. Coverage is excellent within this period with very few notable absences and, as Paul Nicholls notes the volume complements Saffady's annual *Optical Storage Technology: A State of the Art Review* and his own *CD-ROM Buyer's Guide and Handbook* as well as providing a much needed update to Elshami's *CD-ROM: An Annotated Bibliography;* the annotations being a major strength (Nicholls, Paul. 'Book Shelf'. *CD-ROM World* 8 (5) (June 1993) p. 51). Emphasis is on articles dealing with collection development and practical works which avoid the technical aspects. The citations are listed under 39 subject headings ranging from Acquisitions to Use Studies but there is no author index and the subject indexing is minimal.

142. Oppenheim, C. 'Sources of information, and keeping up to date'. *In* Oppenheim, C. (ed.) *CD-ROM: From Fundamentals to Applications.* London: Butterworths, 1988, pp. 293-299.
Provides a descriptive and evaluative guide to the major regularly-held conferences and periodical publications for current awareness purposes. The section on journals and newsletters is especially valuable, listing over fifty sources from major countries and indicating the type of coverage which they provide. Publishers addresses are supplied in many cases. Market research companies and conference organizers are also identified.

143. Saffady, W. *Optical Storage Technology: A State of the Art Review.* Westport, CA: Mecklermedia, 1990-. c.200pp. Annually.
Aimed at information management professionals, this bibliography contains an annual selection of the literature on optical disc storage. This is a bibliography that addresses the technology rather than the applications but is none the less useful for that.

Books

144. Buddine, L. and **Young, E.** *The Brady Guide to CD-ROM.* New York: Prentice-Hall, 1987. 476pp.
Offers a thorough grounding in the technology which underpins CD-ROM databases. The first section explains how CD-ROM databases are produced in a stage-by-stage presentation which covers user interfaces, standard system features and capabilities, retrieval software and mastering techniques. Examples of existing database products are used to illustrate retrieval software in action. CD-ROM technology and standards are the subject of the second part. Appendices list a selection of US manufacturers and describe the subject content of the databases mentioned in the first section.

145. Burton, P. F. and **Moore, C.** (eds.) *CD-ROM: A Practical Guide for Information Professionals.* London: UK Online User Group and the Library Information Technology Centre, 1994. 59 pp.
One of the few publications to offer a British perspective on CD-ROM and now in its second edition, this guide offers valuable advice on a number of issues of concern to information professionals. In the second edition the chapter on networking has been dropped, this being covered in the companion CD-ROM Networking in Practice. Chapters cover database and equipment selection, installation, training and user documentation, management, reuse of downloaded data, copyright and even 'Making your own CD-ROM'. A select bibliography is appended. All chapters are written by

practicing professionals with experience of CD-ROM use and all are written at a practical, introductory level. Most chapters have their own reading lists.

146. Desmarais, N. *The Librarian's CD-ROM Handbook.* Westport, Connecticut: Mecklermedia, 1988. 174pp.
Separate chapters provide advice on selection of CD-ROM databases and hardware, followed by a discussion of management issues. Topics of concern to the CD-ROM industry in 1988 are briefly outlined. The second half of the book indicates the major products on offer – again in 1988 – for a range of library and business or industrial applications. The emphasis throughout is on American experience and products and this is reflected in the bibliography at the end which runs to over 100 references.

147. Eaton, N. L., MacDonald, L. B. and **Saule, M. R.** *CD-ROM and Other Optical Information Systems: Implementation Issues for Libraries.* Phoenix: Oryx Press, 1989. 167pp.
This book addresses a range of issues including user interfaces, staffing, the impact on other library operations, networking, workstation ergonomics and financial considerations. These discussions are supplemented by a series of case studies from US libraries covering the implementing of their systems. Appendices offer a list of producers and distributors of optical information products and a selective bibliography.

148. *Facts and Figures 1995.* London: TFPL, 1995.
TFPL publish the twice-yearly *CD-ROM Directory* and consequently have a ready-made source for this graphical presentation of developments in the CD-ROM and multimedia market over the past nine years in their database of CD-ROM titles. Charts show such information as trends in the growth of titles, formats and subject areas as well as examining pricing. A full commentary by industry expert Julie Schwerin (author of *The OPIA Report*) is included. Interestingly, with consumer titles increasing with a growth rate of over 70%, she notes that, 'Industry output has reached a level sufficient to propel CD-ROM into the mainstream of desktop computing and position it for similar success in domestic set-top systems.' The 1994 volume was 'an excellent publication' according to Phil Bradley in the *UKOLUG Newsletter* 5(4) (July/August 1994) p12.

149. Hanson, T. A. and **Day, J.** (eds). *CD-ROM in Libraries: Management Issues.* East Grinstead: Bowker-Saur, 1994.
Addresses a wide range of topics through a mixture of discursive chapters and case studies. Thus a chapter on Training Endusers is backed up by a case study on the approach taken in a particular library. Covers hardware, management resourcing, marketing, and in-house applications as well as end-user training. General case studies on academic, public and special libraries, and a discussion on the future of CD-ROM conclude the book. A second edition of this book is already in preparation.

150. Holtz, F. *CD-ROMs: Breakthrough in Information Storage.* Blue Ridge Summit, Pennsyslvania: TAB Books, 1988. 208pp.

Describes the capabilities of CD-ROM technology and how it works in terms of information storage. A useful chapter is devoted to CD-ROM drives. Leading companies in the industry in the United States are profiled, while the final chapter consists of a series of contributions by executives from some of these companies on the future of optical disc technology.

151. Jacsó, P. *CD-ROM Software, Dataware, and Hardware: Evaluation, Selection, and Installation.* Englewood, Colorado: Libraries Unlimited, 1992. 256pp. (Database Searching Series).

Replete with screen dumps and sample output, this book serves as both a guide to evaluating CD-ROM products and as a directory of past poor practice. Dealing with the various aspects of the package-as-purchased (Jacsó coins the term, 'Dataware') such as the interface; the search features; set and query management; output features; database scope, content, structure and quality; accessibility; documentation; installation; and price, Jacsó creates a methodology for assessing any CD-ROM product. Final sections on hardware evaluation and CD-ROM application requirements; the selection of CD-ROMs and installation procedures complete this review of characteristic features of CD-ROM databases; a review, as he says in the Introduction, intended to help the librarian in the evaluation, comparison, selection, installation and operation of CD-ROM products. Appendices with check-lists or evaluation forms for software, dataware, database and hardware complete the book. This excellent book should be compulsory reading not only for the would-be user of CD-ROMs but for those involved in their publication and production.

152. Nicholls, P. T. *CD-ROM Buyer's Guide and Handbook* (3rd ed). Wilton, CT: Pemberton Press, 1994. 500pp.

A users' guide containing in-dpeth reviews of over 100 core databases plus a bibliography of 'virtually every CD-ROM product review ever published'. The guide is of value to anyone involved in purchasing CD-ROMs and also includes hundreds of facts, tips and checklists as well as explanations of new technologies in CD-ROM and multimedia.

153. Oppenheim, C. (ed.) *Applications of Optical Media.* London: Aslib, 1993. 141pp.

Given the centrality of CD-ROM technology, this book should interest most readers – but especially those from the library and information profession who will be able to relate to the management issues discussed. The nine chapters include an introduction to the technology, a chapter which the editor admits draws heavily on an ICC report on the marketplace for CD-ROM, a practical account of the issues faced when a library installs CD-ROM for the first time, a dip into the virtual library and networked CD-ROMs, an account of 'the pains, pleasures and pitfalls' of running a Help Desk, a look at business applications, a case study for those thinking of creating a CD-ROM, a chapter on CD-ROM use in developing countries and one on multimedia – something with which the chapter author predicts librarians will shortly be involved.

154. Oppenheim, C. (ed.) *CD-ROM: From Fundamentals to Applications.* London: Butterworths, 1988. 308pp.

The advantages and disadvantages of CD-ROM in relation to other media for distributing information are explored largely from the perspective of publishers. This collection concentrates on technology and includes contributions which examine the range of optical storage media, CD-ROM production methods, the economics of CD-ROM publishing, likely markets, the design of user interfaces, and examples of CD-ROM publishing activities. In addition, an annotated list of published sources of information describes the major current awareness publications in the field.

155. Pahwa, A. *The CD-Recordable Bible: An Essential Guide for Any Business.* Wilton, CT: Eight Bit Books, 1993.

For those planning to produce their own optical-disc products, this guide covers all aspects of CD-R in fourteen chapters including: an introduction to the recordable revolution, applications, hardware, selecting a system, manufacturing, standards, reviews, software evaluation, new product announcements and a glossary.

156. Parker, D. and **Starrett, B.** *Technology Edge: A Guide to CD-ROM.* Carmel, IN: New Riders Publishing, 1992. 426pp.

This book is an introduction to CD-ROM technology for the IBM-compatible microcomputer user written at an elementary level. Chapters deal with the general technology; the hardware and networking; practical uses of CD-ROMs; and, in the final section, the future for the technology, multimedia and other related topics such as CD-I, CD-ROM XA, DVI, Photo CD and CD-WO. The volume is well illustrated and handy hints are highlighted in the text. Also included are a directory of companies involved with CD-ROM and a glossary.

157. Roth, J. P. (ed.) *CD-ROM: Applications and Markets.* Westport, Connecticut: Mecklermedia, 1988. 147pp. (Supplement to Optical Information Systems; 3).

Investigates trends in CD-ROM product and market development. Individual chapters examine the library, science and medicine, government and law, and general education sectors in terms of the major products and applications in each. A list of relevant company names and addresses is supplied at the end of each of these chapters. An additional chapter looks at marketing strategies and future trends. The work concludes with an index which provides access to companies, organizations and products discussed in it.

158. Roth, J. P. (ed.) *Essential Guide to CD-ROM.* Westport, Connecticut: Meckler, 1986. 189pp.

A primer which introduces the principles of CD-ROM technology, with its associated hardware, software and applications. A series of appendices provides guidance on standards, terminology, organizations and publications.

159. Schwerin, J., Kaikow, H., Bailey, C. and **Lightbown, P.** *CD-ROM Standards: the Book.* Oxford: Learned Information; Pittsfield, Vermont: InfoTech, 1986. 53, 80pp.
Provides an overview of the early debate on creating technical standards for CD-ROM production and of initiatives taken by major optical publishers, including, in an appendix, the full text of a detailed working paper proposing the High Sierra standard. A bibliography is included.

160. Sherman, C. *The CD-ROM Handbook* (2nd ed.). New York: McGraw-Hill, 1993.
Technical aspects of CD-ROM are emphasized throughout this publication. It consists of a series of chapters by experts in the United States on CD-ROM technology. The past, present and future of CD-ROM are discussed, as are hardware and software, techniques for manipulating data for different applications and the various processes involved in producing discs. An annotated bibliography and list of CD-ROM titles concludes the handbook.

161. Stewart, L., Chiang, K. S. and **Coons, B.** (eds.) *Public Access CD-ROMs in Libraries: Case Studies.* Westport, Connecticut: Mecklermedia, 1990. 311pp.
The book presents over twenty case studies from public, academic, school and special library in the United States, Canada and Europe, which installed CD-ROM workstations in the public access area. Designed as an aid to planning, implementing and staffing, it emphasizes issues associated with public access philosophy, administration and the maintenance of such workstations. Separate sections also address user fees, networks and remote access.

Conferences: Proceedings

162. Ensor, P. and **Nicholls, P.** (eds.) *CD-ROM for Library Users: A Guide to Managing and Maintaining User Access.* Oxford: Learned Information, 1994. 200pp.
Following a 'CD-ROM and Library Users' track at the Washington Computers in Libraries conference, the editors have brought together the fourteen papers presented that day with some additional studies and a selected bibliography. Accepting end users as 'the bottom line of the whole CD-ROM effort', the editors have focused on the use of CD-ROM resources in meeting the needs of the end user.

Dictionaries

163. 'Glossary of Basic CD-ROM Terms'. *CD-ROM Professional,* 7 (1), January 1994, pp. 122-126.

Supercedes the previous 'Glossary of frequently used CD-ROM terms' in the *Laserdisk Profesional* of January 1990, with nearly treble the number of terms (116 terms). Between times, glossaries of local networking terms (January 1993. pp. 80-84), multimedia (January 1993. pp. 106-111) and sound boards (July 1993. pp. 20) have also appeared. A supplementary list of 28 terms dealing mostly with disc production appears in the March 1995 issue (Parker, D. J. 'Standard Terminology: A Lexicon of CD-ROM Jargon'. *CD-ROM Professional* 8 (3) March 1995. pp. 76-78).

164. 'Glossary of CD-ROM-related technical terms and acronyms'. *Optical Information Systems,* 6 (3), May-June 1986, pp. 230-234.

The journal name is now *Document and Image Processing,* but the near 100 technical terms concisely defined in this earlier volume stil make a useful summary provided that users remember newer terms exist too.

Directories: CD-ROM/Diskette

165. *CD-ROM of CD-ROMs.* Resource International Publishing Company, 1993-. Monthly.

CoC lists every title for which full information on contact and pricing can be found. In addition, colour photographs of the front and back of the packaging/jewel box, manufacturer's information, full screen shots in colour, and reviews of the title are included. Resource International try to provide multiple reviews by different authors in order to provide different perspectives. A Who's Who of the industry with names, addresses, telephone and fax numbers on companies involved in multimedia and CD-ROM worldwide, working demonstrations of some titles, sound samples from some titles, shareware and freeware that relate to CD-ROMs and/or multimedia, press releases, news and information on the industry are also included. A serialised version of Professor Paul Nichols' book is also included. The software allows automatic facilities to connect the user with the sellers of CD-ROMs by either telephone, fax or letter so that orders can be initiated. Each monthly disc cumulates until some of the 'older material falls off the edge'.

Bibliographies

166. **Elshami, A. M.** *CD-ROM: an Annotated Bibliography.* Englewood, Colorado: Libraries Unlimited, 1988. 138pp.

Valuable and well arranged compilation of 725 references, representing literature on CD-ROM up to the end of 1987. Abstracts are provided in each case. Most of the references are articles from journals, newspapers or newsletters, the majority of which are published in the United States. Computing titles feature prominently alongside publications in information science. A selection of conference, dissertation and report literature is also included. All aspects of CD-ROM are covered and are assigned separate sections in the bibliography. Twelve parts, further subdivided into more specific sections, deal with CD-ROM technology, types of optical media, comparisons with other media, production, applications and markets. Applications receive most attention, with nearly 300 references listed in forty categories. Indexing is by author, title and subject. Alternatively, the bibliography can be purchased in diskette format for use on IBM and Macintosh computers.

Handbooks

167. Pivovarnick, J. *The Complete Idiot's Guide to CD-ROM.* Indianapolis: Alpha Books, 1994. 297 pp.

A guide for both IBM and Macintosh owners to using CD-ROMs. Covering everything from selecting hardware and installing software to troubleshooting and understanding error messages, the book is written in simple terms in plain English. A reviewer on the Internet noted that the book covered all the essentials of getting started with CD-ROMs: compatibility, standards, accessories, sound cards and multimedia – a bargain at twice its price from which much could be learned.

Journal Articles

168. Guenette, D. R. and **Nicholls, P.** CD-ROM and Multimedia Industry Newsletters. *CD-ROM Professional,* 7 (6), November/December 1994, pp. 154-161.

A resource guide to newsletters covering the CD-ROM and multimedia industries. Newsletters are included which are targetted at the general user, the professional and the producer, ranging from *CD-ROM Newsletter* and *Computers in School Libraries* to *Digital Media: a Seybold Report* and *Pits and Lands.* Each reference (there are 41) has a short descriptive paragraph, the address of the publishers, the name of the editor and the frequency and cost.

169. Harry, V. and **Oppenheim, C.** 'Evaluations of Electronic Databases, Part I: Criteria for Testing CDROM Products; Part II: Testing CDROM Products'. *Online & CDROM Review,* 17 (4), August 1993, pp. 211-222 (Part I) and 17 (6), December 1993, pp. 339-368 (Part II).

A detailed methodology for the evaluation of CD-ROM databases. In the first part the various criteria by which CD-ROMs might be judged are discussed with references to earlier literature covering similar aspects. A review should contain comments on costs, user needs, collection development and hardware platforms as well as basic issues such as vendor details and the product evaluation itself. Harry and Oppenheim subscribe to the school of thought which gives marks for various aspects of the product being reviewed and this is demonstrated in Part II where four CD-ROMs are reviewed. The authors stress, however, that these reviews do NOT include contact with the vendors and in no case was installation evaluated so that the sample reviews should not in any way be construed as representing a real review of the product. Two appendices give the Test Manual with questions for consideration and the marking scheme, and the actual Evaluation Form. This pair of articles cover the business of evaluating a CD-ROM product in considerable depth and, with the appendices, provide potential purchasers and reviewers with an excellent methodology which this editor, as a long-time reviewer, has no hesitation in recommending.

170. Jacsó, P. 'Have I Got a Deal for You: The State of the Art in CD-ROM Marketing and Pricing'. *Information Today* 10 (4) (April 1993) pp. 28-29.
The article explains why 1993 was a good year for purchasing CD-ROMs, looking at discount manufacturer prices for both CD-ROMs and CD-ROM drives, superseded and discontinued databases, special subscriptions, special user deals and bundle deals where CD-ROMs are supplied with the hardware.

171. Large, A. 'The User Interface to CD-ROM Databases' *Journal of Librarianship and Information Science* 23 (4) (December 1991) pp.203-217.
The article looks at CD-ROM search interfaces (for example, command, command menus, drop-down menus), input devices, display features, and user assistance as well as reliability and robustness. Large suggests that software users are becoming more discerning and that there was – at the time of writing – much to be accomplished in interface design. The article makes a good basic guide to CD-ROM software evaluation and there is a useful list of references.

172. Nicholls, P. T. and **Sutherland, T.** 'CD-ROM Databases: a Survey of Commercial Publishing Activity'. *Database* 15 (1) (February 1992) pp. 36-41.
Based on the same methodology as used in four previous surveys, this review reports on commercially available CD-ROM titles for 1985 – 1991 and plots comparative growth of titles, database trends, subject distribution, hardware platforms, and update frequency trends.

173. Paster, A. 'CD-ROM Versus Online: 1980 – 1994'. *CD-ROM Professional* 7 (5) September/October 1994. pp. 137-144.
A useful article tracing the rise of CD-ROM as a competitor and subsequently as an equal to online systems. Quotation from many well-known writers over the years are used to demonstrate how opinions change with time. An interesting review showing how problems were first noted (they contained too little data) and then, by 1990, accepted (multimedia was the major advance needed to give CD-ROM viability), it demonstrates very well the snowball effect of technology. The final pages look at other contenders: CD-ROM versus the Internet or are locally-mounted databases making a comeback? The conclusion is summed up in the one word, co-existence.

174. Shear, V. 'CD-ROM and Metering: an Overview'. *CD-ROM Professional* 5 (2) (March 1992) pp. 85-87.
The article argues that the cost constraints of CD-ROM subscriptions have limited the market and that a meter-based charging mechanism could avoid this. Four critical elements of a metering system are given as encryption techniques, securely managed search histories, maximum usage limit formulae and support of database functionality.

175. Sylvia, M. and **Lesher, M.** 'Making Hard Choices: Cancelling Print Indexes'. *Online* 18 (1) January 1994. pp. 59-60, 62-64.
With the popularity of CD-ROMs, print index use goes down. When St Mary's University Library, Texas investigated the possibility of cancelling some of their printed abstracting and index services, they found that it was possible in many cases to do so without impairing services. Factors considered were price, ease of access, usage patterns, end results and retrieval characteristics, quality of indexing and content and ownership. The indexes examined were Social Sciences Citation Index, Engineering Index and Index Medicus.

176. Tamule, H. B.; Gaus, K. and **Desmarais, N.** 'A New Look as CD-ROM Prices'. *CD-ROM Librarian* 7 (9) (October 1992) pp. 22-26.
The article outlines the uncertainty felt in 1992 with regard to new technology prices and attempts to construct a price index by analysing the titles listed in Pat Ensor's *CD-ROM Research Collections: An Evaluative Guide to Bibliographic and Full-Text CD-ROM Databases.* The conclusion suggests that CD-ROM subscriptions are becoming better value.

177. Zink, S. D. 'Towards More Critical Reviewing and Analysis of CD-ROM User Software Interfaces'. *CD-ROM Professional* 4 (1), January 1991, pp. 16-21.
With reference to past literature, the author discusses the various user considerations in software design which render a product either more or less successful, and follows this with a short review of Congressional Information Services's MASTERFILE 2. The short, but critical review demonstrates where this product has failed to take account of its potential users in developing the search interface. Unlike the Harry and Oppenheim work, this review has been passed to the CD-ROM producers and a short response is included on the final page.

Journals

178. *CD-ROM Professional: the Magazine for CD-ROM Publishers and Users.* Weston, Connecticut: Pemberton Press, 1988-. Bimonthly.
Similar in layout and style to *Database* and *Online*, this substantial journal changed its title from *Laserdisk Professional* in May 1990. It continues to offer numerous articles analysing the CD-ROM scene in terms of database products, equipment, standards, publishing, user experiences and management issues. Product reviews

remain a strong feature, with frequent review articles (such as the Genre Report on Magazines on CD-ROM in November/December 1994), short tests of two or three databases per issue in the 'CD-ROM in Brief' section and a further two or three in the 'Multimedia in Brief'. Also of practical interest is 'Questions and Answers', a feature which advises on solutions to problems experienced by users. An extensive news section monitors industry developments and announces new databases and equipment. For the two years to January 1995, this was extended in a parallel newsletter, *CD-ROM News Extra;* but in 1995 this 30-page supplement is being 'rolled into the parent publication'. Other features report on trade shows and conferences and review new books. The full text of the journal has been included in the online database Trade and Industry ASAP since January 1989, while The Online Chronicle has carried news items from it since March 1990.

179. *CD-ROM World.* Westport, CT: Mecklermedia, 1986-
See Multimedia World.

180. *Document and Image Automation.* Westport, Connecticut: Meckler, 1981-. Bimonthly.
US title – formerly, *Optical Information Systems: the Journal of Digital Document Image Automation, Videodisc* and *Optical Disk and Videodisc – Videotex* – whose news and articles describe developments in optical disc technology, more from the publisher's perspective than that of the user of optical media. Articles emphasize applications of optical media for information retrieval and storage possibly in particular sectors such as medicine and education. Articles are a mixture of reports of new hardware and software developments and broader overviews of publication of CD-ROM databases in individual subject areas. Thorough reviews of new CD-ROM databases are sometimes published. Announcements of new publications and forthcoming events are included. The final issue of each year is a buyer's guide and directory.

181. *Inform: the Magazine of Information and Image Management.* Silver Spring, Maryland: Association for Information and Image Management, 1967-. Monthly.
Articles concentrate on information management, image processing and storage rather than the retrieval aspects of optical media, but include CD-ROM. The journal examines micrographic, optical digital computer technology and systems. The journal's conference reports, events listings and book reviews are of more general interest to anyone seeking current awareness on CD-ROM.

182. *Information Media and Technology.* Hatfield, Hertfordshire: Cimtech, 1967-. Bimonthly.
Includes CD-ROM within a broad coverage of document image processing on optical discs and offers a UK perspective on developments. News of new databases and associated hardware or software products is provided, sometimes as part of a conference or exhibition report. A separate section contains short abstracts of recent

articles in related publications. This section is preceded by a keyword index. Book reviews are often published.

183. *Memoires Optiques et Systemes: le journal de la gestion electronique de documents et du multimedia.* Vannes: ARCA, 1982-. Ten issues per year.
A regular reporter of CD-ROM and multimedia developments in France. The emphasis is on product information and new hardware, software and databases are announced, and in many cases illustrated, in each issue. Interviews with executives from leading French companies are another regular feature. The journal is available in French and an international edition bearing the same title is published in English, concentrating almost exclusively on the announcement of new products from US suppliers in most cases.

184. *Multimedia World.* San Francisco: IDG Communications, 1991-. Monthly.
Formerly *CD-ROM Librarian* (and prior to 1987, *Optical Information Systems Update*), *CD-ROM World* was published by Mecklermedia until late 1994 when it was sold to IDG Communications were it has become a part of *Multimedia World.* It offers a mixture of news and practical articles on CD-ROM issues such as implementation and management, reviews of databases in broad subject areas, and announcements of new databases and peripheral products. Some databases are reviewed in detail in each issue and, in the later Mecklermedia years, many half-page reviews covered games and clip art as well as more serious CD-ROMs. Full reviews were critical and include hardware configuration, software performance, documentation, test searches and pricing.

185. *School Library 2000.* Oxford: Learned Information, 1993-. Termly (three issues per year).
School Library 2000 is targetted at secondary school and sixth form college libraries in the UK and focusses on the addition of CD-ROM and multimedia discs to the school curriculum. Each issue contains product reviews — some with resource material for use in class, as well as coverage of multimedia personal computers (MPCs), CD-ROM hardware, school library automation systems, library security, satellite television, and going online. There are also lists of courses, conferences and exhibitions. The emphasis is on a non-technical approach and the journal is written from the teacher/librarian standpoint with discussions, letters news round-ups and 'how-to' tips all intended to simplify the material covered. All UK secondary schools and sixth form colleges may receive the journal free.

Newsletters

186. *CD Computing News.* Boston, MA: Worldwide Videotex, 1988-. Monthly.

A monthly eight-page report consists of short news items relating to the optical disc industry. The intended audience includes both the users and the managers of CD-ROM resources.

187. *CD-ROM Directions.* Bushey, Hertfordshire: Hitachi New Media, 1987-. Irregular.
Essentially a house journal, this newsletter provides a convenient digest of developments in CD-ROM worldwide, coverage being by no means restricted to the publisher's own product range. The emphasis is on hardware, software and accessory products, although new databases are also featured. Directories of databases and companies are sometimes published.

188. *CD-ROM International: Newsletter on International Developments in CD-ROM, CD-I, CDTV, DVI.* Paris: Transtex International, 1987-. 18 issues per year.
Contains the latest company, product, market and standards news internationally, although with an emphasis on Europe, especially France. CD-ROM International profiles CD-ROM publishers, systems integrators, and developers; gives facts and figures from market studies and publishes a regular barometer of optical disc publishing activity within Europe and worldwide; summarises studies carried out by leading consultants and market research organisations; previews and reviews conferences; and review new products – databases for a wide range of audiences are featured including bibliographic files for libraries and products for more general reference purposes which are aimed at industrial users. A French edition is published in parallel as *CD-ROM: la Lettre Mensuelle du CD-ROM, CD-I, CD-V.* (Paris: A Jour, 1987-).

189. *CD-ROM Newsletter.* Alton, Hampshire: Microinfo, 1987-. Bimonthly.
Provides a very useful forum for the announcements, with brief descriptive information, of new and enhanced CD-ROM databases from a range of publishers. Details of workstations, drives and other equipment are often provided, with technical information such as hardware and software compatibility included. News of new optical industry reports and of new licensing arrangements are also included and the short product reports are supplemented by a CD-ROM Jottings column. Aimed at the British market, the pricing information is given in pounds sterling.

190. *CMC News.* Cannon Falls, MN: CMC News, 1979-. Quarterly.
CMC originally stood for *Computers and the Media Center* and the newsletter is intended for library and media school professionals. However, within the normal 20 to 24 pages, users will normally find about six or eight CD-ROM reviews as well as articles and a listing of current CD-ROMs. The main focus is on education.

191. *Electronic Information Report.* Wilton, CT: SIMBA Information. Weekly
Previously known as *IDP Report,* this newsletter – like other SIMBA publications – monitors an industry sector. In this case the areas covered include storage and

distribution media, electronic publishing, multimedia and databases. Items report on the trends and developments in information services.

192. *omni: Optical Media News and Information.* Alton, Hampshire: Microinfo, 1986-. Monthly.
Originally known as *Optical Data Systems,* the newsletter changed names in April 1991 and continued with wider coverage but narrower scope than before. While this news service continues to take in optical disc technology in general, interactive video and document management/image processing, CD-ROM only figures in terms of its technology. Brief news stories contain the latest product and market developments mainly in Britain and the United States, with full contact information in most cases. Major international trade shows are reviewed and product launches are highlighted.

Online and CD-ROM Databases

193. *Macintosh ShowCase.* Metatec Discovery Systems.
Hypercard stacks about CD-ROM technology itself containing descriptions – complete with sound and graphics – of how the information is stored, how the CD drive reads data, etc. Also included are numerous product reviews and the full text of messages on the CD-ROM Forum on the CompuServe Information Service.

Reports

194. **Hendley, T.** *CD-ROM and Optical Publishing Systems.* Hatfield, Hertfordshire: Cimtech, 1987. 151pp. (Cimtech Publication; 26). (BNB Research Fund Report; 25).
Examines the strengths and weaknesses of CD-ROM as a publishing medium, comparing it with other more established media such as print, microfilm and online as well as with other optical publishing systems. Among the topics discussed are standards, the stages involved in CD-ROM production, associated hardware and software and likely markets.

195. **Royce, C., Akeroyd, J.** and **May, L.** *CD-ROM: Usage and Prospects.* London: British Library Research and Development Department, 1989. 84pp. (British Library Research Paper; 71).
A survey of the uptake and usage of CD-ROM and other optical media in the United Kingdom which was carried out between January and April 1989 on behalf of the British Library. Findings are based on questionnaire responses from libraries and information centres and follow-up interviews with academic, public and special library staff and CD-ROM suppliers. A full range of issues is addressed, including databases in use, hardware, user access, expenditure, training and future acquisitions. Consideration is also given to reasons for non-use and prospects for networking and

for new products. A bibliography of more than seventy references on CD-ROM applications is included. A volume which still makes interesting reading, the more especially so, given the accepted use of networks and end-user/public access CD-ROM workstations five years on.

Reviews: Databases

196. Armstrong, C. J. and **Large, J. A.** (eds.) *CD-ROM Information Products: the Evaluative Guide.* Aldershot: Gower/Ashgate, 1990-1992. Annual; 1993. Quarterly.

Initially produced as annual volumes, and in its final year, as sets of four reviews each quarter, this *Guide* has set out to provide in-depth reviews of information-oriented CD-ROM products. Each review is written by a subject specialist and follows a standard pattern beginning with a fact sheet and continuing with discussions of the database and the retrieval software, the documentation and the pricing. Supported by screen dumps and explanations of software functions, reviews tend to concentrate on the quality of the total package as purchased by the user. Following three years in which it was produced as an annual volume, the move to quarterly publications enabled reviews to reach the readers faster – usually while the product reviewed was still available in the same version. The editors suggest that the general methodology for reviewing used could form the basis for any in-house evaluation of CD-ROMs. In its four years, *CD-ROM Information Products* covered some 74 individual products.

Reviews

197. Fox, E. A. 'Optical disks and CD-ROM: publishing and access'. *Annual Review of Information Science and Technology,* 23, 1988, pp. 85-124.

This literature review focuses on CD-ROM rather than on optical discs generally and, within this framework, on the technology itself rather than on its applications for information retrieval. It begins by briefly discussing book, conference and journal publications in the field and proceeds to review thoroughly the state of the art and literature on media and standards, publishing, access, applications and research. A bibliography with 180 references, representing US literature mainly, concludes the review.

198. *Optical Storage Technology: A State of the Art Review.* Compiled by W. Saffady. Westport, Connecticut: Mecklermedia, 1985-. Annually in December.

Aimed at a wide-ranging readership in both the computing and library fields, this publication offers a convenient outline of developments in optical disc technology for those involved in planning, implementing and evaluation of optical storage. Separate sections cover read-only and read/write optical media. CD-ROM still tends to dominate the former section which describes the latest technological developments, equipment, information products and market projections. Issues such as standards, competing optical disc technologies and the relationship between online and CD-ROM access are also addressed. A substantial bibliography of citations from computing and librarianship literature, is included, as is a listing of US-based vendors.

Yearbooks

199. *Microsoft CD-ROM Yearbook.* Redmond, Washington: Microsoft Press. Annual.

An annual review of the CD-ROM industry which commenced publication in 1989, this consists largely of a collection of articles by leading executives and technologists. The articles are a mixture of reprints or excerpts of previous publications and original contributions commissioned specially for the yearbook. Their readability is enhanced by brevity and clear presentation. Reprints come from a variety of librarianship, computing and business journals or newsletters. The articles are grouped under the following six themes: past, present and future; alternative optical media; applications; production technology and processes; legal aspects; and the CD-ROM business. The remainder of the yearbook is devoted to a series of directories. The lengthiest of these lists commercially available CD-ROM titles alphabetically and by subject in a tabular format which contains publisher, a brief description, audience, retrieval system, computer compatibility, minimum memory required, initial release date, update frequency and price. The other directories list drives, retrieval systems, data preparation houses, mastering/replication facilities, publications and conferences. The section on publications includes journals, newsletters, monographs, market research reports and directories, with a brief abstract for each. As in the rest of the yearbook, however, the emphasis is on US resources.

200. *The Optical Memory Report: the Comprehensive Annual Sourcebook of the Optical Memory Industry Worldwide.* San Francisco: Rothchild. Annual.

Compiled by the publishers of the newsletter *Optical Memory News,* this yearbook provides an overview of the optical disc industry, specifications and pricing for 1,000 associated products and systems, company profiles and five-year worldwide market projections for individual product sectors.

CD-ROM NETWORKING

Books

201. Desmarais, N. *CD-ROM Local Area Networks: a User's Guide.* Westport, Connecticut: Mecklermedia, 1991. 175pp.
Addresses the issues associated with networked access to CD-ROM databases, including planning, management, hardware and software options and copyright implications.

202. Wood, M. S. (ed.) *CD-ROM Implementation and Networking in Health Science Libraries.* New York: Hawarth Press, 1993. 165pp.
A concise guide for librarians and information workers concerned with CD-ROM administration, the book is a collection of essays dealing with the basics of the technology, database selection criteria, systems management and future trends. A second part consists of seven case studies of the implementation of stand-alone CD-ROM workstations, software upgrades, user education programmes, cost recovery initiatives and several different networked systems. This is a comprehensive collection which is of interest to both the novice and the experienced CD-ROM administrator. Antony Brewerton noted one reservation on the 'excessively mercenary' section on cost recovery but also – importantly – pointed out that the volume's worth extended well beyond health libraries. 'The examples may be drawn from the medical arena but the lessons learnt are universal.' (Brewerton, A. W. 'CD-ROM Practical Guide'. *Library Association Record* 95 (12), December 1993, pp. 699.)

Conferences: Papers

203. McSéan, T.; Rowlands, J. and **Forrester, W.** 'Becoming a Micro-host: Using Desktop Computers to run an Online Retrieval Service.' *In Online Information 93: 17th International Online Information Meeting Proceedings London 7-9 December 1993.* Edited by D. I. Raitt. Oxford: Learned Information, 1993. pp. 367-376.
The British Medical Association Library now provides a full-scale MEDLINE information retrieval system as a free service to its members. This paper introduces the service – believed to be the first of its kind – and gives a brief technical description. It then goes on to describe problems in implementation, gives a frank but basically favourable analysis of the Library's relationship with their system of choice (CD-Plus) and a discussion of copyright and licensing issues raised by a service of this type. BMA members can now dial into the Library's CD-Plus MEDLINE database from around the United Kingdom and the paper closes with a summary of the benefits and the problems which have been encountered.

Conferences: Proceedings

204. **Armstrong, C. J.** and **Hartley, R. J.** (eds.). *Database 2000: UKOLUG State-of-the-Art Conference 1992.* Oxford: Learned Information, 1992. 125pp.

The United Kingdom Online User Group (UKOLUG) holds a State-of-the-Art conference every other year with, since 1986, published proceedings. The 1992 conference lived up to its name in providing comprehensive updates on telecommunications, CD-ROM networking and post-processing software as well as number of papers looking at current practice in database design and in training. For the first time, a student paper – by the winner of the first UKOLUG Student Award, Cathy Cope – was included in the proceedings. Perhaps as important as any other aspect of the conference or the proceedings is the final section devoted to quality assurance. This section includes a guest lecture by Reva Basch, five short introductions to aspects of quality in the database industry and a summary of discussions. It was as a direct result of this meeting that the UKOLUG/Library Association Centre for Information Quality Management was formed.

205. **Armstrong, C. J.** and **Hartley, R. J.** (eds.). *Changing Patterns of Online Information: UKOLUG State-of-the-Art Conference 1994.* Oxford: Learned Information, 1994. 145pp.

As in previous years, the proceedings contain not only the papers, but summaries of the discussions which took place after the formal presentations as well as a complete programme, delegate list and biographical details of the speakers. The theme in 1994 was reflected both in the title and in the choice of papers which coverd the Internet, Campus-Wide Information Services, SuperJANET, electronic document delivery and CD-ROM networking. A student paper – by the second winner of the UKOLUG Student Award – is also included in the proceedings.

Dictionaries

206. 'A Local Area Network Glossary'. *CD-ROM Professional,* 6 (1), January 1993, pp. 80-84.

Adapted from the glossary in Tom Rugg's book, *LANtastic Made Easy* (Osborne/McGraw Hill, 1992), the glossary defines 76 terms commonly used in discussing networks. The definitions are not technical although, as Rugg notes, some of the concepts are difficult, and the whole makes a useful novice's guide to networking.

Handbooks: Online Format

207. CDROMLAN_FAQ

Users of the Internet may have come across FAQ (Frequently Asked Question) files; this one provides information on such subjects as CD-ROM drives, networking, antivirus software, Microsoft Extensions, menu and tracking software and much more. It is recommended as being both useful and interesting (Bradley, Phil. 'CD-ROM Corner'. *UKOLUG Newsletter* 5(1) (Jan/Feb 1994) 11) and is available from ftp.uga.edu in the pub/doc/ids directory – it is called cdromlan_faq.

Journal Articles

208. **McQueen, H.** 'CD-ROM Servers: An Overview'. *CD-ROM Professional* 6(5) (September 1993). pp. 54, 56-57.

The article reviews various CD-ROM server configurations such as CD-ROMs attached to individual workstations, dedicated CD-ROM servers and dedicated file server/CD-ROM servers. It also covers typical features of CD-ROM server software, management issues and solutions supporting Macintosh and Unix.

Journals: Electronically Distributed

209. Information Networking News.

An electronic journal sent to subscribers to the BITNET list CDROMLAN@IDBSU via Eric Thomas's List Server. To subscribe to CDROMLAN send the following e-mail message to listserv@idbsu.idbsu.edu: SUBSCRIBE CDROMLAN First-name Last-name

Reports

210. *CD-ROM Networking Monitoring, Metering and Control Systems: Report to CD-ROM Standards and Practices Action Group (CD-ROM SPAG).* London: Library Information Technology Centre, 1993

In-depth report looking at standard approaches to running CD-ROMs over networks: methods of monitoring use and charging. The report is available free to members and to the public at a cost which is slightly more than membership of CD-ROM SPAG (£125) – so there may be a message there somewhere.

DATABASE DIRECTORIES

Bibliographies

211. Hall, J. L. *Online Bibliographic Databases: a Directory and Sourcebook.* (4th ed.). London: Aslib, 1986. 509pp.

This work provides a major ninety-page bibliography of published literature on online information retrieval as well as a database directory. This edition of the bibliography lists 1,011 references from the early 1960s through 1985. Most of these references appeared in refereed publications and represent a good proportion of the core journal and conference literature in the field. The emphasis is on publications about specific databases or database coverage in particular subject field, and references are made from database entries in the directory section to relevant papers listed in the bibliography. Retrieval is also assisted by a listing of comparative studies of individual databases in the early part of the work. This listing is in order of author name, as is the bibliography itself. A co-author index and general subject index are also supplied. The directory covers all subject fields and concentration on the most heavily used databases is deliberate in order to keep the work within manageable proportions. Useful features contained in each entry are sample record, file name or number on different hosts, indicative search costs, and references to published work relating to the database in the separate bibliography. Indexing is by database producer, title keyword and general subject. Other sections of note provide contact information for hosts, sample searches on nine major systems, and a statistical profile of available databases.

Books

212. *Databases in Japan 1993.* Tokyo: Database Promotion Centre, Japan, 1993. 102pp.

This report covers the state of the database industry in Japan with sections dealing with Trends of the Database Service Market; Trends of the Database Service Industry; the Present State of Use of Commercial Databases; Database Utilization and Education at Universities; and Database Promotion Policies of the Ministry of International Trade and Industry. According to the executive summary, the market size in Japan has increased by 14.5% over the previous year, topping 200 billion Yen for the first time. Appendices (1) discuss the number of Japanese databases accessible from overseas; (2) list in tabular format Japanese databases accessible overseas by producer; (3) list, again in tabular format, Japanese databases accessible overseas by distributors; (4) list Japanese databases planned for overseas expansions; and (5) give the addresses and contacts for these databases. The details given in Appendices two to four include a brief description of each database, a subject code for science and technology or economics, business and finance or general; the language; the format (online/CD-ROM/Tape/Facsimile) and the main countries in which the database is available. It is important to note that the databases listed include those available in Japan but produced overseas (such as MEDLINE) as well as those produced in Japan.

213. Wolski, K.; Koivula, T.; Lukkari, M. and **Mäkinen, M.** *Data on Display: A Guide to Numeric Databases.* Helsinki, Finland: Central Statistical Office of Finland, 1991. 330pp.
This book consists of a 96-page analysis of over 1,000 numeric databases: Chapters 1 and 2 provide a general overview, Chapter 3 deals with the services of international organisations, Chapter 4 deals with databases maintained by te statistical authorities of various countries, and Chapter 5 provides summaries by subject area. There is a bibliography and a number of appendices, of which Appendix 5 is the most important as it lists some 170 databases alphabetically. Appendices 1 to 4 contain information on magnetic tape or diskette databases supplied by international organisations, on databases from statistical institutions in France and te United States, on data access charges and on search procedure examples. Appendix 6 contains the subject and regional indexes and the final four appendices contain addresses. Database description in Appendix 5 follow a standard format and include information on subject, update period, timeframe, print publications, content, geographical coverage, the number of time series included, host(s), software, auxiliary material and remarks. Databases coverage is international.

Directories: CD-ROM/Diskette

214. *CD-ROM Directory ON DISC* 1994. London: TFPL, 1992-. Biannually.
Details of all products and companies in international CD-ROM market. Includes details of about 6,000 CD-ROM Titles, with access by subject area, language, geographical coverage, updates, price etc. Multimedia titles in all formats are listed – CDTV, CD-I, DVI and CD-ROM XA. It also contains 3,800 company profiles, which can be searched by activity, products, country or any other field. Two 'user' fields are included in each record for the addition of user's own information. Other sections of the disc include information on hardware – details of available products; software – descriptions of that used in the development and use of CD-ROMs, including search and retrieval software; conferences and exhibitions – a diary of relevant forthcoming events; books and journals – details of relevant publications available and a glossary. The search interface functions in Italian, French, Spanish, German and English. While both this directory and Meckler's aspire to comprehensive coverage, a thorough comparative review by Paul Nicholls (*CD-ROM Professional* 6 (4) 1993 81-82, 84, 86-90) noted some minor differences in coverage. TFPL had (in 1993) more title entries but considerably fewer company entries; balanced against this is their coverage of conferences, journals, books, software and hardware. In one test TFPL had more unique titles than Meckler. There are twenty title access

points in TFPL but only nine in Meckler. As Nicholls says, the conclusion is that either source will 'deliver a comparably good single-source search ... there is little to choose between the two'. He does emphasise the need for both in order to be comprehensive and is equally complimentary about the editorial rigour of the two companies. His final analysis is that one cannot go too far wrong with either directory – 'the CD-ROM counterparts are much harder to choose between than the print directories' as they both share the basic strengths of excellent coverage, accurate data, reasonable currency, usable indexing, effective access software and a fair price.

215. *CD-ROM Guide Three.* Updata Publications
Contains details of over 500 CD-ROM products on a wide variety of topics.

216. *CD-ROMs in Print 1994.* London: Meckler, 1992-. Biannually.
Provides information on 2,975 CD-ROMs currently available and 3,040 companies. The information contained includes: Title; Former title; Number of discs; Availability; Demo (availability); Data provider; Publisher; US Distributor; Non US distributor; Software provider; Software; Technical requirements; Update frquency; Price; Language of data; Site licence information; Coverage of data; Equivalent printed version; Subject – Keywords; Description – Short description of data. As Connie Donley noted in *CD-ROM Professional* (6 (2) (March) 1993. p 142-144), the ability to search for this directory-type information on CD-ROM products and companies is very valuable and Meckler are interested in customer feed-back on the product. Search software is stored on the CD-ROM. There are twelve product indexes indexes (title, subject, publisher, search software, language, disc format, etc) and a thirteenth general index which searches globally in free text in all fields of all records. Connie Donley also noted that the global search facility was to be recommended as indexing inconsistencies in other fields can mean that some important records are not retrieved. She 'searched Genealogy as a subject heading and found three records. She then searched Genealogy in the Global Text index and found three additional useful records which had been assigned headings such as Biography or Statistics, Population & Demography.' She also found inconsistencies in the technical details chart which each record contains. In one instance cited she noted that against 'Drives' for ERIC on SilverPlatter, the only area shaded is against 'Other' which would lead a user to believe that none of the other drives listed are compatible — this does not agree with either fact or the print version of the directory (probably because the latter does not mention specific brand names). Although the interface has 'a few rough edges', it is efficient and gets the job done. As the end-user market for CD-ROMs grows, reference librarians can expect more product-information queries – Meckler's disc will be a useful reference tool.

217. *EBSCO CD-ROM Handbook on CD-ROM.* Topsfield, MA: EBSCO
Contains a directory of commercially available CD-ROMs, information includes: Publisher; Database description; Markets and applications; System requirements; File format; Update frequency; Price; Availability; and Supplier information.

218. *Online Manual on Disk.* Oxford: Learned Information, 1993-. Biannual.
The Online Manual is a comprehensive guide to over 2,000 English-language databases or 60,000 source publications. Using Headfast software, The Online Manual on Disk is a fast and effective reference tool which can pinpoint relevant databases and provide information on such topics as 'the databases which will give information on food in the USA'; 'the databases which have coverage of Spain'; 'the account items that particular databases hold'; or 'whether a particular journal is available online'. Searches are possible by subject, source, geographical coverage, financial details, database and host. There are, in fact over 100 searchable account items. With the December 1994 edition, the software has become Windows-based. The electronic version is available on diskette or CD-ROM. A comparative review can be found in the *Journal of Information Science* 20 (4) (1994) pp. 260-269 although readers should note subsequent correspondence between the editors of *The Onlie Manual* and the reviewer.
Originally available from Disclosure First Contact, the consultancy who produce the *Manual*, all forms (bound, CD-ROM and diskette) became available from Learned Information in mid 1994.

Directories: Online Format

219. ACBAS. Yves Balbure
Descriptions of over 1,400 publicly available French, German and English language databases of interest to business managers. Coverage includes on-line business directories, industry sectors, economics, finance, law, politics, technology. Database details include names, type, producer details, access. Corresponds partly to *La téléinformation 19xx pour une gestion stratégique* and *YB Téléinformation Stratégique.* Available online on SLIGOS.

220. *ADDA.* Hawthorn, Victoria: Australian Database Development Association. Twice yearly.
Corresponds to the printed *Directory of Australian and New Zealand Databases* but updated more regularly. Information provided includes the database name, producer, online service(s), type of data, file size, update frequency, time span, sources of data, corresponding print publications, prices and conditions of access, subject terms and general notes. Access is offered via AUSINET. Planned as well as existing databases are included.

221. *AERONET Data Locator.* Washington: US National Aeronautics and Space Administration (NASA), Scientific and Technical Information Facility
References to scientific and technical computer-readable numeric databases available to users within NASA and its contractor organisations. Each record contains a description of the database and contact name and address information. The database is accessible through NASA only in the US, to NASA Research Centers and

contractors, NASA-sponsored Industrial Application Centers, other US government agencies and contractors, and to universities with aeronautics and space-related scientific and engineering activities.

222. *Alphaline Database of Databases.* Bad Vilbel: Holger Mayer Unternehmensberatung für Informationsverarbeitung. Monthly.
A guide to over 3,000 databases accessible from the Federal Republic of Germany. All subject areas are covered and full details of each database are provided in a tabular format, including current search costs. These costs are given in the original currency but can easily be displayed in any other currency required, a useful feature for purposes of comparison. Other information includes the producer name, a content description, updating frequency, time span, and search aids available. Alphaline can be accessed via GENIOS, the German Economic Network, on which it can be searched in German or English and Gesellschaft für Betriebswirtschaftliche Information mbH (GBI).

223. *Databas.* Madrid: Instituto de la Pequena y Mediana Empresa Industrial. Annual.
Provides details of databases produced worldwide which can be accessed from Spain. The language of the database itself is Spanish and it can be searched by arrangement with the producer.

224. *DIANEGUIDE.* Luxembourg: European Information Market Development Group. Updated continuously.
More up to date than the printed *Directory of European Databases and Databanks,* the database can be searched through ECHO. Databases are described in more detail online and searches can be conducted through a variety of access points including host, database type, timespan of coverage and language. Each database record contains a descriptive abstract which, as in the case of the descriptors used, can be searched in any of six European languages (English, French, German, Italian, Portuguese and Spanish).

225. *DUNDIS: Directory of United Nations Databases and Information Services.* New York: United Nations Advisory Committee for the Co-ordination of Information Systems. Irregular.
Available in printed form and offered for searching by ECHO. As in the hard copy publication, indexing is in English, French and Spanish. Online retrieval can be restricted to those records which describe online databases. A user manual can be obtained free of charge from the host and is published in English and French.

226. *Gale Directory of Databases.* Detroit: Gale. Twice yearly.
The online version of the printed directory with the same title is offered by KR Data-Star with quarterly updating and by Questel/Orbit (both systems). It is also available on CD-ROM, diskette and magnetic tape from the publishers. The online version

allows specific subject retrieval through free-text searching of terms contained in the content summary which accompanies each database description. Other search criteria which can be specified online but not so easily searched in print are geographic coverage, time span, database type (for example, bibliographic or numeric) and language.

227. *NORD*. Esbo, Finland: SCANNET. Twice yearly.
Jointly produced by all Scandinavian countries, this database updates the printed *NordGuide*. It can be searched in any of the Nordic languages and is made available for searching via a national host in each Scandinavian country, namely VTKK (Finland), NSI (Norway), DAFA (Sweden) and FEK (Denmark). Recent updates are available via the Internet at address gopher://nordinfo.hut.fi

Directories: Print

228. *Books & Periodicals Online: a Directory of Periodicals Found Online and CD-ROM*. New York: Library Alliance, 1987-. Annually.
This publication includes four separate directories: the *Directory of Periodicals Online – News, Law and Business; the Directory of Periodicals Online – Medical and Humanities;* and the *Directory of Periodicals Online – Science and Technology,* as well as *Books and Periodicals Online*. Covering sources online and on CD-ROM, the directories cover over 43,000 publications in nearly 1,800 databases. Publications include newsletters, magazines, newspapers, conference proceedings, reference books and newswires and online services covered include LEXIS/NEXIS, Westlaw, CompuServe, DIMDI, NewsNet, Dow Jones and CDP Online. Appendices offer listings by subject and publisher, titles by database, and vendor and producer listings. Books and Periodicals Online is also available on CD-ROM.

229. *Business and Legal CD-ROMs in Print 1993*. Westport: Mecklermedia, 1993. 360pp.
Marketed as a 'comprehensive' directory of CD-ROM and CD-based multimedia products in business and law, the subject coverage includes economics, patent information, taxation, finance, related government information and management. The directory is based on information gathered for Mecklermedia's *CD-ROMs in Print: an International Guide* and is the first in an annual series of subject-specific reference guides. The editors admit to having 'cast the net widely' in order to make the directory a stand-alone guide and the 1,234 titles include many from peripheral areas such as advertising, almanacs, the automotive industry, forestry, government information, pollution, railways, telecommunications, and trade. Even allowing for such an inclusion of specific industries, it is difficult to see why titles such as Digital Chart of the World, the Sea-D series of marine navigation charts and the American Heritage Illustrated Encyclopedic Dictionary have been included. Each listing includes up to 31 items of information about the product including a short description

and full price, contact and ordering information. Making due allowance for its generous inclusion policy, this is a useful and informative directory sensibly targetted at a precise sector. The directory includes a company index in which products are listed under contact details of producers (this is useful as with no cross-referencing, users might not find DIALOG (KR OnDisc) discs which are all listed in the main alphabetic sequence under 'DIALOG ONDISC'); separate title lists of Macintosh, multimedia and Electronic Book products and a subject index. No indexes refers to page or item numbers, rather they list products by producer, by style or within subject categories.

230. **Campbell, H.** (ed.) *CINFOLINK Directory of Information Services in China 1993-1994.* Toronto: Espial Productions, 1993. 120pp.
The directory covers selected, publicly available databases in China and Hong Kong, as well as printed information sources and publicly available services selected as being key sources of information products related to the databases. Almost all of the publications and databases are in the Chinese language but those which are in English have been identified. For each entry the database name (in English and Chinese), acronym, language, size, updating frequency, year of commencement and type of data (factual, bibliographic, etc) are given as well as a short description and full contact details. Some 325 information sources have been identified, of which 171 are databases – many on diskette or CD-ROM. In the Preface, the editor acknowledges the difficulties in locating information for the directory and points to the growing market-orientation among Chinese information sources which means both that the number of such products is increasing and the sale of information products has a growing place in China's economy. There are already some 30,000 consulting firms registered and 2,500 specialised research institutes.

231. *CD-ROM Databases.* Boston: Worldwide Videotex. Monthly.
This monthly database directory service provides details of CD-ROM databases currently marketed. Coverage is international with brief descriptions which contain subscription terms, price, subject area and supplier name, address and telephone number. There are four sections, the first three arranged by title, vendor and subject area, and the last offering a separate directory of all vendors with addresses and telephone numbers. Can be searched online and on the NewsNet service.

232. *CD-ROM Market Place: an International Guide.* Westport, Connecticut: Meckler. Annually in March. 225pp.
Published annually, this volume gives librarians and industry professionals a guide to organizations, individuals and products in the CD-ROM industry. Detailed information on over 3,500 organizations worldwide with Geographic, Subject (over 150 terms) and Names/Numbers Indexes.

233. *CD-ROMs in Print: an International Guide.* Westport, Connecticut: Mecklermedia. Annual.

An alphabetical listing of CD-ROM databases. Information provided includes distributor, search software, hardware and memory required, price, and a brief product description. Addresses and telephone numbers are supplied for data providers, publishers, distributors and software producers. Databases are indexed according to these organizations and also by type and broad subject area. Until 1994, details of new databases released between editions are announced in a separate section of the publisher's journal *CD-ROM Librarian.* This section served as a supplement to the directory, with entries listed in the same format, and was established in May 1990. Since 1992, a CD-ROM version of the directory, updated every six months, has also been available.

234. **Cousins, J.** and **Robinson, L.** *The Online Manual: A Practical Guide to Business Databases* (3rd edition). Oxford: Learned Information, 1994. 900+pp.
Described in *Aslib Information* as scoring favourably in comparison with the Cuadra/Gale *Directory of Online Databases,* being much easier to use, *The Online Manual* is a comprehensive guide to over 2,000 English-language databases or 60,000 source publications. In reality, although both list databases, *The Online Manual* serves a different purpose as its principle listing is by print publication rather than by database. Here, details of the actual databases are scant, being limited to a list of hosts, geographical coverage and a single-letter code for Type of Information equating to Marketing, Scientific, Economic, Financial or Technical. Financial databases only are dealt with in more detail. The second edition has seven main sections: How to Use the Manual; Hosts – contains contact details, costs and access times; Technical Requirements – gives details of hardware and software required for accessing databases; Financial Databases – a section providing comprehensive details on each of the financial databases covered by *The Manual;* Thesaurus which provides listings of databases by subject; Database to Host – a section containing an alphabetical list linking databases to hosts; and the 800+ page Source Guide which contains an alphabetical list of source publications (journals, newspapers, etc) showing on which databases on which hosts they may be found. *The Online Manual* is also available twice per year on diskette or CD-ROM.
Originally available from Disclosure First Contact, the consultancy who produce the *Manual,* all forms (bound, CD-ROM and diskette) became available from Learned Information in mid 1994.

235. *DataBase Directory.* White Plains, New York: Knowledge Industry in association with the American Society for Information Science. Annual, with monthly updates and inter-edition supplement.
Contains descriptions of full-text, numeric and bibliographic databases in all subject areas. Coverage is international but there is a definite emphasis on files produced in the United States and Canada. Descriptions are detailed and include information on subject coverage, thesauri or classification schemes in use, file size, source coverage, price data and printed search aids. A notable feature is the wide range of hosts covered, among them business corporations, government departments and universities. Ar-

rangement is alphabetical by database name, with indexes by host, producer and subject, while a list of database alternate names facilitates retrieval. The directory is part of the DataBase Directory Service which includes monthly updating via the newsletter, *DataBase Alert.*

236. *Directory of Australian and New Zealand Databases.* Hawthorn, Victoria: Australian Database Development Association. Every two years.
This directory provides details of over 200 databases in all subject areas which are produced in Australia or New Zealand. The description in each entry includes producer, host, type, printed equivalent and price. Contact information is supplied for major Australian hosts. Additional features are a review of developments in the Australian online information scene and lists of acronyms and thesauri.

237. *Directory of European Databases and Databanks.* Compiled by the European Community Host Organisation. Luxembourg: ECHO Customer Service. Irregular.
Generated from the DIANEGUIDE database on ECHO, this directory is published at irregular intervals. Hosts range from the major commercial operations to smaller organizations such as universities and government bodies active in individual countries. Databases are listed alphabetically by acronym. The only information provided is a brief subject description and the host or hosts through which searching can be conducted. Databases are indexed by general subject headings and by host. Full contact data, with network user address (NUA) in many cases, is supplied in a separate section for hosts. The final section gives addresses and telephone and telex numbers for the national telecommunications networks in the European countries.

238. *Directory of United Nations Databases and Information Services (DUNDIS).* (4th ed.) Compiled by the Advisory Committee for the Co-ordination of Information Systems (ACCIS). New York: United Nations. 1990.
The directory gives detailed descriptions of a total of over 547 selected databases, and 325 information services operated by, or in association with, the thirty eight organizations of the United Nations. A wide range of subjects and countries is covered, reflecting the many activities of the United Nations, and many statistical databanks are described. Entries indicate whether a file is available to external users and through which United Nations organization or commercial host it can be accessed. Other information given includes the year the database was established and its timespan, the database type (for example, bibliographic), the subject scope and geographical coverage, languages, indexing or classification tools used, any printed products and the computer, operating system and software used. Indexes are provided by name or acronym and, in English, French and Spanish, by subject. Can be searched online via ECHO.

239. *Espial Canadian Data Base Directory.* Toronto: Espial Productions. Every two years, with annual supplement.

Provides information on over 520 databases containing Canadian information. These databases are evaluated and ranked in a four-part classification scheme according to the amount of data they contain about Canada. Information includes an indication of the language, and evaluations of the amount of Canadian material contained. All subject areas are covered and a title and name index provides access. French and English editions are available. The 1992 edition has separate indexes to CD-ROMs and database distributors and producers.

240. *FullText Sources Online: for Periodicals, Newspapers, Newsletters and Newswires.* Needham Heights, Massachusetts: BiblioData. Twice yearly.
Lists over 4,000 periodicals, newspapers, newsletters and newswires offered in full text online with their years of availability and the databases which contain them on any of fifteen host services. The start of a typical entry might appear as:

FORBES
Not all files contain FYI and ASAP supplements.

▲	**Data-Star:** INFO	01/93 to Present
	Data-Star: INDY: TRADE & INDUSTRY	01/83 to Present
	Data-Star: MAGS: MAGAZINE DB	01/83 to Present
	Data-Star: PTSP: PROMT	12/89 to Present
	DataTimes: DOW JONES (BUSLIB:FB)	01/85 to Present
▲	**Dialog:** 15: ABI/Inform	01/93 to Present
	LEXIS/NEXIS: NEXIS (FORBES)	01/75 to Present
	Freq: Bi-weekly; Lag: 1 wk	

where the '▲' indicates that a publication is available as selected-articles-only, as opposed to cover-to-cover inclusion. In some cases the update frequency and time that the online publication lags behind the print publication are shown indented on the line following a database entry. All subject areas are included and a subject index facilitates access.

241. **Hall, J. L.** *Online Bibliographic Databases: a Directory and Sourcebook.* (4th ed.). London: Aslib, 1986. 509pp.
This work provides a major ninety-page bibliography of published literature on online information retrieval as well as a database directory. This edition of the bibliography lists 1,011 references from the early 1960s through 1985. Most of these references appeared in refereed publications and represent a good proportion of the core journal and conference literature in the field. The emphasis is on publications about specific databases or database coverage in particular subject field, and references are made from database entries in the directory section to relevant papers listed in the bibliography. Retrieval is also assisted by a listing of comparative studies of individual databases in the early part of the work. This listing is in order of author name, as is the bibliography itself. A co-author index and general subject index are also supplied. The directory covers all subject fields and concentration on the most

heavily used databases is deliberate in order to keep the work within manageable proportions. Useful features contained in each entry are sample record, file name or number on different hosts, indicative search costs, and references to published work relating to the database in the separate bibliography. Indexing is by database producer, title keyword and general subject. Other sections of note provide contact information for hosts, sample searches on nine major systems, and a statistical profile of available databases.

242. Hoffmann, E. (ed.) *Directory of Special Data Bases in Israel.* Tel-Aviv: National Centre of Scientific and Technological Information, 1986. 38pp.
Issued in both English and Hebrew, this directory provides details of fifty databases produced in Israel. Separate sections list databases in the social sciences and in science and technology. Many of the files listed cover very specific subjects and are factual or numeric rather than bibliographic. Entries contain full contact data for the producing organization, its staff size, a description of the main subjects of the database, publications generated from it and its public or private accessibility. Indexing is by subject and jointly by producer and database name.

243. Hogan, K. and **Shelton, J.** (eds.) *CD-ROM Finder: The World of CD-ROM Products for Information Seekers.* (6th ed. 1994/95) Medford, New Jersey: Learned Information, 1994. 585pp.
This is the sixth edition of the guide formerly known as *Optical Publishing Directory* – an irregular directory containing in this edition some 2,000 CD-ROM product descriptions. CD-ROM Finder includes only those products which are currently generally available and omits prototypes or demonstration products as well as CD-ROMs prepared for specific industry applications. Entries contain the address of publisher, a description of subject content which, for products included in previous editions, has been extended and for new products is as full as possible, hardware and software requirements, a history of the product, updating frequency, availability and price. Following the body of the directory arc three useful indexes: the product index includes data on the type of database (statistical, bibliographic, full-text, etc); the applications index has been expanded to provide users with titles grouped into one of 85 categories (medicine, science, law, etc); and the address index lists CD-ROM publishers, distributors and search software suppliers.

244. Marcaccio, K. Y. (ed.) *Gale Directory of Databases.* Detroit: Gale Research, 1991- (previously, Cuadra). Twice per year.
Gale Research took over the former Cuadra *Directory of Databases* in 1991 and merged it with their own *Computer-Readable Databases* and the Cuadra/Gale *Directory of Portable Databases* to form a new two-volume product with profiles of some 9,800 databases available in a variety of electronic formats. Volume 1 covers online databases and Volume 2 databases in portable formats such as diskette, CD-ROM, magnetic tape and handheld products. Each volume contains a master index and subject and geographical indexes as well as a statistical analysis (updated

annually) written by former editor and leading industry expert Martha E. Williams. Descriptive entries contain such details as producer name and contact information, a summary of the content, language, geographic coverage, time span and updating. Each volume also contains a producers section and a vendors section containing complete contact information. The directory is also available online, and on CD-ROM, diskette and magnetic tape.

245. *Newspapers Online.* Needham Heights, Massachusetts: BiblioData, 1992-. Annual.
The 1993 edition covers more than 150 newspapers that are online in full text and full coverage and includes online search tips for each newspaper, online and CD-ROM hosts and the availability of telephone help from the newspapers and online vendors. Coverage of the USA and Canada has been expanded and international coverage has been expanded to include an additional eighteen European, Middle Eastern, Asian and Australian newspapers. Looseleaf format with two updates during the year.

246. *NordGuide: Nordic Databases.* Esbo, Finland: Nordinfo. Every other year.
The 1994 edition contains some 704 databases, either produced in a Nordic country or available through a Nordic online service. Entries are listed alphabetically by database name, with Denmark accounting for 138 databases, Finland for 221, Norway for 173, Sweden for 171 and Iceland for one. Descriptions are in English and provide standard details for databases of all types in all subject areas. Directory-type information is also supplied for producers and hosts. A main subject and a geographic index is provided and contact information for both producers and host organizations in separate listings. Can be searched online and recent updates are available via the Internet at address gopher://nordinfo.hut.fi

247. **NTIS.** *US Government Datafiles for Mainframes and Microcomputers.* Springfield, VA: NTIS. Annually.
The directory describes datafiles which are available from NTIS' Federal Computer Products Center and lists text and data files in subject areas such as agriculture and food, banking, business, communications, employment, energy, environment, health care, logistics, personal wealth and employment, and vital statistics. Each entry summarizes the data and provides complete specifications.

248. *The CD-ROM Directory.* London: TFPL. Bi-annually.
A major information sourcebook on CD-ROM internationally. The two main sections are: 'CD-ROM Products', listing (in the 11th edition of December 1993) about 6,000 existing or announced databases (CD-ROM, CD-ROM XA, CDTV, CD-I, etc) and including details of information provider, supplier, recommended hardware and drive, and price; and 'Company Information', in which the activities and specialisms of more than 3,800 companies involved in the industry are described. The other sections describe hardware, software and relevant books, journals and forthcoming events. Six indexes allow retrieval by subject, information retrieval software and

organization type. Since 1992, this directory has been available on CD-ROM, updated every six months.

249. Tookey, D. A. (ed.) *Accessible Databases: a Directory of Online and Machine-Readable Information Sources.* London: Spicer and Pegler, 1987. 262pp.
The number of databases listed, 799, illustrates the selective nature of this directory. All types of machine-readable database are included, bibliographic, numeric and full-text. The term 'accessible' allows the inclusion of some files on tape or disk as well as online. Over one hundred host services internationally are listed, ranging from the well known to the obscure. Subject emphasis tends towards files of business, commercial and financial information, some of which are very specific and unlikely to be listed elsewhere. Entries are detailed and include data on geographical coverage, record content, size, and methods and costs of access. The list of databases is alphabetical with indexes by vendor, producer and subject.

Handbooks

250. Berkman, R. I. *Find It Online!* New York: Windcrest/McGraw-Hill, 1994. 380pp.
An all-embracing approach to finding information in electronic (online, CD- ROM or Internet) database sources. Written for the end user in a 'popular' style, the book's mission is described as 'to cut a clear path through the thicket of data sources by clearly describing and comparing competing electronic services and sources.' Despite that hyperbole, *Find It Online!* does accomplish much of what it sets out to do, although very much for an American audience covering, as it does, America Online (not quite in Europe at the time of writing), Delphi, GEnie, Prodigy and CompuServe in addition to the Internet and CD-ROM sources. The first section deals with online sources and the second with those on CD-ROM; both have almost more screen shots and examples than text but both cover the ground well although there is a tendency to use front-end search software (such as CompuServe's CIM) in the figures. Charging information will date rapidly. The final section and chapter lists databases under some forty broad topic headings such as Address and telephone directories, astronomy and space, business and company information, and travel. For each category the section lists three 'major types' of electronic database: consumer CD-ROMs, CD-ROMs found in libraries and online services. It is not comprehensive but provides a 'quick look up and contact information for many of the most broadly useful and popular electronic databases'. The cover suggests that the book will allow readers to 'Do your own online searching'; and find 'fast facts and answers from around the globe'; and is 'compatible with all hardware and software' – it is quite definitely aimed at the home user and contains a wealth of information to help him or her find and use appropriate sources.

DATABASE INDUSTRY

Abstracting and Indexing Services

251. *ABI/INFORM.* Louisville, Kentucky: UMI/Data Courier, 1971-. Monthly.
A general business database, with no print equivalent, which includes coverage of the database industry. About 1,000 periodicals are indexed, with an emphasis on US publications, for articles which reach over a column in length. Journals include *Online, Database* and *CD-ROM Professional.* Lengthy abstracts have always been provided and time lag from publication to inclusion in the database is relatively short – often less than two months. Over half of the journals included on the database now have the full text of articles included as well. The online database can be searched on over a dozen hosts, while a CD-ROM version is produced by University Microfilms International. It should be noted that the journals included in full text may vary from host to host.

252. *Business Periodicals Index.* New York: H. W. Wilson, 1958-. Monthly, with quarterly and annual cumulations.
A worthwhile source of articles and features on business aspects of the database industry, including information on specific companies and products. Over 350 business journals and newsletters in the English language are indexed. Most of these sources are published in the United States. Entries are arranged under subject headings, the most appropriate of which are 'Database Publishers', 'Database Vendors' 'Information Storage and Retrieval Systems' and, since 1989, 'CD-ROM' and 'CD-ROM Drives'. Headings are also provided for individual companies as appropriate. Available online and on CD-ROM as Wilson Business Abstracts.

253. *F & S Index Europe.* Foster City, CA: Information Access Company, 1978-. Monthly, with quarterly and annual cumulations.
Offers the same type of information for business and company activities in Europe as that provided for the United States, described in the entry for that part of the service, although coverage of the database industry is less extensive for Europe. Three sections provide access by Standard Industrial Classification, country and company, the country section being the most comprehensive. Available online.

254. *F & S Index International.* Foster City, CA: Information Access Company, 1967-. Monthly, with quarterly and annual cumulations.
Provides company, product and industry information for countries outside Europe and the United States. Arrangement is the same as in the European section of the service and further details of the nature of the coverage provided for the database industry can be found in the entry for F & S United States. Can be searched online.

255. *F & S Index United States.* Foster City, CA: Information Access Company, 1960-. Weekly, with monthly, quarterly and annual cumulations.
The United States receives the most extensive treatment of any country covered by the three parts of the F & S Index series, which also consists of separate volumes for Europe and the rest of the world. Company, product and industry information are the main province of this service. All industries are covered and the database industry is accorded a separate section, titled 'Database Vendors'. Another section, arranged alphabetically by company name is also included in the service and can be used to trace information on specific companies, some of which is exclusive to this section. Basic bibliographic details, without abstracts, are provided for references in each section. Source coverage embraces over 750 financial publications, business-oriented newspapers, trade magazines and special reports. This part of the service deals with business activities in the United States. The activities of US companies in other countries can be traced through the European and international parts of the service. Included in the online database PROMT.

256. *FINDex: the Directory of Market Research Reports, Studies and Surveys.* New York: FIND/SVP, 1979-. Annual, with semiannual supplement.
Although the emphasis is on indexing US market research reports and industry surveys, this is the most detailed printed source for tracing these publications worldwide in that it provides full abstracts in each entry. A variety of industry sectors is covered and reports are listed under broad headings representing industry sectors and, within these, more specific subheadings. Most publications on the online industry are grouped under the subheading 'Computer Services and Information Systems' within the 'Data Processing Systems and Electronics' heading. CD-ROM can usually be found under the same main heading in a section titled 'Computer Storage and Peripherals'. Comprehensive access can, however, be gained through the indexes which are by subject, geographic area and company. Reports are also listed by publisher and there is a separate directory of publishers, offering address, telephone number and a person to contact, in order to facilitate ordering of reports.

257. *FINDex.* Bethesda, MD: Cambridge Scientific Abstracts, 1972-. Quarterly.
Corresponds to the printed *FINDex* directory and is available on KR DIALOG and MAID Researchline online and on SilverPlatter and KR OnDisc CD-ROMs.

258. *Marketsearch.* London: Arlington Management Publications, 1976-. Annual, with semiannual supplement.
This service complements *FINDex* with wider non-US coverage although abstracts are much less detailed. Entries are arranged in tabular format under the numerical code supplied by the British Standard Industrial Classification scheme. The code number can be obtained from the alphabetical product index at the beginning of the work. Relevant codes for online are 3668, 'Computer Applications' and 8651, 'Computer and Database Services' and, for CD-ROM, 3652, 'Audio, Video and Hi-FI Equipment'. Publishers are listed, with address, telephone number and telex numbers, at the

end, according to the alphabetical code assigned in the main body of the directory, the listing of publications. Entries in the main section provide bibliographic details (apart from publisher's name), cost, geographical coverage and, usually, brief keyword summaries.

259. *Wilson Business Abstracts.* New York: H. W. Wilson, 1982-. Twice weekly.
The online version of *Business Periodicals Index* can be searched back to June 1982 via WILSONLINE. Updating is more frequent than in the printed index and information can be retrieved through over forty access points. Access is also available via the Internet and through OCLC and CDP Online. Both the publisher and SilverPlatter also offer CD-ROM versions, although updating is only monthly.

260. *World Publishing Monitor.* Leatherhead: Printing Industries Research Association, 1983-. Monthly.
Formerly *Electronic Publishing Abstracts* from Pergamon Press, with subject coverage which emphasized the input, transmission, storage and retrieval of data and images in non-print form. A remit which included online and optical disc databases, networks and electronic mail, with a tendency towards technical and market developments. In its new form, the coverage is the technical, scientific and business literature of publishing which includes such aspects as publishing office hardware and software, desktop publishing, communications, pre- and postpress and products. While the coverage is now not explicitly electronic, the former aspects are still included to some extent. All entries contain abstracts and can be accessed via author and subject indexes. Sources include some of the major journals in the online field along with a number of general computing titles, newspapers, books and market research reports. Most source publications are in English, although some French, German and Japanese items are included. Online and CD-ROM access is also offered by way of PIRA Abstracts/PAPERBASE.

Books

261. *Databases in Japan 1993.* Tokyo: Database Promotion Centre, Japan, 1993. 102pp.
This report covers the state of the database industry in Japan with sections dealing with Trends of the Database Service Market; Trends of the Database Service Industry; the Present State of Use of Commercial Databases; Database Utilization and Education at Universities; and Database Promotion Policies of the Ministry of International Trade and Industry. According to the executive summary, the market size in Japan has increased by 14.5% over the previous year, topping 200 billion Yen for the first time. Appendices (1) discuss the number of Japanese databases accessible from overseas; (2) list in tabular format Japanese databases accessible overseas by producer; (3) list, again in tabular format, Japanese databases accessible overseas by distributors; (4) list Japanese databases planned for overseas expansions; and (5) give the addresses and

contacts for these databases. The details given in Appendices two to four include a brief description of each database, a subject code for science and technology or economics, business and finance or general; the language; the format (online/CD-ROM/Tape/Facsimile) and the main countries in which the database is available. It is important to note that the databases listed include those available in Japan but produced overseas (such as MEDLINE) as well as those produced in Japan.

262. **Durieux, B.** *Online Information in Europe.* Luxembourg: EUSIDIC, 1989. 176pp.
Provides an introduction to the online information industry in Europe and to its major players. Separate chapters examine the information market, the structure of the online market, the database industry, the demand for online information and the present and future role of the search intermediary. This publication has its origin in the author's doctoral thesis and the statistical data which it contains are somewhat dated – as are the references which tend to date from the early- to mid-1980s. EUSIDIC has heavily edited the text in order only to improve readability. Durieux notes that the online industry in 1989 was still largely dominated by the United States and that the online market is a challenge for information providers: both true but not surprising; of more interest is his comment that information providers need to improve their products 'by focussing less on technology and more on content, ease of use and ease of access' – as the quality debates of the 1990s show, this is still largely true. There are some interesting tables in the section on the database industry: figures not often seen in print such as the revenues (admitedly for 1985) of top players like Reuters, Quotron, McGraw-Hill and Dow Jones and the gowth in the numbers of passwords for major hosts. An interesting read which provides a good historical picture of the online industry; CD-ROM does not figure at all.

263. **East, H.** *Designing and Marketing Databases.* London: British Library, 1986. 146pp. (British Library Research Paper; 7).
The report examines the role and activities of the database producer in the design, production and marketing and distribution of online and CD-ROM databases. Interactions between producers and their distributors are studied, along with their marketing and legal implications. Although this report is becoming dated, it continues to have some importance as one of the few studies looking at this area (it is to some extent brought up to date by Oppenheim's 1990 report, *The Relationship between Online Hosts and Database Producers.* The bias is largely British and examples draw on UK experience.

264. *Facts and Figures 1995.* London: TFPL, 1995.
TFPL publish the twice-yearly CD-ROM Directory and consequently have a ready-made source for this graphical presentation of developments in the CD-ROM and multimedia market over the past nine years in their database of CD-ROM titles. Charts show such information as trends in the growth of titles, formats and subject areas as

well as examining pricing. A full commentary by industry expert Julie Schwerin (author of *The OPIA Report*) is included. Interestingly, with consumer titles increasing with a growth rate of over 70%, she notes that, 'Industry output has reached a level sufficient to propel CD-ROM into the mainstream of desktop computing and position it for similar success in domestic set-top systems.' The 1994 volume was an excellent publication according to Phil Bradley in the *UKOLUG Newsletter* 5(4) (July/August 1994) p12.

265. Hartley, J.; Noonan, A. and **Metcalfe, S.** *New Electronic Information Services: An Overview of the UK Database Industry in an International Context.* Aldershot: Gower, 1987. 147pp.

The volume reports on research undertaken in late 1985 and early 1986 and seeks to redress the dearth of publicly-available statistical information on the database industry. Much of Chapter 1 is based on material originally presented by Dr J Michel of Telesystemes Questel at Information Policy Seminar in Luxembourg in 1986. The remaining chapters deal with the Economics of Tradeable Information, UK Databases and Users, Technology Developments, The Industry View and National Policies for the Database Industry. The major threads are drawn together in the final summary chapter which noted that clearer delineation of the relative legal positions of hosts, database producers and data providers was a matter of urgency and that, along with Japan and other European countries, the UK had cause for concern over the near monopoly control over access to information invested in the United States. At that time, the UK database industry had 'considerable growth potential but was in a fragile, infant stage'.

266. Jones, C. and **Dowsland, W.** *Online Sources of European Information: Their Development and Use.* Aldershot: Avebury (Gower), 1990. 125pp.

The work examines the current and future role of electronic information services in Europe with particular emphasis on the provision and use of online information relating to European matters from both commercial and official sources. The work compares the European information industry to that of USA, UK, France, West Germany and Italy and notes the influence of CD-ROM technology before looking at business use of online information, European Community information, European telecommunications and harmonization, European Community policies, the Information Market Observatory, programmes such as RACE and ESPRIT and looking at the future – noting the importance of ISDN, the authors think that the success of the industry depends largely upon whether national interests can be put aside to allow the development of an integrated and harmonised telecommunications network. Appendices list abbreviations and glosses; Euroinfo Centres addresses; European Documentation Centres in the UK; Online systems produced by Eurostat; Commercial hosts holding EC databases; European data networks; Packet switching exchanges in the UK; and give details of Packet standards and OSI; ESPRIT; and RACE. There is also a bibliography and an index.

267. Saunier, F. *Marketing Strategies for the Online Industry.* Boston: G. K. Hall, 1988. 224pp. (Professional Librarian Series).

The author critically evaluates the marketing strategies employed by the online industry, noting a tendency to market unevenly or to under-market and urges a deeper understanding of marketing communications. Full use is made of illustrative examples of the industry's advertising and mailing.

268. Wolski, K.; Koivula, T.; Lukkari, M. and **Mäkinen, M.** *Data on Display: A Guide to Numeric Databases.* Helsinki, Finland: Central Statistical Office of Finland, 1991. 330pp.

This book consists of a 96-page analysis of over 1,000 numeric databases: Chapters 1 and 2 provide a general overview, Chapter 3 deals with the services of international organisations, Chapter 4 deals with databases maintained by te statistical authorities of various countries, and Chapter 5 provides summaries by subject area. There is a bibliography and a number of appendices, of which Appendix 5 is the most important as it lists some 170 databases alphabetically. Appendices 1 to 4 contain information on magnetic tape or diskette databases supplied by international organisations, on databases from statistical institutions in France and the United States, on data access charges and on search procedure examples. Appendix 6 contains the subject and regional indexes and the final four appendices contain addresses. Database description in Appendix 5 follow a standard format and include information on subject, update period, timeframe, print publications, content, geographical coverage, the number of time series included, host(s), software, auxiliary material and remarks. Databases coverage is international.

Conference: Proceedings

269. Armstrong, C. J. and **Hartley, R. J.** (eds.). *Database 2000: UKOLUG State-of-the-Art Conference 1992.* Oxford: Learned Information, 1992. 125pp.

The United Kingdom Online User Group (UKOLUG) holds a State-of-the-Art conference every other year with, since 1986, published proceedings. The 1992 conference lived up to its name in providing comprehensive updates on telecommunications, CD-ROM networking and post-processing software as well as number of papers looking at current practice in database design and in training. For the first time, a student paper – by the winner of the first UKOLUG Student Award, Cathy Cope – was included in the proceedings. Perhaps as important as any other aspect of the conference or the proceedings is the final section devoted to quality assurance. This section includes a guest lecture by Reva Basch, five short introductions to aspects of quality in the database industry and a summary of discussions. It was as a direct result of this meeting that the UKOLUG/Library Association Centre for Information Quality Management was formed.

270. NFAIS Annual Conference: Annual Conference of the National Federation of Abstracting and Information Services. Selected papers usually published in *Information Services and Use.*

The conference has been held annually since 1959 and is reported in the *NFAIS Newsletter.* Database producers and online hosts are among the members of the Federation and are a likely source for papers. For example, in the 1988 conference whose theme was 'The Database Business: Managing Today – Planning for Tomorrow', there were presentations on industry concerns such as online pricing policies, full-text information provision online, gateway services, quality assurance and document delivery.

Journal Articles

271. **Fletcher, L. A.** 'DIALOG Price Restructuring Evaluation: Tentative Steps on the Road to Value-Based Pricing'. *Searcher,* 2 (8), October 1994, pp. 44-46, 48-52, 54-56, 58-59.

In the wake of the major price restructuring by KR DIALOG, many users were left unsure as to whether this was a 'good thing' or not. Certainly the new pricing places more emphasis on the value of information (generally seen as good) but there is still a connect time charge (admittedly reduced) and a new fixed 'View Fee' charged against every type, print or display (definitely bad). Fletcher's article looks in some depth at the pricing structure, compares searches on the old and new charging systems and generally looks at pros and cons. He notes the savings to be made with a flat fee pricing plan (for heavy users) and finally asks, 'Will the View fee Backfire on KR DIALOG?' – his conclusion is that users will avoid it (and he has his own suggestions) whenever they can. KR DIALOG may have sought revenue neutrality but in their View Fee they may well have inconvenienced users just too much.

272. **Nicholls, P. T.** and **Sutherland, T.** 'CD-ROM Databases: a Survey of Commercial Publishing Activity'. *Database* 15 (1) (February 1992) pp. 36-41.

Based on the same methodology as used in four previous surveys, this review reports on commercially available CD-ROM titles for 1985 – 1991 and plots comparative growth of titles, database trends, subject distribution, hardware platforms, and update frequency trends.

273. **Paster, A.** 'CD-ROM Versus Online: 1980 – 1994'. *CD-ROM Professional* 7 (5) (September/October 1994) pp. 137-144.

A useful article tracing the rise of CD-ROM as a competitor and subsequently as an equal to online systems. Quotation from many well-known writers over the years are used to demonstrate how opinions change with time. An interesting review showing how problems were first noted (they contained too little data) and then, by 1990, accepted (multimedia was the major advance needed to give CD-ROM viability), it demonstrates very well the snowball effect of technology. The final pages look at other contenders: CD-ROM versus the Internet or are locally-mounted databases making a comeback? The conclusion is summed up in the one word, co-existence.

Journals: Online/CD-ROM Full-text

274. BookQuest. ABACIS Inc
A magazine covering online databases and search systems, optical disc products and computer hardware and software for information retrieval and management. Covers technical developments, new product announcements and reviews, search techniques and industry trends. Corresponds to *Online Magazine.*

Journals

275. *Managing Information.* London: Aslib, 1993-. Ten issues per year.
A well-designed journal with the usual mix of news items, articles and reviews. Typically, subject coverage might include online and CD-ROM databases, publishing CD-ROMs in-house and education for information, plus several well-written book and journal reviews, two or three CD-ROM reviews and general, Internet and European news items. Articles are not over-long and are practical in nature. In the issue before the December Online Conference in London, every news item was flagged with stand numbers.

276. *Searcher: The Magazine for Database Professionals.* Medford, New Jersey: Learned Information, 1993-. Nine issues per year.
Edited by Barbara Quint, *Searcher* centres on the needs of the professional searcher and combines evaluations of data content with discussions of delivery media: its scope includes all electronic media from CD-ROM and diskette and tape leasing to online. Regular sections include News Flashes, Tools of the Trade (short hardware reviews with Best Buys), (inevitably) The Internet Express and Searcher's Voice – the editorial. Coverage and style have a distinctly USA feel, but the content is relevant to any 'database professional'.

277. *Videotex International: Fortnightly International Newsletter on the Videotex Industry.* Paris, France: Transtex International. Twice monthly.
The newsletter provides up-to-date worldwide news on videotext applications and markets, including policies of European telecommunications organisations, US RBOCs and other operators of public and private videotex networks; policies and trading results of the main international concerns (network equipment suppliers, engineering, software, hosts and services); worldwide market figures; and regular reports on major EEC programmes.

Newsletters: Online/CD-ROM Full-text

278. *I'M GUIDE.* Luxembourg: Commission of the European Communities. Directorate General for Telecommunications, Information Industries and Innovation, 1989-. Five times per year.

Offers the full text of the Directorate's news publication *I & T Magazine* for online searching free of charge via ECHO.

279. *PROMT.* Foster City, CA: Information Access Company, 1972-. Daily.

PROMT represents Predicasts Overview of Markets and Technologies and includes the three printed Predicasts F & S Index publications which cover the United States, Europe and the rest of the world although the USA accounts for about 80% of the database. The file is updated daily and contains over two million records from more than 1,100 sources – some 300 of which are in full text. It provides a single source of worldwide product, company and market information in all manufacturing and service industries, including the online and CD-ROM sectors. Company news is a particular strength. A wide variety of sources is indexed, mainly comprising trade and business journals and newsletters, news releases and industry studies. Although coverage aims to be international, US developments are more strongly featured. Abstracts are included and contain tabulated numeric data where appropriate. Searching is most efficiently conducted through the IAC's unique coding system of product, event and geographic codes. PROMT is searchable on KR DIALOG from 1972 and on KR Data-Star from 1978; FT Profile and I/PLUS Direct offer the file from 1988; LEXIS/NEXIS from 1985; MAID from 1990; Questel/ORBIT from 1991 and GENIOS from 1992. All have either weekly or daily updating.

Newsletters

280. *Data Storage Report.* San Jose, CA: Jonas Press, 1985-. Monthly.

Aimed primarily at CD-ROM producers rather than users, this newsletter offers brief news sections on optical disc technology trends, legislation, finance, marketing and production techniques. Its full text is included in the PTS Newsletter Database.

281. *Digital Information Group's Information Industry Bulletin.* Stamford, Connecticut: Digital Information Group, 1985-. Weekly.

Formerly just the *Information Industry Bulletin,* this newsletter concentrates on a combination of brief news and more detailed analysis of markets and companies in all sectors of the US information industry, including online service providers. It includes financial and competitive statistics and a monthly mergers and acquisitions table summarizes developments containing details for each transaction of seller, buyer, market and, where known, price.

282. *Electronic Information Report.* Wilton, CT: SIMBA, 1979-. Weekly.
Formerly the *IDP Report: Information and Data Base Publishing Report* and briefly after that *Electronic Information Week, EIR* monitors, analyzes and reports on information services. This could include storage and distribution media, databases, electronic publishing, value-added facsimile services and online and voice services. Each issue provides a series of brief news items on US companies active in the information industry as print or database publishers. The emphasis is on company financial performance, supplemented by reports of mergers and takeovers, pricing policies, marketing opportunities and new database products. Can be searched online in the Trade and Industry ASAP database.

283. *Electronic Marketplace Report.* Wilton, CT: SIMBA Information, 1994-. 24 issues per year.
Previously and less-snappily entitled *Electronic Directory and Classified Report,* the change of title reflects a wider remit and the newsletter now gives analysis and opinions for the emerging business of electronic shopping and commerce, *EMR* addresses new technologies, advertising, busines and consumer education on commercial online networks and Electronic Data Exchange (EDI) systems. Each issue covers the latest developments and company ventures or mergers. *EMR* is more than just a news service, commentaries cover such topics as the 1994 interactive TV shopping service, US Avenue, announced by West and examine their chances of success and follow them up over the following weeks. News and analysis can be expected on industry alliances, financial data and market forecasts, marketing technologies and products, industry efforts to enter and build markets, the Internet, and delivery and hardware platforms such as CD-ROM. The bias of the newsletter is clearly North American; but in this area, Europe may well follow were the United States leads so it could provide valuable insights.

284. *Electronic Services Update.* Boston: Link Resources, 1982-. Monthly.
Provides coverage of news in business networks, consumer electronics, interactive entertainment and electronic messaging. Contains some analysis of international online database markets, descriptions of new databases, reports of recent meetings and news of companies and people in the database industry. Its title changed from *Electronic Information Report* in 1988. Searchable online on the PTS Newsletter Database.

285. *Friday Memo.* Washington, DC: Information Industry Association, 1986-. Twice weekly.
A source of up-to-date news on industry developments for members of the Information Industry Association. The IIA also produce the the quarterly *Information Times.* Can be searched online via NewsNet.

286. *I & T Magazine*. Luxembourg: Commission of the European Communities. Directorate General for Telecommunications, Information Industries and Innovation, 1976-. Quarterly.

Formerly known as *XIII Magazine* and formed from the merger of *I & TT, IES News* and *I'M: Information Market* (formerly *Euronet Diane News*), this newsletter acts as a regular channel for communication of news on electronic information exchange from Directorate General XIII of the European Commission whose purview includes telecommunications and the information industries. Directorate initiatives in these areas are regularly discussed and research reports announced. The *I'M* newsletter included coverage of service developments from ECHO, the European Communities Host Organisation, and of new commercially available online and CD-ROM databases but this has been largely discontinued. *I & T Magazine* remains relevant as many of the programmes deal with information handling. The journal comes in two parts: a glossy portion containing between six and eight articles and a blue-paper *News Review* with short press releases on the internal market, programmes of action, standardisation and publications. Although most of this publication is in English, news relating to a single European country is often published in the native language. Available online.

287. *Information Times*. Washington, DC: Information Industry Association, 1974-. Quarterly.

Like the *Friday Memo,* available only to members of the Information Industry Association, this publication contains news of developments in government policy with implications for the US information industry, along with details of company and people movements in the industry and forthcoming events organized by the Association. Special columns deal with international news and with electronic and database information services. The Association includes businesses involved in the creation, distribution and use of information and representatives of the online sector sit on its board of directors.

288. *Monitor: an Analytical Review of Current Events in Electronic Information.* Oxford: Learned Information, 1981-. Monthly.

Monitor takes a critical view of the information industry which, along with its products and services, it has been tracking since 1981. Reports of meetings and conferences are a regular feature, as are reviews of trends in the online industry in terms of its legal and political environment and market developments and interviews with leading figures. With a wide-ranging coverage, *Monitor* is of potential value to database producers, network operators, online service operators, publishers and policy makers in the information industry worldwide. The customer's perspective is also represented in articles on telecommunications and the value for money of online services. Every second issue contains a twelve-month author and subject index.

289. *Newsidic: Newsletter of the European Association of Information Services.* Luxembourg: EUSIDIC, 1970-. Bimonthly.

The newsletter acts as a channel for news of initiatives and reports of meetings of EUSIDIC, the European Association of Information Services. All members of EUSIDIC are providers or corporate users of electronic database services, so that the meetings, including an annual conference, provide a forum for both sides to come together. Newsidic consequently reflects the views of both the information industry and its larger customers. It consists of short features rather than full-scale articles, although occassional longer contributions are included. Regular themes are telecommunications, regulations affecting the information industry and news from the major host services of new databases or services.

290. *NFAIS Newsletter.* Philadelphia: National Federation of Abstracting and Indexing Services, 1958-. Monthly.

Usually contains short contributions on industry concerns such as pricing of online and CD-ROM information and user training. Profiles of companies in the United States and worldwide are included in many issues and describe origins, products and future developments. Other regular features are reports of conferences and meetings, database news, announcements of new appointments and company developments and listings of forthcoming events. For members of NFAIS, this publication is supplemented by *NFAIS Notes.*

291. *Optical Memory News.* Potomac, MD: Phillips Business Information, 1982-. Twice monthly.

Primarily of interest to industrialists, this newsletter concentrates on industry developments, company news, installations, contracts and market moves in the optical storage arena. It also usually features new CD-ROM hardware, software and database products and monitors technological advances internationally. Full contact information is supplied at the end of most stories. Conference and trade show reports are a feature of many issues, as is a calendar of forthcoming events. Incorporates *Optical and Magnetic Report.*

Reports

292. **Blake, P.** (ed.) *European Information Users: A Three-Part Briefing.* Oxford: Learned Information, 1993. (Three parts available separately or together.)

Published during 1993, the three reports covering Germany and Central Europe; the UK and Northern Europe; and France and Southern Europe each profiled some twenty information users. Dealing with such questions as how much money do Europeans spend on electronic information services? How are existing services rated? What influences their purchasing decisions? and what new products and services would they like to see? each report contains an executive summary highlighting regional issues and trends as well as a directory of services. The panel of some sixty information users across Europe included the budget conscious and top end spenders, private companies and public bodies, and users in science and business.

293. Bubley, D and **Bennett, P.** *Information Superhighways: the new information age*. Camborne: FT Management Reports, 1995.

This management report published by the Financial Times assesses and analyses the nature and status of both the technology and its management issues. It examines participating industries, key regulatory issues, existing and emerging technologies, the role of the business sector as a key user, the potential of the consumer market place, and the changing involvement of government. Chapters on technology (ISDN, ATM, frame relay, LANs), regulatory issues (the impact of technical standards, deregulation, copyright, etc), corporate networking, public telecommunications networks, cable television networks (the role of cable operators in the wider communications/ media marketplace and the use of fibre optic networks as a delivery mechanism for new services), satellite and mobile communications (the status of traditional service providers and the potential for broadband and universal services via the planned emergence of global mobile satellite networks), applications (vertical markets, uses of the superhighway and the differing views of business, the general public and academia), strategic issues (government development of the sector, investment requirements, competitive dynamics) and trends are followed by a full glossary of industry terminology.

294. Collier, H. *Strategies in the Electronic Information Industry: A Guide for the 1990s*. (2nd ed). Calne, Wiltshire: Infonortics, 1993. 105pp.

Two years on from the first edition of this study, this complete revision looks at the nature and background of information and its markets, the technology and the key delivery mechanisms, and information pricing and legal issues, before concluding with a summary of the commodity and its problems. Appendices cover Information strategies: key decision points (initial questions, online and CD-ROM) and industrial statistics. The second edition covers new areas such as multimedia and computer games and aims to provide an essential briefing of this huge subject area. A worthy aim surprisingly achieved in only just over a hundred pages, it provides background information for companies considering entering the electronic information arena and should help clarify thinking for those already involved.

295. East, H. and **Tilson, Y.** *The Liberated Enduser: developments in practice and policy for database provision to the academic community*. (CCIS Paper 4; British Library R&D Report 6100). London: University of Westminster Press, 1993. 62pp.

Following work at the Centre for Communication and Information Studies, the report covers research undertaken into the use of online services, BIDS and CD-ROM at universities and, at what were then, polytechnics. Four chapters examine market forces, the demand, strategies and politics, and future research. In retrospect it is not surprising that the findings included trends towards an increase in end-user services and the centralisation of supply in 'academic datacentres'. The Foreword points out that the title, *The Liberated Enduser,* looks forwards to where the authors think technology is leading rather than describing current practice.

296. *Information Market Indicators: Information Center/Library Market.* Compiled by M. E. Williams. Monticello, Illinois: Information Market Indicators, 1983-. Quarterly.

A regularly updated source of statistical data relating to the US online information industry. Figures are provided for the amount of usage of online database services by libraries, information centres and other corporations, and the distribution of revenue, based on hours of connect time, among the major US hosts and database producers. There is also commentary on patterns of usage, pricing policies and the entry of new hosts and database producers into the market. The full report is produced on a subscription basis but a summary of findings appears annually in the opening paper, presented by the author of the report, of the National Online Meeting.

297. **Mansell, R.** and **Tang, P.** *Electronic Information Services: Competitiveness in the United Kingdom. A report prepared for the Department of Trade and Industry, Textiles and Retailing Division.* Brighton: Science Policy Research Unit, 1994. pp. 49.

This report summarises the state of the UK database industry in 1994. Beginning with statistics covering sectors, revenues, market participants, and number of databases, the report goes on to look at issues affecting the market environment such as copyright, data privacy and the information industry structure. The section assessing competitiveness is only five pages long and the main conclusion is that there is considerable scope for cooperation within the sector, particularly with government to stimulate long-term competitiveness and with greater advantage being taken of the European Commission's programmes such as the National Awareness Partners Network. A general conclusion is that British information services are well placed to compete internationally although caution should be exercised in over-reliance on the financial and professional sectors.

298. *On-Line Databases.* Hampton, Middlesex: ICC Information Group, 1983-. Annual. (Key Note Report: an Industry Sector Overview).

This report has been published in 1983 and 1985 and annually since 1987. A general overview of the online information business in Britain is provided, with commentary on industry structure, market size and trends, the impact of recent and projected technological developments, and one-page financial profiles of the major companies. The report closes with a section on further sources of information, including recent articles on the industry, addresses of organizations, and lists of journals and directories.

299. *Online Services: 1994 Review, Trends & Forecast.* Bridgeport, Connecticut: SIMBA Information, 1994. 550pp.

A useful addition to a number of reports published on both sides of the Atlantic forecasting futures for the online industry, the database industry or optical publishing. The SIMBA report, focussing exclusively on online, includes a summary of of subscribers and revenues and forecasts that worldwide online service sales will reach $17.8 billion by 1999, a 57% increase compared with 1993. It also predicts that the greatest growth will be in business and professional services which, as Paul Blake of *Information World Review* suggests, is surprising. The report includes analysis of six business and professional sectors and in-depth coverage of 15 professional online services. SIMBA predict that the efforts to woo end users will show results over the next ten years, but result will be slow; with new services from the likes of Apple and Microsoft the consumer market will grow more than 20% annually to 1998. The trend towards value-priced searching will continue but, according to the report, this will not compensate for increased searcher efficiency. At $695, the report itself makes no small contribution to revenues!

300. Schwerin, J. *Optical Publishing Industry Assessment (The OPIA Report).* Columbus, Ohio: InfoTech, 1988-. Irregular.

Analyzes the worldwide market for optical publishing in terms of various criteria which include number of titles, publishing patterns in subject areas and installed base of CD-ROM drives. Now in its 6th edition, this quantitative market research report by Julie Schwerin covers the period 1986-1999 and includes over 150 pages of detailed graphs (272 unique charts and figures) and text. Data in both volume and value is reported in terms of global, regional and national statistics for units sold, disc masters produced, commercial versus in-house markets, languages and platforms.

301. *State of the CD-ROM Industry: Applications, Players and Products.* Alexandria, Virginia: Information Workstation Group, 1987-. Annual.

Published in two volumes, the first of which includes technology and market forecasts for CD-ROM and related technologies. It contains comparative tables of industry participants, product characteristics, storage capacities, relevant markets and available databases. The second volume profiles over 250 applications, players and products, including hardware providers, library services and systems integrators.

302. *The CD-ROM and the Online Database Markets.* Monticello, Illinois: Information Market Indicators, 1989-. Annual.

A mine of statistical data and analysis of CD-ROM usage and purchase. Data are obtained by surveying organizational users of databases and this reveals the impact of CD-ROM on the established online database market. Tables are provided extensively and these include data on the leading CD-ROM vendors and databases, expenditure on online and CD-ROM by organization type, and types of organization using and not using CD-ROM databases. The same publisher analyzes the online industry in its quarterly Information Market Indicators series.

303. *The European Market for Online Databases*. London: Frost and Sullivan, 1995. c.350pp.
Concentrates on business information online, finding the European market in a state of constant flux but predicting a continuing expansion in revenue growth from 1993 to 2000. National markets are examined in terms of current and projected revenues. Britain is seen as the largest player in the single market which is estimated to reach US$ 7.25 billion by 2000. Financial databases accounted for about 62.3 per cent in 1993 but this is expected to fall to 60.9 per cent by 2000 while news databases become more important. Business information databases will perform best and are expected to account for 22.8 per cent by the end of the period.

304. *The Online Database Market in the US*. New York: Frost and Sullivan, 1989. 290pp.
A survey of the US online information industry which offers market forecasts and trends to 1993 by number of databases, number of users and revenues. Selected hosts and producers are profiled with analysis of their marketing strategies, products and approaches to distribution and promotion. The size, nature and structure of the industry are examined, along with the segmentation of the market by types of users and databases. A tripling of 1988 revenues is predicted by 1993, representing nevertheless a slowing of previous growth rates which is largely attributed to competition from CD-ROM. Unlike the European equivalent, this report has not yet been updated.

Yearbooks

305. *Information Industry Factbook: the Information Industry's Annual Report*. Stamford, Connecticut: Digital Information Group. Annual.
A statistical yearbook for the information industry in general which includes chapters on the online and CD-ROM sectors. Information given for the online industry includes revenue estimates, number and type of subscribers and online usage for selected US companies, pricing trends, movement into new markets and developments in online technology. For CD-ROM, sales figures and market projections are provided, along with pricing policies, technology trends, and a directory of available CD-ROM titles and publishers. An additional feature is a month-by-month review of company news from all sectors of the information industry. The directory is supplemented by the *Factbook Data Disk* which can be purchased separately. It contains a variety of statistical data in Lotus 1-2-3 format for direct importation into most spreadsheets and database management systems which run on IBM-compatible microcomputers.

DATABASE INDUSTRY: LEGAL ISSUES

Books

306. **Brinson, J. D.** and **Radcliffe, M. E.** *Multimedia Law Handbook.* Menlo Park, CA: Ladera Press, 1994.

Aimed at developers and publishers, this volume covers legal issues such as the Compton NewMedia patent dispute and the idea that copyright law will have to be fundamentally altered to address multimedia. According to the review in *CD-ROM World* (Liebman, H. 'Legal Ease review'. *CD-ROM World* 9(7) (July/August 1994) p. 107) the book is laid out in a clean and logical style that makes finding relevant information easy. There are four main sections: Building Blocks; Production Relationships; Other Production Issues; and Post-Production Issues, together covering basic legal precepts, development agreements, rights and licences, naming the product and protecting intellectual rights. Almost a third of the books is taken up by the appendices – sample licences, model release forms, etc. An online preview of the book can be obtained by way of the Internet at obs@marketplace.com so it is possible to see if the US$74.95 will be money well spent. A bimonthly newsletter on related issues is promised.

Conferences: Papers

307. **White, A.** 'Copyright Law, Information Services and the Challenge of Multimedia'. *In Online Information 93: 17th International Online Information Meeting Proceedings, London, 7-9 December.* Edited by D I Raitt. Oxford: Learned Information, 1993. pp. 243-252.

The paper sets out the basic principles of UK copyright law and highlights certain areas where existing law is placed under strain by multimedia. White argues that if solutions to some of these problems are not found soon, the multimedia industry and the application of multimedia to information services will be significantly inhibited. Andrew White covers legal issues in a semi-regular column for *Information World Review.*

Handbooks

308. **Bremner, J. P.** *Guide to Database Distribution* (2nd ed.) Philadelphia: National Federation of Abstracting and Information Services, 1995.

A guide which reviews the process of licensing machine-readable databases and addresses the issues involved in negotiating database agreements, including intellectual property protection. Topics covered include: distribution schemes for intellectual works, the legal relationship between the various members involved in the distribution scheme, sample contractual language, contractual issues, royalty arrangements and site licensing. An appendix includes a complete model agreement that can be used to check the content and style of agreements. The guide is said to be intended for the executive or lawyer involved with distribution of information in online or CD-ROM formats and is written by an attorney with experience in copyright law; it covers the issues and options needed for negotiating a licence agreement. As the NFAIS publicity notes, 'If you are considering producing an electronic information product, this book will bring you up-to-date on the methods that database producers are using to protect their intellectual property in an electronic environment.'

Journal Articles

309. Cornish, G. P. 'Copyright protection for materials in electronic forms: the CITED solution'. *Learned Publishing* 6 (2) April 1993. pp. 15-18.

The article describes one means of allowing access to electronically stored copyright materials under controlled conditions: Copyright in Transmitted Electronic Documents (CITED). The system monitors the use of the store and permits the downloading of copies of documents to authorized users (Original abstract).

Reports

310. Jones, D. *Liability of Information Service Providers.* London: The Library Information Technology Centre, 1990. 11pp. (Library & Information Briefings, No. 25)

Library and information Briefings collect essential material on particular topics and present state-of-the-art reports in easy-to-read formats. The Briefing covers contract, negligence (tort), product liability and copyright as they impinge upon the information industry. Following a brief example of the inadequacy of the law prior to the Computer Misuse Act 1990 and using case examples and legal citations by way of support, Dick Jones covers Liability in Contract (privity of contract, Sales of Goods, Supply of Services); Liability in Negligence, Product Liability (Consumer Protection Act 1987, What is a product? What is a defective product? What is damage?); Liability for Defective Services (economic damage); Copyright (compiler produced-abstracts, author-produced abstracts). He concludes that the law of contract and tort relating to information service providers is reasonably clear while copyright and likely defective services await clarification by way of proposals from the European Commission.

311. Oppenheim, C. *The Legal and Regulatory Environment for Electronic Information.* Calne, Wiltshire: Infonortics, 1992. 131pp.

With particular focus on Europe, this study covers the international arena in matters such as intellectual property, copyright, data protection, liability for information provision, freedom of information and confidentiality. There are, as Professor Oppenheim points out, a highly complex set of relationships governing information provision and use, and most information providers and users are doing their best to understand the current legal and regulatory environment – a task that will be aided considerably by a detailed reading of this briefing. Although recommended reading, it must be remembered that this is an area which can and will change – this briefing dates from 1992.

312. Oppenheim, C. *Electronic Copyright.* London: Library Information Technology Centre, 1992. 12pp. (Library and Information Briefings, No. 35)

Library and information Briefings collect essential material on particular topics and present state-of-the-art reports in easy-to-read formats. The copyright issues of machine-readable records are complex and still-debated, and Charles Oppenheim brings to bear much experience in this introductory text – a less detailed version of his Infonortics report. Definitions of copyright, fair dealing and literary works lead to a discussion of databases. Citing the Feist Decision, the Magill Decision and Microfor versus Le Monde it is suggested that the trend is to reducing the protection given to databases which comprise non-copyright material. The conclusion that the copyright status of the database is confused leads naturally to the corollary that the thing to do is rely on contracts. However, the following three-page section on Recent EC Initiatives (including the EC definition of database and extracted highlights) belies this to some extent. The penultimate section on Multimedia Copyright may well be somewhat out of date due to the Patent action by Compton NewMedia. Although some of the points made have been overtaken by events, this is still a useful and relevant briefing.

313. Oppenheim, C. *The Relationship between Online Hosts and Database Producers.* London: The Library Information Technology Centre, 1990. 10pp. (Library & Information Briefings, No. 24)

Following a short definition of the players in the information industry arena, this Briefing sets out to explain the legal and, to some extent, the financial relationship between database producers and online hosts. It looks at a typical license agreement or contract, giving definitions of typical issues such as copyright, restrictions on use, royalties, marketing, the law under which the contract runs, and confidentiality. An excellent summary of a relationship which the author thinks will remain broadly the same for some time to come despite changes in the information industry itself. The Briefing makes no claim to cover the technical and logistical side of the relationship.

314. UK Monopolies and Mergers Commission. *Historical Online Database Services: a Report on the Supply in the UK of Services which provide access to Databases Containing Archival Business and Financial Information: Presented to Parliament by the Secretary of State for Trade and Industry, May 1994.* London: HMSO, 1994. 96pp.

While the issue of copyright is discussed in many of the other documents referenced in this section, this report makes particularly interesting reading as it has a rather different starting point. Sir Bryan Carsberg, the Director General of Fair Trading noted in his referral to the Commission that, 'although ownership of copyright automatically bestows an inherent monopoly advantage ... I am concerned that the restrictions on copyright material may be inhibiting effective competition'. For a discussion of competitiveness, the report by Mansell and Tang makes interesting reading [297].

DATABASES: ALTERNATIVE HOSTS

Conferences: Papers

315. **McSéan, T.; Rowlands, J.** and **Forrester, W.** 'Becoming a Micro-host: Using Desktop Computers to run an Online Retrieval Service.' *In Online Information 93: 17th International Online Information Meeting Proceedings, London, 7-9 December 1993.* Edited by D I Raitt. Oxford: Learned Information, 1993. pp. 367-376.

The British Medical Association Library now provides a full-scale MEDLINE information retrieval system as a free service to its members. This paper introduces the service – believed to be the first of its kind – and gives a brief technical description. It then goes on to describe problems in implementation, gives a frank but basically favourable analysis of the Library's relationship with their system of choice (CD-Plus) and a discussion of copyright and licensing issues raised by a service of this type. BMA members can now dial into the Library's CD-Plus MEDLINE database from around the United Kingdom and the paper closes with a summary of the benefits and the problems which have been encountered.

Directories: Online Format

316. **Hallman, J.** *Campus-Wide Information Systems (CWIS).* Chapel Hill, North Carolina: University of North Carolina.

Compiled by Judy Hallman, this directory is available via anonymous FTP on FTP.OIT.UNC.EDU in the PUB/DOCS directory, filename CWIS-L.

E-Mail Lists

317. CWIS-L@WUVMD (BITNET)

Discussion forum/e-mail list on campus-wide information systems. To subscribe, send an e-mail message to LISTSERV@WUVMD:

SUBSCRIBE CWIS-L First name Last name

Journals

318. *Campus-Wide Information Services.* Bradford: MCB University Press, 1995- (Mecklermedia, 1983-1994). Quarterly.

Originally *Academic and Library Computing,* Mecklermedia changed the name in 1993 and then sold the journal along with other library titles at the end of 1994. Under

Mecklermedia, the journal averaged four or five articles each issue, a news section and book reviews. Articles range from the technical to the theoretical. The journal is indexed in The Microcomputer Index, Information Science Abstracts and Computer Database.

Journal Articles

319. East, H. 'National Datasets Selection: Pragmatism in Pursuit of Policy.' *Journal of Information Networking* 2 (1), 1994, pp.1-12.

The article examines issues arising from the evolution of a national datasets policy in the UK Higher Education community and questions some recent interpretations of it; particularly how the composition of a portfolio of 'core' databases is to be determined. It provides data indicating those databases for which expenditure on mediated online services and CD-ROM subscriptions is highest and for which the largest economies of scale are possible. It suggests that the imposition of flat rate charging is likely to disadvantage some sections of the Higher Education community and runs counter to the concept of 'equal access to all' which is basic to the policy.

320. Law, D. 'The Development of a National Policy for Dataset Provision in the UK: a Historical Perspective.' *Journal of Information Networking.* 2 (2), 1994, pp.103-116.

Records some of the issues surrounding the development of a policy for central funding of dataset provision in the UK academic and research community. It describes the work of the Information Services Committee's Datasets Working Group and its predecessor the Computer Board's National Task Group on Datasets, and how their recommendations have been taken forward by the Information Systems Sub-committee (ISSC) of the Joint Information Systems Committee (JISC) of the Higher Education Funding Councils (HEFCs) which now has responsibility for implementing the policy. It also reviews implications for institutional service provision and sketches potential service outcomes of the policy.

321. Morrow, T. 'BIDS – The Growth of a Networked End-user Bibliographic Data Service'. *Program* 29 (1) (January 1995) pp. 31-41.

Outlining the development of the BIDS service and the facilities on offer, the article reviews the growth of the service, the lessons learned from user feedback and their use in re-implementing the service on a new platform. Finally it looks at future developments: the use of the Internet and the World Wide Web to offer a support service; more databases; document ordering; and – something not 'just around the corner' – full-text services.

Reports

322. Breaks, M. and **Wood, S.** *SuperJANET.* London: The Library Information Technology Centre, 1993. 14pp. (Library & Information Briefings, No. 47)

Following a brief introductory background to JANET (Joint Academic NETwork), the Briefing goes on to describe the high-performance SuperJANET. After listing the sites to be connected at each phase and mapping the network links, there is a summary of SuperJANET multimedia projects – the high speeds make such things possible – such as Pathnet, a pilot to explore the potential for remote consultation of pathologists. Library and information applications include access to manuscripts, information delivery and electronic journals while humanities potential includes access to museums and galleries: all are covered. The report ends with a brief section on issues to be addressed and the thought that SuperJANET is only limited by the imagination of its users.

323. Scanlon, S. *BIDS: The Revolution in Database Access.* London: The Library Information Technology Centre, 1991. 11pp. (Library & Information Briefings, No. 29)

Library and information Briefings collect essential material on particular topics and present state-of-the-art reports in easy-to-read formats. Written relatively early in the life of the Bath ISI Data Service (BIDS), this Briefing summarises its growth by way of JANET, the UK Office of Library Networking and the Combined Higher Education Software Team (CHEST). It details the four ISI databases available in November 1991, the facilities available, and the participating sites. There is also a list of further readings and a glossary.

324. Scanlon, S. *The UK's Networked Dataset Revolution Continues.* London: The Library Information Technology Centre, 1993. 13pp. (Library & Information Briefings, No. 50)

Library and information Briefings collect essential material on particular topics and present state-of-the-art reports in easy-to-read formats and this Briefing updates much of the material in Briefing 29 (*BIDS: The Revolution in Database Access*). BIDS now stands for Bath Information and Data Services and encompasses many more than the original four databases; there are now 76 sites and six services: BIDS-ISI, BIDS-EMBASE, BIDS-INSIDE INFORMATION, BIDS DOCUMENT ORDERING, BIDS COMPENDEX and CHEST-FIRSTSEARCH (OCLC) which offers access to seven databases including ERIC and MEDLINE as well as (optionally) to the Wilson databases (12) and some nineteen others. The Briefing gives the background to BIDS, a note on BIDS copyright, lists the services and some databases that 'got away', and in the conclusion notes that although end-users are demanding more databases, it is difficult for CHEST to pursue future services wholeheartedly when its own source of future funding is also in doubt.

DOWNLOADING

Books

325. Jameson, A. *Downloading and Uploading in On Line Information Retrieval.* Bradford: MCB University Press, 1987. 64pp.

Issued as *Library Management,* 8 (1), 1987, this is a valuable review of downloading and uploading practices in online searching, with an emphasis on downloading. Software packages are reviewed, with details of their special features, operating requirements, suppliers and costs. Another chapter surveys applications for downloaded data such as reformatting of records and database creation. In addition legal issues are fully discussed and the prevailing attitudes of the information industry are represented. The bibliography at the end of the volume has 168 references.

Journal Articles

326. Stigleman, S. 'Bibliographic Formatting Software: a Buying Guide'. *Database* 15 (1) February 1992. pp. 15-27.

Bibliographic formatting software takes records downloaded from an online or CD-ROM database and formats them into another specified citation style. Forty-three bibliographic formatting programs are identified and listed with supplier information. Each producer was asked to supply answers to eight questions and these are published in full and in a series of tables.

ECONOMIC ASPECTS

Books

327. **Bysouth, P.** (ed.) *The Economics of Online.* London: Taylor Graham, 1987. 229pp. (Foundations of Information Science; 2)

Twenty-six contributions, published as journal articles or conference papers between 1976 and 1984, are arranged under the following themes: choice of search equipment and host system; calculation of search costs; cost-benefits; charging policies; and future trends, including pricing for online access. A typical Taylor Graham collection with papers brought together by their common theme but separated by their approach – some papers are very technical while others are almost simplistic in approach. As, for the most part, the papers deal with generalities of charging rather than specifics, much of the content is still relevant today although their vintage must be born in mind.

Guides to Charges

328. *Online Files: Comparative Cost Analysis.* Humberston, Grimsby: Effective Technology Marketing, 1993-. Quarterly.

Taking into account search costs, connect time costs, display and print format costs, currency manipulation and the availability of SDI searches, OFCCA enables users to identify which hosts provide the required database and locate the most cost-effective, to identify which display and print formats are available at what cost and thus to estimate online search costs in advance. The computer-print, landscape layout offers eleven columns: database name, host abbreviation, file label, average search cost (7 minutes of connect time and 15 comparable-format online prints), browsing search cost (20 minutes connect time and 27 minimum-format online prints), minimum and maximum charges for both online and offline prints, and SDI availability. Three pages of explanation precede the table. An enhanced diskette-based version (OFCCA) is also available.

Guides to Charges: Diskette

329. *OFCCA.* Humberston, Grimsby: Effective Technology Marketing, 1993-. Quarterly.

An enhanced electronic version of *Online Files: Comparative Cost Analysis* which gives instant access to search cost comparisons, display/print formats costs and allows currency exchange rate manipulation. OFCCA enables users to identify which hosts (of the 16 included) provide the required database and, from the listing supplied, locate the most cost-effective access and identify which display and print formats are available at what cost. Searching is by database name or part name. OFCCA has been developed jointly with First Contact Ltd (the company responsible for *The Online Manual* and *The Online Manual on Disk*) and runs under DOS 3.3 or higher and requires 250K free RAM and 2 Mbytes of fixed disk space. It is possible to configure OFCCA to remind users of the hosts to which they have access.

Journal Articles

330. Bates, M. E. 'Cost Control: Using Automatic Accounting Features to Monitor Search Costs'. *Online* 17 (1) (January 1993) pp. 39-43.

Microcomputers can be used to track search costs and DIALOGLINK Commuications Manager provides each terminal with its own log and compilation of costs, however, the article notes that it is still necessary to cross check the monthly invoice against the log. Bates goes on to discuss the relative merits of system-specific accounting software and that supplied with communications packages such as CROSSTALK or ProComm. Online accounting features are also noted.

331. El-Hadidy, B. 'The Breakeven Point for Using CD-ROM versus Online: a Case Study for Database Access in a Developing Country'. *Journal of the American Society for Information Science* 45 (4) (May 1994) pp. 273-283.

The article discusses the extent to which publicly available CD-ROM databases can satisfy the information needs of a particular information requirement in a developing country and looks at the economics of an alternative system of CD-ROMs supplemented by online searching. The relative costs of the two media are investigated and a breakeven analysis of the costs is discussed as a potential approach to a cost-effective system for accessing databases. The article also discusses the implications of the law of core and scatter on the volume of use of databases and its effects on the economics of searching CD-ROM versus online.

332. Fletcher, L. A. 'DIALOG Price Restructuring Evaluation: Tentative Steps on the Road to Value-Based Pricing'. *Searcher* 2 (8) (October 1994) pp. 44-46, 48-52, 54-56, 58-59.

In the wake of the major price restructuring by KR DIALOG, many users were left unsure as to whether this was a 'good thing' or not. Certainly the new pricing places more emphasis on the value of information (generally seen as good) but there is still a connect time charge (admittedly reduced) and a new fixed 'View Fee' charged against every type, print or display (definitely bad). Fletcher's article looks in some depth at the pricing structure, compares searches on the old and new charging systems and generally looks at pros and cons. He notes the savings to be made with a flat fee pricing plan (for heavy users) and finally asks, 'Will the View fee Backfire on KR DIALOG?' – his conclusion is that users will avoid it (and he has his own suggestions) whenever they can. KR DIALOG may have sought revenue neutrality but in their View Fee they may well have inconvenienced users just too much.

333. Gregory, A. 'Pay-as-you-go vs. All-you-can-eat: Trends in Online Pricing'. *In* Martha E. Williams (ed.) *Proceedings of 14th National Online Meeting 1993. Learned Information New York 4-6 May 1993.* Medford, NJ: Learned Information, 1993. pp. 165-169.

The conference paper concludes that the online database hosts and providers have failed to match the needs of their users by clinging to old pricing strategies instead of following the lead of CD-ROM databases in providing subscription-based services. The author suggests that the future of centralized online hosts lies with a more flexible approach to pricing.

334. Hawkins, D. T. 'In Search of Ideal Information Pricing'. *Online* 13 (2) (March 1989) pp. 15-29.

An overview of different past, present and future approaches to the pricing of information retrieval from online databases, with twenty-four references.

335. Jacsó, P. 'Have I Got a Deal for You: The State of the Art in CD-ROM Marketing and Pricing'. *Information Today* 10 (4) (April 1993) pp. 28-29.

The article explains why 1993 was a good year for purchasing CD-ROMs, looking at discount manufacturer prices for both CD-ROMs and CD-ROM drives, superseded and discontinued databases, special subscriptions, special user deals and bundle deals where CD-ROMs are supplied with the hardware.

336. Rowley, J. E. 'Pricing Strategies for CD-ROM Products'. *Online & CD-ROM Review* 18 (2) (April 1994) pp. 87-93.

The article investigates the variety of pricing strategies adopted by CD-ROM database publishers and identifies some of the issues that have yet to be resolved. The author points out that the original simplistic view of CD-ROM database pricing which assumes the CD-ROM to be a single self-contained product has become compromised by the emergence of networking and downloading. She considers the influence on CD-ROM pricing strategies and the difficulties facing CD-ROM publishers in predicting key indicators such as the proportion of their market that will migrate from online and print to CD-ROM; the effect on their market of other publishers starting to offer CD-ROM products; and the speed at which such migration will take place. The conclusion is that the complexity of pricing structures reflects the fact that electronic information can be neither clearly identified or marketed as either a product or a service. It should be recognised that CD-ROM's complex pricing strategies are inevitable but some standardisation of approach would be useful.

337. Shear, V. 'CD-ROM and Metering: an Overview'. *CD-ROM Professional* 5 (2) (March 1992) pp. 85-87.

The article argues that the cost constraints of CD-ROM subscriptions have limited the market and that a meter-based charging mechanism could avoid this. Four critical elements of a metering system are given as encryption techniques, securely managed search histories, maximum usage limit formulae and support of database functionality.

338. Tamule, H. B.; Gaus, K. and **Desmarais, N.** 'A New Look as CD-ROM Prices'. *CD-ROM Librarian* 7 (9) (October 1992) pp. 22-26.

The article outlines the uncertainty felt in 1992 with regard to new technology prices and attempts to construct a price index by analysing the titles listed in Pat Ensor's *CD-ROM Research Collections: An Evaluative Guide to Bibliographic and Full-Text CD-ROM Databases.* The conclusion suggests that CD-ROM subscriptions are becoming better value.

339. Whitaker, B. 'The Pricing of Online'. *Database Searcher* 5 (1) (January 1989) pp. 12-20.

Examines factors considered by database producers and online hosts in setting search costs and the effects of technological developments such as faster data transmission rates, front-end software and CD-ROM. Searchers are encouraged to exercise their influence by communicating their concerns to the database industry.

Reports

340. Davison, P. S., McDonagh, M., Meldrum, J. P. D. and **Moss, A.** *International Bibliographic Review on Costs and Modelling in Information Retrieval: Report on Completion of Data Collection, Assessment of the Efficiency of Searching, and on the Means of Indexing Information.* London: British Library Research and Development Department, 1988. 29pp. (British Library Research Paper; 37).

This report compels attention on two separate counts. Firstly, it analyzes the performance of forty different information science sources in compiling a major bibliography of 6,098 references on the costs and economics of all aspects of information transfer. Bibliographies, card files, printed indexes and online services were searched. The interesting conclusion is that, in terms of unique references retrieved, bibliographies proved to be the most successful source, with online searching offering fewest references but being the most expensive method. Secondly, as an adjunct to the report, 320 of the references are listed by author, with a selectively permuted title keyword index, as a pilot for indexing the whole database. This bibliography represents a cross-section of the literature internationally since sources searched included the major indexes from Britain, the United States, France, Germany, the Soviet Union, Poland and Hungary. Some of the citations published here deal with online retrieval, while the whole database of 6,098 references is held by the Scientific Documentation Centre Ltd., Halbeath, Dunfermline, Scotland.

Review Publications

341. Spigai, F. 'Information Pricing'. *In* M E Williams (ed.) *Annual Review of Information Science and Technology* 26 (1991) pp. 39-73.

While Pricing has been a previous topic in the *Annual Review,* this is the first time that Information Pricing has appeared, reflecting recent concerns. The focus is on events and literature surrounding the pricing of research and professional materials in libraries and as it covers 1986 to 1990, the chapter includes electronic formats as libraries 'are charged with obtaining information regardless of format'. A useful coverage of a transitional period where electronic information become an equal partner to print information while methodologies for charging for it were being explored. The review contains about 120 references.

ELECTRONICALLY DISTRIBUTED TEXTS/JOURNALS

Directories: Print

342. *On Internet 94: An International Guide to Electronic Journals, Newsletters, Texts, Discussion Lists, and Other Resources on the Internet.* Westport, Connecticut: Mecklermedia, 453pp. 1994-. (Annually ?)

Given the increase in scholarly and commercial electronic publishing over the Internet in the last two years, with an estimate of around 1,500 discrete publications and discussion lists, this directory provides a comprehensive guide to the full range of electronic documents available as of late-1993 – nearly 6,000 entries. The directory is divided into eight sections: Discussion Lists and Special Interest Mailing Lists; Electronic Journals and Newsletters; Electronic Texts, Text Archives, Selected FTP Sites, and Internet Resource Guides; Freenet and Other Community-Based Information Services; Campus-Wide Information Systems; Commercial Services on the Internet; Usenet Newsgroups and Other Mailing Lists; and WAIS-Accessible Databases. For each publications, details are include on access, subscriptions and submission instructions; there is also a brief description, listings of contents, and reviews. The Subject Index lists entries under subject headings such as 'Astrophysics' or 'Austen, Jane'; each publication entry directs readers only to the appropriate section of the directory.

Reports

343. Feeney, M. *Electronic Texts.* London: The Library Information Technology Centre, 1993. 11pp. (Library & Information Briefings, No. 40)

Electronic texts range from products such as The Voyager Company's 'Expanded Books' to archives such as the Oxford Text Archive or corpora such as Thesaurus Linguae Graecae and the subtle differences between these is explained in the *Briefing*. Giving a taxonomy of electronic text as well as examples of applications and products scarcely pins the term down as it can be seen to include CD-ROM products such as the *Oxford English Dictionary* or *Grolier's Encyclopaedia.* However, the Briefing does see a considerable future for electronic texts – probably due to the increasing use of the Internet, Hypertext systems and the blurring of the distinction between the reader and the writer. One important point to note: at the time of writing there is no coordinating initiative in the UK concerned with the creation of an electronic version of the national heritage.

END USERS

Bibliographies

344. **Efthimiadis, E. N.** *Online Searching Aids: a Subject Bibliography on Front-Ends, Gateways....* London: British Library, 1989. 52pp. (British Library Information Guide; 11).

Resulting from a British Library-funded research project at City University, this bibliography contains 540 references obtained by searches in March 1989 of the COMPENDEX, INSPEC, Information Science Abstracts and LISA databases. The subject of the project, and of the bibliography, is a review of systems which in some way intermediate between searchers and databases or other information retrieval systems. The entries cover descriptions of technology and its implementation and reviews of individual systems or software packages. References are arranged according to five main subject areas: gateways; downloading and uploading; front-end systems; intermediary systems; and post processing of search results. In each case these subject divisions are further divided (for example, post-processing systems and methods; reported post processing; and post-processing products and descriptions). Full bibliographic details, without abstracts, are provided for each entry, with indexes by author and product name. References belong mostly to the period from 1983 to the end of 1988.

Books

345. **Albright, R. G.** *A Basic Guide to Online Information Systems for Health Care Professionals.* Arlington, Virginia: Information Resource Press, 1988. 296pp.

Written by an end user *for* end users, this publication devotes individual chapters to a number of online medical information services, including CompuServe, MEDLARS, DIALOG Medical Collection and Knowledge Index, and the, then, BRS/Colleague. Sample screens are used as illustrations in each chapter. Other chapters and appendices briefly explain modems, communications software and telecommunications networks and provide a glossary.

346. **Benson, J. A.** and **Weinberg, B. H.** (eds.) *Gateway Software and Natural Language Interfaces: Options for Online Searching.* Ann Arbor, Michigan: Pierian Press, 1988. 204pp. (Library Hi Tech Special Studies Series; 2).

The bulk of this work consists of a series of critical evaluations of individual telecommunications and gateway software products which facilitate end-user searching. Other sections offer chapters on gateway services and on applications of natural language interfaces and artificial intelligence in information retrieval. Although many of the products will by now have undergone revisions and upgrades, most will have essentially the same features so that this is an invaluable guide. Some newer products such as the CompuServe Information Manager (CIM/WinCIM) or the Ameol off-line reader for Compulink Information Exchange (CiX) are, of course, not mentioned and all the products included are pre-Windows versions. An extensive bibliography of 715 references is provided, with a bias towards US literature. There is also a glossary of major terms and a directory of gateway and telecommunications software with US suppliers. There is also a subject/product/author index which includes authors mentioned in chapter bibliographies.

347. Kesselman, M. and **Watstein, S. B.** *End-User Searching: Services and Providers.* Chicago: American Library Association, 1988. 300pp.
Invaluable handbook for librarians involved in devising end-user programmes and services for their clients. The first three chapters identify and discuss the issues and implications of end-user searching in terms of staffing, product selection, promotion and user training. The remaining chapters describe in some detail available systems and services specifically aimed at end users, mainly in business, science and the home. The emphasis is on online systems but separate chapters are devoted to front-end and gateway software and to optical disc media. An extensive annotated bibliography concludes the work, with an appendix which provides contact information in the United States and Canada for the products and services described earlier.

348. Mount, E. (ed.) *End-User Training for Sci-Tech Databases.* New York: Haworth Press, 1990. 128pp.
This monograph, published simultaneously in *Science and Technology Libraries* 10 (1) (Fall 1989) contains four contributions which illustrate methods of promoting and teaching end-user searching and its practice in science, engineering and medical settings in the United States. Both academic and industrial research organizations are featured. Online rather than CD-ROM searching dominates.

349. Pfaffenberger, B. *Democratizing Information: Online Databases and the Rise of End-User Searching.* Boston: G. K. Hall, 1990. 193pp.
Examines the value of end-user searching for society as a whole, concluding that the application of artificial intelligence and expert systems will be necessary to make information retrieval from databases a more helpful tool in decision making.

350. Wasik, J. F. *The Electronic Business Information Sourcebook.* New York: Wiley, 1987. 208pp.
Written by a journalist, this is a guide to the general research and business databases on offer on a range of US hosts. The book emphasizes the end user and describes a number of appropriate services aimed at this market. Appendices provide annotated lists of further reading, information brokers, hosts, and selected databases.

351. **Wood, M. S., Horak, E. B.** and **Snow, B.** (eds.) *End User Searching in the Health Sciences.* New York: Haworth Press, 1986. 290 pp.
Published as a monographic supplement to volume 5, 1986, of the journal *Medical Reference Services Quarterly,* this work consists of sixteen contributions grouped in three sections on the environment of end user searching, existing programmes in the United States and the user's viewpoint. Although the emphasis is on the health sciences, many of the issues discussed, notably educational materials, implications for library planning, information management and user attitudes are of general interest. Also included are an annotated bibliography and glossary. The bibliography consists of 170 references, mostly representing mainstream journal literature in the period from 1983 to 1985, which are divided into eight subject sections on topics such as the role of the librarian and computer interfaces.

Conferences: Proceedings

352. **Armstrong, C. J.** and **Hartley, R. J.** (eds.). *Changing Patterns of Online Information: UKOLUG State-of-the-Art Conference 1994.* Oxford: Learned Information, 1994. 145pp.
The United Kingdom Online User Group (UKOLUG) holds a State-of-the-Art conference every other year with, since 1986, published proceedings. As in previous years, the proceedings contain not only the papers, but summaries of the discussions which took place after the formal presentations as well as a complete programme, delegate list and biographical details of the speakers. The theme in 1994 was reflected both in the title and in the choice of papers which coverd the Internet, Campus-Wide Information Services, SuperJANET, electronic document delivery and CD-ROM networking. A student paper – by the second winner of the UKOLUG Student Award – is also included in the proceedings.

353. **Mensching, T. B.** and **Stanger, K. J.** (eds.). *Bibliographic Instruction and Computer Database Searching: Papers Presented at the Fourteenth Library Instruction Conference Held at Eastern Michigan University 8 and 9 May 1986; and Numerous Examples of Current Instructional Materials Collected in Late 1987.* Ann Arbor, Michigan: Pieran Press, 1988. 173 pp.
This publication is divided into five main sections. The first consists of eight papers delivered at the conference. Their theme is the integration of training in online information retrieval into existing instruction programmes in US academic libraries. Poster session abstracts are featured in the next section. This is followed by a collection of handouts and sample instructional materials produced by US libraries. Two appendices offer suggested objectives for library instruction in online information retrieval and a series of guidelines for online training sessions which address issues such as length of session, equipment, handouts, evaluation and follow-up. The final section is a set of separate bibliographies.

Handbooks

354. Berkman, R. I. *Find It Online!* New York: Windcrest/McGraw-Hill, 1994. 380pp.

An all-embracing approach to finding information in electronic (online, CD-ROM or Internet) database sources. Written for the end user in a 'popular' style, the book's mission is described as 'to cut a clear path through the thicket of data sources by clearly describing and comparing competing electronic services and sources.' Despite that hyperbole, *Find It Online!* does accomplish much of what it sets out to do, although very much for an American audience covering, as it does, America Online (not quite in Europe at the time of writing), Delphi, GEnie, Prodigy and CompuServve in addition to the Internet and CD-ROM sources. The first section deals with online sources and the second with those on CD- ROM; both have almost more screen shots and examples than text but both cover the ground well although there is a tendency to use front-end search software (such as CompuServe's CIM) in the figures. Charging information will date rapidly. The final section and chapter lists databases under some forty broad topic headings such as Address and telephone directories, astronomy and space, business and company information, and travel. For each category the section lists three 'major types' of electronic database: consumer CD-ROMs, CD-ROMs found in libraries and online services. It is not comprehensive but provides a 'quick look up and contact information for many of the most broadly useful and popular electronic databases'. The cover suggests that the book will allow readers to 'Do your own online searching'; and find 'fast facts and answers from around the globe'; and is 'compatible with all hardware and software' – it is quite definitely aimed at the home user and contains a wealth of information to help him or her find and use appropriate sources.

Journal Articles

355. Efthimiadis, E. N. 'Progress in Documentation. Online Searching Aids: a Review of Front Ends, Gateways and Other Interfaces'. *Journal of Documentation* 46 (3) (September 1990) pp. 218-262.

The article reports on the then-current state and the potential of tools and systems designed to aid online searching. Intermediary mechanisms are examined in terms of both the end user and the intermediary and different forms of user-system interaction are discussed. The review looks at the functions of online search aids, from logon procedures to query reformulation, database selection and post processing as well as discussing costs briefly. Future trends such as Distributed Expert Based Information Systems (DEBIS), standard generalised markup language (SGML) and client-server models are also looked at. A useful overview and summary leading to some 160 further references. The section on future trends is particularly interesting in the light of progress over the last five years in such areas as client-server systems.

356. Martin, H. and **Nicholas, D.** 'End-Users Coming of Age? Six Years of End-User Searching at The Guardian'. *Online and CD-ROM Review* 17 (2) (April 1993) pp. 83-90.

The article presents the results of a questionnaire survey administered to journalists who had access to online databases over a ten year period. Many of the journalists had taken to doing their own searching. Results show that journalists are generally high-volume users with a tendency to quick-and-dirty searches. Most journalists are satisfied with the results of their searches and most showed no interest in viewing electronic facsimiles of cuttings. This was generally echoed by the student paper by Margaret Katny in *Changing Patterns of Online Information: UKOLUG State-of-the-Art Conference 1994.*

357. Mularski, C. A. and **Bradigan, P. S.** 'End-User Searching: Review of a Modular Program'. *Bulletin of the Medical Library Association* 81 (1) (January 1993) pp. 61-63.

This article updates an earlier report on an end-user instruction programme for medical students.

358. Tilson, Y. and **East, H.** 'Academic Scientists' Reaction to End-User Services: Observations on a Trial Service giving Access to MEDLINE using the Grateful Med Software'. *Online and CD-ROM Review* 18 (2) (April 1994) pp. 71-77.

The article reports on the results of a one-year study of free end-user access undertaken in 1993 and covering twenty bioscientists in two universities. Responses were viewed in the light of independent factors affecting user attitude and behaviour such as familiarity with information technology and a perceived need for bibliographic data. Most users used the software in a simplistic way not venturing beyond keyword searching and comments concerning the quality of the data or deficiencies in the software were few. Quality of network connections and access to the microcomputer received more attention.

Reports

359. Efthimiadis, E. N. *A Review of Online Searching Aids.* London: British Library, 1990. 69pp. (British Library Research Paper; 86)

Resulting from a British Library-funded research project at City University, the review indicates the (then) current state and the potential of tools and systems designed to aid online searching; it also covers areas other than information retrieval in a selective manner and makes some suggestions concerning future areas of development. The functions and features (such as automatic logon or database selection) are discussed with exemplar systems described. Of course, some of the examples are long since departed (UserKit and TomeSearcher, for example). A 155-entry Bibliography completes a useful report.

360. Wood, F. E. *Guidelines for Teachers of Online Information Retrieval.* Paris: United Nations Educational, Scientific and Cultural Organization, 1988. 81 pp. (UNESCO Report; PGI-88/WS/7).

Offers guidelines to anyone involved in teaching online information retrieval either to library school students or to potential end users of databases. The report proper is divided into seven sections which identify online searching topics, offer sample teaching programs and discuss necessary teaching facilities and equipment. A series of appendices includes an extensive listing of English-language readings on the seventeen online searching topics identified in the fourth section of the report, a glossary and list of acronyms.

Review Publications

361. Drenth, H., Morris, A. and **Tseng, G.** 'Expert Systems as Information Intermediaries'. *In* M. E. Williams (ed.) *Annual Review of Information Science and Technology* 26 (1991). pp. 113-154.

A review of the use of expert systems as online search tools with a brief general introduction and overview of the components and types of knowledge representation used in expert systems followed by an examination of prototype systems and a review of operational intermediary systems covering front ends and user-friendly interfaces for commercial online services. (152 references.)

362. Shaw, D. 'The Human-Computer Interface for Information Retrieval'. *In* M. E. Williams (ed.) *Annual Review of Information Science and Technology* 26 (1991). pp. 155-195.

The Human-Computer Interface is often the single most important factor in determining the success or failure of a system. It is also one of the most expensive. The review defines it as 'what the user sees, hears, and touches in interfacing with a computer system' and includes basic interface models, topics related to navigation, interaction styles and screen design. Topics on user interface engineering such as general guidelines, help facilities and interface evaluation are also covered. Every topic is oriented towards information technology and retrieval. The chapter begins with a review of advances in general interface design. Major application areas include online catalogues, online searching and CD-ROM products with an emphasis on working systems. (188 references.)

INFORMATION NETWORKING

Books: Electronically Distributed

363. Sternberg, S. *Business Use of the Internet.* Available via the Internet, 1995. 500pp.

A completely public-domain resource and resource guide which, if printed extends to some 500 pages, has been made freely available online. Eleven chapters discuss all aspects of business use with about half of the volume devoted to listing specific reports and resources. The chapters are: Communication Services and Resources; Improving Business Communication; Improving Internal Operations; News Sources and In-Company News Services; Resources of General Business Interest; Net Facilities by Types of Business; Net Resources for Global Commerce (in three parts covering business opportunities, information by geographic location and information about the United States); Business Research on the Internet; Developing Your office on the Net; Small Business; and The Future of Business. The full text of the book is available from servers: gopher:\gopher.phoenix.caor or ftp:\ftp.phoenix.capubor or http:\www.phoenix.cawhats-newas as well as by anonymous ftp from FTP:\gopher.epas.utoronto.ca/epas anonymous ftp directory/pub/datalib/misc/sternberg.txt.

Books

364. Dempsey, L.; Law, D. and **Mowat, I.** (eds.) *Networking and the Future of Libraries.* London: Library Association Publishing, 1995. c.288pp.

Published in association with UKOLN: The UK Office for Library and Information Networking, this collection of papers deals with the increasing proportion of intellectual record that is in electronic form and accessed through a network. The overall theme of managing the intellectual record is divided into four sections: Transforming the Organization; Producing the Intellectual Record; Accessing the Intellectual Record; and Preserving the Intellectual Record – all matters which the library community must take on board in order to handle systems of the future.

365. Harries, S. *Networking and Telecommunications for Information Systems: an Introduction to Information Networking.* London: Library Association Publishing, 1993. 247pp.

The impact of computer networking on the lives of anyone involved with information handling in the 1990s has to be dramatic and this volume examines the development of, current state of and future plans for all forms of network. The basic introduction to the technology is followed by a consideration of its impact on the information activities of users, and on the delivery of integrated information services. Particular emphasis is given to the role of networking in the public domain, to library and bibliographic networking and to the development of open systems approaches to message transfer and document delivery. High-bandwidth network requirements for multimedia are reviewed and the body of the book ends with a note on current developments in networking taking place in Europe and the USA. Appendices cover both the Internet and JANET, and contain a glossary of terms.

366. Kehoe, B. P. *Zen and the Art of the Internet: A Beginners Guide.* Englewood Cliffs, New Jersey: Prentice Hall, 1993.
This widely recommended book has its text made available on the Internet itself via anonymous FTP on FTP.CS.WIDENER.EDU in the PUB/ZEN directory. See their README file for more information on access.

367. LaQuey, T. L. and **Ryer, J. C.** *The Internet Companion: A Beginner's Guide to Global Networking.* Reading, Massachusetts: Addison-Wesley, 1993. 196pp.
The Preface states that, 'if you want to stay current in the nineties, and even into the next century, you need to learn about the Internet.' This is probably largely true and this book provides an excellent and easy-to-read introduction. The first two chapters describe the Network of Networks and the following chapters describe various aspects of its use: e-mail, finding information, finding e-mail addresses, getting more information, and getting connected. If the book has any faults, they lie in leaving the user wanting more – but then more is probably only available with actual use of the Internet – and, for the UK reader, in the North American slant. There is a useful bibliography and twenty-page list of resources. For those who collect names, the Foreword is by USA Vice President, Al Gore.

368. Marine, A.; Kirkpatrick, S.; Neou, V. and **Ward, C.** *Internet: Getting Started.* New York: Prentice Hall, 1993. 360pp.
According to the authors, the book is intended for local area network administrators who need to connect to the Internet. The first section defines the network and discusses various types of access as well as costs of connecting and data on service providers. The remainder of the book deals with the Internet itself, covering protocols, applications, and national and international Internet organisations. There is an historical backgrund and a physical description with the section on appications including electronic mail, mailing lists, File Transfer Protocol (FTP) and information on services such as Archie, Prospero and the Internet Gopher.

369. Quarterman, J. and **Carl-Mitchell, S.** *The Internet Connection: System Connectivity and Configuration.* Reading, Massachussetts: Addison-Wesley, 1993. 256pp. (A title in the UNIX and Open Systems Series).
A concise reference for system designers, system administrators and individuals trying to gain access to the Internet, the book offers assistance in setting up naming, mail and news systems. It describes the use of tools such as Archie, WAIS and Gopher; explains the many kinds of Internet access and discusses security issues and will serve

as a central source of information about the Internet with answers to technical and administratve questions.

Conferences: Papers

370. Hallam, S. 'Introducing the Internet: a Case Study'. *In Online Information 93: 17th International Online Information Meeting Proceedings, London, 7-9 December 1993.* Edited by D I Raitt. Oxford: Learned Information, 1993. pp. 443-452.
The paper deals with the author's experience of teaching Internet skills to students at The Nottingham Trent University. It describes the teaching materials and methods used to introduce students to the Internet and offers practical advice to those teaching in what can be an unpredictable environment. In discussing the problems of access from sites not supporting the full suite of utilities necessary to use the Internet to the full, Susan Hallam introduces Guest Telnet, Guest ftp, FTPMAIL and the publicly-available Gopher services. Finally, there are suggested additional readings which can be located on the Internet itself.

Conferences: Proceedings

371. Armstrong, C. J. and **Hartley, R. J.** (eds.). *Changing Patterns of Online Information: UKOLUG State-of-the-Art Conference 1994.* Oxford: Learned Information, 1994. 145pp.
The United Kingdom Online User Group (UKOLUG) holds a State-of-the-Art conference every other year with, since 1986, published proceedings. As in previous years, the proceedings contain not only the papers, but summaries of the discussions which took place after the formal presentations as well as a complete programme, delegate list and biographical details of the speakers. The theme in 1994 was reflected both in the title and in the choice of papers which coverd the Internet, Campus-Wide Information Services, SuperJANET, electronic document delivery and CD-ROM networking. A student paper – by the second winner of the UKOLUG Student Award – is also included in the proceedings.

372. Geh, H. P. and **Walckiers, M.** (eds.) *Library Networking in Europe: Proceedings of the conference held in Brussels in October 1994.* London: TFPL, 1995.
A collection of papers from leading experts which form a state-of-the-art review of achievements and likely future developments in library netwroking. An excellent reference book with chapters on document delivery, multimedia, retrospective conversion, empowering the end user, sharing and extending bibliographic services, electronic publishing, platform integration as well as networking challenges themselves. The conference was conceived to help libraries make the best use of networks and other technical developments and to share experiences at European level by the European Foundation for Library Cooperation (EFLC) in cooperation with the European Bureau of Library, Information and Documentation Associations (EBLIDA)

and Ligue des Bibliotheques Europeennes de Recherche (LIBER) with support from the European Commission.

Conferences: Regular

373. *Networking and the Future of Libraries 2.* Organized by UK Office for Library and Information Networking (UKOLN). Bath: UKOLN, 1995. Irregular.
The UK Office for Library and Information Networking (UKOLN) at Bath holds conferences frequently and this is the latest, held in April 1995. The programme reflects the issues that most interest UKOLN, the issues that librarians must face as they develop strategies for managing the intellectual record in an electronic environment. The programme centres on four topics: Transforming the Organisation; Producing the Intellectual Record; A Distributed Resource: Accessing the Intellectual Record; and Preserving the Intellectual Record and is organised into four half-day session with speakers on topics such as: 'An ordered migration? the publisher and the network'; 'Resource discovery and systematic change: a UK perspective' and 'A policy framework for legal deposit in a networked age'.

Dictionaries

374. 'A Local Area Network Glossary'. *CD-ROM Professional* 6 (1), January 1993, pp. 80-84.
Adapted from the glossary in Tom Rugg's book, *LANtastic Made Easy* (Osborne/McGraw Hill, 1992), the glossary defines 76 terms commonly used in discussing networks. The definitions are not technical although, as Rugg notes, some of the concepts are difficult and the whole makes a useful novice's guide to networking.

Directories: Online Format

375. *Directory of Scholarly Electronic Conferences.* Compiled by Diane K. Kovaks. Kent, Ohio: Kent State University Libraries.
A useful directory of lists on the Internet or BITNET in several subject areas. Users must have electronic access to receive the directory and may do so by anonymous FTP on host ksuvxa.kent.edu, directory library (get ACADLIST.README file for more information) or by sending the following e-mail message to LISTSERV@KENTVM.KENT.EDU:

```
GET ACADLIST README F=MAIL
GET ACADLIST File1 F=MAIL
GET ACADLIST File2 F=MAIL
GET ACADLIST File3 F=MAIL
GET ACADLIST File4 F=MAIL
GET ACADLIST File5 F=MAIL
```

GET ACADLIST File6 F=MAIL
GET ACADLIST File7 F=MAIL
GET ACADLIST File8 F=MAIL

For further information about the directory contact the author at DKOVAKS@KENTVM.

376. **Hallman, J.** *Campus-Wide Information Systems (CWIS).* Chapel Hill, North Carolina: University of North Carolina.

Compiled by Judy Hallman, this directory is available via anonymous FTP on FTP.OIT.UNC.EDU in the PUB/DOCS directory, filename CWIS-L.

377. *Internet Resource Guide.* Cambridge, Massachusetts: NSF Network Service Center, BBN Laboratories.

Available via anonymous FTP on NNSC.NSF.NET in the RESOURCE-GUIDE directory. A README file contains instructions.

378. **Silva, S. da.** *Publicly Accessible Mailing Lists.*

Compiled and maintained by Stephanie da Silva, this directory is posted regularly to USENET newsgroups, NEWS.LISTS, NEWS.ANNOUNCE.NEWUSERS and NEWS.ANSWERS. It is also available via anonymous FTP on PIT-MANAGER.MIT.EDU in the PUB/USENET/NEWS.ANSWERS/MAILING-LISTS directory as files PART1, PART2 and PART3.

379. **St.George, A.** and **Larsen, R.** *Internet: Accessible Library Catalogs and Databases.* New Mexico: University of New Mexico.

This directory is available via anonymous FTP on ARIEL.UNM.EDU in the LIBRARY directory. The text version is INTERNET.LIBRARY and a postscript version is LIBRARY.PS.

380. **Yanoff, S.** *Special Internet Connections.* Milwaukee, Wisconsin: University of Wisconsin.

This directory is posted regularly to the USENET alt.internet.services newsgroup and is also available via anonymous FTP on CSD4.CSD.UWM.EDU in the PUB directory with filename INET.SERVICES.TXT.

Directories: Print

381. **Bailey, C. W. jnr.** 'Library-Oriented Lists and Electronic Serials'. *ITs News: The Journal of The Library Association Information Technology Group* 28, (November 1993). pp. 36-41.

In order to use BITNET or the Internet effectively, users need to know how to connect with the various conference areas which are potentially of interest to them. This short article lists the network addresses of selected lists and electronic serials that are of interest to librarians. The list is dated August 1993 and includes two entries which will give more comprehensive information: Diane Kovaks' Directory (lists in many subject areas) and Michael Strangelove's Directory (electronic serials).

382. *Gale Guide to Internet Databases.* Detroit, MI: Gale Research Inc, 1995-. 600pp.
This new directory covers some 2,000 'authoritative' databases which are available on the Internet. Focussing on major government, academic, research and educational databases containing material in a range of formats from bibliographic to image and from textual to software bulletin boards or directories of property, the Guide gives details of all means by which the database can be accessed – gopher, telnet, ftp, e-mail and URL addresses and entries contain the database name and acronym, data providers, main file names, a database description (scope and contents), geographic coverage, charges, languages, related lists, database type, updating frequency and special instructions or search routines. Five indexes – a master index, and subject, host provider, white pages and alternative formats indexes – provide access to the databases.

383. Newby, G. B. *Directory of Directories on the Internet: A Guide to Information Sources.* Westport, Connecticut: Meckler, 1994. 153pp.
A guide to help users navigate the maze of data available on the Internet and find the resources of interest to them. The introductory chapters explain resources and use of the Internet and the various tools which can be used to locate them. The remaining chapters deal – although not comprehensively – with Resource Guides, OPACs, Mailing Lists, FTP Directories, etc. Each chapter has a brief explanation of the resources listed in it before the directory entries- proper which are quite detailed and conform to a fixed pattern. Frequently there is a sample entry. Definitely a good guide for beginners with clear explanations of the various resources.

384. Notess, G. R. *Internet Access Providers: An International Resource Directory.* Westport, Connecticut: Meckler, 1993. 230pp.
A directory of electronic bulletin boards, private companies and regional networks that offer dial-in access to the Internet. Covering Internet access providers worldwide, the directory is particularly useful for those with no current access or looking for home access.

385. *On Internet 94: An International Guide to Electronic Journals, Newsletters, Texts, Discussion Lists, and Other Resources on the Internet.* Westport, Connecticut: Meckler, 453pp. 1994-. (Annually ?)
Given the increase in scholarly and commercial electronic publishing over the Internet in the last two years, with an estimate of around 1,500 discrete publications and discussion lists, this directory provides a comprehensive guide to the full range of electronic documents available as of late-1993 – nearly 6,000 entries. The directory is divided into eight sections: Discussion Lists and Special Interest Mailing Lists;

Electronic Journals and Newsletters; Electronic Texts, Text Archives, Selected FTP Sites, and Internet Resource Guides; Freenet and Other Community-Based Information Services; Campus-Wide Information Systems; Commercial Services on the Internet; Usenet Newsgroups and Other Mailing Lists; and WAIS-Accessible Databases. For each publications, details are include on access, subscriptions and submission instructions; there is also a brief description, listings of contents, and reviews. The Subject Index lists entries under subject headings such as 'Astrophysics' or 'Austen, Jane'; each publication entry directs readers only to the appropriate section of the directory.

386. **Rosenfeld, L., Janes, J.** and **Vander Kolk, M.** *The Internet Compendium: Guides to Resources by Subject.* London: Mansell, 1995 (in press).
A comprehensive, three-volume set of Internet resource guides in over forty subject areas. Compiled by a team from the University of Michigan Internet Clearinghouse, the Compendium provides critical analysis of the content of the various sites, with listings in each subject chapter for Gopher Collections, World Wide Web servers, electronic journals, list servers, Usenet Newsgroups, full-text items, images, indexes and databases, selected library catalogues, FTP sites, government (US) agencies, Frequently-Asked Questions (FAQ) and other subject sites and fee-based services. Each chapter begins with a short introduction to the topic. For added value, an introductory section covers all the basics of the Internet – addresses, search methods and navigation – with comendable clarity and detail. All chapters in the three volumes as well as some additional subject guides are also electronically available on the Internet from the clearinghouse.

E-Mail Lists

387. BUBL (Bulletin Board for Libraries). gopher://ukoln.bath.ac.uk:7070/11/BUBL_Main_Menu
This UK-based bulletin board system has, with the spread of JANET, become an important source of news and communications between librarians in many sectors – although possibly academic librarians constitute the largest group. BUBL will give information on conferences, workshops and meetings, news items and much more. A regular subject index is posted on appropriate lists. For more information, contact Dennis Nicholson at The University of Strathclyde, Andersonian Library, 101 St John's Road, Glasgow G4 0NS; e-mail address: cijs03@vaxa.strath.ac. uk.

388. *Current Cites.* Berkeley, CA: Library, University of California, Berkeley, 1994-. Monthly.
Current Cites is an e-mail publication containing annotated citations from around thirty journals in library and information technology. Articles included cover optical disc technologies, computer networks and networking, electronic publishing, hypermedia and multimedia. The service is free and subscribers to PACS-L and

PACS-P will receive it automatically. The most current six issues are archived and can be accessed by telnet to a.cni.org with login as 'brsuser'. Current Cites is also printed in the journal, *Computers in Libraries* and some references contribute to the current awareness section in the *UKOLUG Newsletter.* To subscribe to Current Cites send a message 'sub cites your name' to listserv@library.berkeley.edu and this will lodge your Internet address on their computer.

389. INFO-NETS@THINK.COM
A mailing list for general discussion of networks, focusing in internetwork connectivity and covering worldwide netwroking questions, connections to particular sites and announcements of new networks and services. Archives are maintained and can be accessed via anonymous FTP to THINK.COM, directory MAIL. All subscription requests should be sent to info-nets-request@think.com.

390. NETTRAIN@UBVM (BITNET)
Internet and BITNET network trainers discussion list. To subscribe, send an e-mail message to LISTSERV@UBVM: SUBSCRIBE NETTRAIN First name Last name

Handbooks

391. Bradley, P. *UKOLUG Quick Guide to the Internet.* London: UKOLUG, 1995.
Like the UK Online User Group's other major publication, the *Quick Guide to Online Commands,* this volume is an attempt to de-mystify and simplify a potentially complex area for information professionals. Covering all aspects of searching the Internet with sections on FTP, World Wide Web, Veronica, etc. as well as a comprehensive glossary, this concise guide also lists resources relevant to the library professional's use of the Internet.

392. Dern, D. P. *The Internet Guide for New Users.* New York: McGraw-Hill, 1993
Described as the Internet Safety Net, this is a definitive, step-by-step guide to joining, understanding and using the Internet. Discusses the similarities with other services such as CompuServe or DELPHI and covers the methodology of logging in, file transfer, electronic mail; using tools like Archie, Gopher or WorldWideWeb; how to find out what resources are available; using online database services via the internet; and being a responsible user – the 'netiquette' of use. 'An excellent all-round guide to networking that even intermediate and advanced users will find helpful' (*UKOLUG Newsletter* 4(6) (November/December 1993) 28).

393. Fisher, S. *Riding the Internet Highway: A Complete Guide to 21st Century Communications.* Carmel, Indiana: New Riders Publishing, 1993. 266pp.
A book intended for readers with a reasonable knowledge of personal computers and possibly some experience of Bulletin Board Systems or commercial services such as CompuServe but no experience of the Internet. Recommended by one reviewer – it

'meets its goal by being a concise introductory book with enough – but not too much – information. It will best suit those who want enough information to get started but want to disciver more on their own' – the book covers connecting to the Internet; what to expect when setting up an account and how to act as a good Internet citizen. With concise explanations of basic Unix commands, security measures and guides to using e-mail, file transfer and a computer at another location, Riding the Internet Highway – replete with many screen illustrations – is a particularly valuable book. (Cady, G. H. Review in 'Internet Bookshelf'. *Internet World* 5(1) (Jan/Feb 1994) 106.)

394. Gilster, P. *Finding it on the Internet.* New York: Wiley, 1994. 288pp.
A realistic and practical guide to search tools on the Internet. A review by Robert Slade posted to the NETTRAIN list noted, 'Among the larger resource-oriented guides to the Internet, I hold Gilster's The Internet Navigator to be the best overall: clear, balanced and mature. ... Gilster has now affirmed his preeminent position on the Internet Bookshelf with this second work.' He treats Telnet as the major access route and notes e-mail servers for all applications except two. The above reviewer also noted that Gilster's enthusiasm for Gopher and World Wide Web 'is not allowed to get in the way of a fair presentation and the weaknesses of the various tools are considered briefly towards the end of the book.' All serious users should have the book at their side of their terminal.

395. Hahn, H. and **Stout, R.** *The Internet Complete Reference.* New York: Osborne/McGraw-Hill, 1994. 817pp.
Another guide to the Internet which is particularly suited to the new user. However, Robert Slade, reviewing the book on the Internet on the Internet began, 'You have to warm to the enthusiasm of a book which says that the Internet is more impressive than the pyramids, more beautiful than Michelangelo's David and more important than the inventions of the industrial revolution in the first paragraph of the Introduction.' and the book certainly does have merit. Although the book does not contain great technical insights, it does go into some depth with no less than seven chapters dealing with Usenet news, for example. Well and humourously written, the book covers everything necessary for the new or beginning user and appendices usefully list Archie servers and gopher, World Wide Web and WAIS sites.

396. Kochmer, J. *The Internet Passport: NorthWestNet's Guide to Our World Online.* NorthWest Academic Computing Consortium, 1993. 516pp.
'Competent and experienced guidance through the jungle of Internet' (Williams, D. Review in 'Internet Bookshelf'. *Internet World* 5(1) (Jan/Feb 1994) 107), which includes a well-structured outline, an extensive, outlined table of contents and a substantial index to 23 chapters focusing on how to use the Internet. Each chapter begins with a description of the topic, what it does and how to use it, and goes on with sample sessions and step-by-step instructions; most end with a bibliography. Recognising that most users still have text-only terminal connections, the author uses text-only versions of Archie, WAIS and WorldWideWeb in the examples. Williams

describes this book as 'a valuable and useful guide' with only a few minor omissions to be expected in a topic so fluid and dynamic as the Internet.

397. Krol, E. *The Whole Internet User's Guide and Catalogue.* (2nd ed) Sebastopol, California: O'Reilley & Associates, 1994.

Highlighted by Hallam (see 'Introducing the Internet: a Case Study', a paper given at *Online Information '93*) as being a comprehensive and accessible guide to Internet resources, Krol's book is already in its 2nd edition. It claims to be the complete guide to the Internet for experienced and novice users alike and is aimed at professionals in all spheres of work who could benefit from use of the Internet in their work. It is a substantial book and includes explanations of what the Internet is, how it works and what is allowed as well as of such things as remote log-in, e-mail, and file transfer. This is then extended to cover specific access methods such as gopher, WAIS, Archie, Veronica and World Wide Web. To complete the book there is a substantial directory of resources available over the Internet. Despite the American bias, the book is an excellent introduction. Only a minimal knowledge of computing is required. The book is also frequently to be seen recommended on Internet lists.

398. Tseng, G.; Poulter, A. and **Hiom, D.** *The Library and Information Professional's Guide to the Internet.* London: Library Association Publishing, 1995. c.144pp.

Claimed to be the first book written by information professionals for information professionals, this volume should take any mystique out of the Internet while providing a manageable guide to what is on offer. Contents include: Networking Fundamentals; What is Available on the Internet; How to Contact Other Users (e-mail, conference systems and live, interactive systems); Resources (text and non-text files, reference materials, information servers and OPACs); Essentials of Finding and Using Resources; and a Resource Guide with a UK Perspective.

399. Veljkov, M. and **Hartnell, G.** *Pocket Guides to the Internet* (6 volumes). Westport, Connecticut: Meckler, 1993.

Designed to provide quick and practical guidance for Internet use, the guides may be purchased separately or (at a cost saving) together. Volume 1 deals with Telneting; Volume 2 with Transferring Files with File Transfer Protocol; Volume 3 with Using and Navigating News Nets; Volume 4 with the Internet E-Mail System; Volume 5 with Accessing Internet front Ends and General Utilities; and Volume 6 with Physical Connections.

Journal Articles

400. McClure, C. R., Bertot, J. C. and **Zweizig, D. L.** *Public Libraries and the Internet: Study Results, Policy Issues and Recommendations – Final Report.*

Washington: National Commission on Libraries and Information Science, June 1994.

The report is the final result of a challenge from Vice-President Gore to US public libraries to investigate how they could act as a safety net, ensuring universal access to the information and services being made available over the rapidly expanding networks. In a rather different approach to that of the UK government, the study commissioned surveyed public library access to the Internet and noted librarians as 'rather passive novice users rather than active facilitators', identifying relevant issues as cost, staffing and the availability of appropriate skills. The quality of the material available, the security of the networks, confidentiality and copyright were not addressed. As the President is reported to have said, 'We must work with the private sector to connect every classroom, every clinic, every library and every hospital in America to a national information superhighway by the year 2000', the statistics showing that only 20.9% of public libraries have Internet access make interesting reading. As David Byrne notes, the report will make interesting reading in the UK for the range of information provided but the report would be more interesting if it had looked beyond the traditional to the virtual public library. (Byrne, D. 'The Internet: where public libraries come in ...' *Library Association Record* 97(3) March 1995 167.)

401. **Winship, I.** 'Academic and Research Networks' Column. *UKOLUG Newsletter* 5(2), March/April 1994, pp. 20-22.

This is a consistently useful column which appears regularly in the *UKOLUG Newsletter;* the particular column cited here is a good introduction for new users – especially those of us who are not fortunate enough to be connected to an academic institution with access via JANET. It addresses the problem of how to locate addresses on the Internet, how non-JANET aspirants can connect, and gives – as it generally does – some information on a few information sources which are available.

Journals: Electronically Distributed

402. *Internet Business Journal*

A free version of the journal which does not include all of the contents of its commercial forebear. In order to subscribe, send the following message to LISTSERV@PONIECKI.BERKELEY.EDU: SUBSCRIBE IBJ-L First name Last name

403. *Network News*

In order to subscribe send the following message to LISTSERV@NDSUVM1: SUBSCRIBE NNEWS First name Last name

Journals

404. *Internet Research: Electronic Networking Applications and Policy.* Westport, CT: Mecklermedia, 1991-. Quarterly.

One of the more serious journals devoted to the Internet with four of five scholarly articles in each issue tending to look at the social, political or even ethnographic issues of information networking. A section on Resource Reviews provides lengthy reviews and a final summary of 'Noted Resources'. The final issue of the year includes a comprehensive index.

405. *Internet World: The Magazine for Internet Users.* Westport, Connecticut: Mecklermedia, 1990-. Ten issues per year.

Provides a popularist selection of articles and columns on successful use of the Internet with hints and tips, book reviews and product/service reviews. Articles are sometimes illustrated with Internet Mosaic or gopher-menu screen dumps to ease the path for new users. Curiously, the magazine is still not available on the Internet itself, but the editor claims that as most access is via text-only terminals this would mean dropping their many illustrations (actually mostly artwork to liven up the pages) and would in any case limit the readership to existing Internet users; also, as he explained in answer to a reader's letter, 'the technology to make it available in a way that will pay for the labor of the participants isn't quite there yet' (Dern, D. P. Answer in Letters to the Editor. *Internet World* 5(1) (Jan/Feb 1994) 11). Which might say a lot about the Internet.

406. *Internet: The Practical Guide to What's On and Where To Go.* Ruislip: emap Business Communications, 1994-. Monthly.

A new journal covering, as its title suggests, access to resources available on the Internet. Composed mainly of regular columns, the What's On section forms a valuable, regular directory to new sites, each categorised by topic and each briefly evaluated. This, more than anything else, raises the journal above its contemporaries, demonstrating a real involvement with the Internet rather than an attempt to gain something by association. The Get On section introduces access routes and searching to the novice while Hands On is targetted at the 'more confident' user. Business users have their own section too: Who's On contains articles such as Who's Doing Business on the Net and How to do Business.

407. *New Review of Information Networking.* London: Taylor Graham, 1993-. Monthly. (Formerly: *Journal of Information Networking)*

The *Journal of Information Networking* is devoted to the use of computer networks in universities and higher education and in research for the transfer of information – networks typified by JANET and Internet. The editorial board includes experts from the UK, Europe and Canada and the content is to be mostly full-length researc articles and essay-length book reviews. A regular section, Network Resources and Access

Tools, will deal with user-oriented approach which does not presume on too much expertise. The journals contents are listed on the Bulletin Board for Libraries.

Reports

408. Arnold, S. E. *Internet 2000: The Path to the Total Network.* Calne, Wiltshire: Infonortics, 1994. 105pp.

The publicity flyer notes that between July 1992 and July 1993, the number of networks connected to the Internet rose from 5,739 to 13,293 while between July 1993 and October 1993 the number of Internet hosts rose from 1,776,000 to 2,056,000 – compelling reasons for anyone seeking information to consider the Internet. The briefing covers the history of the Internet and gives a general description of it as it is today; other sections cover Government Information on the Internet; American States' Internet plans; Doing Business Today via the Internet; International Applications; Network Technology; Protecting Intellectual Property and Information; Internet's Impact on Software Innovation; and The Path to the Total Network. There is also a glossary, a bibliography, tables and figures showing the growth of the Internet, comparisons of billing structures and network architecture bandwidth, as well as an index. In her review (*Library Association Record* 96 (10) (October 1994) p. 561), Gwyneth Tseng points out that this is neither a practical guide nor an academic study; rather, it is a readable and well- researched briefing giving a strategic overview of the potentials and pitfalls of the Internet. Stephen Arnold sets out to identify the political, economic, technological and legal and social imperatives that will 'shape the face of the Internet towards the year 2000.'

409. Breaks, M. and **Wood, S.** *SuperJANET.* London: The Library Information Technology Centre, 1993. 14pp. (Library & Information Briefings, No. 47)

Following a brief introductory background to JANET (Joint Academic NETwork), the Briefing goes on to describe the high-performance SuperJANET. After listing the sites to be connected at each phase and mapping the network links, there is a summary of SuperJANET multimedia projects – the high speeds make such things possible – such as Pathnet, a pilot to explore the potential for remote consultation of pathologists. Library and information applications include access to manuscripts, information delivery and electronic journals while humanities potential includes access to museums and galleries: all are covered. The report ends with a brief section on issues to be addressed and the thought that SuperJANET is only limited by the imagination of its users.

410. Bubley, D. and **Bennett, P.** *Information Superhighways: the New Information Age.* Camborne: FT Management Reports, 1995.

This management report published by the Financial Times assesses and analyses the nature and status of both the technology and its management issues. It examines participating industries, key regulatory issues, existing and emerging technologies, the role of the business sector as a key user, the potential of the consumer market place, and the changing involvement of government. Chapters on technology (ISDN, ATM, frame relay, LANs), regulatory issues (the impact of technical standards, deregulation, copyright, etc), corporate networking, public telecommunications networks, cable television networks (the role of cable operators in the wider communications/media marketplace and the use of fibre optic networks as a delivery mechanism for new services), satellite and mobile communications (the status of traditional service providers and the potential for broadband and universal services via the planned emergence of global mobile satellite networks), applications (vertical markets, uses of the superhighway and the differing views of business, the general public and academia), strategic issues (government development of the sector, investment requirements, competitive dynamics) and trends are followed by a full glossary of industry terminology.

411. Parker, A. and **Attwood, R.** *Business Applications of the Internet: Commercial Opportunity or Media Hype?* London: Financial Times Telecoms & Media Publishing, 1995.

In the light of the comment in their own paper, the *Financial Times* (26 July 1995), noting that while many business people had left the Internet to students and academics because they were unsure how to make money out of it, even sceptics cannot ignore it forever, this report sets out to analyse the scale and nature of the opportunities offered by a global network. The report offers an unbiased coverage of the Internet: its nature, its practical realities for commerce, existing opportunities for profit, the position of the Internet in terms of its competition, existing successful business activity, and benefits and pitfalls. An introduction and a conclusion surround nine chapters on Background, Growth and Commercialism; Commercial Potential; Services and Software – Commercial Activity and Opportunity; Internal Business Applications; Business-to-Business Commercial Activity; Consumer-Oriented Commercial Applications; Enhanced Versatility Through Technological Change; Assessment of Regional Issues; and Commercial Online Systems: an Alternative to the Internet?

INFORMATION RETRIEVAL SYSTEMS

Books

412. Ellis, D. *New Horizons in Information Retrieval.* London: Library Association Publishing, 1990.

Not a textbook but a book which introduces major themes which have preoccupied information retrieval researchers in recent years. There is a chapter on the origins of information retrieval research: the Cranfield tradition; this is followed by chapters on statistical and probabilistic retrieval, cognitive user modelling, expert intermediary systems and, finally, a chapter on associations, relations and hypertext. At the time of compilation, the book is out of print but a new version called *Prospects and Problems of Information Retrieval* is expected in 1996 or 1997.

413. Gerrie, B. *Online Information Systems: Use and Operating Characteristics, Limitations and Design Alternatives.* Arlington, Virginia: Information Resources Press, 1983. 189pp.

Addresses a range of factors which influence the performance of online information retrieval systems, especially database design and structure, vocabulary control, the process of retrieval and the search strategies employed by different users. In his Foreword, F. W. Lancaster notes that for a long time (in 1983) there had been a need for a book dealing with the overall design of information retrieval systems and factors affecting their performance – Gerrie's book 'has done an admirable job' in examining such systems from both the viewpoint of the designer and that of the user, and successfully demonstrating the range of factors – intellectual, rather than mechanical – which govern their performance. Although now not the most current of books, its breadth of coverage in the area of the design of information systems merits its retention here.

414. Judge, P. and **Gerrie, B.** (eds.) *Small Scale Bibliographic Databases.* Sydney: Academic Press, 1986. 198pp. (Library and Information Science).

Eleven contributions address aspects of planning, managing and marketing a database. Full consideration is given to making provision for comprehensive and flexible information retrieval.

415. Kemp, D. A. *Computer-Based Knowledge Retrieval.* London: Aslib, 1988. 399pp.

Examines the different components of computer-based information retrieval systems: the users, retrieval software, knowledge representation, expert systems, database management systems, hardware and user interfaces. The remaining chapters cover the evaluation of systems and software, controlled vocabularies and the characteristics of ideal information systems. The work is of interest to systems designers, database producers and online searchers and includes an extensive glossary and a bibliography of almost 1,000 references which is indexed by subject and author.

416. Lancaster, F. W. and **Warner, A. J.** *Information Retrieval Today.* (revised ed.) Arlington, VA: Information Resources Press, 1993. 341 pp.
A revised, retitled and expanded version of Lancaster's well-known text, Information Retrieval Systems: Characteristics, Testing and Evaluation. It provides a good broad account of the current state of information retrieval and thus places the searching of OPAC, online and CD-ROM databases in a broader context by looking at the problems of indexing, the factors affecting retrieval performance and the evaluation of IR systems. Topics include automatic indexing, linguistics, semantics, evaluation and quality control and input and output processes.

417. Rowley, J. E. *Organizing Knowledge: an Introduction to Information Retrieval* (2nd ed.). Aldershot: Ashgate, 1992. 510 pp.
Designed as a standard introductory textbook for students on postgraduate and undergraduate courses in librarianship and information management, the second edition – a 'significant re-write' – incorporates such topics as networks for online retrieval, computer databases and international telecommunications networks. It is an integrated overview of information retrieval with a practical approach which explains common principles. Chapters of particular interest here are those dealing with indexing and those in Part IV on online, optical discs and networks. This is a thorough book with a huge scope; necessarily, and as suggested by the title, the relevant chapters are an introduction to their particular specialities.

Conferences: Papers

418. McSéan, T.; Rowlands, J. and **Forrester, W.** 'Becoming a Micro-host: Using Desktop Computers to run an Online Retrieval Service.' *In Online Information 93: 17th International Online Information Meeting Proceedings, London, 7-9 December 1993.* Edited by D I Raitt. Oxford: Learned Information, 1993. pp. 367-376.
The British Medical Association Library now provides a full-scale MEDLINE information retrieval system as a free service to its members. This paper introduces the service – believed to be the first of its kind – and gives a brief technical description. It then goes on to describe problems in implementation, gives a frank but basically favourable analysis of the Library's relationship with their system of choice (CD-Plus) and a discussion of copyright and licensing issues raised by a service of this type. BMA members can now dial into the Library's CD-Plus MEDLINE database from around the United Kingdom and the paper closes with a summary of the benefits and the problems which have been encountered.

E-Mail Lists

419. CWIS-L@WUVMD (BITNET)
Discussion forum/e-mail list on campus-wide information systems. To subscribe, send an e-mail message to LISTSERV@WUVMD: SUBSCRIBE CWIS-L First name Last name

Journal Articles

420. Feldman, S E. 'Searching Natural Language Systems: Searcher Know Thy Engine'. *Searcher* 2 (8), October 1994, pp. 34-36, 38-39.
On the basis that it is necessary to know the search engine if the best is to be got from it, Feldman sets out to explain in lay language what such non-Boolean (or Beyond Boolean) systems can and cannot do. She concludes that personal intelligent digital librarians foraging in cyberspace to bring back precisely what is needed and no more may be the thing of the 'misty future' but today's search engines have a long way to go. Side bars give natural language searching tips ('Throw lots of words at the question. The more the better') and describe four such search engines (Personal Librarian, SMART, ConQuest and TextWise's DR-Link).

Journals

421. *Information Processing and Management: an International Journal.* Oxford: Elsevier, 1963-. Bimonthly.
With text in English, French, German and Italian, this journal concentrates on the publication of detailed research articles on database theory and the design of information storage and retrieval systems. There are occasional critical reviews of the ways in which online databases are structured for searching. Of most interest to search practitioners is the wide range of book reviews in most issues, which includes reference works such as commercial database and software directories as well as textbooks.

422. *Journal of Documentation.* London: Aslib, 1944-. Bimonthly.
A largely theoretical journal dealing with the documentation aspects of librarianship and information science. In more recent years the subject coverage has been less tightly drawn and recent articles have included CD-ROM and hypertext, Welsh-language free-text retrieval, and pictorial information as well as the more traditional citation counting and Lotka's law on self-citing. The journal also contains book reviews and letters. All articles are peer-reviewed.

423. *Journal of Information Science: Principles and Practice.* East Grinstead: Bowker-Saur, 1979-. Bimonthly.

This is the major research journal of Britain's Institute of Information Scientists and offers substantial, theoretical or research articles on the design, operation and evaluation of information retrieval systems. Most issues include brief communications summarizing ongoing or recently completed research and regular space is provided for a column on legal issues of concern to the library and information sector

424. *Journal of the American Society for Information Science.* New York: Wiley, 1950-. Bimonthly.

Consists mainly of research articles on theoretical aspects of information science and information systems evaluation – usually about five or six per issue. Searcher behaviour, search techniques, indexing practices and vocabulary control in databases are regular themes. Book review feature regularly. Each year there are one or two special issues relating to a particular topic: 'Perspectives on...'. Of recent interest are: Human-Computer Interfaces (1992 32(2)); Information Technology Standards (1992 32(8)); and Digital Libraries (1993 33(8)).

MANAGEMENT OF ONLINE INFORMATION SERVICES

Bibliographies

425. *Database Design.* Springfield, Virginia: U.S. Department of Commerce. National Technical Information Service. (NTIS order number: PB92-861665CBY).
Compiled from the INSPEC database, this bibliography contains references with abstracts relevant to the design of databases – both in-house and online. NTIS Published Searches are custom-made bibliographies undertaken in the week of order by NERAC Inc on behalf of NTIS. Thus, up-to-date results from a fixed profile can be dispatched as and when needed.

Books

426. *Code of Practice for Information Brokers.* Luxembourg: EUSIDIC, 1993. 17pp.
As a part of the IMPACT Programme the Commission od the EEC has supported the work of EUSIDIC, the European Association of Information Services, EIIA, the European Information Industry Association and EIRENE, the European Information Research Network in producing this Code of Practice. Following a brief introduction on the importance of information to industry and business and the role of the information broker, the code of practice presents three definitions of the term Information Broker and then lays out the Code under the headings, Ethical Principles (Integrity, Confidentiality, Business Ethics, and Objectivity); and Quality of Service to the Client (Good Business Practice, Professional Competence, Confidentiality, Liability and Advertising, and Competition). The Code is clearly laid out and couched in unequivocable terms: 'The Broker shall: ...' or 'Within the client's budget and time frame, the Broker shall: ...'. The Code of Practice is free and may be obtained from EUSIDIC.

427. **Katz, B.** (ed.) *Reference and Online Services Handbook: Guidelines, Policies and Procedures for Libraries. Volume II.* New York: Neal-Schuman, 1986. 602pp.
Includes a collection of policy statements for online service provision from twenty-nine US libraries, mainly in the academic sector. These statements, acting primarily as guidelines for staff, are supplemented by listings of publicity material aimed at library users from sixteen libraries. This work adds to a similar treatment of online search policies which was issued under the same title in 1982 by the same publisher.

428. Lee, J. H. (ed.) *Online Searching: the Basics, Settings and Management.* Englewood, Colorado: Libraries Unlimited, 1989. 130pp. (Database Searching Series; 3).

Like Janice Sieburth's book, the intention, as expressed in the Preface, is to assist administrators, managers and searchers with the experiences of experts facing the same problems. This collection of contributions by eleven authors updates an earlier edition in 1984 and examines the management of library-based online search services in terms of staffing, training requirements, search evaluation, the search interview, search strategy, analysis and evaluation, finance, and usage monitoring. Management issues associated with end-use searching and CD-ROM are also addressed. Separate chapters discuss the administration of service provision in different types of library.

429. Sieburth, J. F. *Online Search Services in the Academic Library: Planning, Management, and Operation.* Chicago: American Library Association, 1988. 331pp.

The author's career in the online world – from searcher in 1975 to trainer and ultimately coordinator – make her perfectly suited to produce a volume intended to assist the manager of an online service and which offers a comprehensive treatment of the many issues involved in managing an online search service in the academic environment. All stages are covered, from the original proposal to establish a service, through its operation and management, to its expansion into end-user programmes. Among the issues discussed are equipment and software selection, training of searchers, charging policies, budgeting, procedure manuals, statistics keeping and reporting, management of search teams and implications of the service for other library operations. An annotated reading list at the end of the book describes sources of current awareness for searchers.

Directories: Print

430. *Burwell Directory of Information Brokers* (10th ed.) Oxford: Learned Information, 1993. 550pp.

A guide which links those who have a need for information with the experts who specialise in information retrieval and document delivery. The *Directory* includes details of nearly 1,400 information brokers from around the world, with companies listed by country and five indexes offering selection by subject expertise, company, individual name, city and subject.

Journal Articles

431. Bates, M. E. 'Cost Control: Using Automatic Accounting Features to Monitor Search Costs'. *Online* 17 (1) (January 1993) pp. 39-43.

Microcomputers can be used to track search costs and DIALOGLINK Commuications Manager provides each terminal with its own log and compilation of costs, however, the article notes that it is still necessary to cross check the monthly invoice against the log. Bates goes on to discuss the relative merits of system-specific accounting software and that supplied with communications packages such as CROSSTALK or ProComm. Online accounting features arc also noted.

Journals

432. *Managing Information.* London: Aslib, 1993-. Ten issues per year.
A well-designed journal with the usual mix of news items, articles and reviews. Typically, subject coverage might include online and CD-ROM databases, publishing CD-ROMs in-house and education for information, plus several well- written book and journal reviews, two or three CD-ROM reviews and general, Internet and European news items. Articles are not over-long and are practical in nature. In the issue before the December Online Conference in London, every news item was flagged with stand numbers.

MICROCOMPUTER HARDWARE AND SOFTWARE

Abstracting and Indexing Services

433. *Microcomputer Abstracts: a Comprehensive Abstracts Journal Covering Microcomputing and Related Subjects.* Medford, New Jersey: Learned Information, 1980-. Quarterly, with annually cumulated indexes.

Each year contains some 12,000 abstracts of articles and 6,000 software, hardware and literature reviews from more than eighty magazines and journals, mostly from the computing field but including some of the major titles on online information retrieval and library automation. Entries are arranged in eight sections according to article type, the most valuable being those for buyer's guides, hardware reviews, software reviews and product announcements. Relevant subject headings within these categories include 'CD-ROM', 'Data Communications', 'Information Retrieval' and 'Online Information'. Five indexes allow access by author, company name, product name, compatible hardware and software and subject. The Company Name index provides access to citations to articles on the activities of over 4,000 companies. Available online and on CD-ROM.

Bibliographies

434. 'Bibliography of Text Information Management Software for IBM Microcomputers and Compatibles'. Compiled by P. Nieuwenhuysen. *The Electronic Library* 8 (4) (August 1990) pp. 254-278.

This bibliography was first published in the August 1988 issue of *The Electronic Library* and updated in the December 1989 issue. Its coverage focuses on software for online or documentation work, the major applications being communications, data reformatting, database creation, and word processing. Entries in the original bibliography are arranged alphabetically by author with software name and application indexes. Source coverage is international.

Books: Chapter

435. Tseng, G. 'Expert Systems and Online Information Retrieval'. *In The Application of Expert Systems in Libraries and Information Centres.* Edited by Anne Morris. East Grinstead: Bowker-Saur, 1992. pp. 167-193.

An in-depth review of the literature and applications of expert systems used to enhance online searching and retrieval. Following a brief look at online information retrieval systems, the chapter moves to front-end search aids such as REX, CONIT and the theoretical model, MONSTRAT before exploring the domain and problems which have to be addressed by such systems: establishing the information needs, user modelling, the selection of online sources and the planning and the formulation of the search. The penultimate section briefly describes four front-end systems (including the ill-fated TOME SEARCHER) and the final section looks to the future: as Tseng says, so far virtually everything has been a research prototype and has yet to prove its commercial viability. 'Perhaps with investment and backing from the information industry itself, they yet might.' The chapter includes 69 references.

Books

436. Alberico, R. *Microcomputers for the Online Searcher.* Westport, Connecticut: Mecklermedia, 1987. 299pp. (Supplement to Small Computers in Libraries; no. 3).

Explains in detail how the component elements of microcomputer hardware and software for online searching work, including system units, modems, printers, operating systems, utilities, software for communications and post-processing, front-ends, gateways and expert systems. The work is enhanced by illustrations of hardware and by examples of individual software packages in action. In general, the emphasis is on ways of making the most of the capabilities of microcomputers in online searching. A glossary of communications, hardware and software terms is provided, along with a directory of US suppliers of products described in the book. Advances in telecommunications mean that references to modem speeds, etc are dramtically out-of-date but, apart from this, the book offers good coverage.

437. Benson, J. A. and **Weinberg, B. H.** (eds.) *Gateway Software and Natural Language Interfaces: Options for Online Searching.* Ann Arbor, Michigan: Pierian Press, 1988. 204pp. (Library Hi Tech Special Studies Series; 2).

The bulk of this work consists of a series of critical evaluations of individual telecommunications and gateway software products which facilitate end-user searching. Other sections offer chapters on gateway services and on applications of natural language interfaces and artificial intelligence in information retrieval. Although many of the products will by now have undergone revisions and upgrades, most will have essentially the same features so that this is an invaluable guide. Some newer products such as the CompuServe Information Manager (CIM/WinCIM) or the Ameol off-line reader for Compulink Information Exchange (CiX) are, of course, not mentioned and all the products included are pre-Windows versions. An extensive bibliography of 715 references is provided, with a bias towards US literature. There is also a glossary of major terms and a directory of gateway and telecommunications software with US suppliers. There is also a subject/product/author index which includes authors mentioned in chapter bibliographies.

438. **Bradley, P.** *CD-ROMs: How to Set Up your Workstation.* London: Aslib, 1995. 50pp.

One of the most often encountered problems for those working with CD-ROMs is that of configuring a microcomputer to access and read one or more disc-based products. This know-how guide provides the basic knowledge – both strategic and practical – for setting up such a CD-ROM workstation. Covering such topics as installation, software and trouble shooting, the guide is intended for the user with no prior knowledge of either microcomputers or CD-ROM technology. For more experienced users, it provides a useful checklist. The contents include: What is a CD-ROM? What computer should I use? What CD-ROM drive should I purchase? Installing the CD-ROM drive; Installing SCSI drives; Installing Microsoft Extensions; Maintaining your system; What to do if you have problems; Ringing technical support; Choosing a CD-ROM publisher; Creating a menu; Networking drives; The future of CD-ROM technology; and Sources of further information. Phil Bradley has been training users in CD-ROM use for many years and is considered one of the most knowledgeable in the field, running frequent training courses for Aslib.

439. **Lane, E. S.** *Microcomputer Management and Maintenance for Libraries.* Westport, Connecticut: Mecklermedia, 1990. 225pp.

Offers practical guidance on the maintenance of microcomputer hardware and software in libraries, outlining associated costs and staffing requirements.

440. **Tedd, L. A.** *An introduction to computer-based library systems.* (3rd ed.) New York: Wiley, 1993. 316pp.

With each edition, Lucy Tedd's text book on the current state of computers in libraries is faced with the problem of reflecting the many changes taking place – as the author herself notes, such changes mean that a text like this can only provide a snapshot of the topic. That the snapshot is in its third edition testifies to the success of the author's eye. The book concludes with a section on local information retrieval and online and CD-ROM databases which, like the other sections, provides the reader with an effective overview. As George Geddes says, this is a book that 'can be confidently recommended to anyone requiring a readable account' (*Library Association Record* 96 (4) April 1994. p. 219).

Conferences: Regular

441. *Computers in Libraries International.* Organized by Learned Information from 1995. (1987-1994: London: Mecklermedia, 1986-.) Oxford: Learned Information, 1995-. Annual.

Meckermedia proceedings for this conference consisted of short versions of papers whose subject scope corresponds closely to that of its sister event in the United States. Papers are mostly presented by speakers from Britain. The conference title changed from SCIL (Small Computers in Libraries) to Computers in Libraries Intenational in

1990, a year later than for the US event. Computers in Libraries International is held in March in London each year.

442. *Computers in Libraries.* Organized by Learned Information from 1995. (1986-1994: Westport, Connecticut: Mecklermedia, 1986-.) Medford, NJ: Learned Information, 1995-. Annual.
Formerly known as SCIL (Small Computers in Libraries), this conference focuses on the integration and application of microcomputers in all aspects of library and information centre management. Mecklermedia published short versions of around sixty papers in the proceedings in alphabetical order of author surnames with an index by session number and title. Speakers' addresses and telephone numbers were listed at the end of the volume for anyone requiring further information. Sessions have been devoted to topics such as the Internet, CD-ROM, microcomputer management and maintenance, operating systems, artificial intelligence and expert systems, optical disc applications in libraries, new software, trends in online information retrieval, local area networks and microcomputer training for library staff. Presenters are mostly from the United States or Canada. British and European experience are the province of Computers in Libraries International.

Directories: Online Format

443. *Buyer's Guide to Micro Software (SOFT).* Weston, Connecticut: Online. Monthly.
Produced by a major publisher in the field of online information, this file emphasizes software for library and information purposes within a wide range of business applications. In each case a full description of the product – including review information – and its operating requirements is provided. Other information includes supplier address, price, documentation, and bibliographic details, with abstracts, of a representative selection of published reviews. The file contains over 6,000 records and can be searched on KR DIALOG who note that the file is 'highly selective' listing packages rated as 'good' by the technical press, all packages from major software producers even if 'negatively reviewed', and packages unique to specific business segments, with special emphasis placed on library and medical software. Until 1990 the database was called Micro Software Directory (SOFT).

Directories: Print

444. *Computers in Libraries Buyer's Guide and Consultant Directory.* Compiled by D Scott Brandt. Westport, Connecticut: Mecklermedia. Annual. 88 pp.
Issued with the July/August issue of the journal *Computers in Libraries,* this directory comprises five sections, the first two of which list over 150 hardware and software product and service categories which are often associated with computer applications in libraries. These sections include the names of supplying companies and the types

of hardware which they support. The next section is arranged by company name and indicates the types of product and service with which each is associated. Remaining sections provide full address data for these vendors and for consultants.

445. Library Information Technology Centre. *European Directory of Software for Libraries and Information Services.* (5th ed.) Aldershot: Ashgate, 1993. 251pp.
Following on from the four editions of the *Directory of Library and Information Retrieval Software for Microcomputers,* this volume concentrates on software that is both actively marketed in Europe and has good background support. (Europe is defined as including both the twelve EC countries and Sweden, Norway, Finland, Switzerland and Austria.) The coverage is restricted to microcomputer software that runs under MS-DOS; PC-DOS; OS/2; UNIX; PICK and the Apple Macintosh operating systems and some 280 packages are described. Descriptions provide supplier name, operating system, hardware requirements, price, a brief description of software features and capabilities and references to published product reviews. The Directory is arranged in a single alphabetical sequence by software name with country, operating system and supplier indexes. Paul Burton (Reviews. *Program* 27(3) (July 1993). p. 318) notes that the reviews are 'non-evaluative, and occasionally a little vendor's hype leaks through' but believes that the new edition will be a useful source 'and may well repay its purchase price ... the first time it is used to answer a question like 'which cataloguing product also offers free-text retrieval?' It will not remove the subsequent task of evaluating suppliers and products for viability and competence, but it makes a good start.'

Journal Articles

446. Efthimiadis, E. N. 'Progress in Documentation. Online Searching Aids: a Review of Front Ends, Gateways and Other Interfaces'. *Journal of Documentation* 46 (3) (September 1990) pp. 218-262.
The article reports on the then-current state and the potential of tools and systems designed to aid online searching. Intermediary mechanisms are examined in terms of both the end user and the intermediary and different forms of user-system interaction are discussed. The review looks at the functions of online search aids, from logon procedures to query reformulation, database selection and post processing as well as discussing costs briefly. Future trends such as Distributed Expert Based Information Systems (DEBIS), standard generalised markup language (SGML) and client-server models are also looked at. A useful overview and summary leading to some 160 further references. The section on future trends is particularly interesting in the light of progress over the last five years in such areas as client-server systems.

447. Stigleman, S. 'Bibliographic Formatting Software: a Buying Guide'. *Database* 15 (1) February 1992. pp. 15-27.

Bibliographic formatting software takes records downloaded from an online or CD-ROM database and formats them into another specified citation style. Forty-three bibliographic formatting programs are identified and listed with supplier information. Each producer was asked to supply answers to eight questions and these are published in full and in a series of tables.

Journals

448. *Computers in Libraries.* Medford, NJ: Learned Information, 1981-. Ten per year.

The main theme of this journal is the optimum exploitation of microcomputers for all library applications, including information retrieval from online, CD- ROM, the Internet and personal databases. Articles are of a practical nature, advising on new applications for general purpose and library software and on software or system selection. New products are announced and reviewed as they emerge. Book reviews and news sections are included in each issue. Until 1989 the journal was known as Small Computers in Libraries and until late 1994 was published by Mecklermedia. It is searchable online in the full-text database Trade and Industry ASAP.

449. *Information Technology and Libraries.* Chicago: American Library Association, 1968-. Quarterly.

Articles fall within the context of information technology applications to library procedures: library automation, communications technology, cable systems, computerised information processing and video technologies. Contributions on database software, expert systems and CD-ROM technology may also be included. Each issue contains a book reviews section in which from five to ten new publications, mostly American and many dealing with online searching, are critically evaluated. Non-print items are also featured.

450. *Library Software Review.* Westport, Connecticut: Mecklermedia, 1981-. Bimonthly.

The major function of this title is to publish review articles which evaluate software packages for the full range of library applications. Each review looks at the software in depth and includes sample screens showing the package in action. The journal also carries a number of articles describing user experience with library software. An additional feature is a book reviews section. The full text of the journal is included in the online database Trade and Industry ASAP.

451. *Microcomputers for Information Management: an International Journal for Library and Information Services.* Norwood, New Jersey: Ablex, 1984-. Quarterly.

This journal carries articles on applications of microcomputers in library and information service environments internationally, sometimes in developing countries. In-house database creation and maintenance are frequently discussed.

452. *Personal Computer World.* London: VNU Business Publications, 1978-. Monthly.

Provides a British perspective on microcomputer technology developments. News pages are followed by articles describing and evaluating new products, including printers, software for data storage and retrieval and utilities for file management, are published in each issue. Book reviews are also a regular feature. Advertising is extensive throughout.

453. *Program: Automated Library and Information Systems.* London: Aslib, 1966-. Quarterly.

A journal of refereed papers on all aspects of information science and automation. Each issue normally contains four articles as well as some brief communications, news items and book reviews. The articles are more or less equally divided between those dealing with library systems implementations; online, CD-ROM and Internet use; and information retrieval.

454. *The Electronic Library: the International Journal for Minicomputer, Microcomputer and Software Applications in Libraries.* Oxford: Learned Information, 1983-. Bimonthly.

Edited since its inception by David Raitt, this journal provides coverage of developments in information technology and their applications or implications for library services. Areas of coverage include networking, expert systems, database searching, online information retrieval and CD-ROM technology. Product information is supplied through an extensive news service and in review sections for hardware and software. Commentary on technological developments and advice on applications can be found in separate columns for IBM and Macintosh computers and in regular technology tutorials. Articles by skilled industry experts and users with practical advice and actual experience supplement other papers. Numerous detailed and critical book reviews appear in each issue, while current awareness is supplied through a feature called 'Peripheral Press' in which articles from a number of journals in the information and computing fields are summarized. A calendar of meetings and trade shows worldwide is also included.

Newsletters

455. *Library Micromation News.* London: Library and Information Technology Centre, 1984-. Five issues per year.

A regular source of practical information on the use of microcomputer equipment and software in libraries and online and CD-ROM searching as well as related areas such as personal bibliographic databases. Coverage usually takes the form of a series of short articles and a news section for the announcement of new products. Articles may offer advice on equipment selection or review specific software packages, frequently with case studies of their use.

456. *T I P Applications: Monthly Information for Libraries and Information Services.* London: Information Partnership, 1987-. Ten issues per year.

T I P (formerly *C & L) Applications* covers the online and CD-ROM fields within the framework of library automation as a whole as well as expert systems, desktop publishing, text and data capture and conversion and communications software. Areas of interest which feature regularly are networks, gateways, CD-ROM, and database software. Contributions are usually brief but lively and practical with a UK slant. Many offer tips on ways of getting the best out of hardware and software for information storage and retrieval. The news section announces new products, software upgrades, databases and research grants. New publications and forthcoming events are listed also.

This newsletter has ceased publication; the last issue was February 1996.

Online and CD-ROM Databases

457. *Computer Database.* Foster City, CA: Information Access Company, 1983-. Weekly.

Searchable on both KR Data-Star and KR DIALOG with no print equivalent as well as on Westlaw, LEXIS/NEXIS and Dow Jones. Full text is included for fifty per cent of the articles currently indexed from January 1988 onwards. The list of source journals has been reduced sharply from over 600 to its present total of 180. The bias is towards the more popular computing magazines and newsletters. Online and CD-ROM technology feature within this coverage with an emphasis on product announcements and software reviews. There are over 40,000 evaluations or reviews of hardware, software and peripherals on the database. A CD-ROM version, updated monthly and containing full text for a limited number of periodicals is offered by Ziff Communications as part of the Computer Select database.

458. *Microcomputer Abstracts.* Medford, New Jersey: Learned Information, 1981-Monthly.

The online version of the printed abstracting and indexing service with the same title can be searched on KR DIALOG while it can be found as one of the three databases on Expert Information's CD-ROM (with Index to Theses and Business Software Database) and on SilverPlatter's CD-ROM. Records from the database also contribute to University Microfilms International's Computer Abstracts CD-ROM.

Overviews

459. *Library Technology Reports: Authoritative Information on Library Systems, Equipment and Suppliers.* Chicago: American Library Association, 1965-. Bi-monthly.

Commissioned by the American Library Association, this series provides detailed reports on areas of technology. Among these have been online services, optical media, and computer printers.

Reports

460. Efthimiadis, E. N. *A Review of Online Searching Aids.* London: British Library, 1990. 69pp. (British Library Research Paper; 86)

Resulting from a British Library-funded research project at City University, the review indicates the (then) current state and the potential of tools and systems designed to aid online searching; it also covers areas other than information retrieval in a selective manner and makes some suggestions concerning future areas of development. The functions and features (such as automatic logon or database selection) are discussed with exemplar systems described. Of course, some of the examples are long since departed (UserKit and TomeSearcher, for example). A 155-entry Bibliography completes a useful report.

461. Ramsden, H. and **Ramsden, S.** *The Use of Information Technology by Information Services: the Aslib Information Technology Survey 1990.* London: Aslib, 1990. 91pp.

Presents the results of a survey which attracted responses from 373 Aslib members on the implementation of information technology in British libraries and information centres. It contains details of hardware and software used for library purposes, including online and CD-ROM information retrieval and associated activities, with brief comments on user experience in many cases. Among the categories of hardware surveyed were microcomputers, printers, modems and CD-ROM drives. Software applications included text retrieval, communications and networking.

Review Publications

462. Drenth, H., Morris, A. and **Tseng, G.** 'Expert Systems as Information Intermediaries'. *In* M E Williams (ed.) *Annual Review of Information Science and Technology* 26 (1991). pp. 113-154.

A review of the use of expert systems as online search tools with a brief general introduction and overview of the components and types of knowledge representation used in expert systems followed by an examination of prototype systems and a review of operational intermediary systems covering front ends and user-friendly interfaces for commercial online services. 152 references.

463. Shaw, D. 'The Human-Computer Interface for Information Retrieval'. *In* M E Williams (ed.) *Annual Review of Information Science and Technology* 26 (1991). pp. 155-195.

The Human-Computer Interface is often the single most important factor in determining the success or failure of a system. It is also one of the most expensive. The review defines it as 'what the user sees, hears, and touches in interfacing with a computer system' and includes basic interface models, topics related to navigation, interaction styles and screen design. Topics on user interface engineering such as general guidelines, help facilities and interface evaluation are also covered. Every topic is oriented towards information technology and retrieval. The chapter begins with a review of advances in general interface design. Major application areas include online catalogues, online searching and CD-ROM products with an emphasis on working systems. (188 references.)

MULTIMEDIA

Books

464. Botto, F. *Multimedia and Your PC.* Chichester, West Sussex: Sigma/John Wiley, 1994. 250pp.

A detailed and practical text covering everything from the development of the multimedia PC (MPC) to authoring sophisticated multimedia combining video animations and stereo sound. The book is said to be comprehensive, covering topics such as authoring, multimedia presentations, courseware, leisure titles, the transcription of books into multimedia, and the setting up of a multimedia workstation. There is in-depth coverage of CD-ROM, CD-R, Photo-CD, CD-ROM XA, DVI, scanners, digital cameras and still video cameras. The work is specific to the IBM PC-compatible family of computers.

465. Botto, F. *Multimedia, CD-ROM and Compact Disc* (2nd ed.). Chichester, West Sussex: Sigma/John Wiley, 1993. 240pp.

The book addresses CD-ROM and interactive multimedia and the new edition includes new techniques of data storage and compression as well as full-motion video. The publishers say that readers of any background will find the book useful with sections including: the Origins of CD-ROM; Platforms and Technology (DVI, CD-I, CD-ROM XA, CDTV, Macintosh HyperCard, Workstations, Image sources); General Applications (Libraries, Point of Sales, Reference, Entertainment); Education and Training; System Development; and CD-ROM Production. There are also appendices of hardware suppliers and sources of further information.

466. Brinson, J. D. and **Radcliffe, M. E.** *Multimedia Law Handbook.* Menlo Park, CA: Ladera Press, 1994.

Aimed at developers and publishers, this volume covers legal issues such as the Compton NewMedia patent dispute and the idea that copyright law will have to be fundamentally altered to address multimedia. According to the review in *CD-ROM World* (Liebman, H. 'Legal Ease' review. *CD-ROM World* 9(7) (July/August 1994) 107) the book is laid out in a clean and logical style that makes finding relevant information easy. There are four main sections: Building Blocks; Production Relationships; Other Production Issues; and Post-Production Issues, together covering basic legal precepts, development agreements, rights and licences, naming the product and protecting intellectual rights. Almost a third of the books is taken up by the appendices – sample licences, model release forms, etc. An online preview of the book can be obtained by way of the Internet at obs@marketplace.com so it is possible to see if the US$74.95 will be money well spent. A bimonthly newsletter on related issues is promised.

Conferences: Papers

467. White, A. 'Copyright Law, Information Services and the Challenge of Multimedia'. *In Online Information 93: 17th International Online Information Meeting Proceedings, London, 7-9 December 1993.* Edited by D I Raitt. Oxford: Learned Information, 1993. pp. 243-252.

The paper sets out the basic principles of UK copyright law and highlights certain areas where existing law is placed under strain by multimedia. White argues that if solutions to some of these problems are not found soon, te multimedia industry and the application of multimedia to information services will be significantly inhibited. Andrew White covers legal issues in a semi-regular column for *Information World Review.*

Conferences: Proceedings

468. Feeney, M. and **Day, S.** (eds.). *Multimedia Information: Proceedings of a Conference held at Churchill College, Cambridge, UK – 15-18 July 1991.* East Grinstead: Bowker-Saur, 1992. 240pp.

Defining multimedia as the integration of data, text, still and moving pictures, and sound within a single digital information system with which users can interact in different ways to access the information, this book emphasises the vital role of research in the creation of successful information systems of the future. The Second International Information Research Conference brought together experts from around the world to discuss multimedia communications and its global implications and the proceedings include both the papers presented and summaries of discussions. Topics covered include the technical aspects of multimedia infrastructures; the implications of multimedia publishing; multimedia applications in public libraries and the arts; teaching information professionals how to use multimedia; and the Scientific Documentary database, a generator of hypertext structures.

469. Stone, S. and **Buckland, M.** (eds.). *Studies in Multimedia.* Oxford: Learned Information, 1992. 263pp. (ASIS Monograph Series.)

Twenty-one papers representing a state-of-the-art study of multimedia computing and information handling. Themes concentrate on seven categories: Indexing and Thesaurus Design; Documents and Images; Sound; Museums and Archives; Medicine; Libraries; and Virtual Reality. While some of the papers were originally presented at the 1991 ASIS mid-year meeting, all have been revised and updated for this volume.

E-Mail Lists

470. *Current Cites.* Berkeley, CA: Library, University of California, Berkeley, 1994-. Monthly.

Current Cites is an e-mail publication containing annotated citations from around thirty journals in library and information technology. Articles included cover optical disc technologies, computer networks and networking, electronic publishing, hypermedia and multimedia. The service is free and subscribers to PACS-L and PACS-P will receive it automatically. The most current six issues are archived and can be accessed by telnet to a.cni.org with login as 'brsuser'. Current Cites is also printed in the journal, *Computers in Libraries* and contributes regularly the current awareness column in the *UKOLUG Newsletter.* To subscribe to Current Cites send a message 'sub cites your name' to listserv@library.berkeley.edu and this will lodge your Internet address on their computer.

Handbooks

471. **Pivovarnick, J.** *The Complete Idiot's Guide to CD-ROM.* Indianapolis: Alpha Books, 1994. 297 pp.

A guide for both IBM and Macintosh owners to using CD-ROMs. Covering everything from selecting hardware and installing software to troubleshooting and understanding error messages, the book is written in simple terms in plain English. A reviewer on the Internet noted that the book covered all the essentials of getting started with CD-ROMs: compatibility, standards, accessories, sound cards and multimedia – a bargain at twice its price from which much could be learned.

Journal Articles

472. **Enser, P. G. B.** 'Progress in Documentation. Pictorial Information Retrieval' *Journal of Documentation* 15 (2) (June 1995) pp. 126-170.

The article surveys the theoretical and practical issues associated with a particular kind of information retrieval problem, namely pictorial information. Technical developments which enable the storage of visual images are reviewed briefly while the body of the article looks at subject indexing and pictorial information retrieval for still and moving images. The four models offered correspond to permutations of the verbal and visual modes for the representation of picture content and information needs.

473. **Guenette, D. R.** and **Nicholls, P.** 'CD-ROM and Multimedia Industry Newsletters'. *CD-ROM Professional* 7 (6), November/December 1994, pp. 154-161.

A resource guide to newsletters covering the CD-ROM and multimedia industries. Newsletters are included which are targetted at the general user, the professional and the producer, ranging from *CD-ROM Newsletter* and *Computers in School Libraries* to *Digital Media: a Seybold Report* and *Pits and Lands*. Each reference (there are 41) has a short descriptive paragraph, the address of the publishers, the name of the editor and the frequency and cost.

474. Large, A. *et al.* 'Multimedia and Comprehension: the Relationship among Text, Animation and Captions'. *Journal of the American Society of Information Scientists* 46 (5) (June 1995) pp. 340-347.
Reporting on research funded by the Social Sciences and Humanities Research Council (Canada) and McGill University, the article covers a cognitive study of multimedia and its effect on children's learning. A sample of 71 12-year olds drawn from three primary schools was exposed to a multimedia sequence drawn from a section of Compton's Multimedia Encyclopedia. Four groups of children viewed either text only, text plus animations, text plus animations plus captions, and captions with animations before being asked to recall what they had learned. No significant difference was found regarding literal recall but the children in the text plus animations plus captions group were more successful in identifying major steps in the procedure viewed.

Journals: Online/CD-ROM Full-text

475. CDROM. Micro Haus.
A multimedia magazine on CD-ROM comprised of a 50/50 split between editorial and advertising. The Editorial includes a Master CD-ROM drive test, a review and demonstration of the best multimedia software currently available, and a multimedia news section. The advertising includes multimedia adverts that can be conveyed in ASCII text, animation, .PCX images and audio. The space used by each advertiser may be a product demonstration or a conventional advert.

Journals

476. *Multimedia World.* San Francisco: IDG Communications, 1991-. Monthly.
Formerly *CD-ROM Librarian* (and prior to 1987, *Optical Information Systems Update*), *CD-ROM World* was published by Mecklermedia until late 1994 when it was sold to IDG Communications were it has become a part of *Multimedia World.* It offers a mixture of news and practical articles on CD-ROM issues such as implementation and management, reviews of databases in broad subject areas, and announcements of new databases and peripheral products. Some databases are reviewed in detail in each issue and, in the later Mecklermedia years, many half- page reviews

covered games and clip art as well as more serious CD-ROMs. Full reviews were critical and include hardware configuration, software performance, documentation, test searches and pricing.

477. *School Library 2000.* Oxford: Learned Information, 1993-. Termly (three issues per year).
School Library 2000 is targetted at secondary school and sixth form college libraries in the UK and focusses on the addition of CD-ROM and multimedia discs to the school curriculum. Each issue contains product reviews – some with resource material for use in class, as well as coverage of multimedia personal computers (MPCs), CD-ROM hardware, school library automation systems, library security, satellite television, and going online. There are also lists of courses, conferences and exhibitions. The emphasis is on a non-technical approach and the journal is written from the teacher/librarian standpoint with discussions, letters news round-ups and 'how- to' tips all intended to simplify the material covered. All UK secondary schools and sixth form colleges may receive the journal free.

Newsletters

478. *Electronic Information Report.* Wilton, CT: SIMBA Information. Weekly
Previously known as *IDP Report,* this newsletter – like other SIMBA publications – monitors an industry sector. In this case the areas covered include storage and distribution media, electronic publishing, multimedia and databases. Items report on the trends and developments in information services.

479. *Interactive Media International Newsletter.* Peterborough: PLF Communications, 1987-. Monthly.
Provides a source of news, project information, market analysis and applications for interactive multimedia technology worldwide. Conference reports, reviews of market research publications and listings of forthcoming events are regular features.

480. *Multimedia Monitor.* Falls Church, VA: Future Systems, 1983-. Monthly.
A newsletter with detailed industry figures (including charts and statistics), news items on hardware and software and conference reports, the previously titled *Videodisc Monitor* analyses and reports on the multimedia industry. Coverage is said to objective and comprehensive and, to keep users up-to-date, the company launched a weekly faxed supplement of news items in 1994. There is also an archive CD-ROM containing the full text and graphic page images from 1983 to 1993. Also available via Newsnet and Information Access Company's newsletter databases.

Reports

481. **Jeffcoate, J.** and **Wesley, I.** *Multimedia Publishing.* London: Ovum, 1995. 250pp.
Publishing companies are seen to be facing stiff competition from IT companies of all sizes who are entering the market with multimedia offerings. This volumc looks at the state of multimedia publishing today and the market opportunities which are becoming available. Beginning with a management summary of multimedia, authoring tools, and network publishing, the report goes on to look at publishers, IT and telecommunications suppliers, market opportunities, markets and models of markets, company profiles for ten key multimedia publishers, and ends with a directory of publishers, a directory of IT and telecommunications suppliers, a section on standards and a glossary.

482. **Jeffcoate, J.** and **Templeton, A.** *Multimedia: Strategies for the Business Market.* London: Ovum, 1992. 350pp.
The Management Summary with which the volume starts defines multimedia, the market for business multimedia, the future for multimedia and strategies for suppliers and users. Following 25 in-depth interviews, it seems clear that uses for multimedia extend well beyond the educational market – point-of-sale information, business presentations and desk-top video communications, for example. The following seven parts to the report deal with the Users, the Applications, the Technology and Standards (converging technologies, the impact of optical storage, compression standards), the Suppliers and Markets (is there a multimedia market? platforms, supplier strategies, market forecasts), Supplier Profiles (Systems and Components), Supplier Profiles (Software and Applications), and User Profiles (case studies covering current applications, implementation issues, views and concerns and future plans). There are also appendices containing a glossary, references and contact information. Like all Ovum reports, this volume is an authoritative analysis of its topic; readers from computing, video and communications industries will find it useful.

483. **Stubley, P.** and **Umney, D.** *Multimedia.* London: The Library Information Technology Centre, 1992. 10pp. (Library & Information Briefings, No. 34)
Following some general definitions of multimedia, the Briefing looks at the formats (CD-I and CDTV), systems and costs of hardware. It is particularly obvious that there is a lack of standardisation. A section on Technical Multinedia covers analogue versus digital video incorporation – the former using the computer to control a video tape/disc is probably already to be seen as inferior and undesirable due to improvements in technology which bring the latter approach within more general means. The following section on design and authoring considers the users, the media and the interface to be used and makes the point that such developments are a lengthy processes. Somewhat cynically, the conclusion suggests that given the investment, research and development committed to multimedia, it must have a future (do I hear

an echo from Douglas Adams here, 'Multimedia is an invention looking for a necessity to mother it'?) but goes on to point to business and education – higher education in particualr – as strong markets.

Yearbooks

484. *Multimedia Yearbook 1995.* London: Interactive Media Publications, 1995. 1000 pp.
Incorporating a 'free' CD-ROM version of both the 1994 editorial and the entire 1995 book (presumably as multimedia), the *Yearbook* contains articles on technology, markets, national profiles, publishing and applications, interviews, details of nearly 200 company profiles and over 1,000 products, a glossary of over 400 terms and directories of books, periodicals, organisations and events. Some thirty per cent larger than the previous year, the 1995 version covers the USA for the first time and has indexes for companies (by country and application as well as by company name) and products by product, producer and distributor. The *Yearbook* sums up the state-of-the-art in multimedia. For anyone involved with multimedia, it is a necessary source of information – the 1994 version was called an 'all-encompassing, easy-to-use, and invaluable reference' (*European Multimedia Bulletin*) and 'an incredibly adept wrap-up of the entire multimedia industry' (*Multimedia & Videodisc Monitor*).

OPACS

Books

485. Aluri, R., Kemp, D. A. and **Boll, J. J.** *Subject Analysis in Online Catalogues.* Englewood, Colorado: Libraries Unlimited, 1991. 303pp.

A detailed coverage of the complex elements that interact to enable subject access in online catalogues: the database of the online catalogue itself, the subject analysis components (indexing/classification), the user, the hardware and the software. The chapters – which reflect the interaction of these components – deal with the database; language in information retrieval; subject indexing process and policy; subject heading systems; keyword subject access and citation indexing; bibliographic classification; Dewey Decimal and Library of Congress Classifications and online catalogues; users and user needs; user-system interaction; and evaluation of subject retrieval in online catalogues. A useful books on OPACs for librarians and students alike, providing much which is of use for those of latter who have, as the authors say, to learn about information retrieval methods ab initio. The book would be even more valuable if it included more detailed consideration of searching OPACs. Nevertheless the material it presents on the subject representation options with which an OPAC searcher might be faced makes this a valuable book.

486. Hildreth, C. R. (ed.) *The Online Catalogue: Developments and Directions.* London: Library Association Publishing, 1989. 212pp.

In at least one library school, one of the key texts on courses dealing with Online Public Access Catalogues, Hildreth's collection of papers by leading figures in the OPAC world (Hancock-Beaulieu, Markey, Tague, Walker, etc.) successfully demonstrates the importance of online access to library catalogues while it details developments and research. With contributions from both the UK and USA, the book is a ready source of ideas for those involved with OPACs. Chapters deal with such topics as the Okapi project, human-computer interaction, the use of transaction log data, subject searching and, of particular interest here, with access to periodical literature within an online catalogue environment (Mischo and Moore).

Conferences: Papers

487. Hancock-Beaulieu, M. 'New Ways for Subject Searching: the OKAPI Retrieval System'. *In* C J Armstrong and R J Hartley (eds.) *Database 2000: UKOLUG State-of-the-Art Conference 1992.* Oxford: Learned Information, 1992. pp. 51-58.

The limitations of OPACs in providing subject access are discussed and lead into a talk on the work undertaken by City University to improve the functionality of an

OPAC without increasing the load on the user. OKAPI is based on 'best match' retrieval with a number of automatic features such as spelling correction, stemming, cross-referencing and query expansion built in. This short paper includes sample screens and a discussion on the future prospects for the system.

Directories: Online Format

488. St.George, A. and **Larsen, R.** *Internet: Accessible Library Catalogs and Databases.* New Mexico: University of New Mexico.

This directory is available via anonymous FTP on ARIEL.UNM.EDU in the LIBRARY directory. The text version is INTERNET.LIBRARY and a postscript version is LIBRARY.PS.

E-Mail Lists

489. PACS-L (Public Access Computer Systems Forum). Houston: University of Houston, Library and Information Technology Division.

PACS-L is a moderated list that deals with all computer systems that libraries make available to their patrons. This means that in addition to OPACs, subscribers may encounter messages dealing with CD-ROM databases microcomputer laboratories or expert systems. Acquisitions, cataloguing and other 'staff-related function' are not covered. This important list has been running since about 1989 and members can expect to receive in the order of ten to twenty messages each day.

To join PACS-L send the following e-mail message to LISTSERV@UHUPVM1.UH.EDU, 'subscribe pacs-l first-name last-name'.

Journal Articles

490. Crawford, J. C., Thom, L. C. and **Powles, J. A.** 'A Survey of Subject Access to Academic Library Catalogues in Great Britain.' *Journal of Librarianship and Information Science* 25 (2), June 1993, pp.85-93.

Reports results of a questionnaire survey of UK academic libraries to determine the level of use of online public access catalogues (OPACs) and the development of in-house subject indexes. 75 respondents reported having commercial systems and 7 reported in-house systems. Data includes: named systems in use and numbers of libraries using each system; percentages of bibliographic records in machine readable format; types of materials; and record formats (UKMARC, LC MARC, etc). Reports the most common access points for searching the OPACs (author, keyword), methods of generating terms to be used for subject searching, subject heading sources (LCSH, MeSH, PRECIS) and classification schemes (Dewey, UDC). Results show that all universities and polytechnics now have OPACs and only the smaller colleges do not.

OPACs are moving towards comprehensive coverage of academic library stocks with the MARC record the most popular format.

491. Larsen, G. 'Advances in OPACs in Europe: an Overview.' *Proceedings of the 16th International Essen Symposium: Resource Sharing: New Technologies as a Must for Universal Availability of Information. 18-21 October 1993.* Edited by Ahmed H. Helal and Joachim W. Weiss. Essen, Germany: Universitatsbibliothek Essen, 1994, pp.237-252.

The acronym OPAC should perhaps stand for Open, Public, Accessible and Cooperative. Looks at how the OPAC modules available in major European library systems live up to this definition. Discusses third-generation OPAC development areas: network access; document types and services included; document ordering and delivery; user interface; retrieval models; communication language; and record enhancements.

492. Su, S-F. 'Dialogue with an OPAC: how visionary was Swanson in 1964?' *Library Quarterly* 64 (2), April 1994, pp.130-161.

In 1964 Don Swanson published an article, 'Dialogues with a Catalog' (*Library Quarterly,* 34 (1), January 1964, pp.113-125), in which he presented a personal prescription for what a library catalogue should look like at some future date. He was in many ways remarkably visionary; some of the features he recommended have still not been implemented, although writers are again referring to their desirability. Despite its visionary qualities, Swanson's article seems to have been quite forgotten in the sense that it is rarely cited. This article traces the development of online public access catalogues (OPACs) from the time they were first introduced into libraries and compare what has occurred with Swanson's recommendations. Remarks on the fact that an article written 30 years earlier could still offer a suitable framework within which to review virtually the totality of OPAC developments. Concludes that the lesson which emerges most clearly from this is that the library profession should prescribe performance goals for tools and services that are not constrained by existing technologies.

493. Tillotson, J. 'Is keyword searching the answer?' *College & Research Libraries* 56 (3), May 1995, pp.199-206.

Examines three aspects of keyword searching to see if defaulting to keyword searches might serve as a solution to the problems users find when performing subject searches in online public access catalogues (OPACs). Investigates whether keyword searching produces useful results; if people who use keyword searches to find information on a subject report that they are satisfied with the results; and how keyword searching and controlled vocabulary searching are offered and explained in currently available OPAC interfaces. Concludes that both keyword and controlled vocabulary searching ought to be easily available in an OPAC, and that improvements need to be made in explanations and help offered to subject searchers.

494. Werf-Davelaar, T. v. d. 'Access to Library Services by Means of End-User Technology.' *IFLA Journal* 20 (4), 1994, pp.462-77.
State-of-the-art review of end-user access to computerized information services to establish the future role likely to be played by PIT (personal information technology) based access in library services. Reports results of a questionnaire survey of 50 national libraries, academic libraries, public libraries, special libraries and affiliated library organizations in Europe and the USA, to determine the degree of end-user access to computerized information services. The scope of the survey embraced: CD-ROMs; online information retrieval; library automation (online public access catalogues (OPACs)); and associated issues, such as charging.

Journals: Electronically Distributed

495. Public-Access Computer Systems News.
Sent to subscribers of the PACS-L and PACS-P lists. PACS-L is the Public-Access Computer Systems Forum while PACS-P gives publications only. The addresses are PACS-L@UHUPVM1 and PACS-P@UHUPVM1.

Review Publications

496. O'Brien, A. 'Online Catalogs: Enhancements and Developments'. *In* M E Williams (ed.) *Annual Review of Information Science and Technology* 29 (1994). pp. 219-242.
The review deals with enhancements to online catalogues in the early 1990s. Articles referenced are those which deal with problem areas such as subject access and user-searching behaviour or those which deal with the future of catalogues – new interface developments and network access, for example. As the author says, many of the topics are very broad and widely covered in the literature. The chapter is divided into sections and starts with topics such as bibliographic standards and cataloguing rules before moving onto subject access (some 26 references), enriching the content of bibliographic records (7) and understanding catalogue users (7). Multilingual access and interface developments are also covered. In all there are 83 references.

497. Shaw, D. 'The Human-Computer Interface for Information Retrieval'. *In* M E Williams (ed.) *Annual Review of Information Science and Technology* 26 (1991). pp. 155-195.
The Human-Computer Interface is often the single most important factor in determining the success or failure of a system. It is also one of the most expensive. The review defines it as 'what the user sees, hears, and touches in interfacing with a computer system' and includes basic interface models, topics related to navigation, interaction styles and screen design. Topics on user interface engineering such as general guidelines, help facilities and interface evaluation are also covered. Every topic is

oriented towards information technology and retrieval. The chapter begins with a review of advances in general interface design. Major application areas include online catalogues, online searching and CD-ROM products with an emphasis on working systems. (188 references.)

PERSONAL BIBLIOGRAPHIC SOFTWARE

Bibliographies

498. *Database Design.* Springfield, Virginia: U.S. Department of Commerce. National Technical Information Service. (NTIS order number: PB92-861665CBY).
Compiled from the INSPEC database, this bibliography contains references with abstracts relevant to the design of databases – both in-house and online. NTIS Published Searches are custom-made bibliographies undertaken in the week of order by NERAC Inc on behalf of NTIS. Thus, up-to-date results from a fixed profile can be dispatched as and when needed.

Books

499. **Hanson, T. A.** (ed.). *Bibliographic Software and the Electronic Library.* Hatfield: University of Hertfordshire Press, 1995. 136pp.
During the nineties, several software packages designed specifically to manage bibliographic references came into their own. Terry Hanson is an acknowledged expert on their use and his book demonstrates how they can provide a solution for users of CD-ROM and online databases who wish to maintain their own, personal databanks. Part 1 is an introduction to bibliographic software and its use for importing downloaded records into personal databases. Part 2 provides five case studies covering four packages – Pro-Cite, Reference Manager, EndNote and Papyrus – and a trial of PC bibliographic database and formatting packages. The case studies are chosen not only for their softwares but for the contrasting types of libraries involved. Rounding off the book in Part 3 are two chapters on copyright implications of such information re-use. Appendices list contact addresses, relevant Internet discussion lists, criteria for the evaluation of bibliographic software, a user trial questionnaire, and notes on reformatting records from the (UK) BIDS service. There is also a useful bibliography.

500. **McCarthy, S.** *Personal Filing Systems: Creating Information Retrieval Systems on Microcomputers.* Chicago: Medical Library Association, 1988. 167pp.
Describes the different types of software package available for personal database creation and management on microcomputers and discusses considerations in software selection and evaluation. Database planning and design principles are also emphasized. Appendices include an evaluation checklist and details of individual packages. A useful introduction to the topic although many of the packages being marketed today have capabilities well in advance of what was possible in 1988.

501. Tenopir, C. and **Lundeen, G.** *Managing Your Information: How to Design and Create a Textual Database on Your Microcomputer.* New York: Neal-Schuman, 1988. 226 pp. (Applications in Information Management and Technology Series, 5)

Provides a thorough grounding in database design, creation and management for anyone involved in setting up a personal or in-house database using a microcomputer. Discussions of search features, record definition and software evaluation are supplemented by a case study which shows the principles of database design in practice. Additional sections list selected software packages with supplier addresses, software directories and sources of software reviews. There is also a glossary of database terminology.

Directories: Print

502. Wood, J. and **Moore, C.** (eds.) *European Directory of Text Retrieval Software.* Aldershot: Gower, 1993. 410pp.

Following on from *Text Retrieval: a Directory of Software* but with a new European emphasis, the Directory is designed to provide a comprehensive source of information for the selection of text retrieval software. It describes some seventy mainframe, minicomputer and microcomputer packages. Some of the packages are suitable for the creation of personal bibliographic databases while others could be used such large-scale and complex applications as crime information. Reflecting the latest trends, software is included which handles images as well as text, and much can be used for the retrieval of data on CD-ROMs. The level of detail varies from entry to entry but usually includes information about price, hardware and operating system requirements, input and retrieval of data, indexing, interfaces with other software, user support and, in some cases, published reviews or articles on the software. All the information has been acquired from detailed questionnaires sent to producers. The supplier index contains company information on the software producers and products are indexed by descriptor, operating system and country in which the software is actively marketed and supported.

E-Mail Lists

503. BIBSOFT@INDYCMS (BITNET)

Discussion forum on software for citations and bibliographies. To subscribe, send an e-mail message to LISTSERV@INDYCMS: SUBSCRIBE BIBSOFT First name Last name

504. CDS-ISIS@HEARN (BITNET)

Discussion forum/e-mail list on UNESCO's CDS/ISIS text retrieval software. To subscribe, send an e-mail message to LISTSERV@HEARN: SUBSCRIBE CDS-ISIS First name Last name

505. ENDNOTE@UCSBVM (BITNET)
Discussion forum/e-mail list on the EndNote and EndLink software packages. To subscribe, send an e-mail message to LISTSERV@UCSBVM: SUBSCRIBE ENDNOTE First-name Last-name

506. PRO-CITE@IUBVM (BITNET)
Discussion forum/e-mail list for the Pro-Cite personal bibliographic software. To subscribe, send an e-mail message to LISTSERV@IUBVM: SUBSCRIBE PRO-CITE First name Last name

Journal Articles

507. Bellarby, L. 'Personal Bibliographic Packages: a Comparison of End-Note and ProCite'. *C&L Applications* 6 (7) March 1993 pp. 3-4.
A brief evaluation of personal bibliographic packages which assesses End-Note and ProCite according to interface, capacity, indexing, searching, output formats, in-text citations and downloading. The article also offers advice on selecting personal bibliographic software.

508. Hill, R. J. 'Using personal bibliographic data bases to keep up with the engineering literature'. *IEEE Transactions on Professional Communication* 32 (3), September 1989, pp. 189-193.
Describes the steps to be followed in setting up a bibliographic database on a microcomputer. Database design, data entry, record structure and report formats are discussed and the author's experience in compiling a database of railway engineering literature is documented.

509. Stigleman, S. 'Bibliographic Formatting Software: a Buying Guide'. *Database* 15 (1) February 1992. pp. 15-27.
Bibliographic formatting software takes records downloaded from an online or CD-ROM database and formats them into another specified citation style. Forty-three bibliographic formatting programs are identified and listed with supplier information. Each producer was asked to supply answers to eight questions and these are published in full and in a series of tables.

510. Wolff, T. E. 'Personal Bibliographic Databases: an Industrial Scientist's Perspective'. *Database* 15 (2) April 1992. pp. 34-40
Four proprietary software packages – Library Master, Notebook2, Papyrus and ProCite – are reviewed against 49 requirements. The requirements classify according to database file features, importing of downloaded records, searching, browsing, editing, sorting and search set handling and reporting output.

Reviews: Software

511. Grumling, D. and **Nelson, D.** Pro-Cite 2.0 for the IBM and Biblio-Link to USMARC Communications Format Records, by Personal Bibliographic Software. *Cataloging & Classification Quarterly* 16 (2), 1993. pp. 125-127.

A short software review describing the use of Biblio-Links to import OCLC MARC-format records. Any or all MARC fields can be transferred or ignored. An 'unscientific e-mail survey' showed the variety of uses to which Pro-Cite with Biblio-Links is put.

512. Lundeen, G, 'Software for managing personal files'. *Database* 12 (3), June 1989, pp. 36-48.

Describes and compares four packages for creating and searching personal research databases. These packages are AskSam, Notebook II, ProCite and Reference Manager. Each is compared in terms of its speed in loading, retrieving, indexing and sorting references from a test file of over 3,000 records from the ERIC database. The operation of each package is described with respect to its ease of use and features supported. User interface, file maintenance, retrieval capacities, output capabilities and documentation are evaluated and record display screens are illustrated.

513. Lundeen, G. 'Bibliographic Software Update'. *Database* 14 (6) December 1991. pp. 57-67.

This article is an update of an earlier article in which four database management system software packages were reviewed: AskSam, Notebook II, Reference Manager and ProCite. The present article reviews new versions of the first three plus three additional products – dms4cite, Library Master and Papyrus. The text database of 3,149 records used in the previous comparisons was used again in the new evaluation.

514. Sieverts, E. G. and **Mastenbroek, O.** (eds.) *Microcomputer Applications for Online and Local Information Systems: a Test and Comparison of 30 Software Packages: Report of a Software Evaluation by Members of VOGIN.* Leiden: VOGIN, 1987. 107 pp.

Although dated and no longer comprehensive, this review remains valuable as it sets out criteria by which microcomputer database- and online-related software can be evaluated. Based on two reports originally published in Dutch as supplements to LOGIN, the periodical of VOGIN (The Netherlands Association of Users of Online Information Systems), the report evaluates packages for terminal emulation and communication, data reformatting and information storage and retrieval in local databases. Test criteria include price, memory required, documentation, presence of particular functions, ease of use, and reliability. Data are presented in tabular format in each section, with an introductory overview of functions and operations and a narrative account of results for each package. Appendices offer addresses of producers or suppliers and a bibliography of literature on software for the applications discussed in the report.

QUALITY AND EVALUATION

Books

515. Jacsó, P. *CD-ROM Software, Dataware, and Hardware: Evaluation, Selection, and Installation.* Englewood, Colorado: Libraries Unlimited, 1992. 256pp. (Database Searching Series).

Replete with screen dumps and sample output, this book serves as both a guide to evaluating CD-ROM products and as a directory of past poor practice. Dealing with the various aspects of the package-as-purchased (Jacsó coins the term, 'Dataware') such as the interface; the search features; set and query management; output features; database scope, content, structure and quality; accessibility; documentation; installation; and price, Jacsó creates a methodology for assessing any CD-ROM product. Final sections on hardware evaluation and CD-ROM application requirements; the selection of CD-ROMs and installation procedures complete this review of characteristic features of CD- ROM databases; a review, as he says in the Introduction, intended to help the librarian in the evaluation, comparison, selection, installation and operation of CD-ROM products. Appendices with check-lists or evaluation forms for software, dataware, database and hardware complete the book. This excellent book should be compulsory reading not only for the would-be user of CD-ROMs but for those involved in their publication and production.

Conferences: Papers

516. Minkoff, D. 'Quality: Participation plus Change'. *In Total Quality Management (The Information Business: Key Issue 92). (Based on the papers given at a one day conference on Total Quality Management in Library and Information Services held at the Library Technology Fair at the University of Hertfordshire on 9th September 1992).* Hatfield: University of Hertfordshire, 1992. pp. 70-81.

Datastream, of which David Minkoff is the Director of Data Services, has had a quality programme operational since 1987. This paper briefly describes the various processes – such as, Self Managing Teams and Action to Prevent Recurrence – which have gone into their quality initiative, amd looks at the elements which go to make up the Small Wins (the stage-wise implementation of the quality programme) approach which they adopted. In quality terms, Datastream is perhaps best known for its 'Data Guarantee' which offers £10 to any customer who spots an error. Database quality is only achieved through involving everyone, and with continuous improvement and continuous innovation, with only minor setbacks, Datastream seems to have been successful.

Conferences: Proceedings

517. **Armstrong, C. J.** and **Hartley, R. J.** (eds.). *Database 2000: UKOLUG State-of-the-Art Conference 1992.* Oxford: Learned Information, 1992. 125pp.
The United Kingdom Online User Group (UKOLUG) holds a State-of-the-Art conference every other year with, since 1986, published proceedings. The 1992 conference lived up to its name in providing comprehensive updates on telecommunications, CD-ROM networking and post-processing software as well as number of papers looking at current practice in database design and in training. For the first time, a student paper – by the winner of the first UKOLUG Student Award, Cathy Cope – was included in the proceedings. Perhaps as important as any other aspect of the conference or the proceedings is the final section devoted to quality assurance. This section includes a guest lecture by Reva Basch, five short introductions to aspects of quality in the database industry and a summary of discussions. It was as a direct result of this meeting that the UKOLUG/Library Association Centre for Information Quality Management was formed.

Journal Articles

518. **Armstrong, C. J.** CIQM Report on Database Quality. *Database* 17 (6) (December 1994). pp. 45-48.
An article summarising the state of the information industry with respect to the quality of databases, reporting on the work of the Centre for Information Quality Management and proposing a way forward that will provide users with an instant indication of how much they can 'trust' a database. In operation for about a year at the time of writing, CIQM has received sufficient calls dealing with database quality to form an impression of where problems lie. By labelling databases in the same way as food and drugs are labelled, information providers will enable users to see exactly what is and what is not covered by the database and at the same time will publish the quality criteria to which their database adheres. As these are instantly verifiable, the label will effectively be a self-policing standard. CIQM hopes to be working on this project during 1995.

519. **Basch, R.** 'Measuring the Quality of the Data: Report on the Fourth Annual SCOUG Retreat'. *Database* 6(8) (October 1990). pp. 18-23.
The Southern California Online Users' Group (SCOUG) spent their annual retreat in 1990 developing a list of criteria by which database quality could be assessed. This article reports on the retreat and gives details of the checklists developed under the broad headings: consistency, coverage/scope, timeliness, error rate/accuracy, accessibility/ease of use, integration, output, documentation, customer support and training, and value-to-cost ratio. It is important to note that beyond these criteria, the group recognised that there were both points specific to particular types of database and points which needed adjusting to match different types of searcher (end user as

opposed to information professional). The criteria represent a studied and considered set of metrics rather than a 'wish list' and the article ends with suggestions for a way forward – a consumer journal, an appraisal system, or perhaps databases should carry an 'end-user safety stamp'?

520. Basch, R. 'The Seven Deadly Sins of Online Services'. *Online* 16(4) (July 1992) pp. 22-25.

A light-hearted (relatively) look at seven aspects of an online service – an 'evil twin' of other database quality scales, rooted on user satisfaction, the concept of system shortcomings rather than file design and content, and the idea that the customer is more sinned against than sinning. A little tortured at times, this resulted in Avarice (volume is not always value so why should time be money?); Inconsistency (I don't remember that one) which translates as file structure defects due to the inability to fit all types of database into a single set of system stadards; Sloth or sluggishness of the system (perhaps during peak periods) which may be charged as connect time; Uncommunicativeness (no toll-free help line, etc); Pride (where the system providers believe so much of their system that context sensitive help seems unnecessary and the system is unforgiving of errors); Inadequacy (a catchall category covering software-based weaknesses); and Ignorance – a sin for which both systems and searchers must take responsibility. The conclusion – based on the fact that this is a very different list to the one which would have been written even three years ago – is that the online industry IS on the quality track.

521. Dolan, D. R. 'Quality Control at the System Level.' *Online* 16(2) (March 1992). pp. 30-35.

An article which looks at quality control in general and then at testing-by-using online systems. Having established that such a testing process is undocumented, Dolan interviewed three one-time BRS testers to discover how they went about proving new software capabilities. In two sidebars, KR Data-Star and KR DIALOG discuss their quality control procedures.

522. Ebbinghouse, C. 'Information Professionals Face the Internet: The Ninth Annual SCOUG Retreat.' *Searcher: The Magazine for Database Professionals* 3 (9) (October 1995) pp. 48-56.

An article which describes the latest annual retreat of the Southern California Online User Group (SCOUG) and the discussions which took place. In previous years a discussion on database quality by this group gave a considerable fillip to world-wide moves on data quality and in 1995 the group turned to the same topic for the Internet. Many of the same criteria that had emerged for databases were looked at afresh as a means of judging the Internet and, in general, it was found wanting. All discussion groups agreed on certain necessary quality standards and some more specific ideas such as the registration of Web pages and a code of ethics for information providers were also suggested.

523. Fox, C., Levitin, A. and **Redman, T.** 'The Notion of Data and Its Quality Dimensions'. *Information Processing & Management* 30(1), January 1994, pp. 9-19.

This important paper discusses the various aspects of data quality in some depth, having first analysed and defined what exactly is meant by the word 'data'. Having reviewed the literature and rejected five descriptions, the authors are left with the rather technical definition that data may be described as a collection of triples <e, a, v> (where the value <v> is selected from the domain of the attribute <a> to represent the attribute's value for the entity <e>), along with the definitions of data representation (a set of rules for recording triples on some medium) and data recording (a physical instance standing for a set of data items according to a data representation). That out of the way, there is a useful discussion of quality dimensions – accuracy, precision, reliability, currentness, age, timeliness, completeness, duplication, consistency and integrity – before an analysis of further work on data quality which remains to be undertaken. Of importance here are the questions, What should be measured? and How should the measurements be made?

524. Granick, L. 'Assuring the Quality of Information Dissemination: Responsibilities of Database Producers'. *Information Services & Use* 11 (1991) pp. 117-136.

A response from the database producer's point of view to the database quality guidelines published on behalf of the Southern California Online users' Group (SCOUG) in which it is argued that rather than there being no distinction between the information producer and the online service when a user searches/evaluates a database ('the database they want to talk about and evaluate is what they get when they sign on and start to search. ... They don't wish to be bothered with what they see as our problems. In their frame of reference, a user buys a product and when it needs fixing, buck passing andlectures on the other partner's unwillingness to make changes do nothing to fix it'), responsibilities for different aspects of the database lie with either the database producer, the host or both. Granick has surveyed current practices relating to quality assurance amongst NFAIS members and the results are reported here. Two appendices carry the SCOUG Criteria with responsibilities marked for either or both parties and the questionnaire results.

525. Harry, V. and **Oppenheim, C.** 'Evaluations of Electronic Databases, Part I: Criteria for Testing CDROM Products; Part II: Testing CDROM Products'. *Online & CDROM Review* 17 (4), August 1993, pp. 211-222 (Part I) and 17 (6), December 1993, pp. 339-368 (Part II).

A detailed methodology for the evaluation of CD-ROM databases. In the first part the various criteria by which CD-ROMs might be judged are discussed with references to earlier literature covering similar aspects. A review should contain comments on costs, user needs, collection development and hardware platforms as well as basic issues such as vendor details and the product evaluation itself. Harry and Oppenheim subscribe to the school of thought which gives marks for various aspects of the product being reviewed and this is demonstrated in Part II where four CD-ROMs are reviewed. The authors stress, however, that these reviews do NOT include contact with the vendors and in no case was installation evaluated so that the sample reviews should not in any way be construed as representing a real review of the product. Two appendices give the Test Manual with questions for consideration and the marking scheme, and the actual Evaluation Form. This pair of articles cover the business of evaluating a CD-ROM product in considerable depth and, with the appendices, provide potential purchasers and reviewers with an excellent methodology which this editor, as a long-time reviewer, has no hesitation in recommending.

526. Medawar, K. 'Database Quality: a Literature Review of the Past and a Plan for the Future'. *Program* 29 (3) (July 1995). pp.257-272.

The Centre for Information Quality Management (CIQM) was funded by the British Library Research and Development Department to undertake a preliminary study into database quality. This paper is a review of papers dealing with total quality management, quality assurance, quality as it impacts upon the information industry and quality in databases, as well as a short look at work just beginning at the Centre. Written before the completion of the British Library project, only brief mention is made of database labelling – the scheme currently being taken forward by the Centre. More details on labelling – an idea similar to the 'registration' more recently suggested for Internet sites in Ebbinghouse [522] – can be found in Armstrong [518, 536].

527. Nahl-Jakobovits, D. and **Tenopir, C.** 'Databases Online and on CD-ROM: How do They Differ, Let Us Count the Ways'. *Database* 15 (1) (February 1992). pp. 42-50.

In order to decide on how to access a particular database, there are a number of factors to consider. Using Psychological Abstracts (online on DIALOG and on disc on SilverPlatter) as a testbed, the authors compared the two media. The two databases were compared over six search queries in terms of the number of responses, the number of unique records found and the search costs. A similar experiment was undertaken on Sociological Abstracts, likewise available on DIALOG and SilverPlatter. The conclusions reached seem to indicate that online databases give a more consistent or predictable response time and yield greater coverage, content and currency. In an interesting side bar, Péter Jacsó clarifies updating on PsycLIT, showing that there were then delays of up to four months before users can find some articles.

528. Orenstein, R. M. 'How Full is Full Revisited: A Status Report on Searching Full-Text Periodicals'. *Database* 16 (5) (October 1993). pp. 14-23.

The author looks at the coverage of the Forbes newsletter on several vendors and databases including DIALOG, Nexis, Data-Star and the Trade & Industry database. She warns that 'many librarians are considering cancelling their print subscriptions and relying on online full-text sources for articles. Given the variability in currency shown here, this is a strategy that bears rethinking!' and supports this with tables showing currency and completeness.

529. Piternick, A. B. 'Functions and Capabilities of Online Searching Systems: A Checklist'. *Online Review* 13 (6) (December 1989). pp. 457-476.
In developing a checklist of functions and capabilities, the author has provided a convenient list of points for comparison for online searchers; a schematic list of features which could form the basis of an assessment or evaluation; and a starting point for those who are considering developing or enhancing such a system. The checklist is discussed and explained fully in the paper and presented as an appendix.

530. Quint, B. 'The 'Dead' Database: Where do Databases go when they Leave Online?' *Database* 15 (5) (October 1992) pp. 15-31.
Bewailing the lack of information from database producers and hosts when databases are taken off online services, this article examines the reasons for such departures and provides some hints for users – 'sickness precedes death in most cases. Sick coverage degrades user trust. Sick revenues discourage industry commitment' – use the warnings the industry provides in logon banners, etc; learn about the producers; stay in touch with fellow searchers; build contacts among information industry professionals; read between the lines in newsletters and documentation; and communicate (with everyone). Search services have also begun to re-examine policies concerning closed files and it is frequently not possible for files which the producer is not maintaining to be held. The article also contains a major sidebar extending over several pages listing whole databases, full-text titles and search services which have vanished, as well as search service policies on notification.

531. Quint, B. 'The Database Connection: Full of Text'. *Document Delivery World* 9 (3) (April 1993). pp 34-36.
The author examines some of the reasons why full-text databases do not equate to document delivery systems and concludes that the principle reason is simply that full text is NOT full coverage – at the very least images are missing from the majority of databases. A slightly angry look at the shortcomings of online systems which purport to deliver free text but fail to tell users precisely what it is that is available. The article contains several examples of databases which are not quite as users imagine.

532. Richards, T. and **Robinson, C.** 'Evaluating CD-ROM Software: A Model'. *CD-ROM Professional* 6 (5) (September 1993). pp. 92, 94, 96, 98-101.
Following a brief literature review (7 references) of articles dealing with the evaluation of CD-ROMs and a demonstration of the increase in both CD-ROMs and CD-ROM search software, the article describes the authors' model for such an evaluation. The evaluation form itself is given as an appendix and works on the principle of scoring for the various functions which might be expected in good search software. For example, a score of zero for no built-in help; of one for a copy of the

manual ondisc and/or in print; of two for structured help available via a table of contents; and of three for context sensitive help. If help is not available at all times from the F1 function key deduct 0.5 from the score. The evaluation model is described briefly in the text.

533. **Schwartz, C.** 'Evaluating CD-ROM Products: Yet Another Checklist'. *CD-ROM Professional* 6 (1) (January 1993). pp. 87-88, 90-91.
A single-paragraph introduction giving the pedigree of the checklist is followed by a detailed list of evaluation points under such headings as Hardware/Software Requirements; Overall Ease of Use; Search Management; and Content Evaluation. Each heading is followed by a number of more specific points: Search Management, for example, asks if, during a session, sets can be reused, the seesion history can be displayed and/or cleared for a restart, and whether sets can be deleted; if the search is offered for re-execution at a file change; if search strategies can be saved to disk, whether the name and location is system-supplied or user-supplied, what is the maximum size of such searches, whether saved searches can easily be amended, whether a list of saved searhes is available, and whether saved searches can be deleted; whether SDI is available; and whether searches can be moved directly to online. There is also a list of references to support the initial pedigree statement.

534. **Zink, S. D.** 'Towards More Critical Reviewing and Analysis of CD-ROM User Software Interfaces'. *CD-ROM Professional* 4 (1), January 1991, pp. 16-21.
With reference to past literature, the author discusses the various user considerations in software design which render a product either more or less successful, and follows this with a short review of Congressional Information Services's MASTERFILE 2. The short, but critical review demonstrates where this product has failed to take account of its potential users in developing the search interface. Unlike Harry and Oppenheim, this review has been passed to the CD-ROM producers and a short response is included on the final page.

Journals

535. *Searcher: The Magazine for Database Professionals.* Medford, New Jersey: Learned Information, 1993-. Nine issues per year.
Edited by Barbara Quint, *Searcher* centres on the needs of the professional searcher and combines evaluations of data content with discussions of delivery media: its scope includes all electronic media from CD-ROM and diskette and tape leasing to online. Regular sections include News Flashes, Tools of the Trade (short hardware reviews with Best Buys), (inevitably) The Internet Express and Searcher's Voice – the editorial. Coverage and style have a distinctly USA feel, but the content is relevant to any 'database professional'.

Reports

536. Armstrong, C. J. *Database Information Quality*. London: The Library Information Technology Centre, 1995. 14pp. (Library & Information Briefings, No. 62)

The Briefing discusses the kinds of problems that are regularly encountered at the Centre for Information Quality Management (CIQM) and describes the work being undertaken in this field by the European Association of Information Services (EUSIDIC) and the Southern California Online User Group (SCOUG) as well as by CIQM itself, which is investigating the idea of Database Labelling as a solution to the quality issue. The report includes a list of further readings as well as an appendix listing the quality criteria used to assess databases.

SEARCH TECHNIQUES

Bibliographies

537. *Full Text Database Searching.* Springfield, Virginia: U.S. Department of Commerce. National Technical Information Service. (NTIS order number: PB92-860469CBY).
Contains references with abstracts to articles on full-text databases taken from the INSPEC database. NTIS Published Searches are custom-made bibliographies undertaken in the week of order by NERAC Inc on behalf of NTIS. Thus, up-to-date results from a fixed profile can be dispatched as and when needed.

538. **Huston, M. M.** 'Search Theory and Instruction for End Users of Online Bibliographic Information Retrieval Systems: a Literature Review'. *Research Strategies* 7 (1), Winter 1989, pp. 14-32.
Reviews the literature of database search strategy, with seventy one references, in the context of the requirements of end user instruction.

539. On-Line Information Searching Systems and Methods. Springfield, Virginia: U.S. Department of Commerce. National Technical Information Service. (NTIS order number: PB93-852689CBY).
Contains references with abstracts to articles on online databases taken from the INSPEC database. NTIS Published Searches are custom-made bibliographies undertaken in the week of order by NERAC Inc on behalf of NTIS. Thus, up-to-date results from a fixed profile can be dispatched as and when needed.

Books

540. **Chan, L. M.** and **Pollard, R.** *Thesauri Used in Online Databases: an Analytical Guide.* Westport, Connecticut: Greenwood Press, 1988. 268pp.
Serves as an aid to searchers by identifying and examining the different types of indexing vocabularies employed in online information retrieval. Thesauri used by a more than 100 online databases are described in separate entries which include details of the scope, usage and arrangement of each, along with types and forms of headings and subheadings used and sample descriptors. Thesauri are indexed by title, personal name of compiler, organization, subject and database. Although beginning to date, this book is useful not only as a guide to online thesaurus use but as a source guide to thesauri and a guide to thesuarus evaluation.

541. Goldmann, N. *Online Information Hunting.* Blue Ridge Summit, PA: TAB Books (Windcrest/McGraw-Hill), 1992. 236pp.

A thorough and well-rounded introduction to online services and searching which takes readers through basics which include 'The Place of Online Searching', 'Information and the Subject Expert' and 'Records, Files and Indexes' to building a search strategy and running an online search. Finally, the volume covers both academic e-mail networks (as they existed in 1992) and the 'Dos and Don'ts, Step by Step' of online searching. Sample searches are generously scattered throughout the book, the examples being taken from vendor systems available in 1992, including: BRS, DIALOG, ESA-IRS, I P Sharp, Mead Data Central and ORBIT.

542. Harter, S. P. *Online Information Retrieval: Concepts, Principles, and Techniques.* Orlando: Academic Press, 1986. 259pp. (Library and Information Science).

A well-researched and thoroughly referenced work of interest to new and experienced searchers which concentrates on the process of online searching, analyzing in detail search preparation, conduct and evaluation 'with the ultimate goal of helping the reader learn how to think about online information retrieval' (Preface, p. ix). Numerous examples of online searching in practice are employed to illustrate command languages, database structure, search strategy and evaluation. There is also an interesting chapter on the characteristics and behaviour of online searchers. A set of practical exercises is listed at the end of each chapter, while a glossary at the back of the book briefly defines over 150 common terms.

543. McCue, J. H. *Online Searching in Public Libraries: a Comparative Study of Performance.* Metuchen, New Jersey: Scarecrow Press, 1988. 272pp.

Reports on an unobtrusive study in 1984 of the performance of twenty one reference librarians in US public libraries. Each librarian was given a search query to answer with thirty minutes of online time on two databases. The results are analyzed and search quality is evaluated in terms of preparation, search strategy, presearch interview, characteristics of the searcher and the physical environment provided for searching.

544. Vigil, P. J. *Online Retrieval: Analysis and Strategy.* New York: Wiley, 1988. 242pp. (Information Science Series).

The Preface states that a primary theme of the book is that the concepts and principles of online interaction are applicable for both searching and creating a database. Thus, while methods, commands and strategies for online information retrieval are at the core of this work, and the intended audience is 'any computer user ... who is either searching commercial online databases or who is considering to do so', there is also a chapter on database construction. A recurrent theme is the searcher's need to understand the computer's capabilities and limitations. The book also contains chapters on search aid software for non-expert searchers. Search examples from the major US hosts are heavily used. As with any textbook containing examples, the particulars of some searches may no longer be accurate – indeed some of the vendors no longer exist in this form – but the principles remain.

545. Walker, G and **Janes, J.** *Online Retrieval: a Dialogue of Theory and Practice.* Colorado: Libraries Unlimited, 1993.
Curiously titled but excellent training manual for searching online databases. A book intended for the novice searcher which uses hundreds of examples drawn from real searches to demonstrate all there is to know about the practice of online searching but at the same time finds room to cover basics such as Boolean logic, indexing and other 'theoretic' topics. The training is based almost exclusively on KR DIALOG on the basis that skills learned on one system can easily be transferred as the user has to move to new hosts. As Andrew Everest notes in his review (*Managing Information* 1 (11/12) November/December 1994. p.42), 'look no further if you need a plain guide to both the how and the why of online. I would go so far as to say that the guide should be required reading for any library school course covering online.' As this is where the first-named author cut her teeth, it is not surprising that the book is so precisely targetted and well balanced. Most notable is the fact that the Internet gets coverage as an online resource in its own right

Handbooks

546. Armstrong, C. J. and **Large, J. A.** (eds.) *Manual of Online Search Strategies* (2nd ed.). Aldershot: Ashgate, 1992. 699pp.
A reference work packed with information on techniques for optimal searching of databases in a wide range of subject disciplines, aimed at searchers who need from time to time to move outside the databases relating to their own subject specialisms. An introductory chapter offers an overview of database evaluation and selection. The core of the work consists of individual chapters by experienced contributors in broad subject areas in which relevant databases are listed and compared, with profiles of the major files and sample records and searches to illustrate significant or unique features, while two other chapters deal with citation indexing and patents as specialist areas. The subject chapters cover: Chemistry; the Biosciences; Agriculture; Energy and the Environment; Engineering; Computer and Information Science and Technology; Social and Behavioural Sciences; Law: British and European Legal Systems; Law: North American Legal Systems; Business and Economics: United Kingdom; Business and Economics: United States; Humanities; and Databases for Quick Reference. Authors are drawn from both sides of the Atlantic. Some chapters include sample searches from a range of hosts, while others concentrate on one system. Most refer to further reading. An appendix contains a selective list of directories, bibliographies and reference works and there are a Database, Host and Information Provider Index, a Source Material and Search Aids Index; and a Subject Index to complete the work.

547. Basch, R. *Secrets of the Super Searchers.* Wilton, CT: Online, 1994.

Through a series of structured interviews with 23 of the world's top online searchers, Reva Basch brought together a series of tips which will help novice searchers, professional searchers, information brokers, trainers and even help desk staff. Covering topics such as charging, end users, electronic document delivery, LANs, consultant-client relationships, budgets, output formats, the pre-search interview, choosing the best system to search, search strategies, multifile searching, and evaluating a search on the fly. The question-and-answer format enables comparisons to be made between the super searchers.

548. **Berkman, R. I.** *Find It Online!* New York: Windcrest/McGraw-Hill, 1994. 380pp.

An all-embracing approach to finding information in electronic (online, CD-ROM or Internet) database sources. Written for the end user in a 'popular' style, the book's mission is described as 'to cut a clear path through the thicket of data sources by clearly describing and comparing competing electronic services and sources.' Despite that hyperbole, Find It Online! does accomplish much of what it sets out to do, although very much for an American audience covering, as it does, America Online (not quite in Europe at the time of writing), Delphi, GEnie, Prodigy and CompuServve in addition to the Internet and CD-ROM sources. The first section deals with online sources and the second with those on CD-ROM; both have almost more screen shots and examples than text but both cover the ground well although there is a tendency to use front-end search software (such as CompuServe's CIM) in the figures. Charging information will date rapidly. The final section and chapter lists databases under some forty broad topic headings such as Address and telephone directories, astronomy and space, business and company information, and travel. For each category the section lists three 'major types' of electronic database: consumer CD-ROMs, CD-ROMs found in libraries and online services. It is not comprehensive but provides a 'quick look up and contact information for many of the most broadly useful and popular electronic databases'. The cover suggests that the book will allow readers to 'Do your own online searching'; and find 'fast facts and answers from around the globe'; and is 'compatible with all hardware and software' – it is quite definitely aimed at the home user and contains a wealth of information to help him or her find and use appropriate sources.

549. **Hunter, B.** and **Lodish, E. K.** *Online Searching in the Curriculum: a Teaching Guide for Library/Media Specialists and Teachers.* Santa Barbara, California: ABC-Clio, 1989. 219pp.

A handbook for teachers and and school librarians involved in teaching online or CD-ROM searching at secondary or high school level. The core of the book is a set of lesson plans for five major projects, including handouts at the end of each project chapter which can be reproduced for distribution. The introductory chapter describes the rationale for the book, and overview of the projects and includes a list of suitable databases available on diskette at the time of writing and a bibliography of over fifty references from the mid- eighties. The bias is towards the USA both in terms of the projects themselves and the teaching style but, six years on, it could usefully find a place in UK schools. Student prerequisites are noted is the projects are to be undertaken without staff assistance.

550. Maxymuk, J. (ed) *Government CD-ROMs: a Practical Guide to Searching Electronic Databases.* London: Mecklermedia, 1994. 324pp.
A collection of twelve chapters – which, despite the title, include one on setting up a public workstation – on searching US government databases on CD-ROM. An appendix provides an annotated list of about 125 Government Printing Office CD-ROMs. The chapters deal with census data, foreign trade data, geographical information systems (GIS), the National Trade Data Bank (NTDB), the National Health Interview Survey CD-ROMs and the Toxic Release Inventory. In each case, the database is described, search and display options are detailed and a summary of good and bad points is given. Most chapters have short lists of further readings and all are replete with screen dumps.

551. Shuman, B. A. *Cases in Online Search Strategy.* Englewood, Colorado: Libraries Unlimited, 1993. 279 pp. (Database Searching Series)
The work consists of sixty case studies which together illustrate the main points of negotiating reference questions, deciding on an approach and producing a search strategy. The case studies cover many fields – humanities, economics and business, the law, life sciences and science and technology – but each is presented in a uniform format taking the reader from the first presentation of the natural-language query through strategy formulation, file selection and the search algorithm to the results and a short evaluation. A useful handbook on the reference process with the single drawback that all files are selected from KR DIALOG alone. The focus is on conditions where the 'meter is running and mistakes can be costly' so that CD-ROM options are not considered. The author acknowledges both these points in the Introduction where he also notes the online versus CD-ROM argument briefly. Despite the apparently narrow perspective, the case studies – from 'If nuclear winter comes, how long can it be expected to last?' to 'Which musical composers are said to have belonged to the nineteenth-century romantic movement?' – make a very real contribution to the literature on database searching which is ideal for use in library schools.

552. *UKOLUG Quick Guide to Online Commands.* (4th ed.) Compiled by Sheila Webber, Chris Baile, Andrew Cameron and Jonathan Eaton. London: UK Online User Group. 1994. 120pp.
Hugely succesful in its previous editions, this invaluable guide to solving command language queries prior to and during searching lists in an easy-to-use tabular format a variety of commands and features from eighteen major hosts accessed by UK searchers. Commands on each system are illustrated with brief commentary and the use of a standard grid format (with fixed positions for index display, printing or sorting

commands, for example) over six A4 pages per host ensures easy location and comparison of system features. Telephone numbers are listed for the help desks of hosts covered in the guide. The guide provides an ideal way for searchers to 'brush up' on command use in an unfamiliar system and the layout means that a function can be located on a system known to the user and the comparable command for the new system picked up from the same box on the new system pages. Systems covered are BIDS, BLAISE- LINE, BLAISE-LINK, CDP Online, KR Data-Star, KR DIALOG, DIMDI, ECHO, ESA-IRS, FIZ Technik, FT Profile, Kompass Online, LEXIS/ NEXIS, Orbit and Questel, STN International and TOXNET.

Journal Articles

553. Basch, R. 'Decision Points for Databases'. *Database* 15 (4) (August 1992). pp. 46-50.

If users do not simply search across large file groups (as is becoming increasingly possible), how do we determine what databases to use? Using the concepts of relevance and accessibility developed in Barabara Quint's two-part article as a starting point (Quint, B. 'Inside a Searcher's Mind: The Seven Stages of an Online Search'. *Online* 15 (3)/15 (4) (May and July 1991)), this article looks again at some of the areas often explored in the pre-search interview (what are you trying to accomplish with this search?) and discusses the interaction of reliability with accessibility – 'if relevance is a matter of database content, accessibility has a lot to do with design: what kinds of fields compromise the individual records?' Finally, it all has to do with quality – 'quality, like ethics, is situational ... there are some files I will not search ... and yet, face it: We have to use what's available, and that sometimes means using a suspect source if we've found zilch elsewhere.'

554. Tenopir, C. and **Hover, K.** 'When is the Same Database not the Same?: Database Differences Among Systems'. *Online* 17(4) (July 1993). pp. 20-27.

Following a brief introduction illustrating the breadth of choice open to searchers, the article looks at potential differences in any given database on its different host systems. Seven possible differences are discussed: updating frequency and schedule; dates covered; price (both time and prints); subfiles structure and field structure; content; support features (such as the thesaurus); and system search features. A major table compares eleven common databases for update schedule, date range, cost and file structure on their various hosts.

SUBJECT SEARCHING – BUSINESS

Books: Electronically Distributed

555. Sternberg, S. *Business Use of the Internet.* Available via the Internet, 1995. 500pp.

A completely public-domain resource and resource guide which, if printed extends to some 500 pages, has been made freely available online. Eleven chapters discuss all aspects of business use with about half of the volume devoted to listing specific reports and resources. The chapters are: Communication Services and Resources; Improving Business Communication; Improving Internal Operations; News Sources and In-Company News Services; Resources of General Business Interest; Net Facilities by Types of Business; Net Resources for Global Commerce (in three parts covering business opportunities, information by geographic location and information about the United States); Business Research on the Internet; Developing Your office on the Net; Small Business; and The Future of Business. The full text of the book is available from servers:
gopher:\gopher.phoenix.caor or ftp:\ftp.phoenix.capubor or http:\www.phoenix.cawhats-newas as well as from FTP:\gopher.epas.utoronto.ca/epas (directory/pub/datalib/misc/sternberg.txt).

Books

556. Glossbrenner, A. *How to Look it up Online: Get the Information Edge with Your Personal Computer.* New York: St. Martin's Press, 1987. 486pp.

Aimed at the US business end user getting started in online searching but sufficiently detailed to be of continuing use to more experienced searchers. Part I provides overviews of equipment, database structure, search strategy and front-end software. The next part profiles the major US hosts available in 1987, while the final (and most extensive) section addresses itself to where and how to find different types of information online. Appendices explain the importation of retrieved data into commercial software packages for different purposes and discuss sources of information on databases. The strong points of the work are its emphasis on ways of finding factual (as distinct from bibliographical) information, several tips on short-cuts or time-saving measures in searching, its informal style, and the provision of contact data for further details on topics covered.

557. Jones, C. and **Dowsland, W.** *Online Sources of European Information: Their Development and Use.* Aldershot: Avebury (Gower), 1990. 125pp.

The work examines the current and future role of electronic information services in Europe with particular emphasis on the provision and use of online information relating to European matters from both commercial and official sources. The work compares the European information industry to that of USA, UK, France, West Germany and Italy and notes the influence of CD-ROM technology before looking at business use of online information, European Community information, European telecommunications and harmonisation, European Community policies, the Information Market Observatory, programmes such as RACE and ESPRIT and looking at the future – noting the importance of ISDN, the authors think that the success of the industry depends largely upon whether national interests can be put aside to allow the development of an integrated and harmonised telecommunications network. Appendices list abbreviations and glosses; Euroinfo Centres' addresses; European Documentation Centres in the UK; Online systems produced by Eurostat; Commercial hosts holding EC databases; European data networks; Packet switching exchanges in the UK; and give details of Packet standards and OSI; ESPRIT; and RACE. There is also a bibliography and an index.

558. Popovich, C. J. *Business and Economics Databases Online: Environmental Scanning with a Personal Computer.* Littleton, Colorado: Libraries Unlimited, 1987. 276pp. (Advanced Online Searching Series).

The author sets out to review the machine-readable resources available to researchers in the business community, concentrating on the environmental factors (social, technological, economic and political) within which an organisation operates. The process of systematically exploring these factors is referred to as environmental scanning and serves as a basis for an exploration of online searching – from PC hardware and software, through basic commands to the data itself. The book mainly comprises illustrated examples of searches for social, technological, economic and political data on databases on the KR DIALOG and I.P. Sharp hosts. A valuable extra feature shows how downloaded data can be imported into Lotus 1-2-3 software for offline analysis. The final section is a source guide to database directories and two appendices list relevant databases on KR DIALOG and I.P. Sharp.

559. Scanlan, J. M., de Stricker, U. and **Fernald, A.C.** *Business Online: the Professional's Guide to Electronic Information Services.* New York: Wiley, 1989. 368pp.

The purpose of the book is described as twofold: to help business professionals determine whether, and identify which online services would be useful to their work and to help interested readers begin to use these services. The book assumes no prior knowledge on the part of the reader and, 'because many sources of information are available through services that also provide electronic messaging', includes a chapter on electronic mail. This immediately dates the work as BI (Before Internet) and the emphasis in the final chapter is on keeping up to date so readers should be aware that business information is time sensitive and the business information industry itself reflects this in its volatility. After seven introductory chapters, the overall summary of databases is divided into: Company Information, News Databases, Management, Marketing and Industry Information, Legal and Tax Information, Accounting,

Econometric and Demographic, and Patent and Trademarks. More than directories, these chapters describe the main databases in some detail and each ends with a case study of a search in that area.

560. **Wasik, J. F.** *The Electronic Business Information Sourcebook.* New York: Wiley, 1987. 208pp.

Written by a journalist, this is a guide to the general research and business databases on offer on a range of US hosts. The book emphasizes the end user and describes a number of appropriate services aimed at this market. Appendices provide annotated lists of further reading, information brokers, hosts, and selected databases.

Conferences: Regular

561. *European Business Information Conference.* Organized by TFPL. London: TFPL, 1990-. Annual.

A relatively new conference focusing on the future of the business information industry, end-user services, global contracts, international stockbroker research, and capital markets. With the emphasis firmly pan-European, the 5th conference concentrates on problems and applications geared to librarians in Central Europe. A series of workshops – in the 1995 conference, on Benchmarking information services, Business information on the Internet, Eastern European company information, Project management approaches to running an information service, Making money from business information on the Internet, CompuServe, etc, and Integrating information into the business process – round off a conference which has received nothing but praise in previous years.

Directories: CD-ROM/Diskette

562. *Online Manual on Disk.* Oxford: Learned Information, 1993-. Biannual.

The Online Manual is a comprehensive guide to over 2,000 English-language databases or 60,000 source publications. Using Headfast software, *The Online Manual on Disk* is a fast and effective reference tool which can pinpoint relevant databases and provide information on such topics as 'the databases which will give information on food in the USA'; 'the databases which have coverage of Spain'; 'the account items that particular databases hold'; or 'whether a particular journal is available online'. Searches are possible by subject, source, geographical coverage, financial details, database and host. There are, in fact over 100 searchable account items. With the December 1994 edition, the software has become Windows-based. The electronic version is available on diskette or CD-ROM. A comparative review can be found in the *Journal of Information Science* 20 (4) (1994) pp. 260-269 although readers should note subsequent correspondence between the editors of *The Onlie Manual* and the reviewer.

Originally available from Disclosure First Contact, the consultancy who produce the *Manual*, all forms (bound, CD-ROM and diskette) became available from Learned Information in mid 1994.

Directories: Print

563. Armstrong, C. J. (ed.) *World Databases in Industry.* East Grinstead: Bowker-Saur, 1994. 852 pp.

Part of a commissioned series covering all disciplines, *World Databases in Industry* is a comprehensive directory of databases published on diskette, tape, CD-ROM (or any of its variants) and online. Records are very full with each database given a top 'producer record' describing the database as developed by the information provider and as many 'product records' as there are online or portable versions. One of the main aims of the project is to make clear any links between databases so if material from one database can also be found in another this will be shown. Third-party review material is either referenced or quoted. The database from which the print directories are produced will be made available on CD-ROM.

564. Armstrong, C. J. (ed.) *World Databases in Management.* East Grinstead: Bowker-Saur, 1994. 794 pp.

World Databases in Management is a comprehensive directory of databases published on diskette, tape, CD-ROM (or any of its variants) and online which complements *World Databases in Industry* (above). Records are very full with each database given a top 'producer record' describing the database as developed by the information provider and as many 'product records' as there are online or portable versions. One of the main aims of the project is to make clear any links between databases so if material from one database can also be found in another this will be shown. Third-party review material is either referenced or quoted. The database from which the print directories are produced will be made available on CD-ROM.

565. *Business and Legal CD-ROMs in Print 1993.* Westport: Mecklermedia, 1993. 360pp.

Marketed as a 'comprehensive' directory of CD-ROM and CD-based multimedia products in business and law, the subject coverage includes economics, patent information, taxation, finance, related government information and management. The directory is based on information gathered for Mecklermedia's *CD-ROMs in Print: an International Guide* and is the first in an annual series of subject-specific reference guides. The editors admit to having 'cast the net widely' in order to make the directory a stand-alone guide and the 1,234 titles include many from peripheral areas such as advertising, almanacs, the automotive industry, forestry, government information, pollution, railways, telecommunications, and trade. Even allowing for such an inclusion of specific industries, it is difficult to see why titles such as Digital

Chart of the World, the Sea-D series of marine navigation charts and the American Heritage Illustrated Encyclopedic Dictionary have been included.
Each listing includes up to 31 items of information about the product including a short description and full price, contact and ordering information. Making due allowance for its generous inclusion policy, this is a useful and informative directory sensibly targetted at a precise sector. The directory includes a company index in which products are listed under contact details of producers (this is useful as with no cross-referencing, users might not find DIALOG discs which are all listed in the main alphabetic sequence under 'DIALOG ONDISC'); separate title lists of Macintosh, multimedia and Electronic Book products and a subject index. No indexes refers to page or item numbers, rather they list products by producer, by style or within subject categories.

566. *Business Information Basics.* Headland, Cleveland: Headland Press, 1992-. Every two years. 150 pp.
Formed from the earlier *Business Information Sourcebook* and *Business Information Yearbook,* reviews an entire range of UK business resources. In fourteen chapters, the directory examines print directories, market research reports, forecasts and looseleaf services; online, CD-ROM and diskette databases and videotex and audiotext sources; and organisations such as financial data providers, major business libraries, courses and conferences. An appendix lists other useful readings.

567. *CD-ROM and Online Business and Company Databases.* (4th ed.) Compiled by L. English. London: Aslib, 1994. 139pp.
A selective list of those business and company information sources most frequently searched in Britain. Each entry contains a brief description of content and includes details of search costs and user aids. The emphasis is on databases which are of broad potential interest. There are database, subject and host indexes.

568. *CD-ROM and Online Business Statistical Databases.* Compiled by M. Brittin. London: Aslib, 1993. 136pp.
Audiovisual Librarian called this directory 'a must for any business information service point' and given the rapid growth in the business statistics generated by todays marketplace, this guide should prove invaluable. Sections include the Introduction, How to Use this Guide, Database Descriptions, Host Addresses, Producer Addresses and indexes for countries and subjects. Each of the 210 database record contains data on the format, content, language, coverage, time span, updating, producer, distributors, costs and user aids. The coverage includes 119 online databases, 69 on diskette, 55 on magnetic tape and 48 on CD-ROM. There is also a bibliography. The compiler states that databases are included even if only partial details were available and, as Andrew Pinnock (*LA Record* 96(1) (January 1994) 45) states, the result is an impressively wide spread of information – 'an accessible source of information to an often inaccessible field.'

569. *CD-ROM and Online Computing, Electronics and Telecommunications Databases.* Compiled by R. Rouse. London: Aslib, 1994. 130pp.
Covers a wide range of databases with sections on business and company databases and subject, host and database indexes. Each database record contains, in addition to a subject description, details on the type of database, language, coverage, time span, updating, the producer, the publisher or hosts, distributors, the platform, costs, user aids and, if relevant, the number of discs.

570. *CD-ROM and Online Management and Marketing Databases.* (4th ed.) Compiled by N. Parker. London: Aslib, 1993. 92pp.
Places the emphasis on European databases, describing files which cover management techniques and are most heavily used by UK searchers. Descriptions are detailed and in each case cover source and subject content, database structure, updating, producer, hosts, search charges and user aids. Contents include an introduction, List of Databases, The databases, Hosts, and a Bibliography.

571. **Cousins, J.** and **Robinson, L.** *The Online Manual: A Practical Guide to Business Databases* (3rd edition). Oxford: Learned Information, 1994. 900+pp.
Described in *Aslib Information* as scoring favourably in comparison with the Cuadra/ Gale *Directory of Online Databases,* being much easier to use, *The Online Manual* is a comprehensive guide to over 2,000 English-language databases or 60,000 source publications. In reality, although both list databases, *The Online Manual* serves a different purpose as its principle listing is by print publication rather than by database. Here, details of the actual databases are scant, being limited to a list of hosts, geographical coverage and a single-letter code for Type of Information equating to Marketing, Scientific, Economic, Financial or Technical. Financial databases only are dealt with in more detail. The second edition has seven main sections: How to Use the Manual; Hosts – contains contact details, costs and access times; Technical Requirements – gives details of hardware and software required for accessing databases; Financial Databases – a section providing comprehensive details on each of the financial databases covered by *The Manual;* Thesaurus which provides listings of databases by subject; Database to Host – a section containing an alphabetical list linking databases to hosts; and the 800+ page Source Guide which contains an alphabetical list of source publications (journals, Newspapers, etc) showing on which databases on which hosts they may be found. *The Online Manual* is also available twice per year on diskette or CD-ROM.
Originally available from Disclosure First Contact, the consultancy who produce the Manual, all forms (bound, CD-ROM and diskette) became available from Learned Information in mid 1994.

572. *European Business Information Sourcebook.* Headland, Cleveland: Headland Press, 1992-. Every two years. 200 pp.
A one-stop source guide to key European business information resources covering all European Union countries and members of EFTA plus Eastern Europe. All categories

of business information are included: print, electronic and organisations. Many sources are evaluated so that the potential user can assess their worth.

573. Foster, P. (ed.) *Online/CD-ROM Business Sourcebook.* Headland, Cleveland: Headland Press, 1993- . Annually.
Developed from *Which Database?,* this is a single-volume evaluative guide to business databases. With a European bias, the *Sourcebook* selects the most important business databases and analyses the major host systems and CD-ROM publishers. The sections include an introduction; in-depth discussions of online hosts and CD-ROM publishers and details of databases containing company directories, company accounts, credit ratings, mergers & acquisitions, business news, etc.

574. Foster, P. (ed.) *Which Business CD-ROM?* Headland, Cleveland: Headland Press, 1993-. Annually.
An A4 paperback directory which evaluates the best CD-ROM databases for business users. The directory combines the CD-ROM entries from *Online/CD-ROM Business Sourcebook* with the 'testdrives' of products from the monthly newsletter, *Online/CD-ROM Business Information.* Important US files are covered although the directory has a UK/European bias.

575. Foster, P. (ed.) *Which European Database?* Headland, Cleveland: Headland Press, 1992-. Annually.
A directory providing in-depth guidance to the best business databases (company, market research, business news, economics, etc) available throughout the regions and countries of continental Europe: EEC, EFTA and Eastern Europe. Arranged by type of data within country chapters, *Which European Database?* includes database evaluations and descriptions taken from *Online/CD-ROM Business Sourcebook* and by varying the amount of detail differentiates between important and lesser databases.

576. *Handbuch der Wirtschaftsdatenbanken: Inhalte und Anbieter – weltweit.* Darmstadt: Hoppenstedt. Annual.
Typically, describes over 750 sources of business, financial and product information. Entries are arranged alphabetically and include data on source coverage, subject scope, geographical emphasis and subscription terms. A subject index is included and contains broad groupings which are further subdivided by geographical scope, reflecting the fact that the directory goes well beyond listing German databases only. The language of the directory is German.

577. *International Company Filing Requirements.* London: Informed Business Services, 1994.
One of the major problems in searching company databases and in comparing information from more than one country is the varying filing requirements of the different countries. This loose-leaf guide gives details of forms of business enterprise,

company registration, filing and audit requirements and particulars of the public availability of information for 26 countries worldwide, including all the EU and EFTA states. The publishers specialise in European business information.

578. *Market Information.* Headland, Cleveland: Headland Press, 1993-. Every two years. 100 pp.
A new version of the award-winning *Market Research Sourcebook,* this directory guides the market researcher to the best information sources. All sources are evaluated in detail. It contains accurate, up-to-date information on statistics, market research reports, reference publications, consumer data, online and CD-ROM databases, and libraries. A final section details how users can conduct their own market research project.

579. Ness, D. *Fast Facts Online: Search Strategies for Finding Business Information.* Homewood, Illinois: Dow Jones-Irwin, 1986. 548pp.
An information-packed publication for US searchers of business data. The core of the book is a listing in tabular format of databases for thirty-two categories of data. These databases are ranked in separate tables according to the level of coverage they offer. Details provided for each database include hosts, geographical coverage, number of source journals and accessible fields. The same information is provided in a form which is easier to digest in a separate alphabetical listing of databases. These factual data are supplemented by another section which explains and illustrates specialized searching of some databases on one or more hosts. The book also includes advice on search techniques, details of the major US hosts, a glossary and and annotated reading list.

580. Riou, B. *Directory of French Videotex Databases for Companies.* Paris: FLA Consultants, 1991. 265pp.
The directory offers details on more than 250 professional videotex databases available on Minitel. The body of the guide is divided into sixteen main parts: Indexes and directories of companies; Financial, Juridical and legal information about companies; Legal context; Economic and political context; Foreign trade; Stock exchange and finance; Business opportunities; Training; Information on the media; Trade fairs and exhibitions; Building, materials and mechanics; Computers and computing; Transportation; Town and country planning and development; and Other fields. Each section begins with a page on which the constituent subject areas are listed (unfortunately these have not been translated from French in the English edition) and continues with standard format descriptions of each database. Information contained includes the access codes, the size of the database, update frequency, language and types of document included. There is also a sample record. Each description extends to one page. Five appendices provide an analytical table of databases, a list of producers, a list of hosts, an alphabetic list of service codes arranged by access type, and an alphabetic list of the databases.

581. Scott, J. (ed.) *London Business School SourceGuide to East European Information.* (2nd ed.) Andover, Hampshire: Gale Research International, 1994. 400 pp.

The guide includes not only company information but also economic information, details of consumer and industrial markets and key contact organisations such as trade councils and government agencies. With around 1,000 entries containing key data such as contact information, format of the database, coverage, language and update information, business users will find this an important source. There are title and subject indexes. Future SourceGuides are planned for *European Consumer Market Information* (2nd ed.) and *European Industrial Market Information* (2nd ed.).

582. Scott, J. (ed.) *London Business School SourceGuide to European Company Information* (5th ed.) Andover, Hampshire: Gale Research International, 1993. 352 pp.

Compiled by specialists at the London Business School Information Service, the *SourceGuide* includes only those sources of information which they would be prepared to use themselves. In most cases, the material has been evaluated while in others publisher's descriptions are used although where publishers have not responded to requests for information, the source is not listed even though it is believed to exist. The *Guide* is divided into four main parts plus an alphabetical index to sources. Part 1 covers Pan-European Sources such as Dun & Bradstreet and Kompass; while Part 2 contains eighteen individual country sections, each with an introduction discussing legal business types and disclosure regulations followed by a full listing of sources arranged by information format (directories, newspapers, online hosts, CD-ROM databases). Part 3 details firms supplying company information or credit ratings for a fee and Part 4 describes information brokers who can provide clients with company information tailored to their needs. Future SourceGuides are planned for *European Consumer Market Information* (2nd ed.) and *European Industrial Market Information* (2nd ed.).

583. Sims, M. S. (ed.) *Directory of Periodicals Online: Indexed, Abstracted and Full-Text: News, Law, Business.* Washington, DC: Federal Document Retrieval. Annual.

Lists over 8,000 news, law and business periodicals worldwide which are indexed, abstracted or presented in full text in over 200 online databases. Entries for journals contain full bibliographic details, subject coverage and list the databases in which they are covered. The separate section for databases indicates the type of coverage given to journals, with information on indexing, abstracting or full-text presentation. Additional sections are an appendix containing the addresses of database hosts and producers and a subject index to periodicals.

584. Spencer, N. (ed.) *The Instant Guide to Company Information Online – Europe.* (2nd ed.) London: British Library Science Reference and Information Service, 1993. 88pp.

The Guide enables users to identify which online company databases contain the kinds of information for which they are looking. The bulk of the guide – one pan-European and sixteen country sections – is tabular in form and lists selected databases containing information about the country/ies in question with their online host, the number of companies included and codes (S = searchable; D = display only; '-' = no information) for the following categories of information which could be included in the database: company location, status, registration number, date/year formed, management, ownership, subsidiaries, industry/product codes, importer/exporter, number of employees, capital, sales, profit/loss, detailed financials, financial ratios, credit rating, advisors, and full-text annual reports. This is followed by an A-to-Z of databases giving the producer, host(s), a very brief description and notes including geographical coverage, language, updating, etc and an A-to-Z of online hosts. There is also a country-by-country listing of company types and disclosure requirements.

585. *The Guide – A Practical Handbook of Marketing Research Sources in the UK and Western Europe.* Hampton, Middlesex: Key Note Publications, 1992. 763pp.

Replacing *The Source Book* with a more European emphasis, this directory describes information sources which can be used for researching markets, companies and industries. Arrangement is by 300 industry sectors for which online databases are included as information sources where appropriate. Some 5,000 databases are listed with details of subject coverage, source documents, time span covered, updating frequency, producer and host. The emphasis throughout is on databases which contain information on UK industry. Contact information is provided for over forty hosts.

Handbooks

586. James, S. *Manual of Online Search Strategies in Business.* Aldershot: Ashgate, 1993. 300pp.

The contents include definitions of online services as used in business; methods of access, and the hardware and software required; dealing with online vendors; how to market online usage in the organisation; using online business services for specific projects that require considerable data gathering; principles of manipulating data to and from online services; training for business information online; keeping up to date with new services and databases; executive information systems; the market for online business information; the future role of the intermediary in online business searching; company information; industry information; online statistical information for business; sources from and about governmental and supranational organisations for business; technical change databases; and legal information sources for business.

Journals

587. *Advanced Searcher.* Humberston, Grimsby: Effective Technology Marketing, 1991-. Bimonthly.
From 1994, the extended coverage of this newsletter encompasses CD-ROM and optical media, patent news and Japanese and Eastern European news. While maintaining the mix of editorial comment, feature articles and interviews as well as its focus on the business world, product developments and search strategies, the new *Advanced Searcher* is offered at a reduced subscription cost. In the past, articles have covered competitor information, McCarthy on CD-ROM, Mead Data Central in Europe, database copyright and the information broker, real time information services and STATUS IQ.

588. *Business Information Review.* Headland, Cleveland: Headland Press, 1984-. Quarterly.
Articles with a practical slant are published in each issue, many focusing on ways of finding information for particular purposes and taking full account of online business information sources as appropriate. New databases are announced and reviewed in a separate section of the journal. All kinds of business information are included from reference sources to broadcast information and regular columns cover top books and industry profiles of leading business information providers. The US journal, *Choice,* said '...scholarly in content and a pleasure to read'.

589. *Information Advisor.* Missoula, MT: Information Advisory Services, 1987-. Monthly.
A useful journal for business researchers which compares and evaluates resources in both print and database forms. The focus is on data quality, international services and finding the best sources of expertise.

Newsletters

590. *European Business Intelligence Briefing.* Headland, Cleveland: Headland Press, 1989-. Eleven times per annum.
Winning second prize in the Aslib EBIG Awards, this is a newsletter which evaluates information sources on companies, markets and products. It covers all information sources (including print) with full-length articles evaluating categories of resource and an update column.

591. *Online/CD-ROM Business Information.* Headland, Cleveland: Headland Press, 1985-. Eleven issues per year.

The major part of each issue are 'testdrives' of major business databases online, on CD-ROM or on diskette such as MAID, ICC Key Notes or Moody's International Company Data. Such evaluations are thorough and analyse source coverage, search fields and record structure, illustrating different types of search. The rest of the publication consists of news of online and ondisc sources as they appear.

SUBJECT SEARCHING – ENVIRONMENT

Directories: Print

592. *CD-ROM and Online Environment Databases.* (2nd ed.). Compiled by J. Cox. London: Aslib, 1994.

An important guide to databases covering all aspects of the environment – air, water, land and mineral – with additional coverage of earth sciences, geology, pollution, chemicals and toxicology, climatology and acid rain, ozone depletion and global warming. Each database record contains, in addition to a subject description, details on coverage, updating, the producer, the hosts, costs, user aids and other formats in which the database may be available.

593. **Lees, N.** and **Woolston, H.** *Environmental Information: A Guide to Sources.* London: British Library, 1993. 180pp.

Although this work lists and evaluates a range of information sources on environmental problems, online and CD-ROM databases are included beside printed publications and key organisations. The contents include technical, government, business and patent information; UK and EC legislation; environmental auditing, assessment and policy; and sources of information on pollution, waste disposal and recycling, energy and transport. There are detailed appendices and indexes.

SUBJECT SEARCHING – GOVERNMENT

Handbooks

594. Maxymuk, J. (ed.) *Government CD-ROMs: a Practical Guide to Searching Electronic Databases.* London: Mecklermedia, 1994. 324pp.

A collection of twelve chapters – which, despite the title, include one on setting up a public workstation – on searching US government databases on CD- ROM. An appendix provides an annotated list of about 125 Government Printing Office CD-ROMs. The chapters deal with census data, foreign trade data, geographical information systems (GIS), the National Trade Data Bank (NTDB), the National Health Interview Survey CD-ROMs and the Toxic Release Inventory. In each case, the database is described, search and display options are detailed and a summary of good and bad points is given. Most chapters have short lists of further readings and all are replete with screen dumps.

SUBJECT SEARCHING – LAW

Directories: Print

595. *Business and Legal CD-ROMs in Print 1993.* Westport: Meckler, 1993. 360pp.

Marketed as a 'comprehensive' directory of CD-ROM and CD-based multimedia products in business and law, the subject coverage includes economics, patent information, taxation, finance, related government information and management. The directory is based on information gathered for Meckler's CD-ROMs in Print: an International Guide and is the first in an annual series of subject-specific reference guides. The editors admit to having 'cast the net widely' in order to make the directory a stand-alone guide and the 1,234 titles include many from peripheral areas such as advertising, almanacs, the automotive industry, forestry, government information, pollution, railways, telecommunications, and trade. Even allowing for such an inclusion of specific industries, it is difficult to see why titles such as Digital Chart of the World, the Sea-D series of marine navigation charts and the American Heritage Illustrated Encyclopedic Dictionary have been included. Each listing includes up to 31 items of information about the product including a short description and full price, contact and ordering information. Making due allowance for its generous inclusion policy, this is a useful and informative directory sensibly targetted at a precise sector. The directory includes a company index in which products are listed under contact details of producers (this is useful as with no cross-referencing, users might not find DIALOG discs which are all listed in the main alphabetic sequence under 'DIALOG ONDISC'); separate title lists of Macintosh, multimedia and Electronic Book products and a subject index. No indexes refers to page or item numbers, rather they list products by producer, by style or within subject categories.

596. *CD-ROM and Online Law Databases.* (4th ed.) Compiled by S. J. Nichols. London: Aslib, 1993. 149pp.

Updates the earlier edition, describing databases in terms of content, time span covered, updating frequency, producers, hosts, cost and user aids. Indexes are for country of coverage and subject. Additional sections provide host and producer addresses and a bibliography.

Journals

597. *Legal Reference Services Quarterly.* New York: Haworth Press, 1981-. Quarterly.

US journal for law reference librarians which includes articles on searching techniques for law databases and occasional comparisons of database sources for categories of information.

SUBJECT SEARCHING – LIFE SCIENCES

Bibliographies

598. *Health Information Systems.* Springfield, Virginia: U.S. Department of Commerce. National Technical Information Service. (NTIS order number: PB92-853324CBY).

Compiled from the NTIS database, this bibliography contains references on relevant to the health services. NTIS Published Searches are custom-made bibliographies undertaken in the week of order by NERAC Inc on behalf of NTIS. Thus, up-to-date results from a fixed profile can be dispatched as and when needed.

Books

599. Albright, R. G. *A Basic Guide to Online Information Systems for Health Care Professionals.* Arlington, Virginia: Information Resource Press, 1988. 296pp.

Written by an end user for end users, this publication devotes individual chapters to a number of online medical information services, including CompuServe, MEDLARS, DIALOG Medical Collection and Knowledge Index, and the then BRS/Colleague service. Sample screens are used as illustrations in each chapter. Other chapters and appendices briefly explain modems, communications software and telecommunications networks and provide a glossary.

600. Rapp, B. A. *Biotechnology Information Sources: North and South America.* Oxford: Learned Information, 1994. 144pp.

Despite the broad scope and rapid expansion of the biotechnology field, the author has succeeded in bringing together a comprehensive list of print and electronic information sources available in North and South America. Because of the broad scope of biotechnology, these sources are likely to prove useful to searchers throughout science, engineering and business. The descriptions of information resources provide concise information to permit readers to make decisions about usefulness and suitability. Each entry is lsted by full name and most common acronym and contact information is given in full.

601. Wood, M. S. R*eference and Information Services in Health Sciences Librarianship.* Medical Library Association and Scarecrow Press, 1994. 394pp. (Current Practices in Health Science Librarianship, volume 1)

This is the first of eight volumes appearing under the series title, Current Practices in Health Science Librarianship – a successor to the *Handbook of Medical Library*

Practice. The series will be a general intorduction to the field for graduate students, a source of basic information and retrieval to the literature of the MLA and a reference work for health science librarians providing basic information in areas peripheral to their own expertise. This volume is divided into six chapters, each covering specific aspects of reference librarianship in the health sciences. Each chapter has been reviewed by a librarian in a hospital library and an academic librarian in order to ensure relevance. The chapters are: General Reference Services; Databases and Database Searching; Microcomputers and the Reference Service; Management of Reference Services; Specialized Types of Reference and Information Services; and Information Technologies – Now and in the Future. There is also a glossary and seven appendices: Position Description: Reference Desk/Inter Library Loan Services Coordinator; Position Description: Information Management Education/Database Services Coordinator; Postion Description: Information Services Librarian; Training Plan: Information Services Librarian; Training Plan: Library Science Graduate Student Intern; Outline of Information Services Manual; and Outline for a Reference Collection Policy.

Conferences: Proceedings

602. Woodsmall, R. M., Lyon-Hartmann, B. and **Siegel, E. R.** (eds.). *MEDLINE on CD-ROM: National Library of Medicine Evaluation Forum, Bethesda, Maryland, September 23, 1988.* Medford, New Jersey: Learned Information, 1989. 506 pp.

The majority of this volume consists of detailed evaluations of seven CD-ROM versions of the MEDLINE database from twenty-one sites in the United States representing a combination of libraries and clinical settings. Findings regarding system performance and user satisfaction are in most cases supported by statistical data from questionnaries. Overall summaries of the evaluations were delivered at the forum and are also included in the volume along with reports of discussion sessions. Two appendices contain a checklist of features of MEDLINE on CD-ROM and a general bibliography of CD-ROM literature which is also available as a separate publication. While the volume is now beginning to date – most of the systems will have upgraded their software by now, for example – the general information on the role of CD-ROM in biomedical information transfer; favoured system features and capabilities; and the impact of CD-ROM on library services still has some relevance to today's professionals.

Directories: Print

603. Armstrong, C. J. (ed.) *World Databases in Medicine.* East Grinstead: Bowker-Saur, 1994. (2 vols) 1646 pp.

The first in a commissioned series covering all disciplines, *World Databases in Medicine* is a comprehensive directory of databases published on diskette, tape, CD-ROM (or any of its variants) and online and the Internet. Medicine is divided up into dentistry, ethics, genetics, handicapped and social medicine, health and safety, hospital administration, nursing, pharmacy and drugs, psychiatry, psychology, toxicology, veterinary medicine, medical devices, specific illnesses, reproduction and child care, age and aging, and forensic science. As with all volumes in the series, records are detailed with each database given a top 'producer record' describing the database as developed by the information provider and as many 'product records' as there are online or portable versions. One of the main aims of the project is to make clear any links between databases so if material from one database can also be found in another this will be shown. Third-party review material is either referenced or quoted. The database from which the print directories are produced will be made available on CD-ROM.

604. **Armstrong, C. J.** and **Fenton, R. R.** (eds.) *World Databases in the Social Sciences.* East Grinstead: Bowker-Saur, 1995. (in press).
Part of a commissioned series covering all disciplines, *World Databases in the Social Sciences* is a comprehensive directory of databases published on diskette, tape, CD-ROM (or any of its variants) and online and the Internet dealing with all aspects of sociology and the social sciences including ethnic studies; urban and rural studies; the elderly, women, children and families; the handicapped and rehabilitation/social medicine; substance abuse; demography; psychology and psychometrics; social policy and services; and opinion polls.

605. *Directory of Online Healthcare Databases.* Los Altos, California: Medical Data Exchange. Annual.
Over 200 databases are included in a standard tabular format which indicates producer, host, cost where known, file size, updating, timespan, and a brief narrative description of subject and source coverage. Other sections include a glossary, directory of host and producer addresses and subject index.

606. *Online Medical Databases.* (5th ed.) Compiled by E. Lyon. London: Aslib, 1991. 96pp.
This basic reference work lists over 100 bibliographic and full-text databases containing information on the biomedical, health care, toxicological and pharmaceutical fields. Detailed profiles of each are supplied and include data such as cost and user aids as well as a full description of subject content. Host, producer and supplier addresses are provided separately, as are a select bibliography and index to databases via hosts and producers. A useful section at the beginning of the directory describes the charging policies operated by different hosts. CD-ROM databases are excluded.

Journals

607. *Bulletin of the Medical Library Association.* Chicago: Medical Library Association, 1911-. Quarterly.

A regular source of information on online and CD-ROM databases in the medical sciences. Many of its articles deal with end-user searching. Numerous detailed reviews of new publications appear in each issue and are supplemented by a lengthy list of books and serials received for review. Recent journal literature from medical and information science sources is surveyed in a separate section which includes the subject heading 'Computers – Systems and Searches'.

608. *Health Libraries Review: a Journal for Medical, Health and Welfare Librarians.* Oxford: Blackwell Scientific, 1984-. Quarterly.

Most issues contain contributions on aspects of online and CD-ROM searching and associated hardware and software. Applications and experience in Britain are emphasized. A valuable current awareness section for recent literature appears in the *Newsletter of The Library Association Medical, Health and Welfare Group* which is included at the end of each issue.

609. *Medical Reference Services Quarterly.* New York: Haworth Press, 1982-. Quarterly.

Contains 'practice-oriented' articles which place a heavy emphasis on online services, especially issues concerned with the practice and management of end- user searching. Experience in the US with individual systems, gateway software and CD-ROM databases is frequently documented. A section, 'Online Updates: a Column for Search Analysts', examines databases or aspects of search technique, while the 'Micros in Medicine' column offers advice on microcomputer applications and maintenance. Other features are evaluative book reviews and abstracts of recent journal articles.

Newsletters

610. *Healthcare Online.* Los Altos, California: Medical Data Exchange, 1985-. Quarterly.

A supplier of news on new online and CD-ROM services, meetings and publications, this newsletter is aimed at end users in healthcare and is published by the producers of the Personal Health Abstracts database. Existing gateway and CD-ROM products are frequently reviewed. Many issues contain a case history of how information obtained in a computer literature search has been applied to clinical practice.

SUBJECT SEARCHING – SCIENCE AND TECHNOLOGY

Books

611. Wherry, T. L. *Patent Searching for Librarians and Inventors.* Washington: American Library Association, 1995. 150 pp.

This book covers the patent search process, detailing the patent tools available in the library and providing background and historical perpective on the US patent system. The text also covers patent forms and fees, patents as an information source and copyrights and trademarks.

Directories: Print

612. Armstrong, C. J. (ed.) *World Databases in Agriculture.* East Grinstead: Bowker-Saur, 1995. 1130 pp.

Part of a commissioned series covering all disciplines, *World Databases in Agriculture* is a comprehensive directory of databases published on diskette, tape, CD-ROM (or any of its variants) and online and the Internet dealing with all aspects of agriculture, aquatic sciences, food science, veterinary medicine and agricultural chemicals. As with all volumes in the series, records are very full with each database given a top 'producer record' describing the database as developed by the information provider and as many 'product records' as there are online or portable versions. One of the main aims of the project is to make clear any links between databases so if material from one database can also be found in another this will be shown. Third-party review material is either referenced or quoted. The database from which the print directories are produced will be made available on CD-ROM.

613. Armstrong, C. J. (ed.) *World Databases in Chemistry.* East Grinstead: Bowker-Saur, 1995. (in press).

World Databases in Chemistry is a comprehensive directory of databases published on diskette, tape, CD-ROM (or any of its variants) and online and the Internet dealing with all aspects of chemistry and the chemical industries. Agrochemistry, biochemistry, food chemistry, forensic chemistry, geochemistry crystalography, chemical processes, reactions and physical chemistry are all covered, and specific sections deal with organic chemistry, inorganic chemistry, analytical chemistry, toxicology and material safety data sheets, pharmaceuticals and cosmetics, surface chemistry and chemical engineering. One of the main aims in this series of directories is to make each one self-sufficient so that, for example agricultural chemicals are dealt with in both the *Agriculture* and *Chemistry* volumes.

614. Armstrong, C. J. (ed.) *World Databases in Geography & Geology.* East Grinstead: Bowker-Saur, 1995. 1255 pp.
World Databases in Geography & Geology is a comprehensive directory of databases published on diskette, tape, CD-ROM (or any of its variants) and online and the Internet dealing with all aspects of geography (geophysics, travel, cartography regional and urban studies, real estate and demography) and geology (mineralogy, oceanography, palaeontology, geochemistry, mining and drilling).

615. Armstrong, C. J. (ed.) *World Databases in Patents.* East Grinstead: Bowker-Saur, 1995. 324 pp.
Part of a commissioned series covering all disciplines, *World Databases in Patents* is a comprehensive directory of databases published on diskette, tape, CD-ROM (or any of its variants) and online and the Internet. Patents databases and their subject-specific subsets are all included, as are databases to do with standards, trademarks, copyright and the laws of intelectual property.

616. Armstrong, C. J. (ed.) *World Databases in Physics & Mathematics.* East Grinstead: Bowker-Saur, 1995. 1085 pp.
Like its companion volumes, *World Databases in Physics & Mathematics* is a comprehensive directory of databases published on diskette, tape, CD-ROM (or any of its variants) and online and the Internet. Despite the title, the directory covers all of science not covered by a separate directory such as chemistry or the biosciences, thus applied science, astronomy, meteorology, materials science and domestic science as well as mathematics, statistics, physics and geophysics are all represented.

617. *Building, Construction and Architecture Databases.* Compiled by J. Cox. London: Aslib, 1991. 76pp.
Covers over sixty databases on building construction, services, civil engineering, structural engineering, health and safety, urban and rural planning to provide a one-stop reference source for the built environment.

618. *CD-ROM and Online Computing, Electronics and Telecommunications Databases.* Compiled by R. Rouse. London: Aslib, 1994. 130pp.
Covers a wide range of databases with sections on Business and company databases and subject, host and database indexes. Each database record contains, in addition to a subject description, details on the type of database, language, coverage, time span, updating, the producer, the publisher or hosts, distributors, the platform, costs, user aids and, if relevant, the number of discs.

619. Fischer, B., Lochar, R. and **Pautler, B.** (eds.). *Libraries, Information Centres and Databases in Science and Technology* (2nd ed.). East Grinstead: Bowker-Saur, 1988. 665p.
This is a combined guide to resources in all areas of pure and applied sciences. While the guide deals with online databases, CD-ROMs are not included.

620. *Handbuch der Datenbanken für Naturwissenschaft, Technik, Patente.* Darmstadt: Hoppenstedt. Annual.

Typically, over 1,000 databases are listed in alphabetical order, covering a broad range of disciplines or document types which includes chemistry, medicine, biotechnology, engineering and patents. Entries provide standard details (Name, producer, host(s), type of database, geographical coverage, language, etc) with a description of the subject and source scope of each file. The major international files are supplemented by those which concentrate on individual countries, with an emphasis on the Federal Republic of Germany, and the subject index subdivides its headings by geographical coverage. A separate section lists host addresses. The language of the directory is German.

621. *Online Engineering Databases.* Compiled by S. Pilkington and R. G. Rhodes. London: Aslib, 1992. 76pp.

A guide to databases covering electronics, computer and control engineering, process technology and mechanical engineering.

622. *Online Patents, Trademarks and Servicemarks Databases.* (4th ed.) Compiled by J. F. Sibley. London: Aslib, 1992. 72pp.

Guides the user through bibliographic and factual databases for patents, servicemarks, trademarks and the protection of property – specialized areas which are closely associated with technology. Also includes a useful history of patent systems development. A narrative description of the content of each database is supplied, along with details of updating frequency, producer, hosts, language, search costs and any user aids. Addresses and telephone numbers for database producers and hosts are listed in a separate section.

623. **Sims, M. S.** (ed.) *Directory of Periodicals Online: Indexed, Abstracted and Full-Text: Science and Technology.* Washington, DC: Federal Document Retrieval. Annual.

Follows the same format for periodicals in science and technology as its longer-established sister volume for news, law and business, indicating databases which include each journal listed and the nature of the coverage offered by the database.

Handbooks

624. **Bawden, D.** (ed.) *Computerised Chemical Information: A Manual of Online and CD-ROM Search Strategies.* Aldershot: Ashgate, 1993. 500pp.

Providing detailed information and advice on the best means of finding chemical information in online and CD-ROM sources, the *Manual* is organised by principally by the subject of the search and by search techniques, although some chapters are devoted to particular files such as CAS Online or Beilstein. Some comparison is made to printed reference tools and there are two background chapters on chemical information and general searching techniques as well as some discussion of in-house systems. All the contributors are practising chemical searchers from both Western Europe and USA.

625. Orton, D. (ed.) *Online Searching in Science and Technology: an Introductory Guide to Equipment, Databases and Search Techniques.* (1995 4th ed.) London: British Library. Science Reference and Information Service. Online Search Centre, 1995. 112pp.

While placing the emphasis on search strategies and providing numerous examples, the Guide includes chapters on equipment and new developments in online and reviews databases in the biomedical sciences, chemistry, engineering and the environmental sciences. There is also a glossary, and a directory of useful UK addresses. The *LA Record* said of the first edition, 'as a practical introduction for someone who wants to find out what can be done and how to get started, this is the one to read' and Inform noted 'no jargon, all plain speaking. This short guide is excellent for the beginner and/or first courses in Library School.' Sections include: basic concepts: databases and hosts; basic search techniques; commands and facilities; search strategies; output options and document delivery; hardware, software and telecommunications; training, help and keeping up to date; reviews of databases in general science and technology, biomedicine, chemistry, engineering and the environment; CD-ROM searching overview; and recent developments.

Journals

626. *Journal of Chemical Information and Computer Sciences.* Washington, DC: American Chemical Society, 1960-. Bimonthly.

Publishes research papers in all areas of information applications and computer science relevant to the chemical field, including information communication, processing and retrieval. Most issues include articles which examine databases as information sources and describe techniques for retrieving chemical information. Information retrieval software and small-scale databases for microcomputers are also reviewed in a separate computer software section.

627. *Science and Technology Libraries.* New York: Haworth Press, 1980-. Quarterly.

Each issue is thematic and consists of a series of articles for technology librarians which are usually written by US contributors and sometimes focus on online topics. A notable feature of every issue is 'Sci-Tech Online' which contains news of the latest developments in host and database services in science and technology areas, along with details of new publications, search aids and tools for online education. Also of interest is 'Sci-Tech Collections', a series of guides to information sources in individual subject areas which includes coverage of online databases.

628. *World Patent Information: the International Journal for Patent Documentation, Classification and Statistics.* Kidlington: Elsevier, 1979-. Quarterly.

A refereed journal which provides a worldwide forum for the exchange of information among professionals working in the patent information, documentation and database fields. A regular column 'Online Patent Information' monitors latest developments. A news section provides information from around the world on patent information services, including coverage of new or enhanced databases. Latest journal articles and conference papers are listed, with abstracts, in the 'Literature Review' feature. In-depth analysis is provided by the journal's research articles which often discuss information sources and retrieval techniques and are abstracted in English, French, German and Spanish at the end of each issue.

TELECOMMUNICATIONS

Books

629. Adams, R. *Communication and Delivery Systems for Librarians.* Aldershot: Gower, 1990. 269pp.

Examines developments in electronic communications and their implications for access to and delivery of information services, particularly via local- and wide-area networks. The author claims that the book's stance is forward looking which means that it is probably roughly up to date now – ISDN services such as Perfect Information are beginning to come online, for example. Following a glossary of telecommunication and computing terms, sections deal with the development of communications technology, wide-area networks, local-area network technology, local- and wide-area networks for librarians, large-scale storage devices, library applications for large-scale storage devices, artificial intelligence, new communications technologies, social implications of the technologies, possible scenarios, and libraries and the communications environment. The book provides a thorough overview of telecommunications implications for library and information workers.

630. Glossbrenner, A. *The Complete Handbook of Personal Computer Communications.* (3rd ed.). New York: St. Martin's Press, 1989. 405pp.

Written at an introductory level, this handbook contains practical information for searchers. It offers a clear explanation of online telecommunications and outlines the technology and procedures involved in connecting to online databases via the major US networks. A wide range of online services is also described. The author provides valuable advice on troubleshooting and on cost-saving measures. Contact information and published sources of information are given regularly.

631. Harries, S. *Networking and Telecommunications for Information Systems: an Introduction to Information Networking.* London: Library Association Publishing, 1993.

The impact of computer networking on the lives of anyone involved with information handling in the 1990s has to be dramatic and this volume examines the development of, current state of and future plans for all forms of network. The basic introduction to the technology is followed by a consideration of its impact on the information activities of users, and on the delivery of integrated information services. Particular emphasis is given to the role of networking in the public domain, to library and bibliographic networking and to the development of open systems approaches to message transfer and document delivery. High-bandwidth network requirements for multimedia are reviewed and the body of the book ends with a note on current developments in networking taking place in Europe and the USA. Appendices cover both the Internet and JANET, and contain a glossary of terms.

Conferences: Proceedings

632. Collier, M. (ed.) *Telecommunications for Information Management and Transfer: Proceedings of the First International Conference held at Leicester Polytechnic, April 1987.* Aldershot: Gower, 1988. 194 pp.

Papers investigate the application of telecommunication networks to information management and delivery by libraries and information units. The final chapter is a selected bibliography on telecommunications and libraries. Although beginning to date, papers look at such topics as local-area networks, ISDN, electronic mail in libraries, and developments in facsimile and document delivery – all remain relevant topics today.

Dictionaries

633. Adams, R. 'Glossary'. *In Communication and Delivery Systems for Librarians.* Edited by R. Adams. Aldershot: Gower, 1990, xiii-xxii.

A glossary of some eighty-five telecommunications and computing terms. Although it does not cover librarianship terminology, a useful glossary with short definitions of everything from Asynchronous Transmission to Virtual Circuit.

634. Benson, J. A. and **Beck, S. J.** 'Gateway and telecommunication software: a glossary'. *In Gateway Software and Natural Language Interfaces: Options for Online Searching.* Edited by J. A. Benson and B. H. Weinberg. Ann Arbor, Michigan: Pierian Press, 1988. pp. 179-186.

Contains detailed definitions of more than seventy terms commonly used in relation to gateway and telecommunications software. Some general online searching and computing terms are also included. Acoustic Coupler to User Interface by way of Boolean Logic and Protocols – nothing very surprising here.

Distance Learning

635. *Data Communications and Networks* (2nd ed.) Stevenage, Hertfordshire: Institution of Electrical Engineers, 1993.

This video-based course was originally recorded at Aston University during a Vacation School and reviews modern practice in data communications. The material is intended for use by small groups who have access to a tutor with subject familiarity, but – say the Institution of Electrical Engineers – can successfully be used, in conjunction with the course book, by individuals. The Complete Video Course comprises sixteen video cassettes and a textbook for UK£1,800, while separate video lectures with the textbook can be purchased for UK£120 each.

Journal Articles

636. Connolly, B. 'Review Roundup: High-Speed Modems for Online Searching'. *Online* 17 (2) (March 1993) pp. 34-41.
The article advises on modem purchasing, covering standards, the distinction between V.32 compliance and compatibility and discussing modem technology, transmission speeds, evaluation criteria, and features. Modems for DOS-based and Macintosh computers are discussed as well as platform crossover, the Fax modem alternative, upgrading and the merits of searching at 9,600 bps.

637. Connolly, B. 'The Fax Modem Alternative: New Modems for Online Searching and Electronic Information Transfer'. *Online* 18 (1) (January 1994) pp. 36-44.
An evaluation of high-speed modems including fax/data modems; 14,400 bps modems and standards. Commments on the vast improvements made to modems over a few years yielding greater reliability and affordability.

638. Eglowstein, H. 'Advancing Communications'. *Byte* 19 (2) February 1994. pp. 104-110.
A look at seven data communications software packages which now offer high-speed, scripting and easy-to-use facilities. The packages examined are: Procomm Plus, Telix, White Knight, MicroPhone, Crosstalk for Windows, Procomm Plus for Windows, Term and Communication Solutions.

Journals

639. *Communicate.* London: Economist Newspapers, 1980-. Monthly.
Aimed at users of telecommunications and data communication systems in Britain, this magazine provides updates, articles and product reviews on communications products, systems and services in the UK. Product news on new telecommunciations and networking equipment is supplied in the 'Showroom' section in which brief descriptions can be supplemented by further information from the manufacturer or supplier using the business reply card provided. Forthcoming courses, conferences and exhibitions as well as appointments and contracts are also featured.

640. *Data Communications International.* New York: McGraw-Hill, 1972-. Seventeen issues per year.
Provides a more international perspective on telecommunications developments and products than *Communicate.* The first issue of each year serves as a buyer's guide to telecommunications software and equipment.

Reports

641. *Communications: A Trend Monitor Report.* Portsmouth, Hampshire: Trend Monitor International. Biannual.

One of four Trend Monitor Reports, *Communications* covers Data Communications, Telecommunications, Business and Regulations; Data Communications, in turn, covers networks (network management, local area networks, modems, etc), Open Systems Interconnection (OSI), and Applications (e-mail, electronic data interchange, electronic funds transfer, facsimile, voice mail and mobile data). Within each of these areas the report covers the technology, production and supply, demand, marketing, and available products. Each 150-page report is the result of scanning more than 400 publications and is put together by a team of experts. Links to source material and related subjects are stressed and a list of sources, an index and a selected bibliography of between 1,500 and 2,000 items complete the reports. The Business section in each report deals with corporate strategy, takeovers and mergers, while legislation and litigation are examined in the Regulations section.

TRAINING

Books

642. Convey, J. *Online Information Retrieval: an Introductory Manual to Principles and Practice.* (4th ed.) London: Library Association Publishing, 1992. 310 pp.

An introduction to online searching which is organized in two parts. The first part contains chapters on the development of online information retrieval; databases; the online information retrieval industry; CD-ROM; hardware and software; general principles of searching; the search; the costs; advantages and disadvantages of online; and the future of online. As Sheila Webber points out (Reviews. *Program* 27(4) (October 1993) 443-445), the first and third of these chapters, while providing a useful overview of online history, overlap while all the chapters seem not to have been as thoroughly revised as they might have been. She also points out that a number of topics have not been covered: the Joint Academic Network (JANET); IXI; the Internet; the emergence of academic hosts (eg. BIDS); site-licensing; online public access catalogues; and the emergence of new types of host (eg. the Manchester Host). The second part of the book is designed to 'show practical applications of the principles outlined in Part 1, and to form part of the training programme of searchers new to information retrieval' and describes and illustrates search features on seven hosts: BLAISE-LINE, BLAISE-LINK, KR DIALOG, ESA-IRS, ORBIT, Pergamon Financial Data Services (since closed down) and KR Data-Star. While covering some advanced features (perhaps better left out for new searchers?) some details are glossed over or lost in the search annotations. As Webber says, 'the book has useful, accurate information in it' but also some shortcomings which detract from its intended uses.

643. Walker, G and **Janes, J.** *Online Retrieval: a Dialogue of Theory and Practice.* Colorado: Libraries Unlimited, 1993.

Curiously titled but excellent training manual for searching online databases. A book intended for the novice searcher which uses hundreds of examples drawn from real searches to demonstrate all there is to know about the practice of online searching but at the same time finds room to cover basics such as Boolean logic, indexing and other 'theoretic' topics. The training is based almost exclusively on DIALOG on the basis that skills learned on one system can easily be transferred as the user has to move to new hosts. As Andrew Everest notes in his review (*Managing Information* 1(11/12) November/December 1994. p.42), 'look no further if you need a plain guide to both the how and the why of online. I would go so far as to say that the guide should be required reading for any library school course covering online.' As this is where the first-named author cut her teeth, it is not surprising that the book is so precisely targetted and well balanced. Most notable is the fact that the Internet get coverage as an online resource in its own right

Conferences: Papers

644. Hallam, S. 'Introducing the Internet: a Case Study'. *In Online Information 93: 17th International Online Information Meeting Proceedings, London, 7-9 December 1993.* Edited by D. I. Raitt. Oxford: Learned Information, 1993. pp. 443-452.
The paper deals with the author's experience of teaching Internet skills to students at The Nottingham Trent University. It describes the teaching materials and methods used to introduce students to the Internet and offers practical advice to those teaching in what can be an unpredictable environment. In discussing the problems of access from sites not supporting the full suite of utilities necessary to use the Internet to the full, Susan Hallam introduces Guest Telnet, Guest ftp, FTPMAIL and the publicly-available Gopher services. Finally, there are suggested additional readings which can be located on the Internet itself.

645. Westmancoat, J. 'SOLSTICE: Training for Online Systems via Satellite'. *In Online Information 92: 16th International Online Information Meeting Proceedings, London, 8-10 December 1992.* Edited by D. I. Raitt. Oxford: Learned Information, 1992. pp. 215-224.
The SOLSTICE experiment was designed to demonstrate the feasibility of combining satellite television broadcasts, two-way audio-conferencing and data transfer via satellite to reach online database trainees at remote sites. Using modified BLAISE-LINE courses as well as other material, the reception of the programmes proved that employees' absence from their workplace could be minimised and that training costs could be reduced.

Conferences: Proceedings

646. Mensching, T. B. and **Stanger, K. J.** (eds.). *Bibliographic Instruction and Computer Database Searching: Papers Presented at the Fourteenth Library Instruction Conference Held at Eastern Michigan University 8 and 9 May 1986; and Numerous Examples of Current Instructional Materials Collected in Late 1987.* Ann Arbor, Michigan: Pierian Press, 1988. 173pp.
This publication is divided into five main sections. The first consists of eight papers delivered at the conference. Their theme is the integration of training in online information retrieval into existing instruction programmes in US academic libraries. Poster session abstracts are featured in the next section. This is followed by a collection of handouts and sample instructional materials produced by US libraries. Two appendices offer suggested objectives for library instruction in online information retrieval and a series of guidelines for online training sessions which address issues such as length of session, equipment, handouts, evaluation and follow-up. The final section is a set of separate bibliographies.

Distance Learning

647. BLAISE-LINE Self-Starter. Boston Spa, West Yorkshire: The British Library, 1989.
Developed by Information Automation Limited in 1989 for BLAISE-LINE, the package consists of a brief set of instruction for installation and running and two diskettes containing the software and lessons. The package is self-contained and instructs users on the basic techniques of online database searching and on the commands to use, and the databases available, on BLAISE-LINE. Users should be able to complete successful searches online by the completion of the course. The software runs on a basic IBM personal computer or compatible, requires no additional material and is completely self-contained: no online connection is required during use.

648. Graffiti on a Database. Oxford: Learned Information, 1980.
A tape/slide programme of 65 slides, one audio tape and instructions which introduces users to online searching. Although still available, this product is more than somewhat dated by now.

649. *grips*-Learn 3.0. Aberystwyth, Dyfed: Information Automation Limited, 1989.
Updated for the second time at the start of 1994, *grips*-Learn is a computer-based training package for users of the German biosciences host, DIMDI. Described in full in Armstrong's overview, 'New Approaches in the Training and Education of Online Users', *grips*-Learn is a five-lesson programme which takes potential users with no knowledge of online systems through the fundamentals of database use, simple searching on DIMDI and more complex search procedures (*grips*-Learn junior omits the more complex techniques and contains three lessons only). In addition to instruction, the package contains self-tests, a comprehensive dictionary of online terms, DIMDI commands and databases; demonstration searches and interactive search simulations. The package is available in both English and German versions.

650. Neomatica. Boston Spa, West Yorkshire: Boston Spa Training, 1993.
A multimedia training package supplied on CD-ROM on the availability and use of business information, especially via online commercial databases. Includes built-in tutorials, demonstrations and practise opportunities. Contains a reference guide to business information, together with a database of business and European Single Market materials. Explains search methods for relevant commercial databases, and how to establish online communications. The *Times Education Supplement* said, 'The scope of the software is astonishingly broad. It is an enormous storehouse of business data ... But Neomatica also offers a comprehensive training package on word processing, database and spreadsheet uses. It is the only UK package to provide tutorials and practice in electronic information handling.' The training content of

Neomatica has been agreed by KR DIALOG, KR Data-Star and FT Profile. The database of 'real' information used for training was drawn directly from Reuters, Financial Times, Jordans, ICC, Dun & Bradstreet, Predicasts and ECHO. Runs on IBM MPC (Multimedia Personal Computer) compatibles with a CD-ROM drive under Ask-It and HyperDoc software.

651. Training Hotline. Boston Spa, West Yorkshire: Boston Spa Training, 1993-. Provides low-cost training via interactive training materials accessed using a touchtone telephone and supported by printed prompt cards and workbooks. Users can follow only those parts of the course relevant to them and then complete a problem-solving exercise in their own time. Two modules are available initially: Developing effective sales staff and Information for effective business decision-making.

Handbooks

652. **Hunter, B.** and **Lodish, E. K.** *Online Searching in the Curriculum: a Teaching Guide for Library/Media Specialists and Teachers.* Santa Barbara, California: ABC-Clio, 1989. 219pp.

A handbook for teachers and and school librarians involved in teaching online or CD-ROM searching at secondary or high school level. The core of the book is a set of lesson plans for five major projects, including handouts at the end of each project chapter which can be reproduced for distribution. The introductory chapter describes the rationale for the book, and overview of the projects and includes a list of suitable databases available on diskette at the time of writing and a bibliography of over fifty references from the mid-eighties. The bias is towards the USA both in terms of the projects themselves and the teaching style but, six years on, it could usefully find a place in UK schools. Student prerequisites are noted is the projects are to be undertaken without staff assistance.

653. *MICROtips: A User's Guide to Microcomputer Index Online 1993.* Oxford: Learned Information, 1993. 96pp.

The printed *Microcomputer Index* and the DIALOG file (File 233) both abstract some eighty journals in the area of personal computing, networks, communications, databases, etc. This *Guide* is designed to assist users of the online file and provides field-by-field search tips combined with sample KR DIALOG searches. An Introduction and Overview is followed by a Thesaurus of descriptors with cross-references and a retrospective of the 179 journals covered in *Microcomputer Index* since it began.

654. **Shuman, B. A.** *Cases in Online Search Strategy.* Englewood, Colorado: Libraries Unlimited, 1993. 279 pp. (Database Searching Series)

The work consists of sixty case studies which together illustrate the main points of negotiating reference questions, deciding on an approach and producing a search strategy. The case studies cover many fields – humanities, economics and business, the law, life sciences and science and technology – but each is presented in a uniform format taking the reader from the first presentation of the natural-language query through strategy formulation, file selection and the search algorithm to the results and a short evaluation. A useful handbook on the reference process with the single drawback that all files are selected from DIALOG alone. The focus is on conditions where the 'meter is running and mistakes can be costly' so that CD-ROM options are not considered. The author acknowledges both these points in the Introduction where he also notes the online versus CD-ROM argument briefly. Despite the apparently narrow perspective, the case studies – from 'If nuclear winter comes, how long can it be expected to last?' to 'Which musical composers are said to have belonged to the nineteenth-century romantic movement?' – make a very real contribution to the literature on database searching which is ideal for use in library schools.

Journal Articles

655. Armstrong, C. J. 'New Approaches in the Training and Education of Online Users'. *Online Review* 15(3/4) (July/August 1991) (Festschrift issue in honour of Roger K. Summit). pp. 147-171.

Originally written in 1989 but revised in late 1990, this paper provides a brief introduction to the history of online and online training, surveys current training and, in the main section deals in depth with computer-assisted instruction for online searching with examples drawn from a number of available packages. Some of the techniques, such as self-testing and search simulations, as well as the advantages of this method of instruction are discussed.

VIDEOTEX

Directories: Print

656. **Riou, B.** *Directory of French Videotex Databases for Companies.* Paris: FLA Consultants, 1991. 265pp.

The directory offers details on more than 250 professional videotex databases available on Minitel. The body of the guide is divided into sixteen main parts: Indexes and directories of companies; Financial, Juridical and legal information about companies; Legal context; Economic and political context; Foreign trade; Stock exchange and finance; Business opportunities; Training; Information on the media; Trade fairs and exhibitions; Building, materials and mechanics; Computers and computing; Transportation; Town and country planning and development; and Other fields. Each section begins with a page on which the constituent subject areas are listed (unfortunately these have not been translated from French in the English edition) and continues with standard format descriptions of each database. Information contained includes the access codes, the size of the database, update frequency, language and types of document included. There is also a sample record. Each description extends to one page. Five appendices provide an analytical table of databases, a list of producers, a list of hosts, an alphabetic list of service codes arranged by access type, and an alphabetic list of the databases.

Newsletters

657. *Bases: Connaitre et Bien utiliser les Banques de Donnees.* Paris: Bases Publications, 1986-. Eleven per year.

A twelve-page, French-language newsletter containing a series of short articles for searchers on CD-ROMs, online searching, videotex and databases. The table of contents is divided into fives sections with a major article, a book review, news releases from online hosts and database producers, a section on Videotex and a diary of events.

658. *Videotex International: Fortnightly International Newsletter on the Videotex Industry.* Paris, France: Transtex International. Twice monthly.

The newsletter provides up-to-date worldwide news on videotext applications and markets, including policies of European telecommunications organisations, US RBOCs and other operators of public and private videotex networks; policies and trading results of the main international concerns (network equipment suppliers, engineering, software, hosts and services); worldwide market figures; and regular reports on major EEC programmes.

PART III

Directory of Organizations

Directory of Organizations

This section provides addresses of the principal organizations linked with the database and information industry and references in the body of this book. They can all be contacted for further information about their products and services. They have been divided into six groups although, in some cases, the distinction is not always useful; many of the publishers, for example, are also information providers. The groups are: Advisory and Membership Organizations which can act as unbiased sources of general help and advice and which, in many cases, accept database users as members, provide training and publish newsletters; Industry Associations represent the interests of the companies in the database industry. The next major group, Information Providers/Information Vendors covers organisations which both create and distribute databases; it thus includes CD-ROM publishers and online vendors (or hosts) as well as companies which generate the initial database. The next small section covers Market Research Companies; many of these are publishers of reports within the body of the *Keyguide* and some also publish their reports as databases. The next large section, Publishers, includes most of the major publishers of books and journals mentioned in this bibliography and many of these, too, will be information providers for databases. Where this is the case, the address has not been repeated and has been placed in the section for which the company is best known. The last section provides addresses for providers of the training and post-processing software mentioned in the *Keyguide*. The entries are numbered as follows:

Advisory and Membership Organizations [659] – [672]
Industry Associations [673] – [683]
Information Providers/Information Vendors [684] – [746]

Advisory and Membership Organizations

659 **American Library Association,** 50 East Huron Street, Chicago, IL 60611, USA

660 **American Society for Information Science,** 8720 Georgia Avenue, Suite 501, Silver Springs, MD 20910-3602

661 **Aslib,** 20-24 Old Street, London, EC1V 9AP, UK

662 **Centre for Information Quality Management (CIQM),** Penbryn, Bronant, Aberystwyth SY23 4TJ, UK

663 **Cimtech,** University of Hertfordshire, College Lane, Hatfield, AL10 9AD, UK

664 **Institute of Information Scientists (IIS),** 44-45 Museum Street, London, WC1A 1LY, UK

665 **JANET User Group for Librarians (JUGL),** c/o William Alexander, University of Sussex Library, Brighton, BN1 9QL, UK

666 **Library Association, The,** 7 Ridgmount Street, London, WC1E 7AE, UK

667 **Library Information Technology Centre (LITC),** South Bank Technopark, 90 London Road, London, SE1 6LN, UK

668 **Medical Library Association,** 6 North Michigan Avenue, Suite 300, Chicago, IL 60602-4805, USA

669 **SCANNET,** Helsinki University of Technology Library, Otnäsvägen 9, FIN-02150 ESBO, Finland

670 **Special Libraries Association,** 1700 18th Street NW, Washington, DC 20009, USA

671 **UKOLUG,** Secretariat, Mrs C Baker, The Old Chapel, Walden, West Burton, Leyburn, North Yorkshire, DL8 4LE, UK

672 **VOGIN, The Netherlands Association of Users of Online Information Systems,** Library Gorlaeus Laboratory, PO Box 9502, 2300 RA Leiden, Netherlands

Industry Associations

673 **Association for Information and Image Management,** 1100 Wayne Avenue, Suite 1100, Silver Spring, MD 20910, USA

674 **Association Française des Documentalistes et des Bibliothecaires Specialises,** 25 rue Claude Tillier, F-75012 Paris, France

675 **Australian Database Development Association,** PO Box 53, Hawthorn, Victoria 3122, Australia

676 **CD-ROM Standards and Practices Action Group (CD-ROM SPAG),** c/o Robert Smith (Chair), British Library National Bibliographic Service, Wetherby, West Yorkshire, LS23 7BQ, UK

677 **Confederation of Information Communication Industries (CICI),** 19 Bedford Square, London, WC1B 3HJ, UK

678 **Database Promotion Centre, Japan,** 7th Floor, World Trade Center Building, 2-4-1 Hamamatsu-cho, Minato-ku, Tokyo 105, Japan

679 **EUSIDIC,** 37, Val St. André, B.P. 1416, L-1014 Luxembourg

680 **Information Industry Association,** 555 New Jersey Avenue NW, Suite 800, Washington, DC 20001, USA

681 **National Federation of Abstracting and Indexing Services (NFAIS),** 1518 Walnut Street, Suite 307, Philadelphia, PA 19102-3403, USA

682 **Optical Publishing Association,** 1880 Mackenzie Drive, Suite 111, Columbus, OH 43220, USA

683 **UKOLN: UK Office for Library and Information Networking,** University of Bath, Claverton Down, Bath, BA2 7AY, UK

Information Providers/Information Vendors

684 **ABC-Clio,** 130 Cremona, PO Box 1911, Santa Barbara, CA 93116-1911, USA (also: Clio Press Ltd, Old Clarendon Ironworks, 35a Great Clarendon Street, Oxford, OX2 6AT, UK)

685 **Bath Information and Data Services (BIDS),** Computing Services, University of Bath, Claverton Down, Bath, BA2 7AY, UK

686 **BLAISE-LINE,** British Library National Bibliographic Service, Wetherby, West Yorkshire, LS23 7BQ, UK

687 **BLAISE-LINK,** British Library National Bibliographic Service, Wetherby, West Yorkshire, LS23 7BQ, UK

688 **Bowker-Saur,** Maypole House, Maypole Road, East Grinstead, West Sussex, RH19 1HH, UK

689 **British Library Document Supply Centre,** Wetherby, West Yorkshire, LS23 7BQ, UK

690 **British Library National Bibliographic Service,** Wetherby, West Yorkshire, LS23 7BQ, UK

691 **CAN/OLE** (Service now discontinued), Canadian Institute of Science and Technical Information (CISTI), Montreal Road, Ottawa, Ontario, K1A 0S2, Canada

692 **CDP Online** *see* Ovid Online

693 **Central Statistical Office of Finland,** PO Box 504, SF-00101 Helsinki, Finland

694 **Centre de Documentation de l'Armement (CEDOCAR),** 26 boulevard Victor, F000460 Paris, France

695 **Centre National de la Recherche Scientifique. Institut de l'Information Scientifique et Technique (CNRS/INIST),** 2 allée du Parc de Brabois, F-54514 Vandoeuvre-lès-Nancy Cedex, France

696 **Compulink Information Exchange (CiX),** London House, Ancaster Square, Llanrwst, Gwynedd, LL26 0LD, UK

697 **CompuServe Information Service (CIS),** 5000 Arlington Centre Boulevard, PO Box 20212, Columbus, OH 43220, USA (also: 1 Redcliffe Street, Bristol, BS1 6NP, UK)

698 **Deutsches Institut für Medizinische Dokumentation und Information (DIMDI),** Weißhausstraße 27, D-50939 Cologne, Germany

699 **Dow Jones News/Retrieval,** PO Box 300, Princetown, NJ 08540, USA (also: 10 Fleet Place, London, EC4M 7RB, UK)

700 **EBSCO Information Services,** 83 Pine Street, PO Box 2250, Peabody, MA 01960, USA

701 **ECHO,** Commission of the European Communities, BP 2373, L-1023 Luxembourg

702 **Educational Resources Information Center (ERIC),** 555 New Jersey Avenue NW, Washington, DC 20208, USA

703 **Elsevier Science BV,** Molenwerf 1, 1014 AG Amsterdam, Netherlands

704 **ESA-IRS,** ESRIN, Via Galileo Galilei, Frascati, I-00044 Rome, Italy (also: British Library Science Reference and Information Service, 25 Southampton Building, Chancery Lane, London, WC2A 1AW, UK

705 **European Association for Grey Literature Exploitation (EAGLE),** Bureau Jupiter, Postbus 90407, NL-2509 LK The Hague, Netherlands

706 **FAIRBASE Datenbank GmbH,** Ihmepassage 4, D-30449 Hannover, Germany

707 **FIND/SVP Inc,** 625 Avenue of the Americas, New York, NY 10011, USA

708 **FIZ Technik,** Ostbahnhofstraße 13, D-60314 Frankfurt am Main, Germany

709 **FT Profile,** Fitzroy House, 13-17 Epworth Street, London, EC2A 4DL, UK

710 **Gale Research Inc,** 835 Penobscot Building, Detroit, MI 48226-4094, USA

711 **Gesellschaft für Information und Dokumentation,** Lyoner Strasse 44-48, D-60007 Frankfurt, Germany

712 **Gesellschaft für Mathematik und Datenverarbeitung. Informationszentrum fur Informationswissenschaft und -praxis,** Dolivostraße 15, PO Box 104326, D-64293 Darmstadt, Germany

713 **H. W. Wilson (WilsonLine and WilsonDisc),** 950 University Avenue, Bronx, NY 10452, USA

714 **HMSO Electronic Publishing,** St Crispins, Duke Street, Norwich, NR3 1PD, UK

715 **Hoppenstedt Wirtschaftsdatenbank GmbH,** Havelstraße 9, Postfach 4006, D-64295 Darmstadt, Germany

716 **ICC Information Group,** Field House, 72 Oldfield Road, Hampton, Middlesex, TW12 2HQ, UK

717 **Information Access Company (IAC),** 362 Lakeside Drive, Foster City, CA 94404-9888, USA (also: CD-ROM Products, 13 Baywell, Leybourne, West Malling, Kent ME19 5QQ, UK; Online Databases, Watergate House, 13-15 York Buildings, London, WC2N 6JU, UK)

718 **Institute for Scientific Information (ISI),** 3501 Market Street, Philadelphia, PA 19104, USA

719 **Institution of Electrical Engineers (IEE),** Michael Faraday House, Six Hills Way, Stevenage, Hertfordshire, SG1 2AY, UK

720 **Instituto de la Pequena y Mediana Empresa Industrial,** Paseo de la Castellana 141, 28046 Madrid, Spain

721 **Japan Information Center of Science and Technology (JICST),** 5-3 Yonbacho, Chiyoda-ku, Tokyo 102, Japan

722 **Jordan and Son,** 21 St Thomas Street, Bristol, BS1 6JS, UK

723 Knight-Ridder Information (KRI), 2440 El Camino Real, Mountain View, CA 94040-9620, USA

724 Kompass *see* Reedbase Kompass

725 KR Data-Star, Haymarket House, 1 Oxendon Street, London, SW1Y 4EE, UK

726 KR DIALOG, Haymarket House, 1 Oxendon Street, London, SW1Y 4EE, UK

727 LEXIS/NEXIS, 9443 Springboro Pike, PO Box 933, Dayton, OH 45401-9964, USA (also: International House, 1 St Katherine's Way, London, E1 9UN, UK)

728 Library of Congress, 101 Independence Avenue SE, Washington, DC 20540, USA

729 Market Analysis and Information Database (MAID Systems), The Communications Building, 48 Leicester Square, London, WC2H 7DB, UK (also: 300 North Continental Boulevard, Suite 330, El Segundo, CA 90245, USA)

730 McGraw-Hill Book Company, 11 West 19th Street, 4th Floor, New York, NY 10011, USA (also: Shoppenhangers Road, Maidenhead, Berkshire, SL6 2QL, UK)

731 Moody's Investors Service, 99 Church Street, New York, NY 10007, USA

732 National Library of Medicine (NLM), 8600 Rockville Pike, Bethesda, MD 20894, USA

733 National Technical Information Service (NTIS), 5285 Port Royal Road, Springfield, VA 22161, USA

734 NewsNet, 945 Haverford Road, Bryn Mawr, PA 19010, USA

735 Nordinfo, Tekniska högskolans bibliotek, Otnäsvägen 9, FIN-02150 ESBO, Finland

736 Ovid Online, 333 7th Avenue, New York, NY 10001, USA (also: 1 Lamington Street, London, W6 0HU, UK)

737 Printing Industries Research Association (PIRA), Randalls Road, Leatherhead, Surrey, KT22 7RU, UK

738 Questel-ORBIT, Le Capitole, 55 avenue des Champs Pierreux, F-92029 Nanterre Cedex, France (also: 18 Parkshot, Richmond, Surrey, TW9 2RG, UK)

739 Reedbase Kompass, East Grinstead House, East Grinstead, West Sussex, RH19 1XA, UK

740 Royal Melbourne Institute of Technology (RMIT), GPO Box 2476V, Melbourne, Victoria 3000, Australia

741 **SilverPlatter,** 100 River Ridge Drive, Norwood, MA 02062-5026, USA (also: 10 Barley Mow Passage, Chiswick, London, W4 4PH, UK)

742 **STN International,** Chemical Abstracts Service, 2540 Olentangy River Road, PO Box 3012, Columbus, OH 43210-0012, USA

743 **United Nations Advisory Committee for the Co-ordination of Information Systems,** Palais de Nations, CH-1211 Geneva 10, Switzerland

744 **University Microfilms International (UMI),** 300 North Zeeb Road, Ann Arbor, MI 48106, USA (also: Information Publications International, White Swan House, Godstone, Surrey, RH9 8LW, UK)

745 **US National Aeronautics and Space Administration (NASA), Scientific and Technical Information Facility,** Code NTT, NASA Headquarters, Washington, DC 20546, USA

746 **Westlaw,** West Publishing Company, 620 Opperman Drive, Eagan, MN 55123-1396, USA

747 **Worldwide Videotex,** PO Box 138, Babson Park Branch, Boston, MA 02157, USA

Market Research Companies

748 **Digital Information Group,** 51 Bank Street, Stamford, CT 06901, USA

749 **Frost and Sullivan,** 106 Fulton Street, New York, NY 10038, USA (also: Sullivan House, 4 Grosvenor Gardens, London, SW1W 0DH, UK)

750 **FT Management Reports,** PO Box 6, Camborne, TR14 9EQ, UK

751 **Information Market Indicators,** Box 194, Monticello, IL 61856, USA

752 **Information Workstation Group,** 501 Queen Street, Alexandria, VA 22314, USA

753 **International Resource Development,** PO Box 1716, New Canaan, CT 06840, USA

754 **Key Note Publications,** Field House, 72 Oldfield Road, Hampton, Middlesex, TW12 2HQ, UK

755 **Link Resources,** 79 5th Avenue, 12th Floor, New York, NY 10003, USA

756 **Market Intelligence Research Company (MIRC),** 2525 Charleston Road, Mountain View, CA 94043, USA

757 **Ovum,** 7 Rathbone Street, London, W1P 1AF, UK

758 **Rothchild Consultants,** 256 Laguna Honda Boulevard, San Francisco, CA 94116, USA

759 **Science Policy Research Unit,** Mantell Building, University of Sussex, Falmer, Brighton, BN1 9RF, UK

760 **SIMBA Information,** PO Box 7430, Wilton, CT 06897, USA

Publishers

761 **Academic Press,** 525 B Street, Suite 1900, San Diego, CA 92101-4495, USA (also: 24-28 Oval Road, London, NW1 7DX, UK)

762 **Addison-Wesley,** Finchampstead Road, Wokingham, Berkshire, RG11 2NZ, UK

763 **Allerton Press,** 150 Fifth Avenue, New York, NY 10011, USA

764 **Alpha Books,** 6771 Wilson Boulevard, Falls Church, VA 22044, USA

765 **Archimag,** 9 rue Bleue, F-75009 Paris, France

766 **Ashgate,** Gower House, Croft Road, Aldershot, GU11 3HR, UK

767 **Bases Publications,** 27 rue de la Vistule, F-75013 Paris, France

768 **BiblioData,** PO Box 61, Needham Heights, MA 02194, USA

769 **Blackwell Scientific,** PO Box 40, Hythe Bridge Street, Oxford, OX1 2EU, UK

770 **British Library Research and Development Department,** 2 Sheraton Street, London, W1V 4BH, UK

771 **Burwell Enterprises,** 3724 F.M. 1960, Suite 214, Houston, TX 77068, USA

772 **Butterworth Heinemann,** 8 Industrial Way, Building C, Salem, NH 03079, USA

773 **Datapro Research Corporation,** 600 Delran Parkway, Delran, NJ 08075, USA

774 **Deutsches Bibliothekinstitut (DBI),** Bundesallee 184-185, D-10717 Berlin, Germany

775 **Effective Technology Marketing,** PO Box 171, Grimsby, DN35 0TP, UK

776 **Eight Bit Books,** 462 Banbury Road, Wilton, CT 06897-2126, USA

777 **Elsevier Science Ltd,** PO Box 800, Kidlington, Oxford, OX5 1DX, UK

778 **emap Business Communications,** Meed House, 21 John Street, London, WC1N 2BP, UK

779 **Espial Productions (CINFOLINK),** 85 Roe Avenue, Toronto, Ontario, M5M 2H6, Canada

780 **FLA Consultants,** 27 rue de la Vistule, F-75013 Paris, France

781 **G. K. Hall,** 70 Lincoln Street, Boston, MA 02111-9985, USA

782 **Gower Publishing Company Ltd,** Gower House, Croft Road, Aldershot, GU11 3HR, UK

783 **Headland Press,** 1 Henry Smith's Terrace, Headland, Cleveland, TS24 0PD, UK

784 **HERTIS,** University of Hertfordshire, College Lane, Hatfield, AL10 9AD, UK

785 **Hitachi New Media,** Hitachi House, Station Road, Hayes, Middlesex, UB3 4DR, UK

786 **IDG Communications,** PO Box 9171, 375 Cochituate Road, Framingham, MA 01701-9171, USA

787 **Infonortics,** 9/9A High Street, Calne, Wiltshire, SN11 0BS, UK

788 **Information Intelligence,** PO Box 31098, Phoenix, AZ 85046, USA

789 **Information Partnership,** Suite 4.2, 140 Tabernacle Street, London, EC2A 4SD, UK

790 **Information Resources Press,** 499 South Capitol Street SW, Suite 406, Washington, DC 20003, USA

791 **Information Today** (previously **Learned Information USA),** 143 Old Marlton Pike, Medford, NJ 08055-8707, USA

792 **Information USA,** 10335 Kensington Parkway, PO Box E, Kensington, MD 20895, USA

793 **Informed Business Services,** 25 Old Street, London, EC1V 9HL, UK

794 **InfoTech Research,** Trumanstede 9320, 4436 WE Goes, Netherlands

795 **IOS Press,** PO Box 10558, Burke, VA 22009-0558, USA

796 **JAI Press,** The Courtyard, 28 High Street, Hampton Hill, Middlesex, TW12 1PD, UK

797 **John Wiley and Sons,** 605 3rd Avenue, 5th Floor, New York, NY 10158-0012, USA (also: Baffins Lane, Chichester, West Sussex, PO19 1UD, UK)

798 **Knowledge Industry Publications (KIP),** 701 Westchester Avenue, White Plains, NY 10604, USA

799 **Ladera Press,** 3130 Alpine Road, Suite 200-9002, Menlo Park, CA 94025, USA

800 **Learned Information (Europe) Ltd,** Woodside, Hinksey Hill, Oxford, OX1 5AU, UK

801 **Learned Information Ltd** *see also* Information Today (USA)

802 **Libraries Unlimited,** PO Box 3988, Englewood, CO 80155, USA

803 **Library Alliance,** 264 Lexington Avenue, Suite 4C, New York, NY 10016-4182, USA

804 **Library Association Publishing,** 7 Ridgmount Street, London, WC1E 7AE, UK

805 **Library Automated Systems Information Exchange (LASIE),** Australian Co. Ltd, Australia

806 **Longman,** Westgate House, 6th Floor, Burnt Mill, The High, Harlow, Essex, CM20 1YR, UK

807 **Mansell Publishing,** Wellington House, 125 Strand, London, WC2R 0BB, UK

808 **MCB University Press,** 60/62 Toller Lane, Bradford, West Yorkshire, BD8 9BY, UK

809 **Mecklermedia,** 247-249 Vauxhall Bridge Road, London, SW1V 1HQ, UK

810 **Medical Data Exchange,** 445 South San Antonio Road, Los Altos, CA 94022, USA

811 **Microinfo Ltd,** PO Box 3, Omega Park, Alton, Hampshire, GU34 2PG, UK

812 **Microsoft Press,** 1 Microsoft Way, PO Box 97017, Redmond, WA 98052-6399, USA

813 **MicroUse Information,** 1400 Commonwealth Avenue, West Newton, MA 02165, USA

814 **National Centre of Scientific and Technological Information,** Atidim Industrial Park, PO Box 43074, Tel Aviv 61430, Israel

815 **New Riders Publishing,** 201 West 103rd Street, Indianapolis, IN 46290, USA

816 **Online,** 462 Danbury Road, Wilton, CT 06897-2126, USA

817 **Oryx Press,** 4041 North Central Avenue, Suite 700, Phoenix, AZ 85012-3399, USA

818 **Pemberton Press,** 462 Danbury Road, Wilton, CT 06897-2126, USA

819 **Pierian Press,** PO Box 1808, Ann Arbor, MI 48106, USA

820 **Plenum Publishing,** 233 Spring Street, New York, NY 10013-1578, USA (also: 88-90 Middlesex Street, London, E1 7EZ, UK)

821 **Prentice-Hall,** 1 Golf and Western Plaza, 18th Floor, New York, NY 10023, USA

822 **Research Publications International,** 12 Lunar Drive, Drawer AB, Woodbridge, CT 06525, USA

823 **Resource International Publishing Company,** Route 1, Box 168, Milford, TX 76670, USA

824 **Scarecrow Press,** 52 Liberty Street, Box 4167, Metuchen, NJ 08840, USA

825 **Spicer and Pegler,** 13 Bruton Street, London, W1X 7AH, UK

826 **TAB Books,** PO Box 40, Blue Ridge Summit, PA 17294-0850, USA

827 **Taylor Graham,** 500 Chesham House, 150 Regent Street, London, W1R 5FA, UK

828 **TFPL Multimedia,** 17-18 Britton Street, London, EC1M 5NQ, UK (also: 345 Park Avenue South, New York, NY 10001, USA)

829 **United Nations Educational, Scientific and Cultural Organization (UNESCO),** 7 PLace de Fontenoy, F-75352 Paris 07 SP, France

830 **VNU Business Publications,** VNU House, 32-34 Broadwick Street, London, W1A 2HG, UK (also: PO Box 9194, 1006 CC Amsterdam, Netherlands)

Software Producers

831 **Boston Spa Training,** Clifford Moor Road, Boston Spa, Wetherby, West Yorkshire, LS23 6RW, UK

832 **Crosstalk,** DCA (UK) Ltd, Harvingwell Place, 29-32 Mark Road, Hemel Hempstead, HP2 7BW, UK

833 **EndNote,** Cherwell Scientific Publishing, The Magdalen Centre, Oxford Science Park, Oxford, OX4 4GA, UK

834 **IdeaList,** Blackwell Scientific Publishing, Osney Mead, Oxford, OX2 0EL, UK

835 **Information Automation Limited,** Penbryn, Bronant, Aberystwyth SY23 4TJ, UK

836 **Personal Librarian,** DIAL, 1 Westgate, Skelmersdale, Lancashire WN8 8LP, UK (or: Systematic Upgrade, 58-60 Edward Road, New Barnet, EN4 8AS, UK)

837 **Pro-Cite,** Personal Bibliographic Software (PBS), Woodside, Hinksey Hill, Oxford, OX1 5BE, UK

838 **Procomm Plus,** Shareware Publishing, Unit 12, Berryden Business Centre, Aberdeen, AB2 3SA, UK

839 **Reference Manager,** Research Information Systems, Camino Corporate Center, 2355 Camino Vida Roble, Carlsbad, CA 92009-1572, USA (also: Bilaney Consultants, St Julians, Sevenoaks, TN15 0RX, UK)

Index

Numbers without brackets refer to pages in Part I; numbers in square brackets refer to entries in Part II ([1] – [658]) or III ([659] – [838]), *not* to page numbers.